Jean Améry

Yochai Ataria
Amit Kravitz
Eli Pitcovski
Editors

Jean Améry

Beyond the Mind's Limits

palgrave
macmillan

Editors
Yochai Ataria
Tel-Hai Academic College
Upper Galilee, Israel

Eli Pitcovski
Tel-Hai Academic College
Upper Galilee, Israel

Amit Kravitz
Ludwig-Maximilian University
of Munich
Munich, Germany

ISBN 978-3-030-28094-9 ISBN 978-3-030-28095-6 (eBook)
https://doi.org/10.1007/978-3-030-28095-6

Cover illustration: Peter Horree / Alamy Stock Photo

This Palgrave Macmillan imprint is published by the registered company Springer Nature Switzerland AG.
The registered company address is: Gewerbestrasse 11, 6330 Cham, Switzerland

Acknowledgments

We would like to thank Tel-Hai Academic College for supporting this project.

Contents

Notes on Contributors

C. Fred Alford is Professor Emeritus at University of Maryland, College Park. He is author of over fifteen books on moral psychology, including *Trauma and Forgiveness: Consequences and Communities* (2013), and *Trauma, Culture, and PTSD* (2016). He co-edits the Psychoanalysis and Society Book Series with Cornell University Press and served as Executive Director of the Association for Psychoanalysis, Culture and Society for over ten years. He curates the blog www.traumatheory.com, and www.godblog.org.

Dana Amir is a clinical psychologist, supervising and training analyst at the Israel psychoanalytic society, a faculty member at University of Haifa (head of the interdisciplinary doctoral program in psychoanalysis), poetess, and literature researcher. She is the author of six poetry books and three psychoanalytic non-fiction books: *Cleft Tongue* (2014), *On the Lyricism of the Mind* (2016), and *Bearing Witness to the Witness* (2018). Her papers were published in psychoanalytic journals and presented at national and international conferences. She is the winner of many national and international prizes, including The Frances Tustin International Memorial Prize (2011), the International Psychoanalytic Association (IPA) Sacerdoti Prize (2013) IPA Hayman Prize (2017), and the IFPE (International Forum for Psychoanalytic Education) Distinguished Psychoanalytic Educators Award (2017).

Yochai Ataria is an associate professor at Tel-Hai Academic College, Israel. He conducted his post-doctoral research in the Neurobiology Department at the Weizmann Institute of Science. He is the author of the following books: *The Structural Trauma of Western Culture* (2017); *Body Disownership in Complex Posttraumatic Stress Disorder* (2018); *The Mathematics of Trauma* [Hebrew] (2014); and *Not in Our Brain* [Hebrew] (2019). In addition, he co-edited the following volumes: Interdisciplinary Handbook of Culture and Trauma (2016); Kafka: New Perspectives [Hebrew] (2013); The End of the Human Era [Hebrew] (2016); 2001: A Space Odyssey—50th Anniversary [Hebrew] (2019).

Roy Ben-Shai is Assistant Professor of Philosophy at Sarah Lawrence College in New York. Former recipient of an Andrew W. Mellon post-doctoral fellowship at Haverford College. Co-editor of *The Politics of Nihilism: From the Nineteenth Century to Contemporary Israel* (2014). His essays on Jean Améry and on nineteenth–twentieth-century continental philosophy appear in Telos, The European Legacy, and the Journal of French and Francophone Philosophy.

Grace Campbell is a PhD candidate at the University of Queensland. Her work focuses on the philosophy of self-destructive behavior with an emphasis on the writings of Jean Améry and Sabina Spielrein.

Eran Fish is a post-doctoral researcher in philosophy at Ludwig-Maximilian University of Munich and a fellow of the Minerva Foundation. His fields of research are, in particular, moral and political philosophy. He holds a PhD in philosophy from the Hebrew University of Jerusalem and has studied legal theory at New York University.

David Heyd is Chaim Perelman Professor of Philosophy at the Hebrew University of Jerusalem. He was born in Jerusalem and earned his PhD in philosophy at Oxford University (Wadham College). Since 1976, he has been teaching at the Hebrew University, serving for some time as head of the philosophy department and as director of the university program for outstanding students. Heyd's main areas of research, in which he has published books and articles, are ethics, political philosophy, and bioethics. He has served on many public committees on biomedical issues, leading to regulation and legislation of medical practice in the fields of procreation, genetics, euthanasia, and research.

Amos Israel-Vleeschhouwer is a lecturer at the School of Law at the Sapir Academic College in Sderot, Israel, and has initiated the Sapir Legal Innovation and entrepreneurship Lab. He serves on the board of PICATI—the public committee against torture in Israel—and volunteers at the rape crisis center. Amos holds an MA in Social psychology, and LLM, PhD in law, all from Tel Aviv University. His research interests are Jewish law, law and psychology, and computational legal studies.

Amit Kravitz teaches philosophy at Ludwig Maximilian University of Munich, Munich. His main fields of interest are Kant and German Idealism, most especially Schelling. His papers in German and English were published in *Kant-Studien*, *Archiv für Geschichte der Philosophie*, *Philosophisches Jahrbuch*, and the *Journal for the History of Ideas.* He was also the co-editor of Der Begriff des Judentums in der klassischen deutschen Philosophie (Tübingen: Mohr Siebeck, 2018, together with Dr. Jörg Noller).

Mooli Lahad, PhD is senior medical psychologist dramatherapist and bibliotherapist, is full professor of Psychology and Dramatherapy at Tel-Hai Academic College Israel, and has two PhDs. He is founder and president of the Community Stress Prevention Center (CSPC) and is one of the world-leading experts on the integration of the arts form therapies and psychotrauma/coping with disasters. Lahad is the author and co-author of thirty-five books and many articles on the topics such as the use of creative therapies in post-trauma and grief, communities under stress, and coping with life-threatening situations. Among his models are the following: The Basic Ph integrative model of coping and resilience, See Far Cbt for the treatment of psychotrauma, and the 6PSM. He has received several awards: the Israeli Psychology Association—Bonner Award, the Adler Institute for the welfare of the child Award-Tel Aviv University, the Israeli Lottery Prize, and the world Wizo and WHO for his humanitarian work in disaster areas.

Berel Lang is Emeritus Professor of Philosophy at the State University of New York at Albany, Albany, NY, USA. His books include *Act and Idea in the Nazi Genocide* (1990), *The Anatomy of Philosophical Style* (1990), *Holocaust Representation: Art Within the Limits of History and Ethics* (2000), *Philosophical Witnessing: The Holocaust as Presence* (2009), *Primo Levi: The Matter of a Life* (2014), and *Genocide: The Act as Idea* (2017).

Yael Lavi is a PhD candidate in the School of Philosophy, Linguistics and Science Studies, The Lester and Sally Entin Faculty of Humanities, Tel Aviv University, Tel Aviv, Israel. Her research interests include ethics, phenomenology, existentialism, and epistemology of vulnerability. More specifically, her work focuses at the phenomenology of end of life decisions.

Eli Pitcovski is a lecturer at Tel-Hai Academic College. His main fields of interest are epistemology, philosophy of representation, and ontology including the metaphysics of death. His last papers have been published in *The Journal of Philosophy* (Normal Knowledge, 2018, together with Andrew Peet), Analysis (Lost in Transmission, 2017 together with Andrew Peet), and *Synthese* (Getting the Big Picture 2017).

Oshrat C. Silberbusch holds a PhD in philosophy from Tel Aviv University. Her book *Adorno's Philosophy of the Nonidentical. Thinking as Resistance* was published in 2018 with Palgrave Macmillan. She has written articles on T. W. Adorno, Jean Améry, Günther Anders, George Orwell, post-Shoah philosophy, and German-Jewish history.

Adrian Switzer (PhD) is an associate professor in the Department of Philosophy at University of Missouri-Kansas City (UMKC) and a Faculty Fellow in the Department of Philosophy at Colby College. The co-translator of *Kant's Critique of Pure Reason: The Foundation of Modern Philosophy* (2009) and *Parmenides, Cosmos and Being: A Philosophical Interpretation* (2007), Switzer is the author of numerous book chapters and journal articles on such figures as Kant, Nietzsche, Merleau-Ponty, Benjamin, Foucault, Deleuze, Derrida, Irigaray, and Jean-Luc Nancy. As a research and teaching fellow at Colby, Switzer is completing his book, *The Events of May 1968: The Art and Philosophy of Revolution* (Rowman & Littlefield, forthcoming).

Magdalena Zolkos is Humboldt Research Fellow at Goethe University Frankfurt. She is the author of a monograph *Reconciling Community and Subjective Life: Trauma Testimony as Political Theorizing in the Work of Jean Améry and Imre Kértesz* (2010) and of a forthcoming "Restitution and the Imaginary: Undoing, Repair and Return in Modernity" (Edinburgh University Press, 2020). She is the editor of *On Jean Améry: Philosophy of Catastrophe* (2011) and co-editor with Marguerite La Caze of a forthcoming "On What Cannot Be Touched: Contemporary Perspectives on Vladimir Jankélévitch" (Lexington, 2019).

Introduction

Jean Améry was born Hans Mayer in Vienna, in 1912, the son of a middle-class Austrian mother and an assimilated Jewish father. In 1935, when Nazi Germany instituted anti-Semitic racial Laws, Améry was studying philosophy and literature at Vienna University. Following Germany's annexation of Austria (*Anschluss*) in 1938, he escaped the Nazi regime. He initially fled to France and later to Belgium, where he joined a German-speaking unit of the resistance. In July 1943, Améry was arrested by the Gestapo for spreading anti-Nazi propaganda among the German occupying forces in Belgium. Imprisoned in Fort Breendonk, Améry was tortured and interrogated by the SS for several days. Upon realizing that he was Jewish, not merely a political prisoner, his captors sent him to Auschwitz. Améry endured a year in Auschwitz III, the Buna-Monowitz labor camp. Lacking manual skills, he was assigned to a labor detail at the I-G Farben site, digging dirt, laying cables, lugging sacks of cement and iron crossbeams. As the Red Army advanced, Améry was evacuated first to Buchenwald and subsequently to Bergen-Belsen, where he was liberated in April 1945. Améry did not speak *publicly* about the Holocaust for almost twenty years. He finally broke his silence in October 1964, in a series of radio programs in Germany. These programs subsequently formed the basis for his well-known collection of essays, *Jenseits von Schuld und Sühne* (1966). An English translation, entitled *At the Mind's Limits*, was published in 1980. On October 17, 1978, Améry committed suicide.

* * *

Améry's decision to break his silence and broadcast his first radio program about the Holocaust should be understood on the background of the Auschwitz trials (that began in December 1963), the publication of Primo Levi's book *If This Is a Man* in Germany (1961), and Arendt's contemplations of the Eichmann trial (1963). Améry's views and style offered a unique, challenging, and straightforward perspective on Auschwitz from within. Throughout the years, interest in Améry has grown continuously. Today, it seems that the essays he published based on his radio programs were not only timely but also timeless.

This volume explores various major aspects of Améry's work. While reading Améry *qua* Holocaust survivor is unavoidable, such overgeneralizations may obscure the uniqueness of Améry's voice. In light of this, the essays in this volume collectively contribute to a subtler, more comprehensive picture of Améry's thought and a better understanding of his multifaceted personality.

The volume is divided into three parts. The first, entitled "Limits: Bound to the Past," concentrates on what appears to be Améry's insistence on "facing backwards," not allowing the past slip away. The essays in this part explore various aspects of this stance, according to which the world continued to move forward while Améry's personal clock remained frozen in time. The second part, "The Mind: Torture and Consequences," focuses on the nature of torture, the ramifications of this experience, and the relevant normative implications. The third part, "Beyond: Philosophy and Literature," progresses beyond the discourse of victimization and trauma, examining less well-known aspects of Améry's work, with special attention to his literary work and philosophical views.

* * *

The first part begins with a chapter by **Berel Lang**. Lang compares Améry to a fellow inmate, a man who was imprisoned in the same block as Améry and is considered one of the most important authors to have written about Auschwitz: Primo Levi. Indeed, there are numerous parallels between the lives (and deaths) of Jean Améry and Primo Levi. This essay underscores the differences between the two writers' understanding of their wartime experiences and their reactions to that past in the post-Holocaust reality.

In the second chapter, **Amit Kravitz** explores the issue of testimony, revealing different aspects of Améry's intricate philosophical approach toward it. In particular, Kravitz examines Améry's approach to testimony in light of three philosophical challenges: (a) testimony and the question of historical objectivity; (b) testimony and the reality of evil; and (c) the tension between testimony and the concept of moral kitsch. In addition, this chapter considers the ramifications of the so-called universalization of the Holocaust on testimony.

Subsequently, **Fred Alford** discusses forgiveness in the intergenerational context. According to Alford Améry regarded forgiveness as a virtue only under impossible conditions: when both perpetrator and victim wish with equal intensity that the offense had never occurred; that time could be reset, ensuring a different outcome. However, Améry's approach encounters a further problem: it can apply only to the Holocaust generation. Subsequent generations, on both sides, can no longer wish for the reversal of time, because they are outside of the original time frame.

Magdalena Zolkos offers a comparative analysis of Améry's essay "How Much Home Does a Person Need?" In this essay, Améry argued that the homesickness experienced by assimilated German-speaking Jews during the war was a very specific kind of longing. This chapter, however, goes a step further, examining Améry's notions in the context of Behrouz Boochani's writings—the political memoir of a refugee imprisoned in the Australian detention center on Manus Island. In so doing, it reveals the central role played by the motif of freedom as a means of resisting oppression.In the final chapter of the first part, **David Heyd** discusses one of the central concepts in Améry's writing: Resentments. Heyd argues that in his essay "Resentments," Améry presented a radical position on the fundamental moral role of "ressentiment" that the victim feels toward the perpetrator of the wrong. Heyd examines how Améry turned Nietzsche's concept of ressentiment on its head, revealing surprising similarities between Améry's view and P. F. Strawson's theory of reactive attitudes in moral theory. Améry's ultimate statement concerning the backward-looking attitude of resentment highlights a tragic tension: it is at once the only genuine moral attitude toward Nazi crimes and completely futile, necessarily obstructing the forward-looking tendency of social morality.

The second part, "The Mind: Torture and Consequences," opens with **Eran Fish**'s account of the act of torturing, inspired by Améry. According to Fish, Améry described not only the act of torture and the experience of the torture victim but also the torturers themselves and their particular psychology. Fish's chapter attempts to explain what torture can bring to light regarding perpetrators' mental state and personalities.

Subsequently, **Amos Israel-Vleeschhouwer** explores the various attitudes toward torture found in Jewish law—ranging from total prohibition, through condoning, to advocating the use of torture under certain conditions. According to Israel-Vleeschhouwer, reading Améry's testimony in conjunction with Jewish legal sources relating to torture has significant heuristic value: The vivid impact of Améry's writings on participants in the Jewish normative debate can balance the currently prevailing influences, revealing aspects and sources, raising questions, and accentuating interpretations.

In the third chapter, **Yochai Ataria** presents the phenomenology of the torture victim. Based on his own experience, Améry argued that torture is *the most horrible event a human being can retain within himself*. Ataria's chapter investigates this statement, seeking to ground it more concretely in phenomenology and embodied cognition.

In the fourth chapter of this part, **Dana Amir** focuses on Améry's essay, "How Much Home Does a Person Need?" In contrast to Zolkos, Amir studies this work mainly from a psychoanalytical perspective. She analyzes the language crisis inherent in forced exile.

In the final chapter in this part, **Mooli Lahad** explores the healing power of imagination and suggests a new perspective on Améry as a Holocaust survivor suffering from Post-traumatic Stress Disorder or Complex Grief. Lahad proposes that Améry was aware of the protective role of imagination and playfulness in traumatic incidents, yet he nevertheless rejected this option.

The third part, "Beyond: Philosophy and Literature," begins with a chapter by **Roy Ben-Shai**, examining Améry as a philosopher. The chapter explains Améry's ambivalent relationship to philosophy and his reluctance to identify his work as philosophical. While registering this reluctance, the chapter nonetheless underscores the philosophical aspects and aspirations of Améry's thought—most notably, the rigorous methodology he developed in order to enable thinking to confront its own limits. Ben-Shai claims that to understand Améry's project as a whole not only must we embrace a philosophical perspective, but, moreover, Améry's writing forces us to rethink the very meaning of philosophy.

In the second chapter, **Eli Pitcovski** discusses the value of death. Drawing on Améry's essay "At the Mind's Limits," Pitcovski defends a response to Epicurus' view ("death has no intrinsic value") that at the same time opposes the prevalent contemporary view regarding the value of death (roughly: the degree to which death is bad depends on the extent to which the life prevented by it would have been good). According to Améry, the cause of death can contribute to the degree to which death is bad, and the question concerning the value of dying is more fundamental than that concerning the value of death.

The next two contributions discuss aspects of suicide. As **Grace Campbell** stresses, within Améry's philosophy, suicide functions as an act of human freedom. Freely choosing to commit suicide is an example of the uniquely human ability to act spontaneously and reject the inertia of the logic of life. Campbell argues that this represents the logical conclusion of Améry's philosophical system as well as his ultimate challenge to the logic of the everyday and natural progression of history. However, this challenge occurs within a system that is firmly grounded in Enlightenment notions of autonomy and human rights. In the following chapter, **Yael Lavi** further investigates the meaning of the *anti-logic of death* and its role in Améry's reasoning. In her analysis, she emphasizes Améry's proximity to the Absurd on the one hand and the Enlightenment tradition on the other, which ultimately led him to formulate a challenging position not only regarding the philosophical aspects of suicide but also with respect to the relevant scientific practice.

The final two chapters examine a less-known aspect of Jean Améry's persona: the novelist. **Oshrat Silberbusch** explores Améry's novel-essay *Lefeu* and other unpublished novelistic fragments written in the immediate postwar period, seeking to discover why, after a promising attempt in pre-war Vienna, Améry only twice returned to the fictional form, and on both occasions with little success. The picture that emerges suggests an intimate relationship between the historical events that shattered Améry's life and his abandoned vocation. The chapter explores the implications of this connection, in particular, the close affinity it established between Améry and a philosopher he loved to hate: T. W. Adorno, who famously said, "There can be no poetry after Auschwitz."

In the final chapter, **Adrian Switzer** discusses Améry's last novel-essay: *Charles Bovary, Country Doctor*. Switzer's chapter offers a reading of Améry's work as a contribution to twentieth-century theories of aesthetic realism. In contrast to Gustave Flaubert, for whom literary style was the mark of realism, Améry demonstrated that the 'real' of realism must be the history of a novel's characters. In the case of Madame Bovary, this is the history of the bourgeoisie after the French Revolution.

PART I

Limits: Bound to the Past

CHAPTER 1

Jean Améry and Primo Levi: The Differences in Likeness

Berel Lang

1.1 Overture

At first glance, the intersections of their biographies link Jean Améry and Primo Levi as a natural or at least historical couple. Separated in age by seven years (Améry, born 1912 in Vienna; Levi, in Turin, 1919) and educated in the interwar period, both were touched by the intellectual currents of the time: Améry, by the Vienna Circle and *its* circles, Levi, at the University of Turin. As young adults, both faced the Nazi threat in the 1930s, with Améry's Jewish identity forced on him—he claims—by Austria's 1938 racial rules, Levi's were nurtured earlier in a consciously Jewish household. Against the Nazis, both joined resistance groups and both were captured in their occupied countries (Améry, in his adopted Belgium, Levi, in Italy); both were then deported to camps in the East and, in common, to Auschwitz where they encountered each other (although with differing memories of that). Both survived Auschwitz (Améry was then sent to other camps), and each had a large impact later in their post-Holocaust writings about their wartime lives as well as in their reflections on the

B. Lang (✉)
State University of New York at Albany, Albany, NY, USA
e-mail: blang01@wesleyan.edu

Y. Ataria et al. (eds.), *Jean Améry*,
https://doi.org/10.1007/978-3-030-28095-6_1

Holocaust in the context of European history. Both were also one-time visitors to the new state of Israel whose efforts for independence they had supported although with no inclination before or after their trips for emigrating. And both died by suicide before reaching the age of seventy: Améry in 1978, Levi in 1987. Améry, after more than one earlier failed attempt, also published a book *about* suicide two years before his death; Levi, who wrote about Améry's death in his own last book, published that in the year Levi himself died. Even the inscriptions on their two gravestones are concisely similar, their names and dates joined only by their six-digit Auschwitz numbers [A: 172364; L: 174517]. (Levi's stone also includes the formulaic Hebrew initials: Taf, Nun, Tsadi, Bet, Hay, acronyms for the expression: 'May his soul be bound up in the grip of life'.)

1.2 First Movement

Such external likeness is, however, no assurance of personal affinity or even acceptance, and aside from a few restrained expressions of mutual regard, Améry and Levi recognized their significant differences both in their understanding of their own histories and in their address to the inevitable post-Holocaust question of 'What is to be done *now*?' That is, in relation to the Holocaust's implications for world politics and, still more immediately, for their personal ways forward in its shadow. The differences between them on these questions amount to an estrangement, one that is more revealing *because of* their biographical intersections. These differences surfaced, furthermore, without apology on either side, although with Améry more vocal and sharper in criticizing Levi than the other way round. Améry's anger at history—at his own and at history as such—was closer to the surface, as was his expression of emotion in general. But that same intensity also spurred Améry to a more self-reflective analysis of that reaction's origins than did Levi whose intensity, although no less strong, expressed itself more guardedly. I attempt here to show these features of Améry's thinking specifically in three of Améry's later books in which his sustained reflections on three significant but rarely analyzed in ethical terms—torture, aging, and suicide—warrant attention even apart from his wartime experience on which he drew in addressing them.

One symptomatic difference between Améry and Levi appears in their writing *as* writing: the difficulty of mistaking the sentences written by one of them for the other's. Consider, for example, these brief passages from the Prefaces to their principal books on the Holocaust (Améry's, *Beyond*

Guilt and Atonement [*Jenseits von Schuld und Unsühn*]; in English, as *At the Mind's Limits* (1966) and Levi's *If This Is a Man* [*Se Questo e un Uomo*]; in its English translation, *Survival in Auschwitz*) (1947)[1]: So, Améry: "If in the first lines of the Auschwitz essay [here] I had still believed that I could remain circumspect and distant and face the reader with refined objectivity, I now saw that that was simply impossible". And Levi: "[This book of mine] … has not been written to formulate new accusations; it should be able, rather, to furnish documentation for a quiet study of certain aspects of the human mind". For the one, a rejection of even the possibility of objectivity; for the other, a conscious effort at disinterest. And indeed these respective characterizations of their writing are compelling, with the distancing effect that Améry rejects having been deliberately adopted by Levi in his 'quiet study'. The differences in their expression of what was for both strong emotion provides an unusual lesson in contrasting styles of rhetorical discourse.

An additional contributory factor to the differences between Améry and Levi as authors was their respective economic situations: Levi with a secure post-Holocaust career in a commercial chemical company; Améry hustling for a living as an ostensibly independent novelist and journalist. (In a midcareer interview in 1957, Améry said regretfully, "I wanted to be a poet, and I am a journalist, a reporter".) Whether as cause or effect of this difference, the current world loomed larger in Améry's thought than in Levi's, and this surfaces in the chronology of their writings about the Holocaust. Even before Levi reached Turin after eleven months in Auschwitz, he had begun to compose his thoughts and to write them down. Only a year and a half later, his book, *If This Is a Man*, was not only completed but published, no doubt a result of good fortune but even more of the *author's* urgency. Améry, by contrast, waited twenty years before systematically addressing his wartime experience (he had earlier, in 1945, begun to add to an autobiographical novel about it, but that difference in genre was crucial).

Améry himself commented on his deferral of writing about the Holocaust in his Preface to *Beyond Guilt and Atonement*, explaining that he wrote *then* (1968) in reaction to what he saw as the forgetfulness in Europe of the Holocaust past. That past had obviously been present for Améry in the intervening two decades, and both Améry and Levi had followed the 1961 Eichmann trial in Jerusalem closely (with Levi in a comment exemplifying both the emotional and intellectual gap between the two, that although he agreed with the death sentence on Eichmann, he 'doubted that he could have carried it out himself'). It is notable in any event that Améry chooses in the opening essay of *Beyond Guilt and Atonement* to write not about the magnitude or character of the Nazi crime and guilt, but about 'the Intellectual in Auschwitz', turning then rather to experience *within* the camp as though the quality of the Nazi 'project' had, on the one hand, been so fully analyzed morally as to require no further elaboration and/or, on the other hand, was of such intrinsic quality as to be not only beyond 'redemption' as his book's title asserted, but beyond language or the telling as well. It was his *then* contemporary world, as it was always his immediate surroundings, that triggered his delayed writing—the combination of anger and despair at what he sees *then* as indifference to, even the denial of the history of those wartime years, including of course the torture he had undergone which he saw in retrospect as an intrinsic expression of Nazism.

The focus in that opening essay (titled 'At the Mind's Limits'; note: it is the reaction to the camps from within, not the Nazis that pushes at the mind's limits), is thus on what he sees as a characteristic failing of intellectuals in the camps—the way their will for transcendence and abstraction blocked them in confronting the camps' immediate and urgent contingencies, and the afterlife of which taints still the abstractions by which Nazism has been diluted if not erased. All that in contrast (he claims) to the resilience of captives whose ideological (presumably '*non*-intellectual') visions of history sustained them. It did not matter, Améry insists, *which* political or religious commitments underwrote those ideologies; the commitments themselves were the resource.

Améry does not say in this diagnosis whether he includes himself among the 'disabled' intellectuals, but a more basic issue is his choice of *that* topic as foremost among many possible ones for his systematic analysis—returning us again to the claim in his Preface of Europe's forgetfulness. He is thus writing about the past through the lens of the present, and no less about the one than the other: the role of the intellectual, in other words, as it had been and as it then also *continued*. (Julian Benda's *The Treason of the Intellectuals*[2] was a familiar text to him in lodging this accusation.)

It is not in this context, however, that Améry criticizes Primo Levi as a 'forgiver'—a term of opprobrium for Améry in relation to the Nazis. But Levi's reading of that opening essay saw in it what he took to be the substantive differences between him and Améry. In an opening volley in his essay on Améry, Levi criticizes Améry's definition of the 'intellectual' as excluding Levi's own culture of science as a source for intellectuals (Levi gives that criticism an ironic turn by suggesting that perhaps his survival showed that he wasn't *that much* an intellectual).[3] More directly confronting Améry's charge, Levi, who had no more ideological commitment of the sort Améry commended than Améry himself, reports as key to *his* survival his attentiveness to the minutiae of daily life: bed-making to meet the absurd camp requirements, how to get to the richer bottom of the daily soup ration, and most of all how to avoid being singled out in the frequent selections. All these taken together, he claims, were so consuming as to leave little room for ideological rationalization. This attentiveness to the immediate and the concrete undoubtedly built on Levi's 'hands-on' work as a chemist, but he also finds in *If This Is a Man* no significant differences among fellow captives who did or did not have ideological commitments. Indeed, Levi directs his harshest words for any of his fellow captives at an Orthodox Jew who in praying, thanked God for having spared him from a selection, surely aware that his place there had been filled by someone else. And his warmest words of admiration were for an Italian worker who at risk to himself smuggled extra rations to Levi but cared and knew nothing of ideology.

When Améry does criticize Levi by name as a 'forgiver' (in his correspondence with a common acquaintance), the inadequacies of intellectuals again hover over that charge. And Levi disputes Améry also on that claim, protesting that he continued to hold the Nazis to account, notwithstanding his efforts to *understand* them which were for Améry a first step toward forgiveness. A passage in *If This Is a Man* exemplifies this difference between the two. Here the Kapo Alex, guiding Levi back to his barracks, grasps a greasy cable wire in order to clamber over an obstacle, and then (in Levi's words), "[w]ithout hatred and without sneering, Alex wipes his hand on my shoulder". "He would be amazed," Levi concludes, "if someone told him that today, on the basis of this action, I judge him … and the innumerable others like him, big and small, in Auschwitz and everywhere".[4] But this retelling might only reinforce Améry's charge, given its contrast from Améry's account of having hit a Kapo in the camp who insulted him and then proudly suffering the painful consequences. Levi specifically wrote about *that* incident in his essay on Améry, emphasizing that hitting back physically as Améry had done was not "in" him—almost as if that absence were a genetic trait.

1.3 Second Movement

Améry's most frequently quoted statements from all his writings appear in his essay on 'Torture', the second chapter in *Beyond Guilt and Atonement*, where, twenty years afterward, he describes his torture by the Gestapo following his capture by them in Brussels. His torturers believed that Améry knew the identities of other group members and the group's future plans, but because of the group's secrecy precautions, Améry did not have that information. He admits to his readers that if he *had* had the information, the torture would have brought it out of him; indeed, he reports *inventing* plausible leads in order to interrupt the torture itself. Finally, however and for their own reasons, his torturers concluded that he did not have the information they sought, and stopped the torture. Améry, still alive, was then deported to Auschwitz. (Améry himself mentions the contrasting case of Jean Moulin who did have the information demanded by his torturers and withstood the demands up to his own death). And then we hear Améry's reflections on the phenomenon of torture that have become familiar: "I dare to assert that torture is the most horrible event a human being retains within himself. [It] … has an indelible character. Whoever is tortured stays tortured. Whoever has succumbed to torture can no longer feel at home in the world". And as capstone: "It would be totally senseless to try and describe the pain that was inflicted on me".[5]

One can hardly question these expressions of Améry's experience, but they do include categorical statements about torture that raise formal issues. In asserting the inadequacy of language to describe the pain of torture, for instance, Améry cites the verbal limitations on descriptions of feelings, a common figure of speech recognizable as the 'aporia'. (So, in a classic example, Cordelia's rejection of King Lear's command that she, like her sisters, tell him how much she loves him—her refusal to obey him coming not from will but from inability; so, her line: "I cannot heave my heart into my mouth".) But the most basic feature of torture's distinctiveness is for Améry how the act itself compels the victim who otherwise experiences a balance of person in body and mind to experience himself as *all* body, with the mind or persona first diminished and finally totally obscured. "Whoever is overcome by pain through torture experiences his body as never before. In self-negation, his flesh becomes a total reality … The tortured person is only a body and nothing else beside that".[6] And then too, as he writes in a following chapter, the tortured person becomes alienated, in exile, no longer "at home" in his own self.

Structurally, this description of torture assumes torture as an effect of human agency, inflicted by a person or persons on others. And although conceptual and moral differences distinguish torture between pain from that source and pain caused by 'natural' or impersonal causes, pain from the latter can be no less intense or sustained than the effect of torturers. George Orwell goes even further than this in arguing that however inventive the human infliction of pain, it does not match the extremes contrived by nature. And Améry himself seems also to admit this prospect in a reference to Freud's end-of-life suffering from his cancer of the jaw, when he describes *that* as "torture"—sufficiently all-consuming to lead to Freud's appeal to his physician to bring it (and him) to an end. At least elements of Améry's analysis of torture thus seem to apply to 'natural' torture as well, whatever their other conceptual and moral differences.

If, furthermore, the effect of torture for Améry is understood as the dissolution into a body as caused by physical pain, an additional parallel suggests itself for *psychological* pain and *its* torture, sustained and consuming as also they can be. So, for example, the death of a loved one, perhaps epitomized in the death of a young child for a parent. Certain evident differences distinguish emotional from physical pain, but arguably not in the intensity or duration of the pain involved, extending also to the phenomenon of Post-traumatic Stress Disorder. Like other moments of extreme experience, the conditions and limits of torture are thus not so readily tamed.

1.4 Third Movement

The drama surrounding the occurrence and consequences of torture understandably becomes part of its analysis, and there is evidence that Améry himself was aware of its openness to hyperbole. Both evidence and consequence of that recognition seem to figure in the book that Améry wrote immediately after *Beyond Guild and Atonement* on the subject of aging (*On Aging: Revolt and Resignation*).[7] On the surface, that next topic seems a radical shift from the concepts of Torture, Ressentiment, and Exile at the center of its predecessor. But that new work is no less remarkable than *Beyond Guilt and Atonement*, and it is distinctively related to that earlier book because, quite unexpectedly, it applies categories introduced in the analysis of torture to characterize a much more common period of human experience—in Améry's words, the "tragic hardship of aging".[8] In this new sequence of essays, the differences between Améry and Levi are also on display, as Améry digs deeply into layers of the self and person in relation to which Levi's overriding senses of privacy and propriety (by his own admission) constrained him.

Early in *On Aging*, Améry reminds his readers that although aging is typically spread over the years, it begins of course at birth. To be sure, it is usually accompanied by physical and psychological accommodation that turns its successive stages into normalcy without much notice, certainly without the singular, 'indelible' mark of torture. But it also becomes increasingly clear, Améry argues, that aging exemplifies the same encroachment of the body on the person that torture injects more suddenly. Indeed, Améry points out, in one respect that process is more radical in aging than in torture, because with aging, unlike torture, there is no stopping it. "Aging", he presses the reminder, "is an incurable sickness"—the more notably since so far as agency is involved, the agent is not someone else but one's own self, through one's own body. Améry describes this agency in a voice forcefully resembling Dostoyevsky's Underground Man, with the body parts of a person being addressed as if they were agents: "Miserable leg, weary heart, rebellious stomach: you hurt *me*, you're my adversaries. I would like … to look after you and commiserate with you and also to tear you out of my body and replace you. My head swims with the thought that I *am* my leg, my heart, my stomach …".[9] The notion of finding it impossible to be "at home in the world" that Améry emphasized as a consequence of torture thus surfaces here for the aging body from which the person is also and increasingly exiled. "We become alienated from ourselves", he writes, "doubled and inscrutable". That torture in its usual role is initiated externally 'by another' and aging as initiated by or at least in the self to whom it applies opens the obvious question of how *that* difference affects the experience or its intensity. One can imagine arguments pressing from either side of that comparison: claiming that the fact that it is one's own self that is 'responsible' for the affliction adds emotional weight to it—or claiming the contrary, that the fact that it is not one's self but another human being who decides to torture adds weight to *its* intensity. Améry does not himself take a position on this comparison, and a likely reason for this avoidance is that both conceptually and phenomenologically, the similarity between the two 'moments' of experience is more central to their understanding than any attempt to calibrate them: the key to each is the coercion exerted on the person in both processed to *become* the body that previously had been the person's subordinate.

Now the very juxtaposition of an account of aging to torture may seem a stretch, but Améry's application of terms argues for a meditated connection and at least a compelling analogy. Indeed, recognition of the ecumenical reach of aging—transcultural, apolitical, beyond ideology—is not only consistent with the account of torture but an apparent transposition or even sublimation of his analysis. Admittedly aging may be disrupted, either by accident or intentionally, as in suicide. But the former occurrence is an interruption of its process, not a denial or reversal, and the latter, whatever else it is, is also a protest *against* aging, thus with the process itself still calling the tune. Survivors of torture like Améry himself can retrospectively rehearse and reflect on torture, but no such retrospection is possible for the encroachment by aging on the body, certainly not for the conclusion of that process. However the Post Traumatic Stress Disorder applies to onetime victims of torture, nothing comparable is on the horizon for the 'victims' of aging.

Here too the parting of ways between Améry and Levi surfaces, with the latter committed more steadily to ironies of the concrete external world, and Améry turning inward to raise internally systematic questions. Levi could call attention (in a book of vignettes) to the ability of mosquitoes to jump two and a half times their height from a standing start, something no Olympic high jumper even approximates. And although he certainly recognized morally charged moments and events, he distrusted philosophical abstractions almost as a matter of principle. So, for example, he would leave undeveloped such notable flashes of deep philosophical intuition as his attack on the essentialist theory of human nature that generalized from the competitive, egoistic—Hobbesian—relations among Nazi camp captives as evidence of *that* as defining essential human nature. But no, Levi objects, "We do not believe in the most obvious and facile deduction: that man is fundamentally brutal, egoistic and stupid in his conduct once every civilized institution is taken away ... We believe, rather, that the only conclusion to be drawn is that in the face of driving necessity ... many social habits and instincts are reduced to silence".[10] Put more formally—as Levi does not—competitive egoism in the camps comes no closer to defining *essential* human nature than human conduct does under other conditions.

In his turn, Améry is not indifferent to the alternatives offered by irony that are so constant in Levi's writing. Thus, Améry finds room even in his somber account of aging for a joke about it (admittedly, he tells it as an *example* of a joke, not quite the same as a joke). This one is about the older man who returns home from a hard day in the office to find his younger wife amorous, urging him on, encouraging him and recalling for him past memories of their love life. "You always used to love to bite me when we did it", she reminds him, and she persists and persists until finally he gives in: "Ok, Ok, I'll do it. But first you have to hand me my teeth".

Perhaps this example proves only that aging is not a fertile ground for humor—certainly it does not surface as a dominant feature of aging in Améry's phenomenological reflections on it.

1.5 Fourth Movement

In considering the connections and differences between the lives and thought of Améry and Levi, one can hardly avoid confronting their common deaths by suicide. Such reference, however, comes with a price, because as for so many suicides in the history of authors (Stefan Zweig, Hemingway, Sylvia Plath), readings of their work often become suffused by the manner of their death, like a lens coloring all their accomplishments. But biographical causality is no more easily corralled than historical causality on a corporate scale. Elie Wiesel's summary judgment on Levi's suicide, for example, that "Levi died at Auschwitz, only forty years later", thus seems misdirected, in effect erasing forty years of Levi's creative accomplishment and recognition, his warm family life and his wide circle of devoted friends. Levi himself seemed to have objected beforehand to Wiesel's comment when he (Levi) wrote about Améry's death in *The Drowned and the Saved* that Améry's post-Auschwitz anger "led him to positions of such severity and intransigence as to make him incapable of finding joy in life, indeed of living".[11] That judgment of Améry's post-Auschwitz life is contestable, but the contrast between its characterization of Améry and the same period in Levi's is unmistakable, with Levi himself having realized, even after Auschwitz, the possibility of 'finding joy in life'. (Recall here even the unexpected author whom Levi names as most kindred to himself: Rabelais).

In a second point about Améry's suicide, Levi bluntly asserts that "like other suicides [it] admits of a cloud of explanations"—with a similar 'cloud of explanations' soon afterward of course clouding Levi's own death. A cloud also persists in a different sense for Améry's own distinction in his book on suicide between the conventional term 'Selbstmord' and the 'Freitod' that Améry contrasts with it. 'Freitod' for Améry represents a decision freely made by the agent as both subject and object—thus not at all murder as in Selbstmord. This distinction as a whole warrants further discussion, but an immediate issue is its assumption of a radical freedom of decision as fully independent of the conditions under which it (or indeed any) decision can be made. At the times of their deaths, both Améry and Levi were suffering ill health physically, together with anxiety about their capacity to carry on their work. Levi did not reflect systematically on suicide (or aging), but suicide as an act had touched him not only through Holocaust writer-survivors like Paul Celan and still other contemporary writers like his fellow Turinese, Cesare Pavese, but in his own family, in one grandfather and an uncle. But then too, does not the 'cloud' over suicide that Levi mentions in reference to Améry's suicide apply as well to Améry's conception of a Freitod? Améry assumes in that concept that the freedom in Freitod is independent of any conditions impinging on the person making the decision. It thus epitomizes the existential freedom and imperative of contingency that had earlier drawn Améry so strongly to Sartre's existentialist writings (including Sartre's contentious *Reflections on the Jewish Question*). What, after all, would more fully exemplify a truly free act than one that freely brought that freedom to an end? But as Améry himself felt increasingly hedged in by physical indisposition, the question of how or whether those hedges may affect (*and* limit) a decision involving them is unavoidable: how 'free' *would* that decision be? As directed at Améry's view, this objection is ad hominem, but it at least suggests a formal question about the distinction of which the Freitod is an essential part.

1.6 Coda

In such varied ways, Améry and Levi were present (and absent) to each other in their lives and thinking. Always, however, they wrote *themselves* as both subject and agent, placing themselves, I have meant to show, in the rich tradition of the moral essay—a tradition often patronized as falling into the gaps between philosophy and non-philosophy, between history and non-history, between fiction and nonfiction. It is a tradition that includes such undisputed authors as Montaigne, Pascal, Emerson, Camus, Orwell, and so now, as would be added, Améry and Levi. As authors, to be sure, they were clearly aware of the reach and bite of criticism, and it would be intriguing now to hear what they themselves would have to say in retrospect about their own writings, fifty or sixty years later. Along with that, we would surely be no less interested to hear what each of them would now have to say about the other...

Notes

1. Jean Améry, *At the Mind's Limits*, translated by Sidney Rosenfeld and Stella P. Rosenfeld; Bloomington: Indiana University Press, 1980. Primo Levi, *Survival in Auschwitz*, translated by Stuart Woolf; New York: Touchstone, 1986.
2. Julien Benda, *The Treason of the Intellectuals*, translated by R. Aldington; New Brunswick, NJ: Transaction, 2006.
3. Primo Levi, *The Drowned and the Saved*, translated by Raymond Rosenthal; New York: Vintage, 1989, p. 133.
4. Primo Levi, *Survival in Auschwitz*, pp. 107–108.
5. Jean Améry, *At the Mind's Limits*, p. 34.
6. *At the Mind's Limits*, pp. 32, 36.
7. *On Aging: Revolt and Resignation*, translated by John D. Barlow; Bloomington: Indiana University Press, 1994.
8. *On Aging*, p. 24.
9. *On Aging*, pp. 46–47.
10. *Survival in Auschwitz*, p. 87.
11. *The Drowned and the Saved*, p. 136.

CHAPTER 2

On Historical Objectivity, the Reality of Evil and Moral Kitsch: Jean Améry as a Witness

Amit Kravitz

Die Leute reden über Politik und Geschichte, objektive Vorgänge. Ich bleibe fixiert, bis zum bittersten Ende, an das Erlebnis.
—Améry (*2005*), p. 46)

2.1 Introduction

The uniqueness of Jean Améry, a Holocaust survivor who reflects on his terrible experience, is twofold.

Firstly, Améry was exceptionally attentive—or so it seems to me—to the intellectual and political developments that arose after the Holocaust. In the context of Holocaust survivors this fact should not be taken for granted, for rarely do we expect a Holocaust survivor to have such a keen involvement in such affairs. On the contrary, we do not expect the Holocaust survivor to be bogged down by particular, wearisome political events of the present, which evoke controversy by definition. For notwithstanding the fact that the Holocaust survivor describes his or her concrete, irreducible experience, which is always rooted in a specific, *particular*

A. Kravitz (✉)
Ludwig Maximilian University of Munich, Munich, Germany
e-mail: amit.kravitz@mail.huji.ac.il; amit.kravitz@campus.lmu.de

Y. Ataria et al. (eds.), *Jean Améry*,
https://doi.org/10.1007/978-3-030-28095-6_2

historical context, parallel to it lurks the unavoidable expectation—given the unique symbolic status the Holocaust has obtained in the western consciousness[1] and the moral authority that accompanies the testimony of the survivor—that the survivor would symbolize something *universal* about evil. Put differently, the very notion of 'Holocaust survivor' has gained in our consciousness such a symbolic, universal status—survivors of the 1915 Armenian Genocide, for instance, do not occupy the same status—that we cannot avoid seeing in them a representation of something which lies beyond their particular experience, and certainly beyond the petty swamp of everyday, recent political events. Therefore the moral authority of the Holocaust survivor might be damaged if he were to decide to take a stand on a concrete political controversy instead of expressing a universal message concerning evil (e.g. 'indifference is dangerous!', 'Wehret den Anfängen!' etc.), with which everyone can identify.

A typical illustration of such a tension is the case of Elie Wiesel. Wiesel did not hesitate to take a stand in concrete political issues, for example—to mention two examples which are in many respects still relevant—his decisive contention that Iran endangers the very existence of the State of Israel (this was the reason for his critique of President Obama[2] and for his support of Prime Minister Netanyahu[3]), or his demanding Obama to stop putting pressure on Israel regarding construction in Jerusalem.[4] The discomfort generated by Wiesel's position in some political circles is of no interest to me in this chapter; I only wish to stress that it is in a way *symptomatic*, and as such it is in a way independent of the *specific content* of Wiesel's position. That is, this discomfort is linked to the *very* decision of Wiesel to take a specific stand in an actual political dispute. A clear indication of such discomfort is the fact that those who attacked Wiesel for his positions did not only hold that he was wrong but added that he betrayed his designation as a Holocaust survivor whose mandate first and foremost was to serve as a "symbol of *universal* conscience".[5] Another Holocaust survivor—Paul Celan—of whom it was occasionally said that he identified more with the past horrors experienced by the murdered Jews than with the new, ever-changing challenges facing the living Jews, and who barely took a stance in such burning political debates corresponds, I think, more adequately with our a priori expectation of Holocaust survivors.

It is important for me to stress that I do not condemn or side with either (for the sake of simplicity, for there are many further nuances, of course) the 'Wiesel type' or the 'Celan type'. Moreover, I do not condemn the expectation that, given the uniqueness of the Holocaust, the Holocaust survivor ought to serve as a *universal moral symbol* rather than to deal with the most controversial political issues of the day. To use an Israeli metaphor, one expects the Holocaust survivor to serve as the president of the historical memory, not as its prime minister (or to use a British metaphor, for those who are not familiar with Israeli politics: as the Queen and not the Prime Minister).

It seems to me, however, that within the 'group' of Holocaust survivors who have insisted on commenting on disputed, recent issues—a fact that, as I said, has reduced their moral authority in the eyes of many—Améry's case is unique. It is unique not only because he published many essays on recent events and developments—Améry was, for instance, one of the first intellectuals to define, in a series of revealing essays,[6] 'anti-Zionism' as a new, honorable (*ehrbar*) kind of Antisemitism, and he convincingly showed how the new form of this ancient, persistent hatred is inherently and unexpectedly linked to the political *left*—but also because he did it with a kind of rare intellectual depth, which is directly related to the fact that he spent many years immersed in the major philosophical currents of his time, mainly—but not exclusively—the currents of French philosophy after the war. One can surely find painstaking philosophical aspects in, for example, the Holocaust reflections of Primo Levi as well[7]; however, Levi was not as intensely engaged with the world of philosophy as Améry. And, as I will argue, Améry's deep engagement with philosophy serves as a necessary background for understanding his *position* toward his experience.

This pertains to the second point concerning Améry's uniqueness as a Holocaust survivor; I refer to the way he comprehended the very concept of being a witness. From his philosophical writings—not necessarily from his celebrated writings about the Holocaust, in which he explicitly writes *as* a witness—one can elicit some interesting insights regarding the question: *What does it genuinely mean to be a witness?* As every Holocaust survivor, Améry testifies first and foremost about his subjective experience. However, parallel to his own experience, he struggles—a very unusual struggle, I think, and here I can only give a preliminary description of it—to legitimize or defend, *by philosophical means*, the very institution of testimony (of bearing witness) itself. Moreover, his defense of testimony is not addressed to the usual opponents of testimony in this context (say, the Nazis who try to blur the footprints of their deeds), but to less obvious opponents, as will become clear presently.

Améry's celebrated essays, gathered in his *Jenseits von Schuld und Sühne*, will not stand at the center of my attention here, but rather some of his lesser known, but no less revealing, essays. I will begin by referring to two texts; the first is a letter Améry sent to Sebastian Haffner on July 31, 1978, more or less two months before Améry's suicide (2007, p. 584). The second is an essay written two years before, which is called 'Time for Rehabilitation: The Third Reich and Historical Objectivity'[8] (2005, pp. 91–102).

My chapter entails three parts. I will first (2.2) address the issue of testimony and the question of historical objectivity; I will then (2.3) examine the issue of testimony and the reality of evil; I will conclude (2.4) with a discussion on the relation between testimony and the concept of moral kitsch and its relation to the problem of the universalization of the Holocaust. For, as we shall see, the opponents of testimony to whom Améry is directly addressing his defense are the historian, the philosopher, and the practitioner of the unique kind of moral kitsch characteristic of Heidegger's thought.

2.2 Testimony and Historical Objectivity

In the above-mentioned letter to Haffner, Améry is troubled by the attempt at an "*objectiveness* of experienced history [*Objektivierbarkeit* erlebter Geschichte]" (2007, p. 585).[9] According to Améry, what he terms "a veiled subjectivity [verhüllte Subjektivität]" can better convey the objective facts about Hitler and the essence of the Third Reich than any scientific, cold, disinterested historical effort aimed at an allegedly objective description of the occurrences (p. 584).

Haffner's writings on the war, according to Améry, are a classic illustration of this objective, scientific attitude, an approach which enables Haffner to discuss with equanimity not only Hitler's failures and mistakes but also Hitler's 'achievements', for Haffner's strategy is typical of a historian: To present a balanced, sober ('objective') evaluation of the events and the grounds which enabled those events to come about.

Améry addresses Haffner in the following lines:

> For you, just as for me, not only "history" is at stake, but also the *moral lesson of history* [Moral von der Geschichte]. Here, however, you were not consistent like I wanted you to be. For what you did not see [...] is something that from an historical and philosophical perspective is not only enlightening, but the only legitimate thing: That, as long as the process of historical entropy has not yet begun, Hitler must remain *the myth of evil*

> [*Mythos des Bösen*]. A factual, objective, businesslike [sachlich] demystification of history is nothing but a new and dangerous form of mystification. History as it was experienced [erlebte Geschichte] is more real [wirklicher] than written history, and he who—as a contemporary [Zeitgenosse]—detaches himself from the experience [Erlebnis] separates himself from reality [Realität] and at the same time alienates himself from his destiny [Schicksal]. (p. 587)

There are two approaches to comprehend Améry's point here; each of which represents a different *kind* of reading. According to the first approach, Améry addresses Haffner *as a contemporary*. This means that Améry's position that Hitler and the Third Reich must be seen as an embodiment of the myth of evil—that is, that the Third Reich ought not to be understood in an objective, detached historical perspective—is not an essential assertion concerning the genuine character of that Reich, but rather is subordinated to the concrete historical situation to which Améry and Haffner factually belong (so a future twenty-second-century historian is not obligated to obtain this perspective, for it concerns only the contemporaries). According to this reading, Améry's disapproval of Haffner's attitude concerns only the fact that Haffner begins with being historically objective "too early" (p. 586), meaning, at a point in time in which Hitler and all the terrifying occurrences attached to his Reich are still fresh in the historical memory. According to the second approach, Améry's claim expresses something *essential* about the very nature of historical events and historical understanding, which ought not only to apply to contemporaries such as Haffner; the description of Hitler and the Third Reich must *principally* be carried out in light of the fact that it was a *real* embodiment of the 'myth of evil', since a scientific demystification of history is something which is objectively wrong. As I suggest, it is necessary to consider both approaches together in order to catch Améry's intent here.

The first approach can be easily elicited from Améry's text. For instance, Améry stresses time and again that as long as *he himself* experiences these events as a moral torment [moralische Pein], the exclusion of this feeling is a sin against objectivity (so it is clear that for Améry the subjectivity of his experience *is* the objectivity of the occurrences). At any event, as Améry admits, he sees things in this manner "not only because I cannot do otherwise, but also because I do not want it to be otherwise" (p. 588); so being trapped in his subjectivity, as a contemporary (who is, furthermore, a survivor), is first and foremost a *fact* for him, a fact that he, moreover, does not want to alter (even if he could). However, Améry also writes that "Haffner's grandchildren, I repeat, ought to know Hitler as the myth of evil" (pp. 588–9); here one might be tempted to interpret Améry's view in a more principal way: The generation of the witnesses, to which Améry and Haffner belong, ought to do everything in order to prevent future generations from *mistakenly* missing the point that Hitler and his Third Reich were, indeed, an embodiment, an epitome of the myth of evil. Améry adds:

> *We* [the contemporaries] are responsible for that which will come. And we cannot address this kind of responsibility by means of detracting objectivity [entziehende Objektivität], but rather only by an inalienable insistence on our *subjective* experience [...] anyway everything will appear [in the future] as if it never happened. Precisely because of that we are facing an urgent demand to use the scarce time interval [Zeitspanne] [...] and to testify. (pp. 589–90)

That is, future historians ought to *use* the experienced dimension presented by the witnesses, in order to prevent the above mentioned mistaken objectivity, which is actually, as Améry holds, nothing but a new mystification of history. "I see", as Améry says, "precisely because the wounds are not healed yet, some symptoms in a more sharp manner" (p. 587); from this it follows that the witness sees everything *more* sharply, that is, that he obtains a unique access to the *objectivity* of some historical events, since 'evil' is not a subjective *judgment* of occasions, but rather a *constituent component* of such occurrences. The occasions were *really* evil, as the witness knows, and not: There were events, and the survivor, the witness, who is allegedly trapped in the subjective state of the victim, merely *judges* the occasions as evil.

Thus, moral attributes of evil historical events must be taken seriously, and the witness, among other things, ought to warn the future historian—the historian who, to cite Hegel's celebrated phrase, spreads his wings, like the owl of Minerva, only with the falling of dusk—not to dismiss the way the occasions were *experienced* as an external component of them, which must be allegedly overcome in order to reach the awaited objective perspective. As Améry determines, "the objection according to which moral outrage [Entrüstung] is useless for historical cognition is not valid" (p. 589).

Améry's stronger argument can be clearly found in his essay 'Time for Rehabilitation: The Third Reich and Historical Objectivity', which was written in 1976, that is, two years before his letter to Haffner. In fact, most of the issues Améry mentions in his letter to Haffner can be found in this essay, sometimes in identical formulations.

In this essay, Améry voices a complaint regarding the fact that the rehabilitation time has already begun. What does 'rehabilitation' refer to in this context? Precisely the allegedly distanced attitude toward the historical events: "It seems now that one wants to better understand the Third Reich—which has become a myth because it was founded on myth—by means of the so called historical objectivity" (2005, pp. 91–2). However, Améry asks—and the question he raises is independent of his being a contemporary—whether such a historical objectivity is *possible* at all (and not just if it is *desired*). Améry writes:

> There is without any doubt something like historical entropy; the historical occurrence itself with all its vitality fades [...] however, there exists in the human sense a crucial requirement that the contemplation of history [Geschichtsbetrachtung] [...] would entail an element of *moral judgment*. The real is reasonable [Vernünftig ist das Wirkliche; Améry alludes, of course, to Hegel's celebrated dictum] only if it is moral. And the historicism would become unnatural if it would present itself as value neutral. If we understand things in this manner, the mythos of the Third Reich as a myth of radical evil is more adequate and faithful than the alleged objectivity, which does not set itself against evil and thus, by its indifference, makes itself the advocate [Fürsprecher] of this evil (pp. 92–3) [...] the myth of evil, which was embodied in the Third Reich, obtains a more objective character than the dialectical demystification. (p. 101)

It is clear that Améry explicitly presents here the thesis that to be loyal to the *things themselves* (to the genuine character of the historical occasion) means to describe the Third Reich as the most distilled expression of radical evil. This does not mean that Améry is of the opinion that there is no difference between the work of a fictional author and that of a historian, nor that the historical investigation ought to be fully reduced to the testimony; he only wishes to underscore the fact that the historical investigation—*if it means an absolute moral neutralization of the historical situation, especially concerning an event in which evil is one of its constitutional elements*—cannot be held objective, for it would constitute—given that the moral attribute is not an external, subjective character of the evil event—a new (false) myth.

Améry laments, then, that "no one, or so it seems, is capable of the insight that in some historical constellations the subjective indignation [Empörung] meticulously [haargenau] corresponds with the human reality" (p. 101). Améry was clear-sighted and sober; he had no doubts that the "rehabilitation, once it begins, against morality and history, will take its course [and would not stop]" (p. 100). However, what is important for the current discussion is what Améry says in the parentheses—"against morality and history", that is: That the mistake here is, of course, a moral one, but also an objective—epistemic—mistake, which misses the *objective* characteristics of an (evil) historical event.

To summarize: Historical objectivity is—at least as far as evil occasions are concerned—a moral as well as an epistemic failure, for evil is not a judgment *of* an occasion, but it *is* the occasion itself so to say. Thus, the Third Reich as an epitome of the myth of evil is, in point of fact, not a myth at all; it serves as a myth only in the eyes of those who obtain a misleading preconception regarding the genuine essence of historical occasions generally (and of evil occasions specifically). Haffner, thus, fails not only as a contemporary—it is "too early" to describe the Third Reich from a cold, detached scientific point of view—but also as a historian, for he falls into the trap of the misleading myth of history as a science, which deceives people and make them believe that historical truth can be reached only if the moral dimension of the occasion is seen as external and thus is neutralized.

Thus, we can point to a first sense of the concept of a witness according to Améry: The witness experienced the occasion on his flesh and bones; thus, he is closer to its *objective* character. His vocation is, to use a celebrated formulation of Walter Benjamin, to brush history against the grain, that is: To retain the experienced dimension in order for it to serve as a counterbalance to the natural tendency—which is morally and objectively wrong, and therefore is the true myth, in the bad sense of the word—to contemplate the occasions from a cold, scientific perspective. The fact that the mission is bound to fail—and the so-called historical entropy will eventually gain the upper hand—does not dismiss the witness from the duty of carrying it out.

We now turn our attention to the second sense Améry gives to the concept of testimony and to being a witness. For one of the implied consequences of Améry's position regarding historical objectivity is that evil is *real*. Arguing this is not only a complaint against the historian but also against a long philosophical tradition.

2.3 Testimony and the Reality of Evil

Why is the claim that evil is 'real' not self-evident in the philosophical tradition to which Améry explicitly relates? To grasp this, I will discuss the question of evil not in light of the well-known dichotomy according to which evil is a negation, or a privation, or, at any rate, a kind of absence of the good (whereas the good is the only 'positive' there is), but in relation to a somewhat different dichotomy: The 'common sense' approach to evil, which rests on what *seems* to be the case according to our experience, versus the 'philosophical preconception' of evil, which entails some a priori restrictions. Let me begin with the philosophical point of departure.

Coupling 'evil' with 'freedom' and the claim that evil can be done deliberately and consciously has always generated unique problems for western philosophers. Two typical examples are Plato and Kant. According to Plato's celebrated position—without getting into some subtle distinctions in this regard—no one does evil deliberately and consciously; if the evil agent would have known that his act is evil, he would not have done it in the first place (i.e. knowing evil excludes acting in an evil way). Kant philosophizes in an entirely different systematical context, but things are not easier for him. As is well known, Kant *defines*—at least at some point in his critical writings—free will as will "under the moral law" (1900a, p. 447), that is, a free act in the genuine sense of the word is an action whose ground of determination (or 'motive', or 'driving-force') is the 'respect for the moral law'. Now if a free action *is* an action determined by the respect for the moral law, then an evil act—an act that is not determined, of course, by this respect for the moral law—cannot count as 'free' in that sense. Thus, it is not surprising that Kant faces some serious problems when trying to couple 'evil' with 'freedom', and a clear indication of this can be found in his terminological deliberations; at one point, he terms a morally good action an action 'through' (durch) freedom whereas an evil act is an act 'under' (unter) freedom (1900b, p. 318), and elsewhere he calls a good action an 'ability' (Vermögen) whereas an evil act is an expression of 'disability' (Unvermögen) (1900c, p. 227).[10]

I wish to describe the rationale which stands behind these complicated formulations by using a simple example. According to this perspective, the Nazis must have really been convinced that the annihilation of all the Jews was something good. They were mistaken, of course; killing, for example, 1.5 million innocent children in gas chambers is clearly not something good. However, according to this theory, their evil was actually rooted in a *mistake*, so that they would not have carried it out had they thought that what they were doing was evil (for how can they do something which is, *in their eyes*, a bad thing? Knowing evil *as evil* must exclude the evil act). Incidentally, from this description it does not necessarily follow that the Nazis cannot be held morally responsible for their deeds; someone can honestly think that the Nazis were convinced that what they were doing was something good, and still be of the opinion that they must be severely punished for it.

This philosophical problem casts a much longer shadow than is sometimes assumed. The most illustrative example can be seen in the case of Hannah Arendt, who famously declared that she tackles the question of evil in an utterly different way, freed from the above-mentioned constraints which constitute western philosophy's attitude toward the problem. However, it is easy to see that Arendt's philosophy supports rather than refutes the typical structure I sketched above. For Arendt, too, could not let go of the thought that Eichmann—as a classic example of Nazi evil—did not decide intentionally and knowingly to do evil for the sake of evil, or to do evil *knowing* that it was evil; her attempt to claim that Eichmann was not 'stupid' (dumm), but that he was nevertheless 'thoughtless' (gedanklos) (1986, pp. 56–7; 1998, p. 14) vividly shows that she did not deviate from the tradition mentioned above. For regardless of how we understand the difference between 'stupidity' and 'thoughtfulness' (I myself doubt if this difference was ever properly *conceptualized* in her arguments), both clearly echo the typical problem mentioned above. In this sense, it is not evil which is 'banal', but—given the Western tradition concerning evil—Arendt's theory itself.

The fact that Arendt's psychological analysis of Eichmann's personality is a pure exegetical invention, which bears no relation to the way the actual Eichmann really thought, talked, and acted, even after the war,[11] attests to it: All that can be elicited from the *empirical* evidence, of which Arendt had a very minor interest (e.g. reports of people who actually interrogated him and prepared a psychological profile of him), is fit into the mold of her philosophical a priori preconception. It is as if the suggestive term 'banality of evil' (which incidentally Jaspers, and not Arendt, coined) serves as the *point of departure* of her contemplations on Eichmann rather than its *outcome*.[12]

Contrary to this philosophical tradition there exists what I wish to term the 'common sense position'. In fact, it is not precisely a position, in the sense of something which is the outcome of philosophical deliberations—

though, it can serve as a *basis* for one—but it is rooted more or less in an intuition or in what seems to be our immediate experience. For our *experience* of evil often seems to be free from the above mentioned constraint, according to which one cannot commit an evil act knowingly and deliberately, and seems to support the conclusion that evil for evil's sake can indeed serve as a motive of one's action, and there are indeed people who do evil *and* know perfectly well that what they are doing is evil (and not only legally forbidden). Experience does, therefore, on occasion give us supportive evidence—a hint—that the evil deed is not always the outcome of a lack of knowledge, even if the experience, as such, cannot replace a philosophical demonstration (cases of self-deception regarding the motives of one's own action are always *possible*).

So roughly there are two ways to think of evil: Using a philosophical, a priori preconception, according to which evil cannot be carried out knowingly (i.e. the difficulty to link 'evil' with 'freedom') and to interpret experience in light of it; or to begin with what seems to be the case in experience, in that deeds which philosophy claims to be metaphysically impossible are actually the case. The question is, then, where should we invest our philosophical effort: Should we interpret experience (or what experience *seems* to imply) in light of a prior philosophical constraint, or—as Berel Lang does (1990, pp. 30–62), or Schelling (1997, p. 25),[13] if one wants to take an example from the history of philosophy—should we search for ways to *think* of our experience of evil given the way we experience it.

Thus, Améry's position regarding evil as a real constitutive component of historical occasions stands in contrast not only to the tendency to understand history objectively but also to a whole philosophical tradition concerning evil. Améry deliberately stresses the way things are *experienced* by the subject (the victim of an evil act, in this case), an experience in which the evil which is inflicted seems to be the consequence of a conscious evil intent, and not the outcome of lack of knowledge, misguided judgment of the privation of the good and so on. Though Améry does not suggest a *theory of evil* which would account for our intuition (contrary to e.g. Lang or Schelling), his philosophical instincts and his moral sensibility evidently clearly locate him in the small group which rejects the classical philosophical point of departure. In this sense, reading Améry cannot replace philosophy and does not amount to formulating a philosophical argument concerning the reality (positivity) of evil, of course, but it can evoke philosophical sensitivity which is often absent from professional discussions.

To summarize what has been said thus far: It seems as if objective historians and philosophers both *silence* the witness; the first tell the witness that he (or she) is all too sunk in his subjectivity, thus cannot understand what 'really' took place (but this, according to Améry, is plainly a new form of myth); the second tell him that the way he experienced the events is metaphysically impossible, for no one can do evil intentionally (but this is just an expression of the unwillingness to confront the *Erlebnis*). Thus, we have disclosed a second sense of the concept of testimony according to Améry: The witness experiences evil occasions as evil and not as an outcome of negation of the good, privation of the good, lack of knowledge and so on; the witness stands against the tendency of philosophy to invalidate, by means of its a priori preconception, the realm of experience.

2.4 Testimony and Moral Kitsch

What is *moral* kitsch, and what does Améry—as a witness—have to do with this question? I will present Améry's position in light of his essay on Heidegger from 1968, 'Sie bleiben in Deutschland—Martin Heidegger' (2004, pp. 297–329).

Let me begin with two descriptions which appear in the essay.

The first description—made by Heidegger himself—is the following: In 1934 Heidegger received a proposal to receive a prestigious appointment in Berlin. Améry cites Heidegger's weighing this possibility:

> I came with this deliberation to an old friend, a 75 year old farmer. He had heard from the newspaper about the call I received from Berlin. What would he say? He slowly pointed to me, his sure, definitive glimpse seen from his clear eyes, held his mouth tightly shut, barely moved his head, put his faithful hand on my shoulder. That meant: Absolutely No. (p. 297)

Heidegger's story about the farmer, according to Améry, ought not to be understood merely as an expression of exaggerated poetical sentimentality,[14] in which the hand put on the shoulder is always 'loyal' and 'determined' and the message is always understood in meaningful silence. No; according to Améry, it is also an expression of a lack of authenticity and attests to a moral problem. Despite the fact that, as Améry notes, we did not attend the meeting described by Heidegger, nor can we know what were Heidegger's genuine deliberations concerning the call from Berlin, we can nevertheless take a wild guess and determine that Heidegger did not suspend all his other considerations—concerning, for example, his career, his family, and so on—in order to utterly devote himself to what one—representative—old peasant would say (precisely when—I presume—the sun was sinking down, as if silently confirming the decision). Heidegger's description seems to be subordinated to an all too sweetened image, a sheer cliché, and this is the reason why it does not invoke credibility.

The second description—this time a description of Heidegger, not by Heidegger—concerns not his thought (at least not directly), but rather what Améry terms Heidegger's way of being or living (Lebensform). Améry cites a well-known description of Heidegger in Marburg at the age of 34, written by Paul Hühnerfeld, which concerns Heidegger's strange suit, which seems to be completely detached from the present, from the way people at that time typically dressed. The amusing detailed description of the suit—it was mocked by Heidegger's contemporaries and named 'the existential suit'—is of no interest to me in this chapter, but rather the political and moral issues attached to it. As Améry writes:

> The appearance of Heidegger ought to be understood as a political manifestation. The *Denker*—and this is precisely the way Heidegger wanted to be grasped, not as a philosopher in the usual sense of the word—grown up [emporgewachsen] from the people [Volk], remaining loyal to the people and wearing its garb [Tracht]. However, this mythical "Volk" had so little in common with the real contemporary inhabitants of Germany, who were gripped by passion for industrial and political expansion. The place where he came from—Meßkirch—and the Black Forest [...] were present not only in his language, but also in his [fundamental] feeling of the world [Weltgefühl] [...] this Denker—maybe the most German philosopher among German philosophers—actually lived past Germany [an Deutschland vorbei]. (p. 308)

In these two descriptions Améry wishes to point to Heidegger's tendency toward kitsch[15] (or cliché) and to his distant spiritual remoteness from every *real* (experienced) social and political context (incidentally, there is an essential connection between Nazism and being *apolitical*, and Heidegger's case is, in a way, a vivid illustration of this point; however, I will not elaborate on this issue here).

What is the relation between the kitsch described above—Heidegger depicting his meeting with the farmer regarding his deliberations about whether he should accept the offer from Berlin or not, and Heidegger allegedly dressing "like the (imaginary) Volk", both of which actually prove that he is completely detached from the contemporary Germany of that time—and the question of testimony according to Améry? Kitsch in Heidegger's case is not only an aesthetic issue, but it obtains a political—thus also moral—significance. One can generally define 'kitsch' according to the content represented in it and according to the form in which this content is delivered so to say.[16] Regarding the content, kitsch uses clichéd representations which do not expand our world of associations, but on the contrary, they awaken the obvious in an exaggerated way (e.g. a romantic kitsch: lovers, facing the sunset, holding hands; an intellectual kitsch: the intellectual sitting, his hand holding his chin, gazing seriously to the camera, in the background a library loaded with books; a socialist kitsch: the worker, with a great mustache below his nose, standing, proud and erect, next to his plow, and so on). As for the form, it ought not to serve as an independent obstacle one has to overcome, it should be transparent so to say (if, a hundred years ago, a cat playing with a wool ball was painted in a cubist manner, then, despite the fact that the content is suitable for kitsch—at least in our culture—the painting itself would not have been considered kitsch, because its form would have rendered it difficult to immediately identify the object. This might not be true today, of course, because in the meanwhile, we have gotten used to cubist representations).

In Heideggerian kitsch, similar elements are in play. Take Heidegger's depiction of the scene with the peasant. Regarding the form, it is simple in the inferior sense of the word: the message Heidegger wishes to convey by using this description can be immediately deciphered, and this is precisely why it seems artificial and unnatural (I think that if kitsch has degrees—and I am not sure if this is the case—then Heidegger's kitsch is a *bad* one). Regarding the content, in this description, the concrete details are relevant for Heidegger *only* insofar as they serve as an abstract ideal which *preceded* the scene and of which the occasion is only an illustration. Heidegger who is detached, according to Améry, from the actual social and political reality of his time,[17] falls precisely into this trap: The image of the peasant is depicted by Heidegger as if it were part of a propaganda film, in which the 'authentic' message which ought to be conveyed through the image is obvious and independent of the experience itself. Nothing in this description seems to be *real*, that is, like something which is not *fully reduced* to the message. Put differently: No *experience* seems to be delivered in Heidegger's story; one might get the impression that Heidegger subordinates even his sensual perception to a preceding 'deep' philosophical message, and the experience is there only to ornament—to illustrate—the 'deep' message. To connect it to what troubles Améry concerning history and evil, which appears in the current context as well: It seems as if Heidegger cannot serve as a *witness* to what happened,[18] as if his kitsch comes at the expense of his ability to be present, to attend specific situations (in this sense, I think, something here catches an important component of Heidegger's philosophy in general: Heidegger was deeply troubled by the question of being and the reduction of 'being' to 'presence', so it is no wonder he could not really *attend* a concrete situation). This is the deep reason why this issue obtains a predominantly political-moral aspect for Améry; if Heidegger's failure is not only personal but is essentially attached to his philosophy as well—and this was the position Améry explicitly held (p. 315)—then it is, in fact, a failure of that philosophy that it does not allow a place for *testimony*.

Améry sees Heidegger's *language* as a further symptom in this regard; for not only is it that Heidegger's philosophy clearly "denied every experienced social reality" (p. 309)—his language, as well, did not leave room for such issues. "And when I speak of language", Améry indicates, "I mean more than just vocabulary, diction or metaphor; I refer to a closed [geschlossen] reference system [Referenzsystem]. Within this system there is no room for social reality" (p. 324). So in the case of Heidegger—and Heidegger is just a symptom,[19] however revealing—the language serves as an obstacle to the experience, to testimony itself. It is not the case therefore that Heidegger's language replicates that of a testimony; rather, it comes *at the expense of* testimony (just as kitsch is not a *kind* of bad art; it comes at the expense of art itself). And Améry was highly sensitive toward linguistic fakes, which are never morally neutral. One example, which Améry mentions in this essay in a roundabout way concerns the concept of "inner emigration [innere Emigration]" (p. 319), which many intellectuals—e.g. Karl Jaspers—used as a rejoinder (or better: as an excuse, a justification) which ought to explain why they did not actively protest and act against Hitler while remaining in Germany (or, why they did not emigrate). According to Améry, this concept of inner emigration—regardless of the fact that it cannot be applied to Heidegger—is nothing but a "mystification" (p. 319) (even as an analogy this concept is, in a way, an expression of moral kitsch, I believe). Améry meant more than just saying that this concept is a mystification: It is a mystification *of the experienced*. For a real, forced exile and emigration is not of the same *kind* as Jasper's "inner" emigration.[20]

Similar motives appear in Améry's only attempt—as far as I know—to say something essential about language, that is, in his 1977 essay *Sprache des Menschen* (2004, pp. 533–48). Améry states right at the outset that he neither suggests a theory of communication, nor a linguistic analysis, nor theories in the spirit of Roland Barthes, for whom every act of speech is a "fascistic exercise" (p. 533). Améry presents solely "some consideration, reflection [Erwägungen] on the present linguistic habits [Gewohnheiten], or, more accurately, the *speaking* habits [*Rede*gewohnheiten] and their limits: the going silent [das Verstummen]" (p. 533). In a typical manner, then, Améry begins with *observation*, without using strong theoretical presumptions. In some sense, Améry is in this respect *a witness of the language*, and only consequently—if at all—a theoretician of the language.

We have disclosed, then, a third sense of the concept of testimony and the role of the witness according to Améry: The witness, as a person whose irreducible point of departure is 'the experienced', refuses to use a closed linguistic terminology which does not describe the world (what *occurs*), but obtains the presumption to *replace* the world, or to convey a message (as is done in kitsch). The language of the witness does not fry itself in its own oil and does not doubt—precisely because it is rooted in experience—its ability to reach out to the world. This doubt is, in many respects, a philosophical luxury[21] which cannot be applied to a *witness who experienced evil.*

And since the language is attached to the experience, Améry writes something which might sound like a kind of heresy in some circles today: "the Jews were hunted *because they were Jews*, and only because of that".[22] Every description which tries to *exploit* the Holocaust with a description such as "crime against *humanity*" (in the spirit of Arendt: "a crime against humanity which was carried out on the body of the Jewish people" [Arendt 1986, p. 74]) would have been rejected by Améry simply because it is false: It was not *people* who were hunted in the Holocaust, but *Jews*, and Antisemitism—not some general racism—was the genuine motive for the Holocaust. Put differently: Antisemitism is not a *contingent* outcome of some general hatred, which lurks in every person by definition and which contingently saw the Jew as its ultimate enemy; rather, Antisemitism is a *constituent component* of the Holocaust (the Nazis did not hate and *then* hated Jews; they *hated Jews*). I believe that here lies the ground for the fact that Améry was alert from a very early stage to new forms of Antisemitism, this time from the left wing ('anti-Zionism'). Since for Améry it was not human beings murdering other human beings in the Holocaust, but

Germans murdering Jews (the second determination cannot be fully reduced to the first without missing something essential); since it was not a general hatred or racism aimed at Jews as its contingent victims, but a very particular, sui generis phenomenon (Antisemitism), it is clear why Améry, who refuses to generalize—to universalize—his experience, was able to discern new, surprising forms of that ancient, *particular* hatred.

As I see it, one can only imagine the deep unease Améry would have felt given the current universalization of the Holocaust, rendering it from something which indicates a specific event—first and foremost, the catastrophe of the Jewish people in Europe—to a general symbol of evil, detached from its particular background.[23] The Holocaust, as the witness knows, is a *proper name*, and only afterward—if at all—a *concept*. Such universalistic attitudes—those that come *at the expense of* the particular point of view—silence the witness, and thus are, in fact, a *moral sin*.

To summarize: We have examined how three rivals of testimony threaten to silence the voice of the witness according to Améry—the historian, who seeks objectivity; the philosopher, who denies the possibility of intentional evil; and the tendency toward kitsch, which reveals itself in language. I hope that the discussion suggested here captures at least some of the complexity of Améry's account of this subtle issue.

Notes

1. Regarding the uniqueness of the Holocaust, see, for example, Margalit and Motzkin (1996). Améry himself stresses occasionally the *sui-generis* of the Holocaust; see, for example, his 27.2.67 letter to Horst Krüger: "Ich habe noch immer und trotz der ungeheurlichen Verbrechen in Vietnam […] das Gefühl, als sei das Dritte Reich etwas Singuläres und Irreduktibles" (Améry 2007, p. 271).
2. See, for example, Eilperin (2015).
3. See, for example, Dunham and Chiacu (2015).
4. Benhorin (2010).
5. Bletman (2016).
6. See here a series of papers published by Améry from 1969–1978: "Der ehrbare Antisemitismus" (1969), "Die Linke und der Zionismus" (1969), "Juden, Linke—Linke, Juden. Ein politisches Problem ändert seine Konturen" (1973), "Der neue Antisemitismus" (1976), "Shylock, der Kitsch und die Gefahr" (1976), "Der ehrbare Antisemitismus" (1976), in Améry (2005, pp. 131–200). This issue stood at the center of Améry's attention also in his letters; see, for instance, his public letter to Erich Fried (Améry 2005, pp. 79–83).

7. See here Lang (2013).
8. "Die Zeit der Rehabilitierung. Das Dritte Reich und die Geschichtliche Objektivität".
9. All translations from Améry's works are mine.
10. For different attempts of philosophers after Kant—mainly Reinhold, Fichte, and Schelling—to overcome this Kantian maze, see Noller (2015). The Kantian position is much more sophisticated than presented here, and he developed it further after *Grundlegung der Metaphysik der Sitten*; my aim here was just to point to the *kind* of challenge he was facing.
11. See, for example, Stangeth (2011).
12. An interesting point regarding Arendt's *Eichmann in Jerusalem*, a text which serves according to Arendt as a mere report (Bericht) of the Eichmann's trial, is the fact that the *testimonies of the survivors*—which constituted more than 50% of the court's hearing—are barely mentioned by Arendt. I will address some other aspects of the tension between philosophy and testimony in due course.
13. See, for example, the definition Schelling suggests for freedom.
14. Améry thinks that Heidegger was a lousy poet (2004, p. 321), and more importantly that there is a connection between his being a lousy poet and his philosophical greatness (2004, p. 322).
15. Améry explicitly mentions the term 'kitsch' in this essay; he quotes some lines from Heidegger's *Der Feldweg* and maintains that they would have a place of honor in a book dedicated to German kitsch (2004, p. 321).
16. For a revealing discussion on this issue, see Kulka (1988).
17. For an encompassing account on Heidegger and the political in general, see Grosser (2011).
18. Regarding Heidegger's celebrated—and morally outrageous—comparison between the "mechanized food industry" which is, according to Heidegger, "in essence the same as the manufacturing of corpses in gas chambers and extermination camps", Berel Lang remarks that an hypothetical reader of these comparisons "who was unaware that Heidegger had written [this comparison] [...] after living through—in—the twelve years of Nazi rule might reasonably infer that its author had inhabited a distant land in another age, that he possessed at most second or third hand knowledge of the events he refers to, and that because of *this* he would care only academically about their histories [...]"; in: Lang (1996, p. 19). This corresponds, I think, to Améry's line of thought, according to which Heidegger's writing evokes the impression that he was *not attending* his historical time in a way.
19. For other examples besides Heidegger, see Sluga (1993).
20. This is not to say that Jaspers did not genuinely suffer during the war (his wife was, for instance, Jewish, and Jaspers himself was fired from his job at

the university in Heidelberg and lived in constant peril of being arrested and deported for the duration of the war), or that Jaspers only pretended—post factum—to be an opponent of the Nazis world view and acts (this was surely not the case). Améry simply rejects the *analogy* implied by the use of the same linguistic terminus.

21. This, I believe, might explain, among other factors, Améry's principal rejection of new French philosophy. Améry raises, though, a series of principal (i.e. philosophical) reasons why he thinks philosophers like Foucault or Lévi-Strauss are nothing but a new form of 'irrationalism' ('Ein neuer Verrat der Intellektuellen', 2004, p. 163); however, one cannot help noticing that Améry's existential state as a witness also plays an important role in this rejection. For structuralism assumes, according to Améry, "mistrust in the subject, in the language, in the sense of what is said" (e.g. see in 'Wider den Strukturalismus. Das Beispiel Michel Foucault', 2004, p. 99), and even doubts that something ever happened, that there are occurrences in the world, that the very concept of historical facts has an application ('Fremdling in dieser Zeit. Zu Werk und Gestalt des Strukturalisten Claude Lévi-Strauss', 2004, p. 122). But this means, in fact, to deny the very possibility of being a witness; for the witness is a *subject*, and he tells about something which *took place*, and he does so using *language*. The witness on whom evil was inflicted wants to speak, and it is as if (French) philosophy doubts his ability of doing so, as if philosophy itself cannot, on principal ground, entail 'testimony' as such. In this sense, the witness, by his very existence, *refutes*—in an existential, not in a logical way—these philosophies.
22. "Mein Judentum" (Améry 2005, p. 41).
23. On some major aspects of the generalizations, see Yakira (2010).

References

Améry, J. (2004). *Werke, Band 6: Aufsätze zur Philosophie*. Stuttgart: Klett-Cotta.

Améry, J. (2005). *Werke, Band 7: Aufsätze zur Politik und Zeitgeschichte*. Stuttgart: Klett-Cotta.

Améry, J. (2007). *Werke, Band 8: Ausgewählte Briefe*. Stuttgart: Klett-Cotta.

Arendt, H. (1986). *Eichmann in Jerusalem. Ein Bericht von der Banalität des Bösen*. München/Zürich: Piper.

Arendt, H. (1998). *Vom Leben des Geistes*. München/Zürich: Piper.

Benhorin, Y. (2010, April 17). Wiesel: Jerusalem Is Above Politics. *Ynet*. Retrieved from https://www.ynet.co.il/articles/0,7340,L-3877077,00.html.

Bletman, D. (2016, July 16). The Problematic Legacy of Elie Wiesel [Hebrew]. *Haaretz*. Retrieved from https://www.haaretz.co.il/opinions/.premium-1.3007277.

Dunham, W., & Chiacu, D. (2015, February 13). Nobel Winner Elie Wiesel Lends Support to Netanyahu's U.S. Speech. *Reuters*. Retrieved from https://www.reuters.com/article/us-usa-jews-netanyahu-idUSKBN0LG32Y20150212.
Eilperin, J. (2015, March 3). In U.S.-Israel Dispute over Iran, Elie Wiesel Emerges as Unlikely Protagonist. *The Washington Post*. Retrieved from https://www.washingtonpost.com/news/post-politics/wp/2015/03/03/in-u-s-israel-dispute-over-iran-elie-wiesel-emerges-as-unlikely-protagonist/?noredirect=on&utm_term=.52d6312b66d7.
Grosser, F. (2011). *Revolution denken. Heidegger und das Politische 1919 bis 1969*. München: Beck.
Kant, I. (1900a). *Grundlegung der Metaphysik der Sitten*, AA IV. Berlin: Preussische Akademie der Wissenschaften.
Kant, I. (1900b). *Reflexionen zur Methaphysik*, AA XVII. Göttingen: Preussische Akademie der Wissenschaften.
Kant, I. (1900c). *Metaphysik der Sitten*, AA VI. Berlin: Preussische Akademie der Wissenschaften.
Kulka, T. (1988). Kitsch. *The British Journal of Aesthetics, 28*(1), 18–27.
Lang, B. (1990). *Act and Idea in the Nazi Genocide*. Chicago and London: Chicago University Press.
Lang, B. (1996). *Heidegger's Silence*. Ithaca and London: Cornell.
Lang, B. (2013). *Primo Levy: The Matter of Life*. New Haven: Yale University Press.
Margalit, A., & Motzkin, G. (1996). The Uniqueness of the Holocaust. *Philosophy and Public Affairs, 25*, 65–83.
Noller, J. (2015). *Die Bestimmung des Willens. Zum Problem individueller Freiheit im Ausgang von Kant*. Freiburg/München: Karl Alber.
Schelling, F. W. J. (1997). *Über das Wesen der menschlichen Freiheit*. Hamburg: Meiner.
Sluga, H. (1993). *Heidegger's Crisis. Philosophy and Politics in Nazi Germany*. Cambridge: Harvard University Press.
Stangeth, B. (2011). *Eichmann vor Jerusalem: Das unbehelligte Leben eines Massenmörders*. Zürich/Hamburg: Arche.
Yakira, E. (2010). *Post-Zionism, Post-Holocaust. Three Essays on Denial, Forgetting, and the Deligitimation of Israel*. Cambridge: Cambridge University Press.

CHAPTER 3

Jean Améry and the Generational Limits of Resentment as Morality

C. Fred Alford

Jean Améry performed a remarkable feat, turning trauma, resentment, and melancholy into ethical categories. No one has ever done this in quite such a lucid and pitiless way. Améry's argues that morality means that perpetrator and victim both want the impossible: to undo what has already been done. As he lays out that argument, it becomes clear that it generates a coherent morality, its own categorical imperative, different in content but not form from that of Immanuel Kant (1993, p. 30). Not that the past actually be undone, but that both victim and executioner wish equally that it could be. Only then is forgiveness possible.

The fact that it is limited to a single generation is not necessarily a flaw in Améry's argument. A morality limited to a unique generation of perpetrators and victims has its place. The problem with Améry's morality is that not only does he say nothing about its limits, but he writes as if the problem does not exist. To wish that it had never happened lacks moral gravity when applied to subsequent generations, whose wish can only be an abstract desire, even if strongly held. History moves on, and in the case of the Holocaust, that's good. This is not to say that subsequent

C. F. Alford (✉)
University of Maryland, College Park, MD, USA
e-mail: calford@umd.edu

Y. Ataria et al. (eds.), *Jean Améry*,
https://doi.org/10.1007/978-3-030-28095-6_3

generations of perpetrators and victims should forget the horror, but only that it will always mean something different to them than to the original participants. This becomes truer every generation.

One reason Améry seems so unaware or unconcerned with the limits of generational morality, as I call it, is that he was overwhelmed by his own fear of death, which he described as worse than Auschwitz. I argue that this is because he could not, or simply did not, think in terms of generations.

What can the Holocaust generation, both victims and executioners, pass on to the next generation? How can the next generation morally participate in the experience of their parents, grandparents, and now great grandparents? These questions, addressed in many works on second-generation trauma (Epstein 2010; Sachs 2013; Alford 2015), simply do not arise for Améry, and it is this—not the impossibility of his morality—that is the limit to his argument. Put perhaps a little too simply, resentment at moral horror makes sense. Resentment at death does not. Améry comes too close to equating them.

An argument whose limits are never made clear can nonetheless be an interesting and instructive argument. Above all Améry is honest and down to earth, reminding us of trauma's overwhelming physical reality. His unrest, he tells us, is not because he is oppressed by some vague metaphysical distress, whether it is called Being, or Nothingness, or God, or the Absence of God. It comes from the numbers on his arm, and his awareness that under certain circumstances it could all happen again (Améry 1980, pp. 99–100). Before this reality, every theory pales. At the same time, Améry remains a utopian thinker who would reverse time, holding history at a standstill, so that perpetrator and victim alike might return to a time and place before the offense. Sometimes it is good to wish for the impossible. In Améry's case, this impossible wish becomes the foundation of his ethics.

My primary source is Améry's *At the Mind's Limits: Contemplations by a Survivor on Auschwitz and its Realities*, which was originally titled *Jenseits Von Schuld und Sühne: Bewältigungsversuche eines Überwältigen.* The first part of the title, "Beyond Guilt and Atonement," is easily read as Améry's ironic evocation of Nietzsche (1966). The subtitle presents a problem in translation. The most direct translation would have the subtitle referring to the author himself: the attempts of an overwhelmed man to come to terms. But the content of the book suggests a second way to read the subtitle as referring to German attempts to overcome or overthrow the Nazi past. I prefer to read it both ways.

The title in English, *At the Mind's Limits*, is one of those rare cases where the title of the translation is a better, or at least more subtle title, capturing the essence of Améry's project. It does not refer to an event that is almost unimaginable, the Holocaust. It refers to the way in which the mind, Améry's mind, could no longer transcend its circumstances—for this is what intellectual life was about for Améry, and perhaps it was even more important for him than most, for he was an autodidact and exile who found in literature a new home. Améry (1980, p. 7) tells the story about dragging himself back from the I. G. Farben factory in the Auschwitz complex after a grueling day. A flag waving in front of a half-finished building reminded him of a line from a Hölderlin poem. He tried to recite the poem, to somehow let the poem possess him, to enter the world of the poem, if for only for a moment, but it didn't work. "The poem no longer transcended reality." This is what *At the Mind's Limit* is about, the ultimate dominance of the material over the spiritual, about how relatively easy it is to crush the spiritual, particularly in men who lack religious or ideological commitments. In the end, the mind is so terribly, frighteningly embodied.

The tacit player in this drama is Primo Levi (1996), whose book, known in its American translation as *Survival in Auschwitz* (and in Britain as *If This Is a Man*), was published a couple of years before Améry's. The books have quite a different structure. Levi's is a narrative, Améry's a series of thematically connected essays. However, Levi (1989, p. 146) agrees with Améry that those with spiritual or ideological armor did best in Auschwitz. Where they differ is on the possibility of transcendence. In a well-known chapter in *Survival in Auschwitz*, Levi spontaneously translates a portion of Dante's *Divine Comedy* into French as he and his friend Jean (Pikolo) tramp through the snow carrying a heavy caldron of thin soup to feed the hungry men whom they are working (Levi 1996, pp. 109–115). For Améry, the real truth of the camps is that it made such glorious moments impossible.

3.1 Resentment

Améry (1980, p. 68) writes that "it did not escape me that *ressentiment* is not only an unnatural but also a logically inconsistent condition [*Zustand*]. It nails every one of us onto the cross of his ruined past." Sometimes called the *Zustand* passage, it reveals *ressentiment* to be a violent occupation of the will and the time sense of the person. The result is to so preoccupy Améry with the wish to undo the past, and the equally impossible wish that his tormentors would wish this as much as he, that there is no exit to the future. A future that Améry (1980, p. 68) calls the genuinely human dimension.

Before continuing a word needs be said about the term *ressentiment*, which figures so prominently in Améry's argument. Writing in German, Améry uses the same French term, *ressentiment*, as Nietzsche did (2009, 1.10–12). Améry intends us to see the connection. What does not seem to matter is whether one uses the terms resentment or *ressentiment*, *Verstimmung* or *Groll*. The French term possesses no subtle connotations lost when its English or German equivalents are used. Writing about Nietzsche, Arthur Danto considers some possible distinctions between the French, English, and German terms before concluding that "it may have been one of those expressions that civilized people simply used" (Solomon 1994, p. 103).[1] Whatever is decided about Améry's use of the term *ressentiment*, and the not very subtly implied critique of Nietzsche, does not depend on hidden subtleties of the term itself.

The *Zustand* passage sounds like a definition of trauma. It is, but we need to be careful, for it reveals that the experience of trauma may itself have ethical import. It does, and its import resides in its answer to the question asked by Kai Erikson. "To what extent," he asked, "does it make sense to conclude that the traumatized view of the world conveys a wisdom that ought to be heard in its own terms?" (Erikson 1995, p. 198). A key aspect of this wisdom is now apparent: that the twisted sense of time, the inability to be free of time past so characteristic of trauma, is not just a neurological or psychological phenomenon. It is also an ethical demand: "that the irreversible be turned around, that the event be undone" (Améry 1980, p. 68). In many cases, the traumatized cannot help but make this ethical demand, even if they wished they could, for it traps them in the past.

One might simply argue that the demand is absurd, impossible. There is no choice but to move on. But consider what Herbert Marcuse called the "*promesse de Bonheur*," the promise of utopian happiness, the demand for joy, peace, and contentment, even the freedom from time, all of which become ever more important even as they seem ever more impossible. Referring to the images of Orpheus and Narcissus, Marcuse (1962) wrote,

> They have not become the culture-heroes of the Western world: theirs is the image of joy and fulfillment; the voice which does not command but sings; the gesture which offers and receives; the deed which is peace and ends the labor of conquest; the liberation from time which unites man with god, man with nature. Literature has preserved their image. (p. 162)

It is, of course, ironic that Améry is talking about dystopia, in which the promise of happiness is reversed. But the promise remains: the hopeless hope that one could return to a time before the horror and set it right. Or as Améry (1980) puts it,

> What happened, happened. This sentence is just as true as it is hostile to morals and intellect. The moral power to resist contains the protest, the revolt against reality, which is rational only as long as it is moral. The moral person demands annulment of time. (p. 72)

Améry is not writing about some abstract utopia. In this particular context, he is writing about capital punishment of the mass murderer, no matter how much time has passed since his deeds. "Thereby, and through a moral turning-back of the clock, the latter can join his victim as a fellow human being." But Améry (1980, p. 72) is also writing about something more general: how morality must stand against nature, in this case, the "biological healing that time brings about."

A well-known Kantian (1996, p. 287) maxim about morality states that "ought implies can" ("*sollen impliziert können*"). One should not make ethical demands of people that are impossible to fulfill. An ethical system that assumes that people have the potential to be morally perfect would violate this demand. Entirely aside from whether this dictum about morality deserves to be enshrined as it has, Améry's ethics do not contradict it. Améry is not asking that people reverse time, an impossibility. He is asking that people wish that time could be reversed, and to base their morality on the hypothetical demand that it could be. To ask that offenders and bystanders wish as strongly as he that it never happened, that history could be done over, is idealistic but not impossible. Certainly, no more impossible than asking that everyone consider what would happen if the principle by which he or she were about to act were to become a universal law, what is known as the categorical imperative (Kant 1993, p. 30). Whether Améry's is the best ethical system is another question, but do not be misled because Améry's version of the categorical imperative is extraordinary.

For Améry, morality becomes the science of the impossible, as impossible as the utopia that Marcuse is writing about in the context of what he calls the Great Refusal, the refusal to go along with a world ruled by what he calls surplus repression, repression that preserves privilege, not civilization. We should read Améry in this same vein, as a utopian, writing about an impossibility, the reversal of time, in the hope that those living would come to see how the Hell that was made just a generation or two ago lives on in the tortured bodies and minds of survivors, some of whom seem to have made a decision to hold onto the reality of their experience, with all its pain, rather than to offer cheap forgiveness. For most, of course, holding onto the pain is no choice.

Thomas Brudholm (2008) comes close to capturing aspects of Améry's moral ideal when he writes that

> One can say that to move on is—in fact—possible, but ethically it is "impossible." To undo what has been done is in fact impossible, but wanting to do so saves the ethical possibility—that is, the possibility of relating with moral sensibility to what has been done. (p. 110)

Relating with a moral sensibility in an entirely new way, one might add.

3.1.1 Sources and Consequences of Resentment

The sources of resentment for Améry are not entirely clear. Sometimes Améry writes as if his resentment began only a couple of years after the war, when he became aware that the Germans were trying to overcome their past by ignoring it, forgiving themselves, and moving on, looking only to the future. His resentment, a clinging to the insults and injuries of the past (more precisely put, the atrocity that was the recent past), was a protest against a new Germany that acted as if the Holocaust did not happen, or it happened a long time ago, and it was time to move on. Germans called this *Vergangenheitsbewältigung*, an overcoming of the past, though the connotation is stronger, as in forcefully overcoming or overthrowing the past (Améry 1980, pp. 66–67). This does not seem an entirely adequate explanation of the sources of Améry's resentment, and yet one hesitates to go along with Brudholm's (2008, pp. 98–100) psychological explanation that Améry's resentment is so strong because as a prisoner he could not express his anger and outrage, or feel his horror. Resentment is the result of rage and horror that were repressed in the name of survival at the time they were originally experienced.

This could be true, but it seems unnecessary to explain Améry's resentment. About his experience, Améry (1980, p. 34) wrote that the survivor of torture can no longer feel at home in the world. "Whoever was tortured, stays tortured. Torture is ineradicably burned into him, even when no clinically objective traces can be detected." One result is a strange and totally undeserved shame at being so weak, exposed, and vulnerable.

Another is a loss of trust in humanity that can never be regained, such as the knowledge that the lovely lady next door who greets you every morning would likely turn her head and look away as you are led off to the concentration camp. Undeniable is the knowledge that you live in a world inhabited by fellow men some of whom are really "antimen," torturers and tormenters who would cause you endless pain before going home to dinner with their families. As for the rest of those among whom you live, hardly a one would lift a finger were you to be hauled away again tomorrow. There are exceptions, and Améry names some of them, but he does not draw the line between the SS and the rest, or Nazis and the rest. It is the vast majority of Germans, and French, including neighbors and clerks, versus the very few (Améry 1980, pp. 40, 72–76, 94–96).

To know this now about the world, the world as it was then, and that under certain special but hardly unimaginable conditions the world as it could become again, is to live in a different world forever. It is "knowledge as disaster," as Blanchot (1995, p. ix) puts it. One consequence of having become wise through knowledge as disaster may be to become *aidos* that marvelous ancient Greek word meaning blessed and cursed at the same time. There are, however, certain experiences that so exceed the normal, experiences by virtue of which the victim does not become *aidos*, but *oulomenos*—that is, simply cursed with knowledge. As Améry (1980) puts it,

> Trust in the world includes all sorts of things ... the certainty that by reason of written or unwritten social contracts the other person will spare me—more precisely stated, that he will respect my physical, and with it also my metaphysical being. The boundaries of my body are also the boundaries of my self. My skin surface shields me against the external world. If I am to have trust, I must feel on it only what I want to feel. At the first blow, however, this trust in the world breaks down ... The other person ... forces his own corporeality on me with the first blow. He is on me and thereby destroys me. It is like a rape. (p. 28)

Améry certainly writes about his torture as though it were a rape, a violation of the intimate boundaries of his own person. Contained within this violation is a terrible knowledge from which he will never be free, a knowledge that will undermine his ability to naively trust in the world as he once did.

One might argue that this account of Améry's resentment is not so different from Brudholm's psychological interpretation: then he couldn't express his anger, outrage, and horror; now he can. As far as whether

Brudholm's is a valid psychological interpretation, the question is not whether Améry could *express* his anger, outrage, and horror, but whether he could *know* them. He was in no position to write a contemporaneous diary, and so we look to his writings for evidence. Later writings are not the best evidence of earlier psychological states. Nevertheless, I know of no other essayist (certainly not Primo Levi) who writes with a harder edge about the reality of the Holocaust, particularly his experience as victim of torture, an experience he recounts in excruciating detail. "Torture is the most horrible event a human being can retain within himself" (Améry 1980, p. 22).

One might ask if there were not some way to share this experience. Améry (1980, p. 33) answers that the only way to share the experience would be to inflict it on another, to in effect become a torturer, and that is a moral impossibility. If Améry is correct, the problem is not his repressed outrage and horror, but the nature of torture itself—that the experience cannot be shared but must be contained within one's body and soul forever. Even projective identification, the psychological projection of the experience into another in order to share it, would be evil. This Améry seems to believe, even if some people would, in fact, be able to psychologically share the experience without being overwhelmed, for this is what good therapists, and occasionally friends and lovers, do.

Améry's post-war resentment makes a claim about reality, about the tenuousness of the civilized bond that one can only truly know from the other side, when the bond has been broken, and one is among the victims. His is a truth claim. Améry's everlasting resentment is how he lives with this truth, protesting against it, much as Job protested his innocence against the Lord (Job: 9–10). Only this time there was no Lord of the Whirlwind appearing to Améry to explain that on God's timetable, the timetable of eternity, it all makes sense (Job: 38–42.6). And so, all Améry could do was hold onto his resentment, his protest in the name of life in the face of horror.

If Améry (1980) could respond, he would argue that the term "trauma" is at once too abstract and too clinical. All he is doing is responding to reality in a world in which the bond of civilization can no longer be counted on.

> I ... am not "traumatized," but rather my spiritual and psychic condition corresponds completely to reality. The consciousness of my being a Holocaust Jew is not an ideology. It may be compared to the class consciousness that Marx tried to reveal to the proletarians of the nineteenth century. (p. 99)

Améry considers survivors who do not pursue retribution the true conformists; they lack the Holocaust equivalent of class-consciousness. Consider, says Améry (1980), the man who willingly "submerges his individuality in society and is able to comprehend himself only as a function of the social ... He calmly allows what happened to remain what it was" (p. 71). Implicitly, at least, he forgives, for he does not demand recompense. He appears normal. "His time-sense is not dis-ordered, that is to say, it has not moved out of the biological and social sphere into the moral sphere. As a deindividualized, interchangeable part of the social mechanism, he lives with it consentingly" (1980, p. 71). In effect, the conformist treats fellow Germans as children. Punishing the child long after his misdeed is senseless, for the child cannot make the connection between distant deed and punishment. But are the citizens of Germany really children, asks Améry, or is it just easier to act as though they are, and so avoid the responsibility of resentment?

3.2 To Be Hated: Resentment and Reconciliation

Jean Améry, it seems, would hold onto his resentment forever. He could never see the world as good, not even good enough. Given the torture and torment to which he was subjected, this is understandable. Indeed, perhaps the simplest and most important thing Améry has to teach is the experience of what it is to live daily with those who would annihilate one's being.

All trauma is not, of course, the result of the will to annihilation. The drunk driver who smashes into my car and kills my child is not acting out of hatred. Or at least not out of a particular hatred of me and my kind. The antiman, as Améry calls him, embodies hatred, for he wishes to annihilate Améry and his kind. To live with this knowledge, not only for the duration of the war, but forever, is knowledge as disaster of a particular sort. That there are humans on this planet who only appear human; in fact, they are antihuman, the enemies of life. This is what Améry (1980) means when he argues that torture was the essence of National Socialism.

> Torture becomes the total inversion of the social world, in which we can live only if we grant our fellow man life, ease his suffering, bridle the desire of our ego to expand. But in the world of torture man exists only by ruining the other person who stands before him. (p. 35)

For the Nazis, sovereignty required the physical expansion of so-called Aryan man into everyman, beginning with the ruination of Jews, Romani, and others. For the antiman to exist as he will, you may not exist at all. But first, you must be made to suffer so much that you do not care to exist.

It is hard to imagine worse, unless worse is living with this knowledge. Nevertheless, if one reads the essay on "Resentments" in *At the Mind's Limits* closely, it becomes apparent that Améry too seeks a type of reconciliation with his tormentors (1980, pp. 62–81). What, he implicitly asks, would lead him to abandon his resentment? If his tormentors, as well as those Germans who came after, wished as much as he that which is impossible: that the Holocaust and all that went with it never happened, that time could be erased, that the past could be unmade, remade, done over. If what were impossible were to be wished as deeply by offenders and bystanders, then there would be no need for resentment (Améry 1980, p. 78).

In Améry's history of victims and executioners, there is a moment in which a tiny utopian crack opens, and the light of reparation comes through. It is a light of an impossible wholeness. Not just because time can never be erased, but because even when they both deeply regret the past, victims and offenders can never see the world, and want the same thing in the same way. Still, it is intriguing that even in the midst of Améry's dark vision there is a glimpse of utopian wholeness, evocative of Walter Benjamin's angel of history who "would like to stay, awaken the dead, and make whole what has been smashed," only to be swept up in the violent storm of progress.[2] The moment does not last. Améry's essay and his book closes in darkness, in which he fears that Hitler's Reich will come to be regarded as no better or worse than any other historical epoch, a little bloodier perhaps but that's all (1980, 70).[3] Nonetheless, the fleeting utopian moment speaks to the strength of the ideals of wholeness and reparation that remain in *At the Mind's Limits.* A strength that make Améry's *On Aging* (1994), published only a couple of years later, especially discouraging.

Améry's resentment is a measure of his longing for a relationship with his tormentors and their successors, including those who want to overcome the past (*Vergangenheitsbewältigung*). Améry wants not permanent and unrelenting resentment, but that the perpetrators and those who stood by doing nothing wish as strongly as he that it had never happened. If this were so, then the objective ground of resentment would have disappeared. At one point Améry (1980) imagines that this would be most likely to happen when the antiman finally stood before the firing squad.

> When SS-man Wajs stood before the firing squad, he experienced the moral truth of his crimes. At that moment, he was with *me*—and I was no longer alone ... I would like to believe that at the instant of his execution he wanted exactly as much as I to turn back time, to undo what had been done. When they led him to the place of execution, the antiman had once again become a fellow man. (p. 70)

Like romantics of old, Améry seeks union in death. Unfortunately, there is no reunion to be had there either. Of course, the SS man wishes to turn back time, to undo the past. At the moment of his execution, he probably wishes it as strongly as Améry. I assume he wishes it for his own selfish reasons, not because he sees the wrongness of his deeds (or at least there is no reason to think so), but because the SS man does not want to die the death he has inflicted so many times on others. I don't know this, of course, but neither does Améry (1980, p. 70), who knows only that Wajs was "a repeated murderer and an especially adroit torturer," who beat Améry over the head with a shovel. Isn't that enough? In any case, lack of sincere remorse seems a reasonable assumption about Wajs and many like him; it is certainly Améry's.

If Améry thinks that Wajs' imminent death creates the possibility of some reunion between them, so be it, but it is a reunion of the lowest common denominator, between animals who wish to live. Torture reduces its victims to this status, the status of squealing animals as Améry puts it (1980, p. 35), but this is hardly the plane on which to seek reunion.

In fact, torture, including the torture that was the concentration camps, does more than reduce a man or woman to a squealing animal. It isolates its victim forever. "The experience of persecution was, at the very bottom, that of an extreme *loneliness*. At stake for me is the release from the abandonment that has persisted from that time until today" (Améry 1980, p. 70). Consider Améry's utopian dream, that he and his persecutors could be reunited, whether in life or death (for some such as Wajs it could only be death), as long as they wish as strongly as he that history be rerun, that the past be done over. This fantasy is familiar to those who study of forgiveness, for it is a fantasy of fusion, of the reunion of lost souls, satisfying what Griswold (2007) refers to as the "soul's deepest yearnings," by which he means "deep reunion, love, and harmony" (p. 193).

Ultimately, Améry realizes that a reunion among humans can never happen. *At the Mind's Limits* ends in a tone of resignation. Unable to persuade the world to help him force yesterday's murderers "to recognize the moral truth of their crimes," Améry is "alone, as I was when they tortured me" (Améry 1980, pp. 95–96). One might argue that Améry is hopeless, but that is not quite correct. Resentment, the animating spirit of *At the Mind's Limits*, is subtended by a quest for attachment and understanding in the face of loneliness. Resentment, the dream that time could be reversed so that it would no longer be necessary to live in a world of antimen, their apologists, and successors, makes no sense except as hope that men and women could one day live together in a world worthy of human beings.

This does not make Améry wrong. We (but not he) are fortunate in what his life lacked, for it rendered his intellectual focus intense. For Améry, resentment remained forgiveness that has not yet found a worthy object, for its standards are impossibly high. The term "impossibly high" is not a criticism. Utopian ideals often help us better understand what we can, can't, and shouldn't demand of each other in the real world.

Améry sometimes writes as if he is only concerned with the generation that perpetrated and suffered the Holocaust, but he admits to puzzlement about subsequent generations. "When I ask myself whether I hold against German youth what the older generation inflicted on me, I don't find the answer quite so easily" (Améry 1980, p. 76). Most often he assumes that subsequent generations of Germans inherited their parents' history, but not their guilt. This includes an inherited responsibility for the deeds of previous generations. The question is not so much how far such responsibility goes, for it goes some way, but whether it even makes sense to ask of subsequent generations of Germans that they wish it had never happened with the same fervor as … whom? The children and grandchildren of survivors? It seems as if the morality of resentment, understood as a refusal to accept the past, coupled with the hope that one's persecutors do so with the same fervor, is confined to a single generation. Indeed, there is very little in Améry that connects the generations. The result is a moral theory, for that is what it is, confined to a single generation in unique circumstances, for Améry (1980, pp. 75–76) makes it clear that the Holocaust cannot be compared with "ordinary" mass murder.

3.3 *On Aging*

Améry's *On Aging* (1994) would seem to be about another topic. In fact, it illuminates his perspective on trauma and history. Both books were published within a couple of years of each other.[4] Perhaps Améry's (1994,

p. 116) most puzzling comment is that he found the terror of his experience at Auschwitz more bearable, less filled with the horror and anguish than the experience of aging. In Auschwitz, clambering over dead bodies, hearing people shot, "I was spared from fear." But now, old and tired,

> fear is with me, a deaf feeling that never makes me tremble, just an extremely persistent one, which in a slow kind of way becomes part of my person, so much so that I can no longer say that I *have* any fear. Instead, I say that I *am* fear. (Améry 1994, p. 117)

Add to this that *On Aging* contains not one word about the experience of torture that Améry underwent as a member of the resistance before being sent to a series of concentration camps, and one wonders what has happened, for it is the experience of torture that is the central horror of *At the Mind's Limits.*

What Améry has to say about fear is so striking and puzzling that it deserves elaboration. In the concentration camp, Améry (1994) says:

> I was not brave, because there was a lot that terrified me. I was young. And the death that threatened me came from outside: there is no nicer death in the world than being killed by an enemy. It came from outside, even when it was not the death of a cudgel or gas. Dysentery and phlegmon were attacks by an enemy world, terrifying as such but not causing fear like that slow dying, assigned to me in my decay. (p. 116)

On the page previous to the one in which Améry says that he was spared from fear in the concentration camp, he writes that he was in fact terrified. However, for Améry there is something especially and uniquely terrifying when the threat comes from within. One conclusion could that he is writing from different places, old age decades removed from his torture and torment. It is this change in perspectives that accounts for the difference. Another conclusion, an elaboration of the first, is that for an old and ill man his body itself became a death camp.

What Améry really meant remains unclear. What is clear is that while an ethically based revolt and resistance against forgiveness and moving on from the Nazi horror makes sense, this same revolt and resistance directed at death itself (for that is the theme of *On Aging*) makes no sense. "Since the contradiction of death overshadowing our entire life makes all logic—which is surely always the logic of life—and all positive thinking invalid, ideas of death have to take their shape in opposition to logic" (Améry

1994, p. 115). What made sense in *At the Mind's Limits* as an ethical refusal to accept reality no longer makes sense as an ontological refusal to accept reality. Not death, but an individual's death before his or her time, a death inflicted by hate, or by carelessness, selfish inequality, lack of imagination and empathy: a death from any of these sources contradicts life. But not a death come in its own time, in its own way. That is life.

At the Mind's Limit makes a valid claim for an ethical refusal to accept the reality of time: time passing, time healing, time leading to what passes for forgetting. *On Aging* is notable for the way it is frozen in static time. This is particularly apparent when one notices the complete absence of generations. *On Aging* is populated by single bodies. There are no children, no families, no marriages, no legacies, and no patrimonies, nothing that connects this generation with subsequent (or previous) generations. Death is entropy of the individual body, but without death, the world itself would be trapped in a downward spiral of entropy, as there would be no place for anyone or anything new. Out of death, a natural death, death in its own time, comes life.

As one generation succeeds another, even Auschwitz loses something of its salience for the relatives of survivors, as well as the rest of us. In some ways, this is bad, which is why history of the horror must always be taught. But this too is the way in which the world renews itself.

One must imagine that the terrible trauma suffered by Améry, trauma that he was able to fight in the form of an ethical refusal to accept reality, came back to haunt him as he became aware of his loss of vital powers, the death that he could see coming toward him (but still years away; he would not die until ten years after the publication of *On Aging*, and then by his own hand). This return of the trauma of Auschwitz to take its revenge on the aging body has by now almost become a theme of Holocaust literature, Primo Levi and Jean Améry its leading lights.

Social research supports this observation. Robert Kraft studied the testimony of 125 survivors, concluding that memories of extreme trauma don't change, whereas most memories do. The result is that the context of the traumatic memory changes, as aging survivors lack the distractions of rebuilding a life, raising children, and so forth. As Kraft (2002) puts it,

> the power of distraction is most evident when it diminishes … a fading happier childhood, a decrease in worldly distraction, and the constant, laser clarity of the remembered horror combine to worsen the torment of traumatic memory. (pp. 43–45)

Whether this conclusion applies to traumas less overwhelming than the Holocaust is unclear, but it is a sobering reminder, in this case of how easily Améry's ethics of resentment can become a terror of death. One might speculate that Améry's ethics of resentment was always a defense against the terror of death, but doing so is unnecessary. Améry's ethics of resentment is justified on its own ethical grounds. Grounds that fail, or rather make no sense, when transformed into resentment against a natural death. The ethics of resentment become the ontology of resentment only at the cost of a denial of the legitimate claims of life, which include a natural death.

It is common to hear survivors say that their children and grandchildren are their greatest satisfaction. For many, this claim takes on added poignancy when one learns that they are often referring to second families, the first having all been murdered in the Holocaust. I often felt awkward hearing survivors, predominantly men, refer to their families as their "revenge" against Hitler and his minions, a not uncommon sentiment. In context it makes sense.[5]

Survivors understand that the Nazis were not out to murder them as individuals. There was nothing personal about Auschwitz. The Nazis were out to exterminate the Jewish people. To survive long enough to bring children into the world, to see them raised in the practice of the faith, to marry other Jews, and bring yet another generation into the world. What affirms the continuity of life more than this? Not just individual life, but the life of the Jewish people. It is (at least from my perspective as an outsider) not merely the fact that the Jewish individual is a member of the Jewish people, but that he or she understands him or herself as a member of a community in time that brings meaning to life, and to death. In other words, the renewal of generations is the work of Eros, the alternative to Thanatos as Marcuse (1962, pp. 222–237) reminds us.

Can the reader imagine surviving Hitler's mad dream to die as an old man or woman after having brought forth new generations? Would one not feel that one had achieved a small victory over the senselessness of death? Not, of course, against the senselessness of the ontological death that faces us all, but the death that would come too soon, inflicted by those humans Améry calls antimen.

Améry's problem isn't that he didn't marry and have lots of children. Many survivors didn't. Many couples remained childless. Améry's problem is that the category of children, generations, and patrimony play no role in his thinking about aging and death. The equation by which he lived and died has too few elements: the individual = death. "The ontic density of my existence gets thin and the fear of dying fills up the empty space as pure negativity" (Améry 1994, p. 117). No wonder he was fear. Who could face death so all alone?

3.4 Doubling and Writing

One might imagine that writing about the Holocaust, indeed writing about old age, writing about virtually anything that terrifies us, would be therapeutic. Or cathartic. At least these are terms in common use to refer to the benefits of writing about such terrible experiences. My hypothesis, which is hardly proven by two cases, is that it doesn't work that way at all. Quite the opposite is the case.

Most survivors cope by doubling. About doubling, Robert Kraft (2002) argues that it is the near universal theme of those who give Holocaust testimony.

> Almost all witnesses state that they live a double existence. There is a Balkanization of memory, where Holocaust memories and normal memories are assigned to two, sometimes hostile territories ... Consider a few phrases that witnesses use: "a double existence," "another world," "a schizophrenic division," "two worlds," "two different planets," "double lives." (p. 2)

Doubling isn't bad. It's the way most survivors survive.

The trouble with writing so much about trauma is that it interferes with doubling. Writing isn't cathartic. The *katharsis* about which Aristotle famously wrote (*Poetics*, c. 6) concerns the experience of *watching* a Greek tragedy, not suffering an atrocity and writing about it over the next few decades. The late novelist Philip Roth (2007) has a character in a recent novel say

> When Primo Levi killed himself, everyone said it was because of his having been an inmate at Auschwitz. I thought it was because of his writing about Auschwitz, the labor of his last book [*The Drowned and the Saved*], contemplating the horror with all that clarity. Getting up every morning to write that book would have killed anyone. (p. 151)

Surely it is not so simple. Many survivors write about their experiences. Some presumably find catharsis in doing so. But for Levi and Améry, the

Holocaust became a life's work. Each struggled mightily to come to terms with the experience. Levi struggled for intellectual clarity: clarity of expression, of description, of understanding. Only the last eluded him. Améry struggled for moral clarity: how to be true to his experience of torture and torment and yet find some way to imagine the conditions of genuine forgiveness. He found them in the denial of time, above all the refusal to let time heal his wounds, any wounds. He found these conditions in the refusal to let time, ethical time, move forward from where it had stopped in Hell. Whatever else one may think of such a strategy, it is a full-time occupation, not one to encourage doubling. On the contrary, it leaves its practitioner daily confronted with an experience that cannot be mastered, indeed can hardly be lived with, except by living beside it. This, Améry's art, his philosophy, would not allow, though one should not imagine that he lived the life of a recluse or saint (Heidelberger-Leonard 2010, pp. 246–251).

3.5 Conclusion

It would be easy to say that relationship between *At the Mind's Limit* and *On Aging* is one in which Améry creates a misleading parallel structure between the ethics of resentment and aging. Since there is no logical relationship between the two, the argumentative flaws in *On Aging* do not and should not affect the ethical argument in *At the Mind's Limit*. While there is some value in separating the works in this way, the relationship is more complex. Améry's claim that survivors must preserve their resentment until the Germans long for the annulment of time as strongly as do thoughtful survivors is a valid ethical stance, a stance that refuses to let history heal old wounds. However mistaken Améry is about applying that same attitude toward aging, his ethics of resentful refusal have their own merit.

Trouble is the merit of resentful refusal is limited to a single generation. The ethics of the annulment of time provide no guidance for subsequent generations in dealing with Germans, collaborators, and bystanders. This becomes truer every day. The resentment to which Améry refers can make no sense, or at least nothing like the original sense, when applied to the children of survivors, let alone their age cohort, which includes the children of perpetrators, the rest of us, and subsequent generations. Indeed, it hardly makes sense when applied to anyone but a survivor. To be sure, one can draw some general guidelines, such as don't forget history, don't forgive too easily or too readily, but there is nothing special or particular about Améry's approach in this regard.

Améry's ethics of resentful refusal fails to offer any guidance for subsequent generations because he doesn't seem to believe in subsequent generations. He doesn't deny them, or disbelieve in them. Subsequent generations rarely enter into his calculations. Even as he expresses concern about younger Germans, he cannot demand of them what he plausibly demands of the generation that committed, collaborated, or tolerated mass murder. If subsequent generations cannot be held responsible in the same way, surely it cannot be expected that they wish to undo the past with the same fervor as the Holocaust's victims. This is what the succession of generations means.

Sadly, Améry did not live to see many members of still younger generations demand a reckoning with the Holocaust. Many younger Germans were extraordinarily responsive to Daniel Goldhagen's *Hitler's Willing Executioners: Ordinary Germans and the Holocaust* (1996). The book appeared in 1996, at just that point when a new generation of Germans seemed finally ready to take on the subject in the face of their elders' reticence. Jürgen Habermas' defense of Goldhagen against an older generation of German historians is a particularly fascinating moment in that encounter.[6]

Notes

1. Robert Solomon (1994) cites personal correspondence as the source of this quotation from Danto, reflecting a position with which Solomon concurs.
2. At: walterbenjamin.ominiverdi.org/wp-content/walterbenjamin_concepthistory.pdf. No translator given. *On the Concept of History*, original 1940, thesis 9. The connection to Walter Benjamin's angel of history is suggested by Thomas Brudholm in *Resentment's Virtue* (2008, pp. 109, 115).
3. "Resentments" was the originally the last essay of *At the Mind's Limits*. "On the Necessity and Impossibility of Being a Jew" was added to later editions. It too closes on a note of deep resignation.
4. *On Aging* was first published in 1968, two years after *Jenseits Von Schuld Und Sühne*. *Jenseits* (*At the Mind's Limits*) was a collection of essays originally published over a period of years.
5. I base this statement on having viewed over 200 survivor videos in the Fortunoff Archive for Holocaust Testimony at Yale University over a period of several years. For details see Alford (2009, pp. 58–93).
6. An absorbing account of Goldhagen's reception in Germany can be found in Michael Zank's (2008) "Goldhagen in Germany: Historians' Nightmare & Popular Hero."

References

Alford, C. F. (2009). *After the Holocaust: The Book of Job, Primo Levi, and the Path to Affliction*. New York: Cambridge University Press.

Alford, C. F. (2015). Subjectivity and the Intergenerational Transmission of Historical Trauma: Holocaust Survivors and Their Children. *Subjectivity, 8*, 261–282.

Améry, J. (1966). *Jenseits von Schuld und Sühne: Bewältigungsversuche eines Überwältigen*. Munich: Szczesny.

Améry, J. (1980). *At the Mind's Limits: Contemplations by a Survivor on Auschwitz and Its Realities*. Bloomington, IN: Indiana University Press.

Améry, J. (1994). *On Aging: Revolt and Resignation*. Bloomington, IN: Indiana University Press.

Benjamin, W. (1940). On the Concept of History. Retrieved from https://www.marxists.org/reference/archive/benjamin/1940/history.htm.

Blanchot, M. (1995). *The Writing of the Disaster*. Lincoln, NE: University of Nebraska Press.

Brudholm, T. (2008). *Resentment's Virtue: Jean Améry and the Refusal to Forgive*. Philadelphia, PA: Temple University Press.

Epstein, H. (2010). *Children of the Holocaust*. Lexington, MA: Plunkett Lake Press.

Erikson, K. (1995). Notes on Trauma and Community. In C. Caruth (Ed.), *Trauma: Explorations in Memory* (pp. 183–199). Baltimore, MD: Johns Hopkins University Press.

Goldhagen, D. (1996). *Hitler's Willing Executioners: Ordinary Germans and the Holocaust*. New York, NY: Knopf.

Griswold, C. (2007). *Forgiveness: A Philosophical Exploration*. Cambridge, UK: Cambridge University Press.

Heidelberger-Leonard, I. (2010). *The Philosopher of Auschwitz: Jean Améry and Living with the Holocaust*. London, UK: I. B. Tauris.

Kant, I. (1993). *Grounding for the Metaphysics of Morals* (J. Ellington, Trans.). Indianapolis, IN: Hackett.

Kant, I. (1996). On the Common Saying: That May Be Correct in Theory, But It Is of No Use in Practice. In M. Gregor (Trans.), *Practical Philosophy*. New York, NY: Cambridge University Press.

Kraft, R. (2002). *Memory Perceived: Recalling the Holocaust*. Westport, CT: Praeger.

Levi, P. (1989). *The Drowned and the Saved* (R. Rosenthal, Trans.). New York, NY: Vintage International.

Levi, P. (1996). *Survival in Auschwitz* (S. Woolf, Trans.). New York, NY: Touchstone Books.

Marcuse, H. (1962). *Eros and Civilization: A Philosophical Inquiry into Freud*. New York, NY: Vintage Books.

Nietzsche, F. (2009). *On the Genealogy of Morals* (D. Smith, Trans.). Oxford, UK: Oxford University Press.

Roth, P. (2007). *Exit Ghost*. New York, NY: Houghton Mifflin.
Sachs, A. (2013). Intergenerational Transmission of Massive Trauma: The Holocaust. In J. Yellin & O. Epstein (Eds.), *Terror Within and Without: Attachment and Disintegration* (pp. 21–38). London, UK: Karnac.
Solomon, R. (1994). One Hundred Years of Ressentiment: Nietzsche's Genealogy of Morals. In R. Schacht (Ed.), *Nietzsche, Genealogy, Morality: Essays on Nietzsche's on the Genealogy of Morality* (pp. 95–126). Berkeley, CA: University of California Press.
Zank, M. (2008). Goldhagen in Germany: Historians' Nightmare and Popular Hero. *Religious Studies Review, 24*, 231–240.

CHAPTER 4

Registers of Undesirability, Poetics of Detention: Jean Améry on the Jewish Exile and Behrouz Boochani on the Manus Prison

Magdalena Zolkos

4.1 Introduction[1]

Jean Améry argued in his essay "How Much Home Does a Person Need?" (1977, 1999) that there is a distinctive kind of homesickness, specific to the exile experiences of the assimilated German-speaking Jews during the war. They were dispossessed not only of their homes, citizenship, and cultural community in the present, but also of their past attachments, memories, and identifications. Through a pervasive act of undoing, the expulsion from their homeland, language, and culture meant that their past sense of home as a site of collective belonging had been revealed as a fiction (Améry 1999, pp. 50–52; see also Udoff 2004). In this essay, I ask about the insights from Améry's writings on exile into the contemporary literature on the 'refugee experience' (see e.g. Agier 2008). I suggest a new way of reading Améry's exile essay—one that moves away from the focus on Améry's phenomenology of homelessness and homesickness (as explored

M. Zolkos (✉)
Goethe University Frankfurt, Frankfurt, Germany

Y. Ataria et al. (eds.), *Jean Améry*,
https://doi.org/10.1007/978-3-030-28095-6_4

e.g. by Brudholm 2005; Shuster 2016; Vivaldi 2019; Zolkos 2010), and from its interpretations as a critical commentary on the German idea of *heimat* (see e.g. Greiner 2003; Grøn and Brudholm 2011; Stone1995; Vansant 2001). Rather, I approach Améry's text on in the light of critical theorizing of the politics of exile and border-control, and with a focus on the notions of 'undesirability' and 'expulsion' that underwrite the extreme political precarity of those who, because of their origin, skin color, ethnicity or religion, have become subjects of 'necro-politics'[2] (Mbembe 2003) and of differential distribution of public mourning and grief in democratic liberal states (Butler 2006, 2010).

I argue that when approached from the perspective of the German-Jewish émigrés' pariahdom and the dynamics of 'expulsion', Améry's essay gives insights into the politicized condition of refuge-seekers through racialized registers of undesirability. Here it is useful to point out the double meaning of the word 'register'; first, as a way of listing, or recording, the instances when undesirable bodies appear on the political horizon. The verb 'to register', from the Latin *regerere*, meaning 'to enter' or 'to record', consists of the root *gerere*, derived from the noun *gest*, meaning 'actions, exploits, [and] deeds'. In his essay, Améry displays great sensitivity in noting precisely those moments when fascist genocidal visions of eliminating an entire people coalesce into mundane and ordinary experiences of the refuge-seekers. The second meaning of the term 'to register' is equally important for my reading as it points to how the politics of expulsion and undesirability (quite literally) *impress*, or *imprint*, themselves onto the émigrés' bodies, as a matter of lived experience, feelings, sensations and affects (voluntarily and involuntarily). One of the definitions of the verb 'to register' pertains to musical and scientific instruments, where it connotes the ability to detect and display sounds (etc.), based on the premise that at hand is both a task of great difficulty, in that such registering requires sensitivity, nuance, and attunement—and a risk of failing to do so.

As others have noted, the idiosyncratic trait of Améry's writings lies in his commitment to philosophizing that originates within, and remains faithful to, concrete experiences during (and after) the war as an assimilated German Jew (see e.g. Brudholm 2005; Shuster 2016). At the same time, Améry's writings are interspersed with moments when the philosophic exceeds the documentary, introspective, or autobiographic objectives, which places him in a broader dialogue with the continental tradition of the Enlightenment, to which he was committed, but not without "a degree of qualification, even of ambiguity" (Suchting 1988, p. 141). Brudholm (2005, p. 9) has written of the oscillation between "the concrete [and] the philosophical" and "the common [and] the personal" in Améry's work. My aim in tracing and analyzing the figurations of 'undesirability' and 'expulsion' in "How Much Home Does a Person Need?" is to highlight the political dimension of this oscillation, or textual movement, to which scholars have paid less attention than to its philosophic, epistemological, or literary dimensions. The proposed reading shows that one of Améry's central preoccupations in his writings on exile have been political freedom and the possibility of resistance, as well as their constitutive codependence, in the oppressive context of forced exile, marked by a futility of political action. Here the act of writing becomes that of resistance and a reclamation of voice and language in the face of the fascistic powers aimed at expelling, silencing, and eliminating the 'undesirables'.

I also juxtapose Améry's writings on exile with Behrouz Boochani's *No Friend but the Mountains: Writing from Manus Prison* (2018), which narrates Boochani's firsthand experiences in Australia's offshore 'processing' (or, more precisely, a de facto indefinite detention) system on the Manus Island. Similarly to Améry, in his writings Boochani oscillates, or moves back and forth, between different narrative registers: personal, political, and poetic. While both Améry and Boochani write from the standpoint of political exiles—one an assimilated German-speaking Jew in Belgium, and the other a Kurd writing in Farsi, and detained on a remote pacific island—*No Friend but the Mountains* resonates not only with "How Much Home Does a Person Need?" but also with Améry's essays on torture and on concentration camps.[3] The proposed comparative reading of Améry and Boochani focuses primarily on "How Much Home Does a Person Need?" because it seeks to articulate the two authors' respective insights into the political condition of exile, expulsion and undesirability, and into how that condition registers within the bodily and affective realm. The importance of the proposed approach is not only its harm-centric and experiential orientation as a way of comprehending the political stakes in state failure to protect and grant entry for the refuge-seekers in situations of extreme precarity; it is also to validate and illuminate sites and spaces of resistance undertaken by the victims of these cruel politics, no matter how tentative, short-lived, or, even, failed they might be.

This chapter proceeds as follows. First, I give an overview of two philosophic discussions of Améry's essay on the émigré experience, and suggest that their insights into Améry's phenomenology of exile illuminate his validation of subjective and firsthand perspectives on displacement within refugee studies and genocide studies—not only as a way of illustrating the existing theories but also of pointing the insufficiency of the law-centric approaches to atrocity and displacement. These philosophic readings of "How Much Home Does a Person Need?" bring to the fore the distinctive category of the 'temporality of exile' in Améry's writing, whereby not only the subject's present but also her past is profoundly affected (undone and nullified) by the act of expulsion from the homeland. Subsequently, the question of the subject's future, which Améry idiomatizes as (making) "new home", unfolds within this overarching framework of the lacking "guarantees [of] security" (1999, p. 48). Second, I suggest that what has been insufficiently noted in these interpretations of Améry's text on exile is the political dimension of his essay; Améry illuminates the political effects of 'undesirability' and 'expulsion' from the perspective of the failure of justice in the postwar Germany. Finally, I undertake a comparative reading of Améry's essay and Boochani's *No Friend but the Mountains*, reflecting on how these two texts intersect and illuminate one another, and how they understand the stakes in the politics of undesirability and expulsion of refuge-seekers.

4.2 Thinking with Améry About Exile: From Non-belonging to Expulsion

Critical philosophic scholarship on Jean Améry's collection *At Mind's Limits* has long recognized the importance of his "How Much Home Does a Person Need?" for contemporary phenomenological understanding of exile, asylum-seeking, and homelessness. Among others, Thomas Brudholm (2005, pp. 7–8) interprets it as a contribution to the field of experiential knowledge, produced by those who have been forced to flee their places of residence because of war and genocide, a "thought-provoking addendum to current laudations of the homeless mind and a valuable contribution to current attempts to rethink the meaning of genocide from the perspective of the harm done to the victims". As such, Brudholm argues (2005, p. 10), Améry deliberately uses terms immediately recognizable in German cultural memory, such as *Heimat*, *Ressentiment*, and *Versöhnung* (reconciliation), but, by offering their radical reinterpretation, he simultaneously attempts their 'unsettling' or 'dislocation'. Regarding the idea of homelessness and homesickness (*Hauptwehe*), Améry (1999, p. 42) argues that constitutive of the exile experience of the assimilated German Jews during the war was the violent dispossession of their place of residence and of national community, as well as expulsion from cultural and intellectual tradition, and from the German language. The Jewish expellees' loss of language has to do, partly, with the 'corruption' of the German language by the Nazi jargon, which Améry (1999, p. 52) describes as its disfiguration, or impairment ("the language [...] was being marred").[4] In turn, the adopted language of the host country allows for only "temporary exile"; Améry compares it to a "friend [who acts in] a reserved manner and receives us only for brief formal visits" (1999, p. 53).[5] Perhaps more importantly, Améry assigns great significance to the fact that it is was in German that the assimilated German-speaking Jews 'heard' their death-verdict; the mother tongue announced their death verdict and became hostile toward them.[6]

The compatriots of the expellees, even when not actively pursuing Fascistic genocidal goals, had become "informers, bullies, [...] opportunists". Améry summarizes the effects of the politics of expulsion on the subject's sense of self in an often-quoted poetic statement: "I was a person who could no longer say 'we' and who therefore said 'I' merely out of habit" (1999, p. 44). This is interpreted by Brudholm (2005, p. 15) as radicalization of the idea of homesickness as *Selbstentfremdung*, the subject's alienation from oneself, as well as the internalized desire to direct aggression at oneself.

Importantly, this alienating dynamic in the émigré experience has also a retroactive dimension, because it nullifies her/his claims on, or entitlements to, political home and belonging not only in the present but also in the past. For Brudholm (2005, p. 14), this highlights the importance of the wide "sociopolitical consensus" in Germany and Austria that had enabled and effectuated Nazi genocidal policies.[7] For the émigré, national identity, 'propped' by language, community, customs, and material objects (etc.), become not only unattainable but also, as Brudholm puts it (2005, p. 15), "intolerable" and irreparable. Améry's text offers a much needed corrective to the privileged cosmopolitan positions that romanticize and celebrate the loss of national belonging as a sign of individual's empowerment, intellectual vigor, and adaptability within the rubric of the 'homeless mind'. Instead, it points to the lived realities of displacement and dispossession. It also highlights the importance of recognizing the refugees' subjective perspectives as a way of countering the dominance of law-centric discourses in the field of refugee and genocide studies, while channeling an argument for greater attention to the 'epistemic privilege' (my term, not Brudholm's) of those contributions to knowledge that are grounded in direct experience. More specifically, Brudholm (2005, pp. 18–19) argues that Améry's exile essay points out a flaw at the heart of the international instruments that help to identify and classifying mass atrocities as genocide, which require a demonstration of intent on the part of the state to destroy groups and collectives on religious, racial, or ethnic grounds. The first-person literature on exile and refuge-seeking shifts the attention from state intent to the question of experiential harm, regardless of whether destructive objectives are discernible and apparent, or not (see also Campbell 2012; Kusher and Knox 1999; Tietjens Meyers 2016).

In "A Phenomenology of Home" Martin Shuster (2016) notes the importance of Améry's essay's surpassing of its autobiographical and documentary elements while remaining grounded in the subjective experience of exile, which Shuster interprets as a defining trait of a phenomenological inquiry. Améry's essay should be read not as an inquiry into "the psychological state of homelessness", but, instead, as a study of "the *ontological* quality of homesickness: that human subjectivity becomes a certain way under certain conditions" (2016, p. 118; emphasis in the original). Similarly to Brudholm's Arendtian reading of Améry's preoccupation with the loss of the world as an experience shuttering the subject's social and personal identity (see also Yeatman 2011), Shuster (2016, p. 119) emphasizes that for Améry the subject's knowledge of the world is not acquired theoretically, but experientially, somatically, and holistically, through a sensorial immersion within it. This aspect of Améry's approach is for Shuster both resonant of Heidegger's pre-reflective and pre-intentional *In-der-Welt-sein*, "being-in-the-world", and Merleau-Ponty's phenomenology of perception (2002). Améry's notion of homelessness invokes thus ways in which the violence of political expulsion results in the subject's discordance or incongruity with the world, or, in Heideggerian terms, it marks the collapse of the subject's "entangled absorption in the 'world'" (Shuster 2016, p. 122).

Importantly, this experience of being "out of touch" with the world is for Améry mediated through the sociopolitical contexts of the exile, torture, and imprisonment. For instance, in the first essay in the collection *At the Mind's Limits*, on intellectuals and the concentration camps, Améry famously evaluates the role of religion and ideology as the alleviating factors of the subject's self-alienation. This is because the shared sociopsychological effect of religion and ideology is that they have given the detainees "firm foothold in the world from which they were spiritually unhinged by the SS state" (Améry 1999, p. 13). According to Kitty Millet's perceptive analysis (2011), while religious belief and ideological commitments sustained the prisoners' political imagination in the camps (which was also the site where personal resistance and hope originated), for the "intellectuals in Auschwitz" homelessness as the loss of the world meant a "shock" and a "disable[ment] to constitute himself as a subject". The phrase "intellectuals in Auschwitz" is Améry's term for those inmates who had no recourse to the Kantian sensu *communis*, "[a] membership in a global community of imagined subjects as an effect of [the] 'shared sense'" of transcendental values. At hand, then, is the subject's experience of witnessing her own "dissolution": the "[p]olitical and religious believers have the ability to cross and 'transcend' the mind's limits, but the intellectual feels the experience as a *profound severance*, and *interruption*" (for discussions of Améry's conception of human dignity in situations of political extremity, see Bernstein 2011; Hunt 2010; Millet 2011, p. 30; emphases mine).

In "How Much Home Does a Person Need?" Améry carefully distinguishes between, on the one hand, the experience of exile and refuge-seeking of the assimilated and secular German-speaking Jews, and, on the other hand, that of East European Jews and that of self-exiled (non-Jewish) Germans (see Zolkos 2010, pp. 34–35). The dispossession suffered by Jews from Eastern Europe was profound, and it included loss of residence, income, and possessions, but, according to Améry, it did not involve the loss of language and cultural values. The unassimilated "itinerant Jew", whose collective identity had been shaped by history of violence, antisemitism, and pariahdom in the host countries, as well as by "wandering and expulsion", had found in the émigré identity a "transportable home, or at least an ersatz for home" (Améry 1999, p. 44). The non-Jewish German escapees from the Nazi Reich were different, too, but in different respect: not only had they undertaken their exile voluntarily and on ideological grounds; they also retained access to the national imaginary community and to the philosophy of the Enlightenment, as important political and ideological counter-project to National Socialism. But, Améry writes (1999, p. 45), "[there was] [n]othing like that [for the] anonymous ones. No game with the imaginary true Germany, [...] no formal ritual of a German culture preserved in exile for better days. The nameless refugees [*die namenlosen Flüchtlinge*] [...] knew that they were outcasts and not curators of an invisible museum of German intellectual history." In contrast to both the voluntary German migrants, and to the Ostjuden refugees, the German-speaking Jews were "completely uprooted [*entborgen ganz und gar*]". Here, Améry's use of the word 'entborgen' emphasizes the political stakes in undergoing exile—the loss of public safety—and its constitutive role for the émigré condition.[8]

The dispossession of language is particularly poignant for Améry (see also Zolkos 2010, pp. 39–40). Shuster (2016, p. 120) argues that Améry's view of the social character of language shares important affinity with the tradition of "linguistic phenomenology" of Wittgenstein and Austin. That affinity is conspicuous in Améry's claim that "every language is part of a total reality [*Gesamtwirklichkeit*] to which one must have a well-founded right of ownership if one is to enter the area of that language with a good conscience and confident step" (Améry 1977, p. 91; 1999, pp. 53–54). The reality of the loss of language is, literally, *murderous* in so far as their mother tongue is also the language of the Nuremberg Laws—pronunciation of the Jewish death verdict. Améry thus describes it as "inimical", "oppressive", and "hostile" (1999, p. 53). The linguistic and cultural loss suffered by the German Jews during the war illuminates what Améry means by homesickness: not a nostalgic longing for a lost place (time), but the subject's profound, and in an important respect irreparable, dispossession. Améry's émigré is "impoverished of routes of salience and action" (Shuster 2016, p. 122).

An important element of the phenomenological account of the Jewish émigré experience concerns the temporal dimension of exile. Shuster notes Améry's skepticism about the idea of the émigré acquiring, or making, 'new home' in the future. Améry says that "there is no 'new home'", and that "whoever has lost [a homeland] remains lost himself, even if he has learned not to stumble about in the foreign country [...], but rather to tread the ground with some fearlessness" (1999, p. 48). In this essay, and elsewhere, Améry cautions against an enactment of political future that absorbs and nullifies the subject's catastrophic experience by aiming to achieve normalization and historical closure, as Améry thought was largely the case with the German *Vergangenheitsbewältigung* politics (see Banki 2018, pp. 52–54; Zolkos 2010, p. 41). The distinctive feature of the temporality of exile is the subject's lasting insecurity, a sense of being open to danger or threat of violence. This does not negate the possibility of hope (or what Améry calls "future possibilities"); neither does it deny the creative capacities, recalcitrance, and perseverance exhibited by émigrés and asylum-seekers on daily bases, often within oppressive social conditions (as Behrouz Boochani's book documents). However, making a new home in the future is a project infused with "lacunae, holes of absence and regret, lines of instability, and routes of limitation, emptiness, and dead-end" (Shuster 2016, p. 123). For Améry (1977, p. 98; 1999, p. 58), "[the] horizon [of the exiled subject] presses in on him, his tomorrow and day-after-tomorrow have no vigor [*Kraft*] and no certainty" because such future is necessarily situated within the subject's lived knowledge that any social "guarantees [of] security" are provisional and precarious.

As I have discussed, these selected philosophical-phenomenological readings of Améry's émigré essay rightly emphasize his validation of philosophical reflection grounded in the first-person perspective and his contribution to philosophical knowledge about the temporality of exile. What is conspicuously absent in these interpretations, however, is attention to Améry's more explicitly political preoccupations in that essay. In what follows, I address that lacunae through a 'bodily political' reading of Améry's essay by applying a heuristic lens of two complementary concepts, which aptly characterize contemporary border politics of liberal states: undesirability and expulsion. I suggest that Améry's essay not only explores the structure of experience and of consciousness of the dispossession undergone by the exiled subject, but that it also illuminates how notions of undesirability attach themselves, and continue to adhere, to certain people by the virtue of their place of birth, race, and religion, and how the expulsion of the 'undesirables' operates as a political imperative and political capital.

4.3 Undesirable Bodies, Expelled Subjects

To raise the question of 'undesirability' of asylum-seekers within the contemporary liberal border-politics is to highlight the dynamics of the deeply entrenched global (neo)colonial relations that congeal as social attitudes and ways of experiencing others who are regarded as unacceptable, harmful, and even physically repulsive. Drawing on Hannah Arendt's well-known essay on the human rights of refugees, Giorgio Agamben (2000, p. 30) argues that the failure of the international community of contemporary nation-states to address the needs of asylum-seekers has to do with their loss of "every quality and every specific relation except for the pure fact of being human". The refugees are 'imagined' within the domain of international law as occupying a temporary and liminal status, which "ought to lead either to naturalization or to repatriation" (2000, p. 31). However, it is precisely to the extent that they defy such normalizing liberal logic, that, for Agamben, refuge-seekers represent a "disquieting element" in the order of the nation state, and "bring radical crisis to [its] principles" (2000, pp. 32, 34). They dismantle the assumed synonymity of "the human and the citizen" and that of "nativity and nationality" and, subsequently, "bring [...] the originary fiction of sovereignty to crisis, [and] unhinge [...] the old trinity of state-nation-territory" (2000, p. 32). The refuge-seekers are "sacred" in the sense that Agamben derives from ancient Roman law of *homo sacer*: "doomed to death" (2000, p. 33), set apart, expunged, or removed, from the community.

Further, Saskia Sassen in her book *Expulsions: Brutality and Complexity in Global Economy* helps to understand how such undesirability translates into the violent logic of ejection, or displacement—the 'undesirables' are "expelled from the core social and economic orders" (2014, p. 1). The importance of Sassen's contribution lies in her insistence that expulsions are deliberate political effects, or, in her words, that expulsions are "*made*". The "instruments for this making range from elementary policies to complex institutions, systems, and techniques", that nevertheless reveal an underlying logic: "they are [acts of] acute [...] savage sorting [and] brutality" (pp. 3, 4), which have at their core that of driving out, or forcing out, those whose presence is unacceptable. While Sassen's broad-stroke methodology raises problems of subsuming the international asylum-seeking policies under the larger neoliberal and global sociological trends of mobility and movement, her insight in regard to the mass displacement of populations points to the important element of unleashing a brutal centrifugal force of 'thrusting out' and 'keeping out', which certainly is at play in much of the liberal border politics today and in particular within the institution of the border-industrial complex.

In "How Much Home Does a Person Need?" Améry makes a distinction between the forced exile of Jews from the Third Reich and the voluntary immigration of German artists and intellectuals as demonstrative of the logic of expulsion. For Améry, the expulsion from the home country starts already in 1935 with the Nuremberg Laws, which, literally, 'put out of community' and 'remove out of sight' the German Jews. What he means by this is that the Nuremberg Laws were "the expression, concentrated in legal-textual form, of the verdict 'Death to the Jews!'[...]" (Améry 1999, p. 89). The "homesickness" that Améry invokes is thus synonymous not with nostalgic feelings, but with irreversibility of the violent acts of expulsion (1999, p. 42).[9] Améry uses the term "undesirable aliens" (*unerwünschte Ausländer*) in order to depict the émigré condition as that of "outcasts" (*Verjagte*), who, for sociopolitical reasons, are unable to produce any substitute for the lost home (Améry 1977, pp. 77, 80; 1999, pp. 43, 45). My point here is that, the essay's phenomenological and philosophical tone notwithstanding, the text makes a political argument: Améry's speaks of 'loss' and 'homelessness' not just synonymously with material dispossession, but also with expropriation of citizenship. Contrary to Stone (1995), I think that Améry invokes the notion of *Heimat* not as a figure of sentimentalized national belonging, but as institutional and political security, or peaceful conditions of coexistence. It is when such conditions are lacking, Améry argues (Améry 1977, p. 83; 1999, p. 47), that the subject is thrust into a condition of "disorder, confusion, desultoriness" (*Ordnungslosigkeit, Verstörung; Zerfahrenheit*). These are not depoliticized descriptors of psychological states; rather, I suggest that they are to be understood as bodily and sensory registration of political precarity. It is noteworthy that Améry exemplifies his point about the sense of confusion and disorientation in the foreign surroundings by pointing to his inability to interpret the cryptic nonverbal signs of a police-officer (was he "good-natured, indifferent, or mocking?", Améry asks [1999, p. 47]). The émigré's experience of confusion and uncertainty, while having her identification documents checked, is not an inconsequential occurrence, but, potentially, a foreboding event with highly detrimental effects. The police officer's inscrutability maps onto the moment of judgment whether the exile's presence if 'legitimate' or 'illegitimate'; it is a tool of control and submission.

Améry distinguishes the émigré's constant (unsuccessful) attempts at deciphering the social rules and cultural communications in his new place of residence from the confusion or strangeness frequently experienced by tourists in foreign countries (a "piquant form of alienation" (1999, p. 47)). Rather, Améry argues (1977, p. 82; 1999, p. 47), the émigré's disorientation is made political by the fact that her life, literally, depends on the decipherment of this "world full of riddles" (*diese Welt voll Rätseln*). The extension of welcome toward the refuge-seekers (if there is one) is a precarious gesture that is highly conditional and that can be withdrawn at any moment; for that reasons, Améry argues (1999, p. 47), the officials and residents of the host country are "lords and masters". And, he adds, "[at] times I felt more vulnerable before them then before the SS man at home, because of him I had at least known with certainty that he was stupid and mean and that he was after my life" (1999, p. 47). Behrouz Boochani's book offers a powerful discussion of how the inscrutability and volatility of the Kafkaesque rules and prohibitions governing life in the detention center, operates as a deliberate tactic of control. They bring about intended political outcomes, bodily registered as states of confusion and heightened agitation, in order to ensure the detainees' subordination and placidity, but also, importantly, the take the detainees' suffering as a goal in and of itself.

In elaborating the émigrés' dependence on their hosts, which locks the former into the incessant process of untangling cryptic verbal and gestural signals, Améry comes to articulate what is, I argue, one of the (largely unnoticed) key preoccupations of his exile essay: the meaning of freedom and unfreedom in the context of refuge-seeking. Interestingly, Améry's idea of freedom bears close resemblance to what Quentin Skinner (1998) has called "the third conception of liberty"—not the 'negative freedom' of the lack of direct restraint on the subject's actions, nor the 'positive freedom' of capacity necessary for the subject to act in accordance with her will, but *freedom as non-domination*. Skinner has shown, in regard to Hobbes and the republican tradition of political thought, that the conception of liberty as non-domination, originating in the ancient Roman jurisprudence, consists in the absence of oppressive and subordinating conditions of political life. This also includes situations when an actual infringement of the subject's actions has not occurred, but 'only' figures as the omnipresent condition of possibility. Améry (1999, p. 47) situates this conception of freedom in relation to his political definition of 'home' as security: "[one] feels secure [...] where no chance occurrence is to be expected, nothing completely strange to be feared."

Admittedly, Améry (1999, p. 48) also writes about the émigrés' insufficient familiarity with the novel cultural contexts and their lack of linguistic proficiency in a way that might suggest description of a general trait of diasporic life of those who migrate in the adult age ("[o]nly those signals that we absorbed early, that we learnt to interpret at the same time as we were gaining possession of our external world, become constitutional elements and constants of our personality"). And yet, at hand is bodily registration of undesirability through disorientation and confusion, which is premised on the specific *violence of expulsion*, rather than psychological factors of cross-cultural competency. The goal is erasure of the 'undesirables'—"my home was enemy country," writes Améry (p. 50), and it sought "to wipe me out". In a poignant statement, which supports my argument that the exile essay reinscribes the émigrés' homelessness as a political effect of undesirability, rather than as a nostalgic longing, Améry says (Améry 1977, p. 88; 1999, p. 51): "[the affliction of] genuine homesickness" (*Hauptwehe*—a term he borrows from Thomas Mann's *Doctor Faustus*) is "not self-pity, but rather [...] self-destruction [*nicht Selbstmitleid, sondern Selbstzerstörung*]. It consisted in dismantling our past piece by piece, which could not be done without self-contempt and hatred for the lost self." For Améry 'expulsion' is not only about the subject's driving out from community and from the sphere of public visibility, but also about the subject directing the aggression against oneself through self-harm and, as was eventually the case with Améry and with numerous detainees on Manus and Nauru, attempted suicide.

It is when the political dynamics of undesirability converge with those of longing sentiment that the émigré's condition becomes truly unbearable: "[the] combination of hatred for our homeland and self-hatred hurt, and the pain intensified most unbearably when, during the strenuous task of self-destruction, now and then traditional homesickness also welled up and claimed its place" (Améry 1999, p. 51). For that reason, "[what] we urgently wished, and were socially bound, to hate, suddenly stood before us and demanded our longing [*wollte ersehnt werden*]. A totally impossible, neurotic condition [*ein ganz unmöglicher, neurotischer Zustand*] for which there is no psychoanalytic remedy" (1977, p. 88; 1999, p. 51). It is important to note the language of force that Améry uses to describe this longing; the lost community presents itself and 'demands' to be desired. What follows is a pivotal, though to my knowledge largely overlooked, moment of the exile essay. Améry (1999, p. 51) proposes that the only possible form of repair—or, as he puts it, I believe ironically, "therapy"—is "history in practice". In the original German text the phrase is "*die geschichtliche Praxis*" ('historical practice' or the 'practice of history') (1977, p. 88). What the English translation misses, then, is the rich connotation of the term "praxis" as a political action oriented toward a societal change (which, interestingly, Hannah Arendt has seen as directly related to the questions freedom). I propose that Améry means by it both (a) politics informed by lessons history, or articulated in relation to historical insight (rather than in denial of it), *and* (b) 'politics of the past'—politics of historical justice; reparative interventions into situations of historical harm that effectuates actual social change—a radical 'politics of the past' that its conservative and counter-revolutionary implementations (for instance in Robert Meister's critique of the discourses of 'closure' and 'resolution' in transitional justice [see 2012]).

Améry explains what he means by the phrase "*die geschichtliche Praxis*": "[it is] the *German revolution* and with it the homeland's strongly expressed desire for our return. But the revolution did not take place, and *our return was nothing but an embarrassment* for our homeland, when finally the National Socialist power was crushed from without" (1999, p. 51; emphases mine). In another essay included in the collection *At the Mind's Limits*, Améry (1999, p. 77) has elaborated the idea of a "German revolution that did not take place" as a demand made by a victim from the site of resentment, by which he means a "personal protest against the anti-moral natural process of healing that time brings about", as well as "the genuinely humane and absurd demand that time be turned back". Améry's critique of the 'neutralization' of German history is perhaps akin to what psychoanalysis describes as the defense mechanism of externalization whereby the subject comes to disown its own characteristics and actions. In contrast to the political displays of such collective disowning and externalization of history within the project of *Vergangenheitsbewältigung*, "Hitler and his deeds will [...] continue to be a part of German history and German tradition" (1999, p. 77). The opposite of the 'neutralization' or 'repression' of the Holocaust through its absorption within the larger cultural discourse of reconciliation, is its 'integration' by the collective Germany subject, without the attempted processing, resolution or 'digestion'. The Holocaust, Améry argues, quoting Enzensberger, will remain "Germany's past, present, and future" (1999, p. 78).

While readers of this essay have paid significant attention to its dialectic of the subjective experience of exile and philosophy of displacement, what has remained unnoticed is the significance of its temporal composition and its intentionality: together with the other essays in the collection *At the Mind's Limit,* "How Much Home Does a Person Need?" was composed nearly 20 years after the war, at the background of the Frankfurt Auschwitz trials, or 'the second Auschwitz trials', that run between 1963 and 1965. It was thus part of Améry's critical commentary on what (he thought was) a failure of justice of the German *Vergangenheitsbewältigung* politics in its drive toward closure and normalization. The postwar public debate about collective German culpability was for Améry demonstrative of profound political unwillingness to do justice to the victims of the war crimes and genocide (Heidelberger-Leonard 2010, pp. 133–186; Suchting 1988).

Améry's skepticism about the place of reconciliation and forgiveness within the *Vergangenheitsbewältigung* politics is inextricable from the fact that his central, and perhaps only, focus is "worldly justice" (see also Banki 2018, pp. 43–45, 52–54; in: Wiesenthal 1997, p. 109). This is particularly conspicuous in his provocative contribution to Simon Wiesenthal's book, *The Sunflower: On the Possibility and Limits of Forgiveness* (1997). Wiesenthal, who died in 2005, was a founder of two documentation centers, one in Linz and one in Vienna, with a mandate of gathering information on, and locating the whereabouts of fugitive Nazi war criminals.[10] In *The Sunflower* Wiesenthal, drawing on his experience in Lemberg concentration camp, posed the question to public intellectuals and religious figures on whether a Jewish victim of the Holocaust should grant forgiveness to a remorseful dying Nazi. Rather than provide an answer, Améry *questions the question.* Forgiveness, Améry says (in Wiesenthal 1997, p. 107), "belongs to the realm to guilt and atonement" (the original title of *At the Mind's Limit* is *Jenseits von Schuld und Sühne—beyond* guilt and atonement). Thus, "the problem [of forgiveness] is a theological one, and as such, *does not exist for me* [...]. Politically, it does not make any difference" (in Wiesenthal 1997, p. 107; emphasis mine). Addressing Wiesenthal directly, Améry questions his fixation on forgiveness as a misplaced preoccupation, and even, somewhat offensively, as a potential distraction from Wiesenthal's work on tracing fugitive Nazis:

> Don's trouble yourself. [...] Your SS man [...] and his death don't matter, just as the response of inmate Wiesenthal doesn't matter. What does matter is the activity of the director and founder of the Documentation Center. He has nothing to do with that criminal who dies in the field hospital, but with others [other criminals] who live here among us. [...] The director of the Documentation Center should not allow them to live this sweet life, but rather make sure that the arm of worldly justice, weak and ineffectual as it is, still reaches them. (Wiesenthal 1997, pp. 108, 109)

I refer to the exchange between Améry and Wiesenthal because it shows that the central 'intention' of his postwar writings is to make an uncompromising claim for justice in the face of the failure of the postwar repairitive politics (see also Zolkos 2008). At this stage, it is useful to bring in Vladimir Jankélévitch's distinction between action and its consequences: while past action is irreversible, its consequences are undoable: "if the misdeed itself is repressed into what is non-actual, even if this would only be because all the consequences are reparable and all its traces are erasable, the fact of having committed it, itself, is incurable, unforgettable, and dependent on a free initiative of our responsibility" (Jankélévitch 2015, p. 56; see also La Caze 2019). That distinction helps to show that the central preoccupation of Améry's exile essay is not displacement as an act of the lost (childhood) home and the impossibility of return (i.e. that past act is irreversible), but the failure of justice (i.e. that the consequences of the past act remain unrepaired).

4.4 The Poetics of Detentions: Behrouz Boochani's *No Friend but the Mountains*

Behrouz Boochani's *No Friend but the Mountains* is part a prison memoir in the form of personal account of his detention experience in the Australian offshore immigration processing facilities on the Papua New Guinea Manus island (Manus Regional Processing Centre), part political philosophic dissection of the confluence of Australian coloniality, oppression, and racism under the heading of "the Kyriarchal system"—as well as a more general critique of the institution of border-industrial complex and liberal states' border politics—and part a poetic mediation that Boochani's translator, Omid Tofighian, has aptly described as "horrific surrealism". The genre, or *anti-genre*, of "horrific surrealism" is the overlapping of "horror realism" and "culturally- or ethnically-situated forms of surrealism", where "[r]eality is fused with dreams and creative ways of re-imagining the natural environment and horrific events and architecture" (Tofighian in Boochani 2018, pp. xxix, 368–369). Boochani's book has some resemblance to magical realism, but also diverges from it in significant respects.[11] Boochani himself, in the launch of his book at UNSW, where he spoke from his remote location on the Manus Island, said that he wanted the book to be read "as work of art" (see e.g. Khorana 2018). This bespeaks further what is perhaps the greatest difference between Améry's exile essay and Boochani 'poetics of detention', namely the question of language. While Améry 'performs' his views about the expellees' experience of 'shrinking' and dispossession of language through adopting a sparse and terse modernist style for his essay, Boochani situates his book within the broader Persian tradition of writing that traverses the prosaic and lyrical forms, and is unafraid of bold dramatizations and lurid descriptions.[12]

Boochani conceptualizes the Australian border-industrial complex as "kyriarchy". He borrows that term from Schüssler Fiorenza's book on feminist biblical interpretations (1992), where it functions as a heuristic devise for the analysis of "interconnected, interacting and self-extending" forms of structural domination and submission, that also illuminates, as its etymology suggests (Gr. *kyrios*, meaning "lord, master"), the connection between oppression and power/sovereignty. Referencing the foundational role that excluding the category of 'undesirables' (slaves, women, children) from citizenship played in the historical emergence of Greek democracy, Schüssler Fiorenza coins the term "kyriarchal democracies", where detrimentally invested categories of "gender, race, class, religion, heterosexualism, and age" operate as both social stratifications and power differentials, resulting in a pyramidal structure with those at the bottom "[experiencing] the full power of [...] oppression" (Schüssler Fiorenza 2010, pp. 10, 11). It is here that its usefulness for Boochani's analysis of how the Australian border-industrial complex is produced, governed, and reinforced becomes apparent. Together with a group of academic collaborators, Boochani (2018, p. 370) speaks of "Manus Prison Theory", whereby the Australian border politics operates within the larger contexts of coloniality, "Indigenous genocide [and] anti-Blackness". It is an "all-encompassing system of oppressive governmentality", and "[...] a professional and precise system in which one is registered in a mass of logbooks, a mass of numbers, a mass of figures" (Boochani 2018, pp. 329, 312). It encompasses techniques of surveillance and the carceral organization of place, architecture, and of the detainees' daily routines, as well as the violent 'theatre' of degradation and control. For the system to remain in operation, it also requires the cooperation and complicity of broad social groups—not just the guards, but also medical professionals, translators, journalists, lawyers, and the Australian public at large ("completely mesmerized by the government's dirty politics [they] just follow along" (2018, p. 92)).

Améry describes the experience of exile, torture, and the camp as something that the subject is absolutely and fundamentally *unprepared for* (in the essay on torture, drawing on Proust, he says about the torturer's "first blow" that it never happens "as we hope it will, nor as we fear it will" (1999, p. 25)). Boochani makes a similar point about living in the detention center: its realities bear no correspondence to the detainees past experiences, anticipations, and imaginings, but not as a way of phenomenology of extreme experiences, but as a deliberate political effect. He writes: "The

Kyriarchal System of the prison constructs landscapes the likes of which the prisoners have possibly never encountered in their entire lives" (2018, p. 230). In that particular instance, Boochani describes a situation where a plea by young man (The Father of the Months-Old Child) to make a phone call to his dying father is refused by the guards on the grounds of procedure violation. When three days later The Father of the Months-Old Child is finally allowed to make the phone call, it is too late—the father died. Responding with fury, destroying property and screaming, the young man is violently pacified by the officers. The situation is seemingly also that of ethical failure on the part of the man's companion, The Man With a Thick Moustache, who, while at first making a passionate please to the Australians to allow for the phone call, and "determined to break the rules any means possible to help his friend" (2018, p. 225), ultimately is reduced to a silent impassive observer. However, Boochani argues that at hand is not an ethical failure, or a cowardly withdrawal of friendship and solidarity, but, rather, an intended and deliberate effect of the prisoners' degradation; the friend has to remain impassive and "silent [in order to] allow the thinking organism that is the prison to operate [...]" (2018, p. 232).

Boochani follows the description of the incident with a poetic rendition of the friend's imaginary internal dialogue:

> *Disrupted and fragmented thoughts/*
> *Thoughts that intended the best outcome for his friend/*
> *Just think what would have occurred if his friend had taken a few steps back and stayed put firmly along the fences but shouted with a formidable voice like an angry ram/*
> *Or think what would have happened if his friend had acquired one of the blue-handled razors from somewhere and bloodied himself/*
> *What would have happened?/*
> *Or imagine if he didn't engage in any of these approaches and just ploughed his nails into his face like a woman whose baby has caught fire/*
> *Imagine if he just died/*
> *Imagine if he just screamed/*
> *Imagine if he screamed at the top of his voice/*
> *What would have happened?* (2018, pp. 230–231)

My reading of Améry's essay on exile relates his notion of self-alienation (*Selbstentfremdung*) not (primarily) to the phenomenological rubric of the émigré's distanciation from a positive sense of self, but to the somatic, sensorial, and affective registering of political violence on the émigré's body. The subject that becomes unknowable and intolerable to oneself as a consequence of the displacement from home, past, and community becomes for Améry an entry-point into a 'negative' theorizing of subjectivity (cf. Zolkos 2014). For Boochani, the Manus detainee experiences a similar violent effect of this molding of his inner life, and it is particularly geared toward *shrinking*, or entirely *eliminating*, the domain of imagination, that is the subject's radical capacity to envision things differently (cf. Bottici 2014). This deliberate contracting of the space of imagination is for Boochani is at the core of the passiveness experienced by The Man With a Thick Moustache when confronted with his friend's desperation and rage.

It is at this point, too, that Boochani outlines one of the key preoccupations in his books, namely that of the possibility of resistance against the kyriarchal prison system. He does that by assigning imaginative function to the poetic. Rather than simply making a counter-factual statement, the recurrent poetic incantation "*What would have happened?*" is a gesture of an almost magical conjuration of alternative worlds, and of appearance of seemingly nonexistent or erased possibilities of the detainee's insurgent responses. Boochani's poetics of detention is circumscribed by the goals of political analysis of the carceral state and border-politics, but it is not identical with, or reducible to, the political. Rather, as I argue, *No Friend but the Mountains* establishes a deeper connection between, first, the emotive, lyrical voice of the poet; second, the question of insurgence and political action in oppressive conditions; and, third, a conjuring gesture, understood not only as a way of intertwining the realistic narrative with magical and fantastic elements (as Boochani's undoubtedly does) but also as sudden appearance of what is nonexistent.

Importantly, too, the poet's lyrical conjuration intervenes in the context of the carceral state's aim to eliminate not only any possibility of revolt but also of freedom, through a complex bureaucratic system of regulations, prohibitions, and control. These disorienting, constantly evolving and fluctuating, rules and regulations of the detention, have as their goal, says Boochani (2018, p. 208), the construction of an 'ideal' detainee-subject; one that is "simply trying to cope". I have suggested earlier that Améry's description of the torturous reality of being caught in the constant decipherment of the hosts' cryptic cultural communications in a context of political insecurity is underpinned by a deeper interest in freedom defined as the absence of the conditions of dependence. *No Friend but the*

Mountains depicts the prisoners constantly engaged in the desperate and impossible 'games' of decoding of the system's always fluctuating and perplexing rules and regulations that govern their daily life, and ensure their domination. These carceral "micro-level and macro-level disciplinary measures" (2018, p. 165) include the distribution of food, the use of phones, their access to medical assistance and items of personal hygiene, their movement, conversations, rest, and sleep (Boochani writes poignantly about the "agency [of] queues" in prison that acquire characteristics of "factory production line[s]" (2018, p. 197).

Every prisoner, Boochani says (2018, pp. 208–209; emphasis in the original),

> is convinced that they or their group are the critical theorists of the systemic foundation, the chief analysts of the system's architecture. But the greatest difficulty is that no-one can be held accountable, no-one can be forced up against the way and questioned, no-one can be interrogated by asking them, 'You bastard, what is the philosophy behind these rules and regulations? Why, according to what logic, did you create these rules and regulations? Who are you?'

Améry has written about the émigré being in a permanent state of "disorder, confusion, desultoriness" (the latter term, *Zerfahrenheit*, is perhaps better translated as a state of "incoherence") (1999, p. 47). Boochani uses equally strong terms to depict the fragmenting or disintegrating effect of the carceral kyriarchy on the subject's body: "I am disintegrated and dismembered, my decrepit past fragmented and scattered, no longer integral, unable to become whole once again" (Boochani 2018, p. 265). The only time when the perplexing convolution and bureaucratic opacity of the carceral-industrial system implodes is when it resorts to direct physical violence, thus momentarily discarding its pretense of the ethics of civility. *No Friend but the Mountains* exemplifies Saskia Sassen's characterization of modern 'expulsions' as a binary dynamic of, on the one hand, indirect violence of the global systemic complexity of diverse factors and techniques, such as those that constitute Australia's border-industrial institutions, and, on the other hand, acts of physical and psychological brutality. Direct violence is response to any insubordination, and it acquires its own forms of ritualization and theatricality. When the Strike Force of the Manus detention intervene with force, they always put on their special black gloves, "full of metal spikes around the hand-wraps"—an ominous gesture that signals to the detainees the imminence of physical force, beating, pinning down, and violent pacification. In a nightmarish scene, observed by Boochani from his hiding place, a confrontation takes place between a prisoner whom Boochani calls The Prophet (and who displays unquestionable signs of a breakdown) and the Strike Force, whom Boochani terms Rhinos. The use of direct violence in response to insubordination is central to the "kyriarchal" objective of domination; Boochani says (2018, p. 278) that in the precise moment of violence the Rhinos 'simply' seek to "annihilate [the prisoner]". And he continues, "I think they achieve their purpose to the best of their ability. Just moments earlier he was The Prophet, now he is simply crushed." Once the violent pacification and immobilization of the prisoner is accomplished, the medical team arrives to examine the detainee. The normalized indirect violence of domination and control of the kyriarchal complex resumes.

Boochani shares with Améry the preoccupation with freedom. He narrates the Manus detainees' desperate attempts at carving out narrow and precarious sites of freedom within the oppressive "kyriarchy" of their prison, which remains "committed to capturing [the prisoner's] basic needs and holding them captive, confining those basic needs within its own cage of violence [...]" (2018, p. 216). Importantly, the arduous task of carving out of narrow spaces of freedom through practices that escape or defy the omnipresent surveillance of the guards and/or through searching out locations that remain beyond their access is also that of creating sites of revolt and subversion. Political action, protest against oppression and freedom are conjoined in *No Friend but the Mountains.* This points to another connection between Boochani's poetics of detention and Améry exile essay—not only are both texts concerned with the infringement of freedom as a defining trait of the writers' respective experiences of exile, but they also affirm the double effect of political action as a performance of liberty and as a rebellious or subversive act of noncompliance. Améry's émigré is also a resistance fighter against Nazism. Boochani's detainee is also a courageous and vocal critic of Australian border politics that galvanize racism to ensure social acceptability of torture. Améry's realization that his "home was [an] enemy country [...] *completely* and forever" and that the goal of his fellow citizens was "to wipe [him] out" (1999, p. 50; emphasis in the original), occurs in the context of a neighborly complaint about noise by an Austrian SS officer, disturbed by a chatter of a group of resistance members in the nearby quarters. That scene is often interpreted as instantiation of the *unheimlich* and as a clash of two impulses—one, of

Améry's "trembling fear" in the face of possible recognition of the activities as a work of resistance, and, two, of the "surging intimate cordiality" toward a compatriot encountered in exile (see e.g. Zolkos 2010, pp. 38–40). What also needs to be noted is that the émigré, whose "horizon presses in on him", and who lives in the condition of unfreedom, dependence, and dispossession, simultaneously occupies "the place of subversion" (*den Ort der Subversion*) and undertakes insurgent political action (1977, p. 86; 1999, pp. 58, 49).

An example of carving out a space of rebellious political action in *No Friend but the Mountains* as, also, an act of claiming liberty, is some detainees' carnivalistic celebration sand queer behavior: Boochani describes a prisoner called Maysam the Whore, performing ritualistic sexualized dances and performances in the evenings, thus affording the spectators a moment of respite from the carceral oppression: "[he] is a man who ridicules everything, and his presence, his dancing, his singing, helps us forget the violence of the prison for a moment" (2018, p. 140). Eventually, however, "the pretend celebrations and partying prove to be no match for the oppression of the prison, for loneliness and hopelessness. As days go by in Manus Prison, even Maysam the Whore becomes more secluded and starts to deteriorate. We must find another way to cope with exile" (2018, pp. 147–148).

Another site of respite and freedom for the prisoners in the book are the lavatories. What distinguishes these sites of filth, stink, and abjection is the physical absence of the Australian officers (they are maintained and monitored by the local Papuan population), and as such "they are still probably the only place in the prison where the prisoners feel liberated, if only for a few minutes" (2018, p. 169). This affords the detainees "a sanctuary where people banish the daily psychological struggles and turmoil of all the other places in the prison" (2018, p. 171). The reality of gaining access to such unmonitored and unsurveilled places, however, only affirms further how the detention and expulsion register on the human body; it is in the lavatory that self-harm is inflicted and most suicidal attempts take place. "[In] the end", Boochani writes, in a poignant account of the human cost of Australia's border-policy,

> at sunset or during the darkness of midnight, someone takes hold of one of those razors with the blue handles, chooses the most appropriate toilet, and over there, in the moments that follow, warm blood flows on the cement floor. The cubicles are places for screaming out. Or they are marked as

> chambers of devastation, the devastation constituted by absolute hopelessness. A location of the clash between terror, hopelessness and outbursts of deep anguish. For this reason, the location embodies an uncanny sense of awe, an eerie spirit. (2018, p. 171)

The central imagery of Améry's dispossessed homeland is cultural; for Boochani it is encapsulated by the figure of the mountain of the Kurdish landscape. As such, the figure of the mountain in the book is not only esthetically evocative of the subject's longing, and a repository of emotional and pleasurable childhood associations; the mountain is a distinctively unsentimental and ambivalent figuration in so far as it becomes indissociable from Boochani's childhood experience of the Iraq-Iran war in 1980s. The striking landscape of Kurdistan is not idyllic or sentimental, but always permeated by violence and desolation of war; the mountains were a site of asylum for the civilians fearing attacks by warplanes, but also a place of militant activities by the Peshmerga (the Kurdish freedom fighters), and a battlefield, "sizzled and incinerated" by the war (Boochani 2018, pp. 258–261):

> [...] I am a child of war. Yes, I was born during the war. Under the thunder of warplanes. Alongside tanks. In the face of bombs. Breathing gunpowder. Among dead bodies. Inside silent cemetries [...]
>
> *[...] I have to say it. Hear me as I cry out: I am a child of war/*
>
> *A child of an inferno. A child of ashes. A child of the chestnut oaks of Kurdistan/*
>
> *I'm insane, I am. Where is this place?/*
>
> *Why has the night become so terrifying? And why can't I fall asleep?/*
>
> *Let me say something; let me surrender myself to the realm of the imagination and amnesia.*
>
> Where have I come from?
>
> From the land of rivers, the land of waterfalls, the land of ancient chains, the land of mountains.

The world of exile depicted by Améry is strikingly absent of children and mothers. In "Being a Jew. A Personal Account", Améry (1984, pp. 13–16) includes a mention of his (Aryan) Austrian mother in a strikingly affectionless tone, and only in passing (one could speculate, too, that significant here is the mother's resistance against Améry's decision to marry an East European Jew). However, he does invoke images and memories from his youth that now remains irrevocably lost, not as a matter of phenomenology of childhood per se, but as effect of the cultural and linguistic divestiture undergone by assimilated, German-speaking Jews. Boochani pays great attention to maternal figures and mother-child relations, including his nuanced and moving descriptions of asylum-seekers undertaking a boat trip to Australia together with him: a Sri Lankan couple united in their care for a newborn infant, or an authoritative dignified woman whom Boochani calls Golshifteh, and who resists the temptation to prioritize the well-being of her own children and kin in her display of care and protection of vulnerable others on the boat.[13] In Boochani's narrativization of the camp, the mother is a source of vital energy, but also of traumatic transmission and of the fissured connection to childhood marked by war and escape; it is through the mother that the author "receive[s] the impressions and hurt that arose from the war" (2018, p. 264). His childhood memories of war are inseparable from scenes abounding with children and women; "[o]ut of everything that I can remember about the war, I can't recall the presence of even one man. Only children and women could be seen" (2018, p. 264). Mothers, then, enable life and its preservation in the midst of violence—against violence and from within violence ("Life always means much more than war, much more than destitution, much more than deprivation / Life for me always emerges from within desolation [...]" [2018, p. 264]). The Kurdish mother-son relationship is an "uncanny [incomprehensible] bond, [...] affected by the elements of war" (2018, p. 349).

During the 2014 riot in the Manus Detention, one of the wounded detainees calls for his mother in Kurdish; and it is that interpellation of the absent Kurdish mother that inspires Boochani not only to acknowledge the "profound and complex" son-mother relationship among the Kurds but also to see in this call a transpiring of a "significant existential moment" (Boochani 2018, pp. 348, 349). The significance of this call, in the context of the riots and the violent state response that ensues, is that it performs a kind of rescue and shelter from violence; only, just as with the figure of the mountains, the mother herself is wounded, and the shelter she provides is not immune to violence, but permeated by it. Boochani invokes images of "mothers wailing and soaked in blood [...]", and "[h]orrified mothers ... mothers [who] wrapped their children within the instincts of motherhood" (2018, pp. 258, 259)—an imagery invoking both maternal protection and transmission of profound trauma and woundedness. That internally splintered maternal figure, at once protective and wounded, is for the poet a source of refuge; one that comes from the subject's involuntary, primal, and bodily connection to maternal life-sustenance; "[...] in the same way that I feel blood flowing through my veins, I feel a connection with my mother," writes Boochani (2018, p. 349).

4.5 Conclusions

This essay has taken its starting-point in Jean Améry's argument that there is a distinctive kind of political homelessness that describes the experiences of the German-speaking Jews who, like Améry, sought refuge during the war. These émigrés were dispossessed not only of their national community and language but also of their past collective attachments and identifications. I have outlined an interpretative approach to that essay that moves away from the focus on Améry's phenomenology of homelessness and his critique of the Enlightenment articulation of *heimat*; instead, I have viewed the essay through the prism of its political preoccupations with undesirability, expulsion, insecurity, and failed justice.

This rereading of Améry's essay has illuminated its, perhaps surprising, connections to a contemporary literary text on the refuge-seeking experience and liberal border-politics by Behrouz Boochani, which has served as a basis for my comparative analysis, and has helped to overcome the obstacle of undeniable contextual, temporal, and philosophic differences between these two texts. The comparison with Améry's exile essay illuminates a striking feature of Boochani's book, encapsulated in the bodily and affective dimensions of the narrative—the confluence of the carceral state and of the punitive and exclusionary border politics registers, or imprints, its violence and surveillance onto the bodies of the detainees with the goal of molding them into figures of deterrence and undesirability. As Boochani's book powerfully demonstrates this political effect of sculpting detainees' lives into exhausted, confused, and surrendered forms of existence is that of the *elimination of imagination*; becoming dispossessed of hope and of the possibility of resistance, grounded in the capacity to envision things (and oneself) otherwise. Both for Améry and for Boochani resistance against oppression consists of carving out narrow spaces of political action and reclaiming not only voice but precisely the subject's capacity to imagine and to dream. But the significant difference is that Améry's subject seems dispossessed and exiled from culture, language, and community in ways that also corrupt any possibility of hope. In contrast, Boochani's protagonist, while targeted by deliberate politics of expulsion and abandonment and subjected to the logic of the camp that seeks to eliminate opportunities and sites for practicing freedom (of speech, thinking, enjoyment, and possible revolt), nevertheless draws political and moral energy from sources that remain beyond control of the oppressive border governmentalities. While Améry's émigré subject practices resistance and revolt without endorsing hope, Boochani recurs to the poetic, and to non-sentimental figurations of homeland and the mother, as sites of refuge, subversion, and solidarity from which resistance against the kyriarchal oppression arises.

Notes

1. This chapter was presented as a conference paper at the Annual Meeting of the Australasian Society for Continental Philosophy held at the Western Sydney University in November 2018. For comments and questions that helped to improve my argument, I thank Simone Drichel, Katrina Jaworski, Marguerite La Caze, Ahlam Mustafa, Michael Richardson, Omid Tofighian, Neil Vallelly, and Jeanne-Marie Viljoen. Many thanks, too, to the editors of the volume and to the anonymous reviewer for their careful and constructive engagement with the chapter.
2. Achille Mbembe (2003) has coined the concept of 'necro-politics' ('the politics of death') partly drawing on Foucault's theory of biopolitics, and partly as a corrective for its overt focus on 'life' and sufficient focus on modern state attention to, regulation of, 'death'. For Mbembe, 'necro-politics' includes, but is irreducible to, the state right to kill; it also extends to civil and social death that state imposes on its subjects, which can take the form of disenfranchisement, dispossession, and economic attrition—the subjects of 'necro-politics' are rendered superfluous; they are 'let die'. 'Necro-politics' has been an important conceptual tool for the analyses of contemporary border-politics and forced migration (see e.g. Estévez 2014).
3. In his review of Boochani's book, Jeff Sparrow compares its analysis of the off-short detention centers to Améry's representation of the life in concentration camps (Sparrow 2018).
4. There is an interesting contrast here between Améry's view on the loss of language by German-speaking Jews, and Hannah Arendt's reflections on language, when she says to Günter Gaus: "[the] German language is the essential thing that has remained [for me]," and "I thought to myself, What is one to do? It wasn't the German language that went crazy" (1994, p. 13).
5. In her interview with Günter Gaus, Hannah Arendt makes a similar point in regard to adopting English as the language of her late writings. She says: "I write in English, but I never lost a feeling of distance from it. There is a

tremendous difference between your mother tongue and another language [...]. [T]here is no substitution for the mother tongue" (1994, p. 13; see also Yeatman 2011).

6. This is further reinforced by Améry's descriptions of the camp and of torture as language-destroying experiences.
7. There is an important similarity here between Améry's thinking about and Hannah Arendt's recognition of the importance of civic and political status for politics of resistance (cf. Arendt 1968). Resonant of Arendt's famous statement that "[i]f one is attacked as a Jew, one must defend oneself as a Jew" is Améry's subject of a 'Jew without Judaism'. It isn't only a question of inhabiting an identity devoid of any cultural or religious 'props', as it was the case for Améry and other assimilated and secular German-speaking Jews (what I have called elsewhere Améry's "negative articulation of Jewishness" (see Zolkos 2014)), but also, and perhaps more importantly in this context, closely linked to his understanding of the possibility and necessity of revolt in oppressive social circumstances. In "On the Necessity and Impossibility of Being a Jew" Améry says: "I became a person not by subjectively appealing to my abstract humanity but by discovering myself within the given social reality as a rebelling Jew and by realizing myself as one" (1999, p. 91; for an illuminating discussion of that essay, see Benjamin 2016).
8. The use of the word *entborgen* is both peculiar and significant in this context. It is likely coined by Améry, who replaced the prefix *ge-* (in the word *geborgen*, 'secure'), with the prefix *ent-*, indicative of removing something from the object (as in *entfolgen*, 'unfollow', or *entlarven*, 'unmask') or conversion to an opposite meaning (as in *enterben*, 'disinherit'). Its English translation as 'uprooted' does not quite capture that connection between exile and loss of security. My thanks to Simone Drichel for her illuminating analysis of Améry's use of that word.
9. My thanks to Yochai Ataria for bringing to my attention the importance of Améry's *On Aging* (Améry 1994) for the elaboration of the concept of irreversibility in his oeuvre. The concept of irreversibility frames Améry's reflections on the self-experience of the aging subject; aging is "the burning and just as hopeless wish of those getting on in years for the reversal of time" (1994, p. 19; see also Zolkos 2010, pp. 84–86). It should also be noted that in the essay "Resentments" Améry assigns to the victims' feelings of grievance and resentment the function of making a political demand "that the irreversible be turned around [and] undone" (1999, p. 68).
10. For instance, the Viennese Documentation Centre of the Association of Jewish Victims of the Nazi Regime played a key role in tracking down and preparing a dossier on the notorious employee of the T-4 Euthanasia Program, and commander of the Sobibór and Treblinka concentration camps, Franz Stangl.

11. While there is a great affinity between *No Friend by the Mountains* and the genre of magical realism, including the Boochani's prolific use of "mythical and epic visual imagery, dream visions and mix of fantasy and reality", Tofighian argues that the unique element that distinguishes Boochani's writings from magical realism is the inclusion of "self-reflexive passages in the book [...], [Boochani's] interpretation of the prison [...]" (p. xxix). Importantly, Tofighian delineates a network of literary references and traditions specific to the coming together of Kurdish oral and literary traditions and the Kurdish political struggle (pp. 366–368).
12. I am grateful to Marguerite La Caze and to Omid Tofighian for helping me elaborate this point.
13. One reason why it is important to notice the presence of children and parent-child relations in *No Friend but the Mountain* is that it provides a powerful counter-narrative to the position held by the Australian government who for years denied that there were children among the refugees on Nauru Island. Another reason why it is important is that Boochani makes the reader see the men on Manus as relational subjects—fathers, children, husbands, brothers (etc.)—who are to remain separated from their families by deliberate border policies that seek to make them into figures of deterrence, by imposing on them a pitiful existence and by deteriorating their mental health.

References

Agamben, G. (2000). *Means Without End: Notes on Politics* (V. Binetti & C. Casarino, Trans.). Minneapolis: University of Minnesota Press.

Agier, M. (2008). *On the Margins of the World: The Refugee Experience Today* (D. Fernbach, Trans.). Cambridge: Polity.

Améry, J. (1977). *Jenseits von Schuld und Sühne. Bewältigungsversuche eines Überwältigten.* Stuttgart: Klett-Cotta.

Améry, J. (1984). *Radical Humanism* (S. Rosenfeld & S. P. Rosenfeld, Trans.). Bloomington: Indiana University Press.

Améry, J. (1994). *On Aging: Revolt and Resignation* (J. D. Barlow, Trans.). Bloomington: Indiana University Press.

Améry, J. (1999). *At the Mind's Limits: Contemplations by a Survivor on Auschwitz and Its Realities* (S. Rosenfeld & S. P. Rosenfeld, Trans.). London: Granta.

Arendt, H. (1968). *Men in Dark Times.* New York: Harcourt.

Arendt, H. (1994). 'What Remains? The Language Remains': A Conversation with Günter Gaus. In J. Kohn (Ed.), *Essays in Understanding 1930–1954. Formation, Exile, and Totalitarianism* (pp. 1–24). New York: Harcourt Brace & Company.

Banki, P. (2018). *The Forgiveness to Come. The Holocaust and the Hyper-Ethical.* New York: Fordham University Press.

Benjamin, A. (2016). On Jewish Being. Notes on Jean Améry. *Journal of French and Francophone Philosophy, 24*(3), 157–172.

Bernstein, J. M. (2011). Améry's Body: 'My Calamity ... My Physical and Metaphysical Dignity'. In M. Zolkos (Ed.), *On Jean Améry: Philosophy of Catastrophe* (pp. 39–60). New York: Lexington.

Boochani, B. (2018). *No Friend but the Mountains: Writing from Manus Prison.* Sydney: Pan Macmillan.

Bottici, C. (2014). *Imaginal Politics. Images Beyond Imagination and the Imaginary.* New York: Columbia University Press.

Brudholm, T. (2005, Fall). A Confiscated Past: Jean Améry on Home and Exile. *The Hedgehog Review*, 7–19.

Butler, J. (2006). *Precarious Life: The Powers of Mourning and Violence.* London: Verso.

Butler, J. (2010). *Frames of War: When Is Life Grievable?* London: Verso.

Campbell, J. J. (2012). *On the Nature of Genocidal Intent.* New York: Lexington.

Estévez, A. (2014). The Politics of Death and Asylum Discourse: Constituting Migration Biopolitics from the Periphery. *Alternatives: Global, Local, Political, 39*(2), 75–89.

Greiner, B. (2003). *Placeless Topographies: Jewish Perspectives on the Literature of Exile.* Tübingen: Niemeyer.

Grøn, A., & Brudholm, T. (2011). Nachdenken. In M. Zolkos (Ed.), *On Jean Améry: Philosophy of Catastrophe* (pp. 193–216). New York: Lexington.

Heidelberger-Leonard, I. (2010). *The Philosopher of Auschwitz: Jean Améry and Living with the Holocaust* (A. Bell, Trans.). London: I.B. Tauris.

Hunt, G. (2010). Performing Dignity. *Women in Philosophy Annual Journal of Papers, 6*, 47–61.

Jankélévitch, V. (2015). *The Bad Conscience* (A. Kelly, Trans.). Chicago: University of Chicago Press.

Khorana, S. (2018, October 10). The Aspirationals vs the Burdens: Reading Migrants and Refugees Through No Friend by the Mountains. *Overland.*

Kusher, T., & Knox, C. (1999). *Refugees in an Age of Genocide.* London: Frank Cass.

La Caze, M. (2019). 'I Can't Beat It': Dimensions of the Bad Conscience in Manchester by the Sea. In M. La Caze & M. Zolkos (Eds.), *On What Cannot Be Touched: Contemporary Perspectives on Vladimir Jankélévitch.* New York: Lexington.

Mbembe, A. (2003). Necropolitics. *Public Culture, 15*(1), 11–40.

Meister, R. (2012). *After Evil: A Politics of Human Rights.* New York: Columbia University Press.

Merleau-Ponty, M. (2002). *Phenomenology of Perception* (C. Smith, Trans.). London: Routledge.

Millet, K. J. (2011). Contemplating Jean Améry's Loss of Transcendence. In M. Zolkos (Ed.), *On Jean Améry: Philosophy of Catastrophe* (pp. 21–38). New York: Lexington.
Sassen, S. (2014). *Expulsions: Brutality and Complexity in the Global Economy.* Cambridge, MA: Harvard University Press.
Schüssler Fiorenza, E. (1992). *But She Said: Feminist Practices of Biblical Interpretation.* Boston: Beacon Press.
Schüssler Fiorenza, E. (2010). Introduction: Exploring the Intersections of Race, Gender, Status, and Ethnicity in Early Christian Studies. In L. Nasrallah & E. S. Fiorenza (Eds.), *Prejudice and Christian Beginnings: Investigating Race, Gender, and Ethnicity in Early Christianity* (pp. 1–25). Minneapolis: Fortress Press.
Shuster, M. (2016). A Phenomenology of Home: Jean Améry on Homesickness. *Journal of French and Francophone Studies, 24*(3), 117–127.
Skinner, Q. (1998). *Liberty Before Liberalism.* Cambridge: Cambridge University Press.
Sparrow, J. (2018). A Place of Punishment: No Friend But the Mountains by Behrouz Boochani. *Sydney Review of Books.* Retrieved from https://sydneyreviewofbooks.com/a-place-of-punishment-no-friend-but-the-mountains-by-behrouz-boochani/.
Stone, D. (1995). Homes Without Heimats? Jean Améry at the Limits. *Angelaki, 2*, 91–100.
Suchting, W. A. (1988). Jean Améry. *Critical Philosophy, 4*, 134–147.
Tietjens Meyers, D. (2016). *Victims' Stories and the Advancement of Human Rights.* Oxford: Oxford University Press.
Udoff, A. (2004). Jean Améry: Evil and the Language of Loss. In M. S. Breen (Ed.), *Truth, Reconciliation, and Evil* (pp. 85–94). Amsterdam: Rodopi.
Vansant, J. (2001). *Reclaiming Heimat: Trauma and Mourning in Memoirs by Jewish Austrian Reémigrés.* Detroit: Wayne State University Press.
Vivaldi, J.-M. (2019). *Reflections on Jean Améry: Torture, Resentment, and Homelessness as the Mind's Limits.* New York: Palgrave.
Wiesenthal, S. (1997). *The Sunflower: On the Possibilities and Limits of Forgiveness.* New York: Schocken Books.
Yeatman, A. (2011). Politics and Personal Responsibility: Reflections on Jean Améry and Hannah Arendt. In M. Zolkos (Ed.), *On Jean Améry: Philosophy of Catastrophe* (pp. 61–86). New York: Lexington.
Zolkos, M. (2008). Jean Améry's Philosophy of Resentment at the Crossroads of Ethics and Politics. *European Legacy, 12*(1), 23–38.
Zolkos, M. (2010). *Reconciling Community and Subjective Life. Trauma Testimony as Political Theorizing in the Work of Jean Améry and Imre Kértesz.* New York: Continuum.
Zolkos, M. (2014). Aporias of Belonging: Jean Améry on 'Being a Jew Without Judaism' and the Tradition of Conscious Pariah. *Journal of European Studies, 44*(4), 362–377.

CHAPTER 5

The Ethics of Resentment: The Tactlessness of Jean Améry

David Heyd

Jean Améry's 1966 essay "Resentments" is not only one of the best-known texts in his *oeuvre* but arguably the philosophically deepest.[1] Although Améry was not a professional philosopher, his background in philosophy was solid from his Vienna days in which he showed particular interest in the activities of the "Vienna Circle". However, contrary to the typically analytical, objective, scientifically oriented style of the positivist work of Rudolf Carnap and Moritz Schlick, Améry turns in his writings after the war to a much more personal and emotional tone in his philosophical reflections. Obviously, the war experience influenced that shift in approach from the detached positivist attitude to a highly engaged moral and judgmental perspective.

My aim in this chapter is to examine this personal approach to moral issues as a philosophical statement rather than just a biographical phenomenon. Methodologically this is not an easy task since Améry himself does not explicitly refer to the underlying question of the distinction between personal judgment and general principle. Accordingly, it is not clear to what extent he would be willing to generalize his ethics of resentment

D. Heyd (✉)
The Hebrew University, Jerusalem, Israel
e-mail: david.heyd@mail.huji.ac.il

Y. Ataria et al. (eds.), *Jean Améry*,
https://doi.org/10.1007/978-3-030-28095-6_5

beyond the issue of the moral attitude to the German people after the war. It is not clear whether he is trying to convince the reader with a philosophical view or rather make a plea for understanding his personal position. But even if my analysis is partly reconstructive, it is based on forceful and explicit statements made by Améry in his writings.

In the first part of the chapter, I shortly discuss Améry's idea of the reversibility of time as a unique but paradoxical attempt to moralize history. The second part is devoted to the view that morality is ultimately concerned with personal reactive responses of the individual. In the third and final part, Améry's a propos suggestion that his resentment essay reflects tactlessness is followed and analyzed in some detail. Améry's views are compared to some well-known philosophers who were writing in the years closely preceding his essay—P. F. Strawson, Hans-Georg Gadamer, and Herbert Marcuse.

5.1 I

Améry believes in the uni-directionality of time. There is no way to go back in time or change past events. But this principle, that nothing done can be undone, applies only on the natural level, that of science or ontology. The moral point of view not only can relate to the past but can transform its meaning. In the debate whether morality should be future- or past-oriented Améry takes an unequivocal stand: although being concerned with future states of affairs is the *natural* approach, which is pragmatic and rational, morality focuses on the relations between the wrongdoer and his victim in the past action. It is concerned with the awareness of the perpetrator of his guilt and the victim's attempt to regain his dignity which was violated by the wrong done to him. This requires "going back in time" as the only way in which the two parties to the wrong can meet, and do so on an equal footing, leveling the original relations of superiority of the one over the other. Améry refers to this attempt to relive the past as "moralizing history". The point of resentment is "that the crime become a moral reality for the criminal, in order that he be swept into the truth of his atrocity", and not—as society sees it—to prevent the crime to be repeated in the future (p. 70).

Ressentiment is the epitome of such an attempt to reverse time. It is exclusively a backward-looking attitude which not only ignores future-oriented considerations but is highly suspicious of them, treating them as an obstruction to what might be called a "moral settlement" of the crime.[2]

Financial or political settlements consist of certain arrangements which change the future state of affairs (e.g. by compensating one party or changing power relations); but, at least for Améry, moral settlements are achieved only by transforming the meaning of past events, a change which calls for deep regret (a wish, of both sides, to obliterate the past action). The idea of ressentiment is associated in Améry's mind, as well as in ours, with Nietzsche.[3] However, Améry turns Nietzsche on his head. While for Nietzsche, ressentiment is the original sin in the genealogy of morality, for Améry it is the most authentic moral attitude; while for Nietzsche it is a hypocritical attempt of the weak type of human beings to divest the strong from their natural and deserved power, for Améry it is the most honest response of a victim to the violators of his dignity; whereas for Nietzsche resentment is a typical revolt against life, for Améry it is the only proper attitude of a person of integrity to a massive wrong done to him. Unlike Nietzsche who celebrates life, Améry is concerned with the problem of (moral) survival. Ressentiment may indeed impede the naturally flowing course of life, as Améry admits, but it is the only refuge for the survivor who cannot continue living without remembering the past.[4]

Améry is fully aware that resentment means being stuck in the past in a destructive way, not only because it is psychologically "unhealthy" (having the same feeling again and again, as the term connotes), but because it is philosophically absurd.[5] Reversing time is a hopeless and dangerous fantasy because it tries to achieve two impossible aims: "regression into the past and nullification of what happened".[6] Max Scheler, a close follower of Nietzsche writing on ressentiment, adds the specifically psychological diagnosis of those who suffer from harboring it: it is the response of the "unfit against the fit, of those who are partially dead against the living!"[7] This is a cruelly accurate description of Améry's own self-image.

Both Nietzsche and Améry seem to share the view that the true moral stance involves loneliness. But again, they do so from opposite perspectives. For Nietzsche, the Übermensch leads a solitary life bounded by no social conventions or public opinion. Only the spiritually weak live in herds. For Améry the trauma experienced by the victim and the resentment he feels toward the perpetrators make him existentially lonely, unable even to share his experience and to obtain understanding by all others who are engaged in the business of future-oriented plans to advance life and prosperity. The multitude is perceived by both as unauthentic and self-deluded, but while Nietzsche accuses them for obstructing life, Améry condemns them for preferring life to morality.

Interestingly, Nietzsche and Améry also share the same view about the relationship between revenge and resentment. Nietzsche argues that the weak cannot resort to revenge due to their lack of power; Améry holds that revenge is futile because it will never serve as "a moral settlement" for the victim. They have to likewise find an indirect expression to their hate which does not involve retaliatory action. Ressentiment is a sort of suppressed revenge. Améry opposes revenge for other reasons, mainly because revenge is an external act which as such lacks moral meaning; for revenge may indeed cause pain to the perpetrator but cannot lead to the hoped for change in his moral consciousness. Although Améry is fully aware that the public views his resentment as a vengeful attitude, he tries to convey to the reader the much more subtle case for ressentiment in contra-distinction to revenge. "If I have searched my mind properly, it is not a matter of revenge, nor one of atonement", says Améry. The punishment of the criminal perpetrator (be it a matter of justice or revenge) is meaningful only to the extent that the perpetrator is forced to face his crime directly through the victim's resentment. Only thus he becomes "a fellow man" and is in the same position as the victim in their common wish to reverse time and undo past events. But ressentiment seems to be much more effective in bringing forth an inner search of the kind Améry is after than punishment and revenge which tend to create only further hate or sometimes a false sense of "settlement" ("having paid for one's crimes"). Only forcing the offender to face his evildoing can the victim be released from his loneliness, at least temporarily.[8]

What is also strikingly common to Améry and Nietzsche with regard to ressentiment is their belief in its *poisonous* nature. The internalization of revenge in the form of ressentiment infects the mind and blocks the prospect of normal, future-directed life.[9] Acts of revenge, despite their long-term futility (as we shall see below), can be temporarily satisfying; but ressentiment, being felt but not acted upon, can never be satisfied unless the perpetrator undergoes a genuine moral transformation. Again, the tragedy of *re*ssentiment is that the emotion of hatred and anger is consciously and purposefully *re*felt repeatedly and is even protected from anything that might make it go away (like forgetfulness or reconciliation).[10] This is well expressed by the metaphor of "harboring".

The reversal of Nietzsche's conception of morality is now completed. After having experienced unimaginable suffering, Améry knows full well what "beyond good and evil" may come to. He is concerned only with the morally appropriate *reaction* to the loss of all sense of good and evil and proposes going beyond "guilt and atonement" as the title of his collection of essays declares. In that realm all that's left is ressentiment. Ressentiment is no more the natural human attitude to questions of value, underlying according to Nietzsche herd morality and institutionalized in social rules and conventions; it is rather the paradoxical and desperate revolt against "the natural time-sense" (natürliches Zeitgefühl).[11] An authentic moral stance goes against social interest, vital instincts, and rational life planning. Healing, the most natural physiological and psychological process based on the sheer passage of time, is the enemy of the moral and should be actively countered. The acceptance of natural occurrences is not only extra moral; it is *anti*-moral. How can this make sense? Taking our cue from Nietzsche himself, the idea here is that morality is neither social nor future oriented. It is neither Kantian nor consequentialist. It is subjective, personal, and reactive.

5.2 II

Nietzsche, who is the direct object of Améry's polemics with regards to ressentiment, believes that the fundamental problem with resentment is its *reactive* nature. The strong spirited "Overman" is an individual who takes the initiative in action, who draws from his inner spiritual resources in shaping his life and creating his values. Being only responsive to social and natural circumstances is the sign of the weak. Those are the people whose principal aim in life is mere survival. Améry's perspective is obviously just the opposite. The moral position, at least of the victim of wrongdoing, is necessarily reactive. It consists of the way past deeds are regarded and judged. Future-oriented planning belongs to politics, to social engineering and to the general aim of furthering life and prosperity—not to morality. This is not an easy position in moral theory. However, Améry could have found an interesting ally in the work of Peter Strawson, the Oxford analytic philosopher who was closer to the positivist style of philosophizing with which prewar Améry was associated than to Jean-Paul Sartre who served for postwar Améry as a main source of inspiration. In his classical article "Freedom and Resentment", published just five years before Améry's "Resentments", Strawson relates to the specifically reactive nature of some of our most fundamental moral attitudes. He refers to gratitude, forgiveness, love, hurt feelings, but above all to resentment.[12]

The context of Strawson's discussion is, as implied by the article's title, the philosophical question whether the truth of determinism undermines the very possibility of freedom and responsibility (or perhaps it is even a necessary condition for their ascription). This seems to be a very different background for the discussion of resentment from Améry's. But on second thought, it seems to be exactly what disturbs Améry so much, namely the irreversibility of time, the absurdity of the attempt to undo what has been done. In both Strawson and Améry the fact that nature and history work in ways which are beyond the control of many of those affected by them means that the sphere left for morality is limited to human *response* or reaction to events. For Strawson the fact that the agent could not have done otherwise (determinism) does not entail exemption from responsibility to her action; for Améry the fact that the agent cannot go back in time to undo his crimes does not detract from his accountability. For both thinkers, resentment is the prime moral response to evil which its perpetrator must face.

As Strawson aptly describes, the issue whether determinism should at all be regarded as a problem for morality is usually focused on practices such as punishment and condemnation. Can we punish a person if we believe that his behavior was completely determined? But Strawson points out that punishment is a "detached" response to what is considered by society as undesirable behavior and is fully compatible with a deterministic view of the world. Punishment can be described and justified as another means by which people's behavior is causally determined (primarily by providing an incentive for future avoidance of wrongdoing). So Strawson wishes to focus on a deeper level of human moral response, that which is "non-detached", that is to say, attitudes which are *directly* involved in our interactions with one another. Attitudes of this kind are the reactions of offended parties (typically resentment or forgiveness) and of beneficiaries (gratitude). Moral judgment does not relate to the objective consequences of behavior but to the way, we respond to the good will or the malevolence motivating the action. It has to do with the assessment of intentions. And to put it in Améry's terms, it is concerned with the mutual awareness of the mental attitudes of both actor and recipient of an action. In this respect, it is subjective in Améry's words or non-detached in Strawson's.

Thus, the Oxford philosopher gets unexpectedly close to Améry when he says that we have

> to try to keep before our minds something it is easy to forget when we are engaged in philosophy, especially in our cool, contemporary style, viz. what it is actually like to be involved in ordinary inter-personal relationships, ranging from the most intimate to the most casual.[13]

Both Strawson and Améry do not wish to convey the impression that they deny the force of objective morality—that of justice, reparations, or psychological excuses for wrongdoing. They only want to argue that such morality misses a most important dimension. Strawson says that "if your attitude towards someone is wholly objective, then though you may fight him, you cannot quarrel with him" (p. 79). This is exactly what Améry is looking for, a real moral quarrel with his tormentor on a personal one-on-one basis, a fantasy meeting between him and SS-man Wajs of Antwerp, his torturer. Only "through a moral turning-back of the clock, the [torturer] can join his victim as a fellow human being" (p. 72). The victim is not satisfied with criminal justice, legal executions or other objectifications of the social response to crime. He is insisting on what Strawson calls "the participant attitude", that of "personal antagonism" and is willing to suffer what Strawson calls "the strains of involvement" which are so painfully expressed in the attitude of ressentiment.[14]

Furthermore, Strawson points out, human beings would not be capable of "a sustained objectivity of interpersonal attitude and the human isolation which it would entail" (p. 82). We remember that Améry's deep motive for a personal confrontation with his torturers is ultimately the release from his own existential loneliness. The punishment of Nazi criminals by courts of justice and social policies of reconciliation both leave the victim in his lonely position and with the sense of society's total incomprehension of his moral needs. Only the perpetrator really understands the victim's sense of resentment and hence is the only one with whom the victim can deal on the moral level. Once resentment is generalized, argues Strawson, it becomes "indignation". The victim of a wrong feels resentment; a third party feels indignation. And although indignation is still a reactive attitude, it is vicarious, once removed from the fundamental personal feeling of resentment. It is impersonal and hence more susceptible to being transformed by an objective, detached perspective into an attempt to understand, excuse, acquiesce and be reconciled with—those attitudes so hated by Améry, at least in the context of such crime to which he was victim.[15]

Finally, both Strawson and Améry regard the meaning of the victim's reactive attitude to the other (the offender) only on the background of the possibility of the *self*-reactive attitude of the offender. Strawson refers to it as the offender's full understanding of his offense and his readiness to accept punishment as his due; Améry views ressentiment as having sense only with the (highly unlikely) complement of the perpetrator's full awareness of his guilt. "I demand", says Améry, "that the [torturers] negate themselves and in the negation coordinate with me" (p. 69).

This personal, non-detached view of morality has aroused significant interest in the last few decades. Some of it is directly relevant to Améry's reflections on ressentiment. For example, Jacques Derrida has argued extensively for the paradoxical nature of gifts.[16] Giving opens an endless cycle since the only way for the recipient to acknowledge a true (gratuitous) gift is by reciprocating with a larger gift. This calls for a further increase in the value of the next gift by the original donor to the recipient, thus creating an endless futile attempt to reciprocate by outmatching the previous donation. In the context of our discussion, the reason for this growing cycle is the personal dimension which is constitutive of gifts. They are not owed or deserved but simply the expression of good will of the donor and hence call for a similar good will. But the gift relation involves more than the expression of gratitude; it creates an expectation of return. It must outdo the original act so as to be more than merely a just (proportionate) return which would not include the element of emotional acknowledgment. This logic of the open cycle is even more acutely manifest in revenge, which is typically personal, being constituted by an attempt to express resentment and anger. Revenge often leads to counter-revenge, like in blood feuds which are disastrously costly (but not dissimilar to the waste in reciprocal gifts as noted by the anthropologist Marcel Mauss[17]). But revenge is also futile in the sense that it will always be *just* a reaction to an original act of malevolence and hence will never be able to achieve the same degree of hate or hostility that the original offense expressed.

Améry is aware of this futility of ressentiment and of the immunity of the perpetrator from the full effect of reciprocal grudge. One can punish a Nazi criminal but never reciprocate in full for his initial animosity and contempt, for any such reaction is going to be regarded as explainable by the suffering caused to the victim and thereby lose its bite. There is something pathetic about vengeful thoughts. Revenge can never be satisfying or settle the moral account. Who was first is a decisive matter in giving, forgiving and offending, at least as long as they are seen as personal matters rather than objective events for which there are always means for a fully balanced reward or retaliation.

Ressentiment is particularly poisonous, as Améry says, because it is "stubborn" and one-track minded.[18] "It nails every one of us onto the cross of his ruined past" (p. 68). The personal grudge, despite its moral depth, can never hope to gain long-term respect—not even patience—by society, which is geared to the future and bound by objective and impersonal rules.

Resentment is the opposite attitude to that of forgiveness. Actually, forgiveness exactly means the giving up of resentment. Améry is of course strongly opposed to any show of forgiveness to Nazi criminals or to their passive accomplices.[19] But on the theoretical level, he would agree that the two opposing attitudes belong to the same category of *personal* ethics (as Strawson too classifies them). If (as some philosophers maintain) forgiveness, in general, is supererogatory, that is going beyond the call of duty, the sense of resentment on part of the victim may be justified (as that which is permitted but may be supererogatorily withheld). Améry goes one step further and argues that there are cases in which such a shift from resentment to forgiveness is not only not supererogatory but plainly inappropriate, and accordingly resentment is morally called for. And indeed, there surely are acts that are "unforgivable", and those inflicted upon Améry may be typical examples.[20] This is why Améry was impatient with people like Martin Buber who urged for a forgiving attitude to German criminals like Eichmann and even (unjustifiably) suspected Primo Levy for being "a forgiver".

5.3 III

This impatience of society with individual ressentiment is the key to understanding the short reference of Améry to tact and tactlessness in the fifth paragraph of his essay on resentment:

> I would do well to excuse myself at the start for the lack of tact that will unfortunately be displayed [in this essay]. Tact is something good and important—plain, acquired tact in everyday behavior, as well as tact of mind and heart. But no matter how important it may be, it is not suited for the radical analysis that together we are striving for here … It may be that many of us victims have lost the feeling for tact altogether. (p. 63)

The concept of tact has not received much critical attention. It is not a moral principle or duty on the one hand but is more than just a rule of good manners on the other. Although, somewhat ironically Améry notes that tact is a good practice in "everyday behavior", he immediately adds that it is also expressed on the level of the "mind and heart". He does not elaborate what he means by it but definitely implies that tact is not only "important" and "good" but that, other things being equal, it is a social virtue. However, other things are *not* equal when it comes to dealing with the response of victims to the horrifying crimes of the Third Reich, and hence the justification of tactlessness. But the appeal to the reader's patience, despite the difficult and disturbing essay, makes sense only because Améry takes tact as a deeper requirement than sheer manners or decorum.

A few comments about the nature of tact, in general, may be helpful before showing why it is a philosophical problem for Améry and how it is connected to his ethics of resentment.[21] Tact has two dimensions—the perceptual and the emotional. The perceptual highlights tact as a kind of *sensitivity*; the emotional is marked by its being a sort of *considerateness*. The element of sensitivity goes back to the etymology of the word. Tact is primarily the most basic of the five senses—touch. The emotional factor in tact lies in the attempt not to give offense to others or win good will. This is why tact is the art of "negotiating difficult or delicate situations" (in the language of the Oxford English Dictionary). It requires both discrimination and attentiveness to the other and a motive of sympathy (typically in the attempt to prevent the other from embarrassment or shame). This is why tact is such an important virtue in interpersonal behavior. But although tact smoothes interpersonal interaction, it involves more than good manners. Etiquette is merely conventional. Tact, like considerateness, is deeper in consisting of the personal interest in maintaining the welfare of other people—not just sticking to social norms of behavior in the public space. Tact, like other forms of sensitivity and unlike manners, cannot be formulated in rules and hence cannot be formally required. Its application is ad hoc and elusive (we say, "she has a magic touch"). Like touch, which is the least susceptible to linguistic articulation, tact is something we feel but cannot conceptualize. It is "immediate" in the sense that it is directly felt and can hardly be described. Tact like touch is created by contact.

We are getting closer to the context of Améry's confession of tactlessness when we read Hans-Georg Gadamer's characterization of tact:

> One can say something tactfully; but that will always mean that one passes over something tactfully and leaves it unsaid, and it is tactless to express what one can only pass over. But to pass over something does not mean to avert one's gaze from it, but to keep an eye on it in such a way that rather than knock into it, one slips by it. Thus tact helps to preserve distance. It avoids the offensive, the intrusive, and the violation of the intimate sphere of the person.[22]

Whereas we suggested that it is unlikely that Améry knew the work of Strawson, it is most probable that he knew this particular passage taken from Gadamer's major work written in German just a few years before Améry's collection of essays.

Although tact refers to a wide array of delicate handlings of sensitive situations, Gadamer is right in highlighting the context of leaving things unsaid as the epitome of tact. You do not mention the rope in the hanged person's home. But the problem with tact is that what is unsaid is not only true but might be importantly so. And here exactly lie the limits of tact of which Améry is so acutely aware. His testimony about the behavior of large parts of the German people during the Nazi period is, on the one hand, disturbing and disrupting in the attempt to create a new Germany, a society facing reconstruction and in need of reconciliation with its former enemies, yet on the other hand, must be heard and acted upon. This is the subtle borderline between leaving truth aside as an admirable sign of empathetic sensitivity to the other and the sin of ignoring truth just in order to appease guilty criminals and accomplices.

Silence has been Améry's policy for the first twenty years after the war. He started speaking up in radio talks and in essay writing only in the 1960s. But whatever his reasons for this silence (such as no one would believe us, only part of the German people can be blamed for the atrocities, the rest being victim of mad propaganda), these do not include tact. But in 1966, when "Resentments" was published, tact has become the issue. How can Améry raise these old events when Germany has transformed itself so successfully, overcoming the trauma of the war? Isn't that the time for leaving some truths unsaid? Or so it seems. Améry now refuses to keep his ressentiment to himself. Although he believed that resentment may be regarded (e.g. by his audience) as the proper internalization of "primitive and barbaric" revenge, he is not willing to keep silent about it. The distance he kept from the object of his resentment, as required by tact according to Gadamer, had to be broken and a direct confrontation of the survivors with the perpetrators and their accomplices had to be created. This would also force the whole German people to face their past with no distancing mechanisms.

Ressentiment is not only poisonous to the mind and soul of the individual bearing it but also to society. A resentful individual in a group, someone who would not forget past misdeeds of the group or its members, is like a sore in the eye, a constant obstacle in getting on with the business of living. We may call him "a moral nuisance". This is why the expression of ressentiment is *in itself* a tactless act. It breaks a certain tacit agreement between the writer and his readers from whom the author seeks excuse for his lack of tact. Even if there is no justification for tactlessness, says Améry, it can at least be excused as the outcome of the series of horrors involved in emigration, resistance, prison, torture and concentration camp. And whether justified or not, only by leaving tact aside can the author (and his readers) engage in what he calls "radical analysis". Radical means going down to the *roots* of the matter, and that calls for rejecting any rule of cover up, even when it has the virtues of tact. Radical analysis requires both exposing the guilt and shame of the German people in an honest way and the full and uninhibited personal grudge of the survivors, their personal resentment. And note that Améry is explicitly talking about radical analysis as a project that "*together* we are striving for here". The only way to achieve some moral goal in this project is by removing the separating gap between the author and his readers and that includes renouncing tact. No altruistic sympathy to the other or a subtle understanding of his conditions and motives—so skillfully displayed by the tactful person—can be of any service in the process that Améry wants the reader to undergo. Tact's main goal is to prevent embarrassment, but here embarrassment is the only means through which the German people can come to terms with their (or their compatriots') horrendous past.

Tact is a social virtue. Ressentiment is a moral reactive attitude which often runs contrary to the values of society. Therefore, we may add that by going against the flow of natural and social life, resentment risks losing *touch* with the world, namely that sense of what is possible and what is merely fantastical. Améry is not only highly aware of this risk in 1966. It is touching (to use the tactile metaphor yet again) to see in the end of the resentment essay that Améry recognizes that his bold project of a tactless radical analysis aimed at transforming his German audience has been subverted by the all-powerful social system. Traveling in Germany he is "received everywhere in a friendly and understanding manner".

> What more can people like me ask than that German newspapers and radio stations grant us the possibility to address grossly tactless remarks to German men and women, and on top of this to be remunerated for it? (p. 80)

This passage is strikingly reminiscent of the analysis of another German Jewish immigrant, Herbert Marcuse, who is writing also in the early 1960s, although in California. According to Marcuse, the postindustrial social and economic system has become so powerful that it is able to incorporate and even benefit from its own critics.[23] For example, Marcuse notes that "this liquidation of *two-dimensional* culture takes place not through the denial and rejection of the 'cultural values,' but through their wholesale incorporation into the established order, through their reproduction and display on a massive scale".[24] Compare this to Améry who senses the same phenomenon in the most personal terms: "What dehumanized me has become a commodity, which I offer for sale" (p. 80).[25] It seems that in a social system which lost the value of tact, any attempt to *break* the rule of tact so as to achieve a serious moral engagement is condemned to failure. It is immediately neutralized by the commercialized mass media. By being untactful Améry aimed to make himself a public nuisance; instead, he became a media star!

The last part of the essay returns to the opening theme: the gap between the current state of the German nation—prosperous, confident, liberal, and easygoing—and its shameful past which has not been integrated into its collective consciousness. Strangely, the same feeling of ressentiment, which Améry has first directed at the agents of his incredible suffering, is now passionately aimed at contemporary German society.[26] It is a second-order resentment against those who totally fail to comprehend and sympathize with the victim's first-order resentment against his tormentors. The objects of the original resentment, namely the perpetrators, are expected to undergo the moral process which Améry knows full well they never will. But beyond that, and especially because the moral account must be settled with the whole German people (the accomplices), Améry expects the whole German nation to "moralize" their postwar history. This does not happen either, for the reasons Améry himself so brilliantly explains. Neither form of resentment—toward the evildoers or toward their descendants—can be satisfied.

To end with a more speculative reflection, *suicide* may be regarded as the ultimate act of tactlessness, the most disruptive of social and interpersonal relations. To use yet again Gadamer's definition, suicide is the most dramatic expression of what everybody knows yet must be left unsaid, namely that life, at least for the victim of evil, has no meaning and that no consolation, compensation, acts of atonement, or manifestation of public respect offered by society can ever recover the sense of life lost by people like Améry.[27] The essay "Resentments" ends with the pessimistic prediction that the morality of resentment will never win and that the victims will consequently have to be soon "finished" in the sordid sense of the concentration camp language. The "soon" comes only twenty-two years later when Jean Améry commits suicide, but suicide is definitely the final act of defiance, that is the most conspicuous of Améry's personality traits. It is with bitter irony that we may hypothesize that through his act of suicide—the most personal, lonely, and desperate of human choices, Améry's project of ressentiment has proved to be more effective than all his radio talks and writings.[28]

Notes

1. Jean Améry, 'Resentments', in J. Améry, *At the Mind's Limits*, translated by Sidney Rosenfeld and Stella Rosenfeld (London: Granta Books, 1999), pp. 62–81. The English version of the German original uses the term "resentment" rather than the original *ressentiment* in the essay's title, which may be conceptually justified although it comes with a price. At least in the English language, "resentment" has fewer negative connotations than the French "ressentiment" and has been used to refer to a potentially justified moral response (devoid of the elements of malice and envy that characterize ressentiment and from which Améry wants to distance himself). Such a validation of resentful reaction is what Améry's essay attempts to establish. Yet resentment is usually a temporary response, while ressentiment is in its essence an ongoing, unyielding, and poisonous emotion—features which also capture an important role in Améry's analysis. The problem of translation proves to be typically interpretation dependent, exposing the ambiguities in Améry's text. For a detailed and philosophically sensitive discussion of this subtle difference, see Thomas Brudholm, 'Revisiting Resentments: Jean Améry and the Dark Side of Forgiveness and Reconciliation', *Journal of Human Rights* 5 (2006), pp. 7–26, and his later book *Resentment's Virtue: Jean Améry and the Refusal to Forgive* (Philadelphia: Temple University Press, 2008), pp. 173–176.
2. For the comparison between the natural forward-looking perspective (typically illustrated by Desmond Tutu and the Truth and Reconciliation Commission in South Africa) and the moral backward-looking attitude represented by Améry, see David Heyd, 'Ressentiment and Reconciliation: Alternative Responses to Historical Evil', in Lukas H. Meyer (ed.), *Justice in Time* (Baden-Baden: Nomos, 2003), pp. 185–197.
3. Friedrich Nietzsche, *Genealogy of Morals*, first essay, sections 7, 8, and 10, and second essay, section 11.
4. Susan Neiman emphasizes Améry's basic acceptance of Nietzsche's judgment about the futility of ressentiment despite his attempt to ground morality on it. I believe Neiman is right since this reading highlights the

tragic situation in which Améry finds himself. Susan Neiman, *Evil in Modern Thought* (Princeton: Princeton University Press, 2002), pp. 264–265.

5. Here I differ from Brudholm and Rosoux who try to list four "reasons" for Améry's refusal to forgive (dignity, recognition, accountability, and coexistence). The question for Améry is not only why not to forgive (since forgiveness is not the only alternative to resentment) but whether resentment can at all be justified in rational, universal terms—particularly in the sense used in the discourse of social morality. Resentment is not really a choice but rather a given, although admittedly it involves a decision to maintain it, not to let it fade away ("I neither can nor want to get rid of [resentment]"). But since ressentiment cannot be treated in rational terms of social morality, the direct and tragic contradiction with the point of view of the non-victims in society is inevitable. See Thomas Brudholm and Valérie Rosoux, 'The Unforgiving: Reflections on the Resistance to Forgiveness after Atrocity', *Law and Contemporary Problems* 72 (2009), pp. 33–49.
6. 'Resentments', p. 68. Améry claims that German history cannot be treated by young Germans as consisting of Goethe and Mörike while ignoring Nazi poets and Himmler's atrocities. But in a contradictory tone he believes that all the books printed in the Third Reich should be turned into pulp. There is a tension between the demand to include the Nazi period in German history and the fantasy of completely erasing it.
7. Max Scheler, *Ressentiment*, translated by W. W. Holdheim (New York: The Free Press, 1961), p. 162.
8. It is true that Améry contemptuously rejects calls for reconciliation of the victims with the criminals since he does not believe in a psychological or moral symmetry between the two parties. See on that Arne Johan Vetlesen, 'A Case for Resentment: Jean Améry vs. Primo Levi', *Journal of Human Rights* 5 (2006), pp. 27–44. But note that the ultimate point of the ethics of resentment is exactly the annulment of the humiliating superiority of the perpetrator over the victim by the continuous imposition on him of the awareness of his atrocities.
9. Améry's ambivalence toward revenge is also expressed in the way he characterizes those victims of Nazi crimes who seek reconciliation as suffering from "the masochistic conversion of a suppressed *genuine* demand for revenge" ('Resentments', p. 71). Nietzsche, with some Freudian supplement, could have easily put it exactly this way. But for Améry, revenge here is, originally, the "genuine" and morally correct response.
10. 'Resentments', p. 67; Brudholm, *Resentment's Virtue*, p. 101.
11. Brudholm (*Resentment's Virtue*, pp. 152, 162–166) believes that for Améry social moral reform can be triggered by ressentiment. But since Améry explicitly says that a moral settlement between the victim and the

perpetrator(s) is "absurd", it is hard to see how Améry can be ascribed with such a belief. His whole point is that such a purging effect of resentment is fantastical, in the mind of the victim, going against natural inevitability. The absurdity of trying to go back in time (and bring the perpetrator into this process!) does not, however, mean that resentment is meaningless (even if it is pointless), since, as we shall presently see, resentment is *reactive* in its essential nature and we can coherently and without logical fallacy feel it toward necessary and unchangeable states of affairs. Accordingly, it seems that Améry does not believe in ressentiment as an "instrument" (or a "weapon", as he puts it) in a struggle for a possible moral settlement, but more fundamentally as an *expression* of the highest moral order.

12. P. F. Strawson, 'Freedom and Resentment', in P. F. Strawson (ed.), *Studies in the Philosophy of Thought and Action* (London: Oxford University Press, 1968), pp. 71–96. Thomas Brudholm has also pointed out the similarity between Améry and Strawson (*Resentment's Virtue*, p. 94). However, it is quite unlikely that Améry actually knew Strawson's article.
13. 'Freedom and Resentment', pp. 76–77.
14. Although Strawson focuses on resentment, his personal reactive view of moral relations applies equally to the mirror image of resentment, namely gratitude. No objective theory can account for this important response (the lack of which is considered a grave sin) since it is based on the personal and subjective acknowledgment of the good will of the benefactor. It has been noted by philosophers that resentment, revenge, gratitude and forgiveness, being personal, cannot be shown by a third party (unlike meting punishment or apportioning compensation, which are their objective correlatives).
15. Butler confuses between resentment and indignation since he understood the value of the natural response of resentment to evil as ultimately a *social* good. He argues that it highlights social bonds by being shared by all members of society and by promoting justice. Butler believes that more than virtue, the potential resentment of the offended party is the major disincentive for the offender. This notion of resentment is of course alien to Améry since it lacks any intrinsic value and can be justified only instrumentally. However, Améry acknowledges one aspect of the social perspective of resentment: although it is personal in nature, it must be "publicized" to have any meaning, to have any effect on both the perpetrators and society at large. Resentment, at least for Améry (though not for Nietzsche), is personal but not private. See Joseph Butler, *Sermons*, Sermon VIII.
16. Jacques Derrida, *Given Time: I, Counterfeit Money*, translated by Peggy Kamuf (Chicago: University of Chicago Press, 1992).
17. Marcel Mauss, *The Gift*, translated by Ian Cunnison (London: Cohen & West, 1954).

18. The author of Améry's biography shows in detail how all the major elements of his ressentiment are already expressed in his 1935 novel, *The Shipwrecked*: hate, loneliness, collective identity, physical pain and suicide. Irène Heidelberger-Leonard, *The Philosopher of Auschwitz: Jean Améry and Living with the Holocaust* (London: Tauris, 2010), pp. 35–37. I should add that Améry's book *On Aging* (Bloomington: Indiana University Press, 1994) can also be read in the light of the theme of ressentiment—in this case (again) the irreversibility of time, the physical pain, the loneliness and the futile revolt against a natural process that cannot be changed. The book displays the same tone of anger, redirected from the historical to the natural. Although the grumpiness of old people lacks the specifically moral quality of ressentiment, the two are phenomenologically similar and may be psychologically correlated.
19. See his response to Wiesenthal's famous "question" about forgiveness to a dying SS officer in Simon Wiesenthal, *The Sunflower* (New York: Schocken Books, 1997), pp. 105–109. Actually, Améry denies that forgiveness is a *moral* issue. It is psychological or theological and hence, for Améry, irrelevant. From the political point of view, he is not clear whether forgiveness makes any difference: on the one hand he declares that it "is quite irrelevant"; yet a page later emphatically adds, "Politically, I do not want to hear anything of forgiveness!"
20. There is an ongoing debate whether there are "suberogatory acts", the mirror image of supererogatory acts, namely acts which are wrong although not morally prohibited. I doubt there is such a category. But if there was, resentful actions may have been a good example. See Julia Driver, 'The Suberogatory', *Australasian Journal of Philosophy* 70 (1992), pp. 286–295.
21. See David Heyd, 'Tact: Sense, Sensitivity, and Virtue', *Inquiry* 38 (1995), pp. 217–31.
22. Hans-Georg Gadamer, *Truth and Method*, translated by Joel Weinsheimer and D. G. Marshall (London: Sheed & Ward, 1989), p. 16.
23. Herbert Marcuse, *One Dimensional Man* (London: Sphere Books, 1968), introduction.
24. Ibid., p. 58.
25. This is yet another indication that, unlike Brudholm's reading, Améry does not believe in the power of his ressentiment to bring forth a moral transformation of the German people. The social changes in German society after the war are inevitable and could not have been otherwise. The Marcuse-like description of the laws of the system of postindustrial economy and mass media belongs exactly to the *natural* forces over which Améry says we have no control. This explains the absurdity of his situation in the very act of giving the radio lecture on ressentiment.

26. But as Margaret Walker correctly notes, this resentment is equally futile as that directed at the actual perpetrators. I am less sure though that she is right in claiming that although resentment cannot be "satisfied", it can still be "answered" (according to Améry). See Margaret Urban Walker, *Moral Repair* (Cambridge: Cambridge University Press, 2006), p. 142.
27. I cannot enter here into the question of Améry's suicide which is often discussed in comparison to Primo Levi's. See Arne Johan Vetlesen, 'A Case for Resentment: Jean Améry vs. Primo Levi', *Journal of Human Rights* 5 (2006), pp. 35–40; Heidelberger-Leonard, *The Philosopher of Auschwitz*, pp. 65–72. The two were different in personality and character, as Levi himself clearly remarked. But beyond that, as their correspondence shows, the double experience of homelessness and torture, from which Levi was spared, made it hard for Levi to comprehend Améry and his ethics of resentment. Yet, as Vetlesen notes, no one knows whether Levi's own suicide was not a late concession that Améry was right, which puts his long-time opposition to ressentiment in perspective.
28. I owe special thanks to Eli Pitcovski, the co-editor of this volume, for his sharp comments and constructive suggestions, many of which I have gladly embraced.

PART II

The Mind: Torture and Consequences

CHAPTER 6

Torture and Torturers

Eran Fish

6.1 Introduction

Jean Améry's unsettling testimony of his own torture at the hands of the Gestapo is a detailed account of what torture, in fact, is, what it does to the person tortured, and what makes it uniquely horrifying. But Améry does not only describe the act of torture and the experience of the victim. His description also includes the torturers themselves: who they were and what they were like. In particular, Améry makes a point of correcting a certain image of the perpetrators as merely "bureaucrats of torture" (Améry 1980). The torturers as described are not of the kind theorized by Hannah Arendt—ordinary and lacking in personality and thought (Arendt 1963). They were not mere conformists who tortured because it was their job to do so. Rather, Améry writes, they went about their business "with heart and soul". Their faces were "concentrated with murderous self-realization" as they did it. Furthermore, Améry claims, this was not only the way they acted. It was also the way they were. The brutality of torture was in their character, as well as part of the character of the ideology by which they were guided. They tortured, he argues, "because they were torturers" (Améry 1980, p. 31).

E. Fish (✉)
Ludwig-Maximilian University, Munich, Germany

Y. Ataria et al. (eds.), *Jean Améry*,
https://doi.org/10.1007/978-3-030-28095-6_6

But why are the torturers' specific psychology and character so important? What difference does it make whether they tortured because they were mere bureaucrats, or 'because they were torturers'? Presumably, the pain wouldn't have been any different, or more bearable, had the torturer been 'mere bureaucrats'. Furthermore, whatever was the torturers' specific character, there is no dispute that they had acted deliberately and in full knowledge of what they were doing. 'Mere bureaucrats' can inflict as much suffering, and as intentionally, as those who are more characteristically violent and merciless. And if so, what might Améry's description of the perpetrators add to our understanding of torture? What would we be missing if we did not know what kind of people the torturers were?

In what follows I will suggest two ways in which Améry's account of the perpetrators' character and psychology is important. The first has to do with what makes the act that Améry describes a unique moral evil. Torture, I will argue, is particularly wrong not in its own right, but rather because, and to the extent that, it is a manifestation of cruelty. Améry's depiction of the torturers' psychology serves to show that the act of torture was one of genuine cruelty, as opposed to a more ordinary form of violence. Secondly, Améry's account may be understood as an attempt to establish a lasting connection between the perpetrators and the crime. As I will suggest, the claim is that there is more than an incidental connection between the perpetrators and the crime: the fact that the actions reflected something deep in the torturers' very character explains why these perpetrators remain blameworthy for their deed long after the fact. I shall discuss these two claims in turn.

6.2 Torture

There may be things more painful than torture. The injuries suffered in the battlefield can be far more excruciating than those inflicted in a torturer's chamber.[1] Yet torture is often considered to be categorically wrong and inexcusable, while many other forms of violence are not. The mere infliction of pain, however severe and unbearable, has not been thought of in such absolutist terms even by the staunchest of deontologists.

Some philosophers have attempted to explain this apparent puzzle by pointing out the additional forms of harm caused by torture. The tortured suffers not only physical pain but also unimaginable psychological distress; not only distress but also degradation; and not just degradation but also a damage to one's very agency: torture has been argued to "... [force] its victim into the position of colluding against himself through his own affects and emotions, so that he experiences himself as … complicit in his own violation" (Sussman 2005, p. 4). These explanations are helpful in drawing a fuller and more vivid picture of the horrors of torture. They explain our special sense of dread and repulsion. They demonstrate how torture is even more harmful than we may think.

However, informative as these explanations are, they leave part of the puzzle unsolved. If what makes torture wrong is the level of harm it inflicts on its victim, then these accounts do show why torture is more wrong than one might assume—namely, in virtue of being more harmful than one might assume. But even if torture is monstrously harmful, we still want to know what sets it apart from other forms of monstrous harm. If the evil of torture consists entirely in the harm it involves, one could always conceive of a scenario that is equally or more harmful than torture, and which is not considered equally wrong—thus the question remains.

Indeed, this is what motivates the familiar objection to the absolute wrongfulness of torture—that is, the Ticking Bomb challenge in its various renditions. The objectors, typically, do not deny that the harm of torture is as gruesome as it is said to be. What they argue is that however bad that harm is, inflicting it may sometimes be justified in order to prevent a harm that is graver still. Torture, it is argued, is merely pro tanto wrong, just as other very harmful acts are. There is no reason to regard it as any more wrong than comparable harms, let alone as wrong categorically.

We may not agree on whether or not torture is always and unconditionally wrong—and this question will not be resolved here. But we may agree, I think, on a less controversial claim: cruelty is always and unconditionally wrong. Of course, some questions regarding the nature of cruelty are controversial: for example, philosophers disagree on whether cruelty is the worst thing one can do or just one among humanity's worst vices (Rorty 1989; Shklar 1984). Similarly, there may be some disagreement with respect to the boundaries of the concept—that is, just how much merciless brutality qualifies as cruelty. But very few would question either the fact that cruelty is wrong, or that it is wrong under all circumstances. There seem to be no all-things-considered justifications for cruelty.[2] As I will be arguing, the categorical wrongfulness of *cruelty* might explain why we find torture to be categorical (or nearly categorical) wrong, too. Unlike some other types of violence, most (if not all) instances of torture are cruel. Some reflection on what cruelty amounts to may be helpful.

6.3 Cruelty

Not every infliction of suffering is cruel. An agent may inflict great pain on someone without being cruel or acting cruelly. Indeed, he may inflict the same pain that a cruel person would without being cruel or acting cruelly himself. To borrow an example from Hilary Putnam: "before the introduction of anaesthesia at the end of the nineteenth century, any operation caused great pain, but the surgeons were not normally being cruel" (Putnam 2002, p. 38). That is because cruelty has a necessary psychological component. The cruel act follows a desire to cause pain or at the very least an indifference to the suffering of the victim (Kekes 1996; Sverdlik 1996, p. 340). Arguably, it is because of this desire or indifference to pain that the act merits the label 'cruel'.

It is not always easy to tell just how much desire for causing pain, or how little regard for suffering, qualify as cruelty. Indeed, it is not obvious that even those nineteen surgeons, however well-meaning, were not being cruel. Perhaps, for example, the patient's pain was so unspeakably excruciating that only someone who is utterly cold-blooded wouldn't take it as a reason to stop the operation. But not all cases are difficult to classify. For example, we can readily agree that deliberately starving a child, or beating a pet, are things that require cruelty. They are hard to explain except by the fact that the person who had done these things either wished to cause suffering or was chillingly unmoved by it.

This, I think, is a cue to understanding the difference between torture, at least as commonly understood, and some other forms of violence. For the paradigmatic case of torture, too, is one that is hard to view as other than cruel. Torture is not merely an infliction of pain, but the infliction of pain on the utterly defenseless (Shue 1978). As Améry himself has put it, "[t]he first blow brings home to the prisoner that he is helpless...Whoever would rush to the prisoner's aid—a wife, a mother, a brother, or friend—he won't get this far" (1980, p. 27). The special setting of the torture chamber—the striking imbalance between torturer and tortured; the fact that the victim is completely at his tormentor's mercy; the desperate cry for this all to stop—are such that only a person who is thoroughly unmoved by the victim's suffering could exploit.[3] The violence of the battlefield, however ferocious, is different. It is more than conceivable for this type of violence to be unleashed without cruelty—for example, in the heat of the battle rather than out of lust for suffering. That does not mean, of course, that the violence of war cannot be bad in various other ways, or that this violence, too, cannot be accompanied by cruelty.[4] The point is only that the special badness of the paradigmatic case of torture, as opposed to other forms of violence, can be explained. When torture does merit special condemnation, it is often for the cruelty it exhibits.

I say that the paradigmatic case of torture is one of cruelty, because there may be some other cases as well. Consider a version of the Ticking Bomb scenario. Suppose that a child has been abducted and one of the kidnappers, who was caught by the police, wouldn't disclose his location. The interrogators exhaust every possible method on the protocol, to no avail. As time runs out and the concern for the child's life turns into desperation, the chief investigator decides to tie up the detainee and extract the information by drastic physical force.

Now, many people would find this resort to violence—indeed, to torture—justifiable all things considered. The common diagnosis of the case is that while using severe violence against a detainee is pro tanto wrong, the reasons against doing so are morally outweighed by the concern for the child.[5] On this diagnosis, the example shows that torture is wrong only most of the time. Under some circumstances, as in this case, it may be justified and even morally required.

But the above reflections on cruelty and its relation to torture suggest another way of diagnosing the case: to the extent that this is a case of torture at all, this case is plausibly lacking a key component that other instances of torture have. Unlike paradigmatic torture, applying violence in the abducted child example does not require a desire to cause pain or a disregard for the person being tortured (even if it *can* be accompanied by such attitudes, too). It is, therefore, an action that, while inflicting great pain, is not necessarily cruel.

Thus, according to this alternative diagnosis, the example does not prove that no unconditional wrongness is involved. Rather, we may have simply misidentified the thing that is unconditionally wrong. *Torture* may sometimes be justified, but perhaps it has never been torture itself that was supposed to be categorically wrong. It is cruelty that is wrong unconditionally, and the abducted child example does not show that it is not. At most, the example demonstrates that a case of non-cruel violence could be justified all things considered. But this does not mean that cruel violence—which is what we ordinarily have in mind when thinking about torture—could be justified as well.

The torture that Améry himself experienced in Breendonk was, of course, nothing like the abducted child example. This was an act of aggression carried out by officials of a conquering power against a civilian—an act that did not serve any defensible purpose. Yet even this case of torture could have conceivably been executed without cruelty. For example, it might have been deployed reluctantly, only to obtain information. The torturer might have even detested causing the detainee physical pain. In fact, Arendt's view—the view against which Améry is protesting—comes close to suggesting precisely this possibility. Though she does not address the same case, she does writes the following of a comparable one—that of the *Einsatzgruppen*:

> the murderers were not sadists or killers by nature; on the contrary, a systematic effort was made to weed out all those who derived physical pleasure from what they did ... Hence the problem was how to overcome not so much their conscience as the animal pity by which all normal men are affected in the presence of physical suffering. The trick used by Himmler-who apparently was rather strongly afflicted with these instinctive reactions himself-was very simple and probably very effective; it consisted in turning these instincts around, as it were, in directing them toward the self. So that instead of saying: What horrible things I did to people!, the murderers would be able to say: What horrible things I had to watch in the pursuance of my duties, how heavily the task weighed upon my shoulders! (1963, pp. 105–6)

According to Arendt, even Nazi perpetrators who were directly involved in executing murder and torture might have felt mercy toward their victims. The crimes may have therefore been committed without the mental state that would render them cruel. It could be that the perpetrators recoiled from their victims' suffering, rather than sought it.

This possibility is one that Améry denies. When discussing the similarities and differences between torture under Nazism and torture as practiced elsewhere, he writes that on the one hand, "[t]he Nazis tortured, as did others, because by means of torture they wanted to obtain information for national policy" (1980, p. 31). In some respects, that is, the torture was not entirely unlike other act of violence committed during a war or a police investigation. However, Améry continues, causing pain and subordinating their victims were not only a means for the torturers but also an end (ibid.). He argues—in what may be read as a direct repudiation of Arendt's claim—that the torturers did act out of sadism, albeit of a particular kind: not the sexual-pathological type, but rather one that is intent on causing suffering and destruction (ibid., p. 35). While Arendt suggests that the perpetrator had acted in spite of the misery suffered, Améry argues that they acted for that purpose.

This insistence on the specific psychology of the torturers serves a purpose. The fact that the act of torture was performed with a desire to cause pain means that it was more than just an ordinary act of war—of the kind that could potentially be explained and accepted as legitimate warfare; it was not merely a violent method of extracting information from the enemy. It was an act of genuine cruelty that cannot be legitimized or forgiven.

6.4 Torturers and Mere Bureaucrats

There is more to be said, however. So far I have focused on the significance of the torturers' mental state at the time of the act. But Améry's and Arendt's respective accounts differ also, if not primarily, with respect to the kind of people the perpetrators were. It has been Arendt's central thesis in her *report on the banality of evil* that the character of the crimes committed under Nazism may have been incommensurate with that of the people who had perpetrated them (Arendt 1963). She argued that the perpetrators of evil were people, not monsters. While the crimes were hideous, the criminals were, if anything, normative through and through: they were people who behaved in accordance with whatever was socially normative to do and say. The image that Arendt has made famous is that of an evildoer who is merely a banal official—one who is not particularly inclined toward violence, but simply carrying out the task with which he had been assigned. They were not so much ruthless as they were thoughtless.

Améry, on the other hand, explicitly resists thinking of the torturers as "merely brutalized petty bourgeois and subordinate bureaucrats of torture" (1980, p. 34). While they were, in some sense, ordinary official who did their job, "they were also much more" (ibid., pp. 35–6) than what Arendt's account would suggest. On the picture that Améry is painting, the torture has emanated from and reflect something in the torturers' character: the sadism with which they acted was also a defining component of who they were.

It might be thought that the reason for opposing the image of 'mere bureaucrats of torture' is that it is incompatible with the cruelty of the deed. One could argue that if we accept that the act of torture had been cruel—that is, performed with a cruel mindset—we ought to also accept that the torturers were cruel as well. But such an implication should be rejected. There is nothing in the very idea of a 'bureaucrat of torture' that is inconsistent with acting cruelly. An obedient official of the sort envisioned by Arendt might not desire to inflict suffering, but he may well exhibit heartlessness or indifference. Perhaps a genuine sadist would be more likely to act cruelly than a mere bureaucrat would, but bureaucrats are nonetheless perfectly capable of acting cruelly.

A more serious objection that is sometimes raised against Arendt's view is that the torturers could not regularly act with cruelty without thereby being cruel (Thomas 1993). A non-cruel person may act with cruelty occasionally, just as a miser can sometimes act generously. However, the argument would go, to repeatedly act cruelly is indicative of a more stable disposition. And since a so-called 'bureaucrat of torture' would be routinely engaged in torturing, the implication would be either that the repeated acts of torture are not cruel, or that the torturer is not a 'mere bureaucrat'.

I think that this claim captures something right. But is it strictly inconsistent to act cruelly on a regular basis without meriting the description 'cruel'? Suppose that instead of a Gestapo interrogator, the 'mere bureaucrat' in question is an obedient functionary in a government committed to aiding the needy and to welcoming refugees. He works tirelessly and selflessly to make things better for a great many people in need, and to keep those fleeing danger safe from harm. He is not averse to his job. More often than not, he even actually cares for the people he helps. Yet he would never have been engaged in helping anyone had he not been assigned with this task. In fact, he would have felt just as committed to expelling these refugees if that were the policy in place.[6]

It seems right to applaud the humanitarian work that is being done by this 'bureaucrat of benevolence', just as it would be right to condemn the actions of a bureaucrat of torture. We also needn't deny that this person acts altruistically and kindly, and more than occasionally so. At the same time, applauding this person himself as either altruistic or kind would be an undeserved exaggeration. A kind character would mean a stable disposition to act kindly. But in this example what is, in fact, stable is not his kindness, but the social circumstances under which he is acting kindly. He is acting kindly on a regular basis, but he is not reliably kind, so to speak. His is not the disposition that a truly kind person would have.

Admittedly, the symmetry between kindness and cruelty is not perfect.[7] But it wouldn't be implausible to say something similar with respect to the supposed cruelty of the 'bureaucrat of torture'. A cruel person would be someone who is consistently disposed to act cruelly, even when conditions and social norms change. But 'bureaucrats of torture' need not have such a disposition, even if they routinely act with cruelty. Conceivably at least, the official who acts with cruelty as a functionary of the Gestapo would act compassionately, or indeed in any other way, in a different capacity, and under different circumstances.

The idea of a 'bureaucrat of torture', then, is not incoherent. Nor is it incompatible with the cruelty of the act of torture. Cruel actions can be carried out by people who are not themselves cruel. That is not to say that the Gestapo investigators would have necessarily been better people according to Arendt. Arendt's banal evildoer might not be cruel, strictly speaking, but he is still a deeply morally flawed person: one who follows morally bankrupt social norms and performs heinous crimes. What appears to be the main and principled difference between Améry's account and Arendt's is in the extent to which cruelty had been characteristic of the perpetrators. To Améry, the cruelty and contempt that made the torture what it was were also an aspect of who the torturers were. On Arendt's view, the perpetrators could have acted cruelly without in fact being cruel. In the next and final section, I will discuss the significance of this difference, in general as well as to Améry in particular.

6.5 Character and Enduring Blameworthiness

It isn't always possible to tell whether an action is characteristic of the person who had done it. And at least according to some philosophers, this might not even be a particularly relevant thing to know. It has been argued that we may praise and condemn people for acting cruelly, bravely, cowardly, or generously without appealing to their character and dispositions at all. Thomas Hurka offers the following set of examples:

> Imagine that, walking down the street, you see someone kick a dog from an evident desire to hurt the dog just for the pleasure of doing so. Do you say, 'That was a vicious act' or 'That was a vicious act on condition that it issued from a stable disposition to give similar kicks in similar circumstances'? Surely you say the former … Or imagine that a military committee is considering whether to give a soldier a medal for bravery. Would they say, 'We know he threw himself on a grenade despite knowing it would cost him his life and in order to save the lives of his comrades. But we cannot give him a

> medal for bravery because we do not know whether his act issued from a stable disposition or was, on the contrary, out of character'? (Hurka 2006, p. 180)

According to Hurka, in everyday moral thought we find it natural to apply the terms 'virtue' and 'vice' to acts, rather than to stable character traits or dispositions. This, he believes, is as it should be. A virtuous act is not made any better for having emerged from a stable disposition to act virtuously, nor is a vicious action made worse (Hurka 2006). In the case of the non-characteristically cruel torturer, this sounds plausible. If a person inflicts suffering and does so with either a wish to cause pain or disregard for her victim, then we seem to have all the information we need to establish that she acts cruelly, and to blame her accordingly. The act is cruel irrespective of what this person is usually like.

Yet I would like to suggest one way in which emphasizing the perpetrators' cruel disposition is nevertheless important—important in general as well as important to Améry in particular. The fact that the cruelty was characteristic of its perpetrators—that it revealed something of and emanated from their stable dispositions—means that it is appropriate to blame them for what they had done long after the fact. I should explain what I mean by that.

The basic intuition was captured by David Hume. "Actions", Hume argued, "are by their very nature temporary and perishing; and where they proceed not from some cause in the character and disposition of the person, who perform'd them, they infix not themselves upon him, and neither redound to his honour, if good, nor infamy, if evil" (Hume 1978, p. 411). At a first glance, this claim seems to conflict with what we have just said. The claim appears to be that we can only blame someone for bad actions that are characteristic of her. This reading of the claim may be plausible if the reason for acting out of character had been some mistake, accident, or duress.[8] It is less plausible, however, to say that a person is not to be blamed for a wrong deed which she had done intentionally and freely, simply because she is not usually disposed to act that way. It would seem that we are within our right to blame a person for committing a wrong even if this happened to be the only time in which she had done it (Kauppinen 2015, pp. 54–5).

But the claim being made is different. It is true that the Humean claim is an attempt to explain when blame is called for and when it is not. The thing to be explained is why, if ever, is it appropriate to blame an *agent* for a bad *action*. And the Humean explanation is, roughly, that the badness of the action reflects on the agent because, and to the extent that, it flows from his character. But this Humean claim is best understood as an explanation for a particular aspect of blameworthiness: its diachronic aspect, rather than its synchronic one.[9]

One question we sometimes ask is *whether and to what extent an agent is blameworthy for his actions at the time they are committed*. Another is *whether and to what extent an agent at one point in time is blameworthy for actions performed at an earlier point*. Since actions are short-lived and the persons who performed them usually endure in time and outlast them, it makes sense to ask why should a mere act reflect on something as complex and enduring as the agent himself (Sher 2005). *That* is a puzzle that Hume's claim is better suited to solve. It is also a question that may have been particularly important to Améry, writing, as he did, two decades after the experience. How blameworthy are perpetrators for deeds committed in the past?

To see how the synchronic question is answered differently than the diachronic one, consider the following example. Suppose that Alex betrayed a friend when he was in his twenties. At the time, he acted selfishly and heartlessly—deliberately taking advantage of the friend's trust, and knowingly hurting his feelings. Now compare several alternative scenarios: (1) Alex has always been disposed to act selfishly and disloyally. This hasn't changed to this day when Alex is already in his forties. (2) Alex, now in his forties, has never shown any clear pattern of behavior. He has acted selfishly on occasion, but at other times he had been rather considerate, and even selfless (3) Alex used to be selfish and disloyal when he was younger, but he has changed over the years. Now, in his forties, he is a rather trustworthy and considerate person. (4) Alex is in his forties and has always been trustworthy and considerate, except this one time, in his twenties, that he betrayed a friend.

Now, in so far as blameworthiness in the synchronic sense is concerned, two things can be said. One is that it seems all but irrelevant which of these four scenarios is the case. At the time, Alex was blameworthy for his betrayal whether it was done in or out of character. Secondly and relatedly, appealing to Alex's character is not necessary to explain why he was to blame. The fact that at that point in time he knew what he was doing and did not care enough is sufficient to establish a connection between himself and what he had done.

But when it comes to blaming him for that same action today, there is, I think, a fairly strong intuition that it does matter which scenario is the case. It seems the most appropriate to blame Alex for what he did two decades ago if scenario 1 is the case and the most problematic to do so if scenario 4 is. That is because the fact that he *was* unfaithful and inconsiderate then does not, in and of itself, explain why it is appropriate to keep holding it against him *now*. For example, if the selfishness that has made it appropriate to hold the act of betrayal against Alex is no longer there, it is an open question what if anything connects the person today and the action twenty years ago. Inasmuch as we still find it suitable to resent him for that act of betrayal—as opposed to just resenting the act itself—the explanation is likely to be that we deem the betrayal to have stemmed from something more enduring about Alex. We assume, even if only implicitly, that something that was responsible for the deed is still true about the doer. It is here that the Humean explanation seems particularly potent. The stable traits of character that have been reflected in the act—apart from being a potential object of condemnation in their own right—may be the thing that ties the agent and what he had done over time.

A similar reasoning applies to the endurance of praiseworthiness as well. The egocentric person who had once made a selfless sacrifice deserves praise, but only for so long. As time goes by, it becomes ever less appropriate for him to take pride in this uncharacteristic instance of virtue. He may be continuous with his past self in some metaphysically relevant sense, but the altruism that had made it suitable to praise him for his action may not be part of who he is. As in the case of blameworthiness, the less an act is anchored to some stable trait of personality, the more it is a thing of the past. Some deeds are left unowned.

That is, I think, what Améry is determined to deny with respect to the crime and its perpetrators. One of the central claims he makes in his monumental *At the Mind's Limits* is that the time is not yet ripe—if ever it will be—to let go of the deeds, to move on, and to reconcile. There remains a reason for resentment, and its underlying wish is that the perpetrators would endeavor to disown their crimes—the crimes that are still there to be disowned—and join their victims in their permanent regret.[10] His remarks on the torturers' character are an attempt to establish a lasting connection between the crime and the people who did it.

While his essay on torture is better known for the claim that "whoever was tortured stays tortured" (1980, p. 34), it also has another message:

the torturers remain torturers, too. The torture was not the action of people who have been cruel and heartless at one point, during the war but are otherwise different. This had been an act of cruelty and contempt which was executed by people who are, or at least have been, themselves cruel. And so long as that is the case, the torture has not let go of the torturers.[11]

Notes

1. It should be said, however, that the suffering caused by torture can differ in kind and not only in intensity. For example, the victim of torture is made to anticipate and be fully aware of his pain, in a way that victims of other forms of violence are not. At the same time, it is at least possible in principle for some other forms of violence to cause greater suffering than some forms of torture. I am grateful to Yochai Ataria for pressing me on this point.
2. Arguably, cruelty is analytically wrong: it is what some might call a thick normative concept or a normative concept with some descriptive elements. See discussion in Elstein and Hurka (2009).
3. A person need not be heartless or cruel from birth, as it were. It is quite possible that such characteristics develop gradually in the torturer.
4. Interestingly, Augustine argued that the real evil in war is not the death and suffering, but the love of violence, or cruelty, that is often on display (1994, 22.74).
5. Some may argue that the violence applied in this case does not in fact amount to torture, since the detainee is not entirely defenseless: he is rather in a position of power, while the interrogator is the one struggling to find a way to defend the child. See discussion in Sussman (2005, p. 16), for example.
6. Dana Nelkin is using this thought experiment to examine whether psychopaths can be appropriately described as cruel. See Nelkin (2015, p. 367).
7. For example, kindness requires actively taking other people's interests and well-being as a reason for action. To qualify as cruel, on the other hand, it is enough that a person fails to care about other people's suffering.
8. Indeed, some take Hume's claim to explain moral excuses. See, for example, Brandt (1958).
9. This distinction also applies to the closely related concept of responsibility. See Khoury (2013).
10. In one place, Améry describes his wish that "two groups of people, the overpowered and those who overpowered them, would be joined in the

desire that time be turned back and, with it, that history become moral. If this demand were raised by the German people … [t]he German revolution would be made good, Hitler disowned." See Améry's "Resentments" (1980, p. 78).

11. I am deeply indebted to Dana Gur, Yochai Ataria, and Eli Pitcovski for their helpful comments on earlier drafts.

References

Améry, J. (1980). Torture. In S. Rosenfeld & S. P. Rosenfeld (Trans.), *At the Mind's Limits* (pp. 21–40). Bloomington, IN: Indiana University Press.

Arendt, H. (1963). *Eichmann in Jerusalem: A Report on the Banality of Evil.* Harmondsworth: Penguin.

Augustine. (1994). Contra Faustum. In P. Schaff (Ed.), *Vol. 4 of Nicene and Post-Nicene Fathers* (pp. 155–345). Peabody, MA: Hendrickson.

Brandt, R. (1958). Blameworthiness and Obligation. In A. I. Melden (Ed.), *Essays in Moral Philosophy* (pp. 3–39). Seattle, WA: University of Washington Press.

Elstein, D., & Hurka, T. (2009). From Thick to Thin: Two Moral Reduction Plans. *Canadian Journal of Philosophy, 39*(4), 515–535.

Hume, D. (1978). In L. A. Selby-Brigge (Ed.), *A Treatise of Human Nature.* Oxford: Clarendon.

Hurka, T. (2006). Virtuous Act, Virtuous Dispositions. *Analysis, 66*(1), 69–76.

Kauppinen, A. (2015). Character and Blame in Hume and Beyond. In I. Fileva (Ed.), *Perspectives on Character* (pp. 46–62). New York: Oxford University Press.

Kekes, J. (1996). Cruelty and Liberalism. *Ethics, 106*, 834–844.

Khoury, A. (2013). Synchronic and Diachronic Responsibility. *Philosophical Studies, 165*, 735–752.

Nelkin, D. K. (2015). Psychopaths, Incorrigible Racists, and the Faces of Responsibility. *Ethics, 125*, 357–390.

Putnam, H. (2002). The Entanglement of Fact and Value. In *The Collapse of the Fact/Value Dichotomy and Other Essays* (pp. 28–45). Cambridge, MA: Harvard University Press.

Rorty, R. (1989). *Contingency, Irony, and Solidarity.* Cambridge: Cambridge University Press.

Sher, G. (2005). *In Praise of Blame.* New York: Oxford University Press.

Shklar, J. (1984). *Ordinary Vices.* Cambridge, MA: Harvard University Press.

Shue, H. (1978). Torture. *Philosophy & Public Affairs, 7*, 124–143.

Sussman, D. (2005). What's Wrong with Torture? *Philosophy & Public Affairs, 33*, 1–33.

Sverdlik, S. (1996). Motive and Rightness. *Ethics, 106*, 327–349.

Thomas, L. (1993). *Vessels of Evil: American Slavery and the Holocaust.* Philadelphia: Temple University Press.

CHAPTER 7

Torture: Reading Améry, Rereading Jewish Law

Amos Israel-Vleeschhouwer

The resurgence of religion in the public sphere (Habermas 2005) and of religiously motivated people in positions of power requires religions to account for the use of excessive power and for the positions stated in the name of religions in public discourse. It has renewed interest, among other topics, in religious perceptions of torture, the attitudes toward it, and its regulation (e.g., Reza 2007 (Islam); Harrison 2005 (Catholic theology)).

In this essay, I juxtapose a close reading of the contemplations of Jean Améry, who was tortured by the Gestapo in Belgium and wrote about it 22 years later (Améry 1980/1974), with Jewish sources pertaining to torture. Améry's "Torture" offers another point of view from which to reread the Jewish literature that can serve as a foundation for moral, social, and legal choices between multiple Jewish legal options.

By detailing the impacts of Améry's reflections on my rereading of Jewish law, I offer a subtle way to influence Jewish legal discourse. *Poskim* (rabbis who render Jewish legal decisions), Jewish public intellectuals, and

A. Israel-Vleeschhouwer (✉)
School of Law, Sapir Academic College, Sderot, Israel
e-mail: Aisrael@mail.sapir.ac.il

Y. Ataria et al. (eds.), *Jean Améry*,
https://doi.org/10.1007/978-3-030-28095-6_7

opinion leaders are influenced not only by the facts and laws but also by traditions, conditions, goals, and by cultural, and personal predispositions. Jewish writers on torture were influenced, for example, by the urgent need to enable the state to defend itself and by their commitment to human rights and universal values (Crane 2011). The impact of Améry's vivid experiences and profound insights can be an influencing factor in the debate on torture (Israel-Vleeschhouwer 2016c). The selections cited were chosen in order to enable readers to experience an Améry-inspired perspective on Jewish law and policy, going beyond the mere fact to reflection, and infusing the resulting rational commitment with passion (Améry 1980, xi, preface to the second edition).

It should be clear that this article is not an attempt to bring Améry into the Jewish legal debate as a participating Jew. Even I would want to do so, for most rabbis his contribution would not be considered as integral to the Jewish debate. For them, any "external" text is devalued, as are the academic scholarship of Jewish studies, Israeli jurisprudence and Jewish secular thinkers (compare, Henkin 2000). I likewise do not wish to imply that Améry was aware of the Jewish sources I discuss, or that he had any intention of influencing their interpretation.

Section 7.1 provides a brief outline of the competing Jewish legal opinions regarding torture. In Sect. 7.2 Améry's texts provide a perspective for rereading biblical texts and consider their cultural impacts, while in Sect. 7.3 they serve to enrich a rereading of four Jewish legal debates. Based on the insights of previous sections, I challenge the utilitarian justification of necessity in Sect. 7.4. I conclude with a call for action.

7.1 Torture in Jewish Legal Literature

The international prohibition of torture posed torture as a modern legal and moral issue and as a policy decision in public discourse. Rabbis, Jewish scholars, and Jewish activists sought to find legal and moral guidance in Jewish sources. These were grounded in the multifaceted historical attitude of Jewish law and culture toward torture. In the Bible and through the end of Jewish sovereignty (second century), we find acceptance of what we today would define as torture only in war, together with the criticism of elements of torture, and use of torture, in other contexts (Crane 2011). Most of the subsequent development of Jewish law until recently occurred in the context of Jewish powerlessness (Biale 1986) and oppression. In recent years, Jews have again to decide about using torture, in the context of Jewish (Israel) and non-Jewish (e.g., USA) regimes.

Engaging and analyzing the American rabbinic literature on torture, Crane identifies two distinct and opposing interpretations of Jewish law. He charges that both are biased, skewing sources and ignoring others to reach their respective conclusions. One posits that Jewish law and religion prohibit torture, mainly based on the failure of torture as an investigative tool and on "broad (moral) principles" such as respect for the human body, created in the divine image, and human dignity (Crane 2011, pp. 472–474, notes 10–27). The other interpretation permits and sometimes even necessitates torture (Bleich 2006), based on laws and legal principles, such as exigency and the commandment to save lives at the expense of the pursuer (Broyde 2006a, 2006b, 2007). Most published Israeli rabbis and scholars maintain this last position, practically condoning the use of "special measures" by the Israeli security services in at least some cases (Rechnitz 2016; Unger 2004; Warhaftig 2000; Wygoda 2000). Other opinions are more nuanced, allowing for some (physical) pressure under certain conditions (Zakheim 2007; parts of Wygoda 2000 and Warhaftig 2000) or prohibiting torture with or without an excuse in cases of necessity (Zakheim 2007).

Crane's findings are not surprising when I compare them to my analysis of Jewish legal attitudes to the use of excessive force on civilians. I found a multilayered disagreement regarding the Jewish legal principles and concepts, as well as on the actual ruling in practical cases. I found no congruence between the various principles and the variety of practical applications, that is, those who principally abhor violence intended toward civilians might accept civilian casualties as a fact of war, and vice versa (Israel-Vleeschhouwer 2014). Such tensions recur in the torture debate, as will be seen below.

Crane (2011) concludes, based on texts and narratives that were overlooked or undervalued by both camps, that the "correct" Jewish position on torture is that it is "a non-option." This might be Crane's position but doesn't correctly account for the whole Jewish tradition, insofar as the discovery of additional sources cannot cancel the inherent multiplicity of the texts. Furthermore, one could argue that contemporary historical circumstances (e.g., destructive power of terrorism, asymmetric warfare, and Jewish independence) necessitate the reversal of what he sees as a clear historical trend. Acknowledging multiple legitimate options, the public Jewish debate and rabbinic decisions are influenced by conscious and unconscious construal, the framing of facts, readings of sources and the contexts of experience and conditions. The main influences until now were the needs as defined by the state's security forces, the vivid threat of terrorism on one hand and the human rights discourse on the other. In the following sections I'll offer Améry's testimony and contemplations on torture as a different source of influence.

For the purposes of rational legal argument, a more concise formulation, focusing on the strongest aspects, would be preferable. Doing so would erase parts of the process in which reading Améry influenced the rereading of the various sources and issues. Rearranging the experience of accumulating reflections for formalistic arguments would simplify the important interactions between the experience of torture, the Jewish legal regulation of the act and the related narratives of Jewish culture. My goal is to add Améry's testimony and contemplations into these interactions and offer a look at the resulting forest, not just to look at some trees (Améry 1980, xiii).

7.2 Recognizing Torture and Hearing the Silenced Cries

Jewish legal narrative, especially in the bible and its interpretations, reveals concepts and values on which cultural and legal debates are based (Cover 1983). Rereading these fundamental biblical stories give depth to the rereading of legal issues (Sect. 7.3) and provide Jewish legitimacy and context to these readings and the resulting policy debate (Sect. 7.4).

7.2.1 *The Biblical Use of* "inui" *and the Experience of Torture*

The Hebrew root ע-נ-ה (affliction or torture) is used in the bible to describe the ill-treatment of a slave by her mistress, mistreatment of slaves in Egypt, the prohibition to abuse strangers and weak members of the society and for rape. These uses are different from the modern legal term of torture, for example, in the United Nations' CAT convention (UN 1984, art. 1.1). I originally thought that by applying the term *inui* to diverse and to relatively harmless deeds, the biblical text trivializes the term "torture." Then I read Améry's disclaimer:

> *If one speaks about torture, one must take care not to exaggerate. What was inflicted on me in the unspeakable vault in Breendonk was by far not the worst*

> *form of torture.* [...] *it was relatively harmless* [...]. *And yet,* [...] *I dare to assert that torture is the most horrible event a human being can retain within himself.* (Améry 1980, p. 22)

Améry made a rhetorical decision to communicate the essence of torture by understatement, detailing the effects of its mundane, trivial form. Hypothesizing that perhaps the Bible's ostensibly gratuitous use was similarly significant, I set out to reread the biblical usage of *inui*, searching for a bottom-up working definition of biblical torture. I offer that scripture reserves the term only for deeds that contain a combination of multiple critical elements of what we now call torture, guiding readers to a cumulative definition by using the common term consistently. Three of the elements of torture—imbalance of power, intentionality of the perpetrator, and inescapability—leading to an outcry, are captured in the biblical prohibition of strong members of society ill-treating the weak (Exodus 22:20–23).

The abuse of power and intentional infliction of pain against a disenfranchised person with apparent legitimacy, together with the inescapability from the abuse, has a transformative effect that is more than just the sum of these experiences.[1] As Améry testifies:

> *The first blow brings home to the prisoner that he is* helpless *[...] they will do with me what they want. Whoever would rush to the prisoner's aid—a wife, a mother, a brother, or friend—he won't get this far.* (Améry 1980, p. 27; Compare, Nowak 2017)
>
> *If no help can be expected, this physical overwhelming by the other then becomes an existential consummation of destruction altogether.* (Améry 1980, p. 28)

When it becomes clear that the pain is no prelude to death, and there to stay, pain becomes torture. It then penetrates the individual's autonomy, taking away control and any pretensions of control over body, privacy, borders, thoughts, and spirit (Améry 1980, p. 33; Salcioglu and Başoğlu 2017). Pain penetrates the civilized aspect of being and the civilizing mechanisms. It becomes the sole experience, robbing the victim of the divine image (compare Lichtenstein 1998).

Accordingly, the Bible also uses *inui* to describe rape (Gen. 34; Deut. 22:22–29; 2 Sam. 13), a similar "penetration of ... autonomy" and "existential consummation of destruction." It is caused by the same combination of intentional violence, power imbalance, apparent inescapability and futile outcry, and the resulting loss of trust. The comparison to rape was made, in turn, by Améry, who said:

> *The other person, [...] with whom I can exist only as long as he does not touch my skin surface as border, forces his own corporeality on me with the first blow. He is on me and thereby destroys me. It is like a rape, a sexual act without the consent of one of the two partners.* (Améry 1980, p. 28)

7.2.2 The Outcry, the Scream

The scream, according to Améry's testimony—and the fact that it goes unheard—is part of torture's essence:

> *From there no scream penetrated to the outside. There I experienced it: torture.*
> [...]
> *From other places the screams penetrated as little into the world as did once my own strange and uncanny howls from the vault of Breendonk.* (pp. 22, 23)

The outcry plays an important role in the biblical legal understanding of *inui*, as seen above in Exodus, regarding Hagar's torture by Sarah (Sect. 7.2.3), and as evident in the laws regarding the rape of a betrothed woman:

> But should the man find the betrothed young woman in the field and the man seize her and lie with her, only the man lying with her shall die. [...] For he found her in the field: the young woman could have cried out and there would have been none to save her. (Deut. 22: 25–27, Alter translation)

Explaining why the raped women aren't expected to cry out in the field, one of the most important Jewish biblical exegetes, Nachmanides (Rabbi Moshe ben Nachman), explains that she bears no blame, as there would have been no aid administered. The bible uses the term "field" to imply that a civilization where there is no help for the oppressed is like a field, uncivilized territory (compare Gen. 20:21). Unheeded cries are a major cause of the breakdown of trust and estrangement, described so well by Améry:

> *Whoever has succumbed to torture can no longer feel at home in the world. The shame of destruction cannot be erased.*

> *Trust in the world, which already collapsed in part at the first blow, but in the end, under torture, fully, will not be regained.* (Améry 1980, p. 40)

Therefore, societies should make screams audible by setting mechanisms in place (Carver and Handley 2016). Biblical *inui* (Egypt, oppressed *ger*, rape) consistently elicits silent cries heard only by God, and sometimes loud cries that challenge society. God watches the response of each potential helper and of the society, with its institutions and structures. Failing to actively prevent atrocities, or to respond to an outcry, the bystanders, too, will be called to justice. Jewish law transforms the scream from its role in the biblical text of determining the innocence or guilt of the woman, to an obligation of an alerted individual to intervene ("law of the pursuer"/ "*din rodef*"), to be discussed in relation to torture, below (sec. 7.3.1).

7.2.3 Torture's Impact

A third context in which the Hebrew root *ע-נ-ה* appears is in Genesis 16. God tells Abraham that his descendants will be tortured in Egypt, and God will judge the tormenters. Then Sarah, feeling threatened by the lack of respect shown her by Hagar, Abraham's Egyptian concubine, tortures (*ע-נ-ה*) her. Améry's distinction between mere abuse of power relations and torture (1980, p. 39) caused me to reexamine this seemingly trivial abuse. I realized that here too the bible uses the cognate "*inui*," accentuating the combination of inescapable intentional abuse, by legitimized authority, leading to an outcry. Nachmanides explicitly criminalizes this act. He also introduces bystander accountability, accusing Abraham for letting it occur.[2]

Nachmanides also points out that the biblical story contains a severe, lasting, "eye-for-an-eye" punishment for Sarah's action: "God gave her (Hagar) a savage son (Ismael) to torture the descendants of Abraham and Sarah with all kinds of torture" (Nachmanides, Gen. 16, trans. A. I.). After reading Améry I recognized that Nachmanides was acknowledging not only the long-term impact of this historical event (the common interpretation) but the lasting effects of torture. Améry describes the lasting effects on the tortured individual, and on his interaction with the world:

> *Whoever was tortured, stays tortured. Torture is ineradicably burned into him [...]*

> *It was over for a while. It still is not over. Twenty-two years later I am still dangling over the ground by dislocated arms, panting.* (Améry 1980, pp. 34, 36)

Améry's personal "fear and [...] resentments" "*remain and have scarcely a chance to concentrate into a seething, purifying thirst for revenge*" (Améry 1980, p. 40). In Nachmanides' historiography the results last longer (compare Améry 1980, pp. ix, 78). A seemingly "minor" act of torture is committed by the Jewish people's illustrious ancestors toward a rebellious non-Jew, leading to severe divine punishment—the persecution of Jews by Ishmael's descendants over history.

Reading Améry led to recognizing an aggregation of elements unique to biblical "torture," consistently leading to prohibitions and obligations to prevent. Nachmanides' morally powerful and haunting exegesis added the legitimacy to criminalize torture, and the need to account for torture's lasting effects. These insights offer an alternative framing of Jewish discourse about torture, which can serve as a normative background for the legal discussions. According to this framing torture is a distinct, condemnable, and prohibited act. The memory of being tortured and of being a torturer is embedded in Jewish narrative, raising sensitivity to its unique impacts. This narrative can be, or should be, part of any Jewish debate on torture (on the importance of narrative, compare Améry 1980, pp. xiii–xiv, preface to the first edition, 1966).

7.3 Rereading Foundations of the Torture Debate

In this section I will consider four concepts discussed in the Jewish torture debate to which reading Améry brought new insights: the law of the pursuer (*din rodef*), confessions, corporal punishment and the universality of the prohibition of torture.

7.3.1 Rereading the Law of the Pursuer

The law of pursuer (*rodef*) is an obligation to intervene and prevent murder or rape of another person. If killing the pursuer is the only way to stop the deed, the rule not only allows to do so but commands it. Some use this rule to defend the use of torture in the "ticking bomb" scenario, arguing that if one might kill a pursuer, one can also torture a person who withholds information that is crucial to saving lives (Broyde 2006a, 2006b; Wygoda 2000). Some Jewish law scholars (Broyde 2006b; Bleich 2006) added the argument that potential victims of terrorism expect help, like the rape victim in the original biblical passage.

The *rodef* law sanctions violence in an event of a chaotic nature. Such events are, by definition, fraught with uncertainty and potential misjudgments (compare Bleich 2006 v. Crane 2011). The intervening person might, therefore, without intent, commit a villainous rather than a heroic act.

In order to limit mistakes, the rule includes many caveats. One must intervene only when certain that someone will kill or rape, that the intervention will succeed, that the minimum amount of violence necessary can be determined and not exceeded, and that the need is immediate, and no other means are available. Therefore, justifying torture by state authorities by applying the *rodef* rule is far from simple. Discussing a ticking bomb scenario with even one of the above uncertainties, Warhaftig (2000) holds that Jewish law is not conclusive that the law of *rodef* applies. Wygoda (2000) holds that any of these uncertainties disqualifies physical torture, though he allows for psychological "pressure" (omitting to mention that this amounts at least to prohibited "inhuman and degrading treatment").

Jewish law is clear that any error in judgment renders the hero a well-intended and non-punishable criminal, but a criminal nonetheless (Maimonides, Rotseach Ushmirat Hanefesh, 1; 13). Intervening is a courageous act, as the hero not only faces possible harm from the pursuer but is also subject to subsequent judicial review of his actions, executed in uncertain conditions. The *rodef* rule obligates bystanders to act despite these difficulties, requiring response to the fundamentally important human need for help (Améry 1980, p. 28).

Améry's anguish at the lack of possibility of help made me conscious of the perspective in which the tortured isn't the pursuer, but the victim. The law of the pursuer prescribes the prevention of rape, called *inui*, with any means possible. In Exodus (2: 11–13) Moses prevents the torturing of a slave when he kills the Egyptian, and in a similar vein, implicitly threatens a violent Jew the day after. Torture is an act to be prevented, at great personal and social costs (Simon 2016; compare with Bleich 2006; Crane 2011, p. 483). The "pursuer" in contemporary institutionalized torture isn't the replaceable individual torturer, but the legitimacy of torture. The effective help is "killing" the policy of torture.

7.3.2 Confessions and Coercion: Personality and Truth Under Duress

The assumption that information gleaned through torture can prevent harm and terror is key in defenses of torture. Améry's testimony challenges the claim of torture's utility in securing truthful, useful information. Améry was "guilty" (he resisted the Nazis), yet his torture was futile due to a high level of compartmentation in the resistance. His contemplation on who could and couldn't resist torture accentuates the complexity of utilitarian torture (Améry 1980, pp. 36–38). Torture is useless when the victim has no information, or when he has but can resist. Torture is harmful if the victim provides wrong information, whether to escape pain or purposefully mislead. According to Améry the futility or utility of torture depends on unpredictable personal characteristics and situational circumstances, precluding simple ex-ante utilitarian justification of torture.

This complexity invites a rereading of the inherent tension in Jewish law. Jewish classic criminal procedure prohibits any use of confessions, whether coerced or voluntary, even from righteous, truth-speaking, people. According to Kirschenbaum, this creates a system-wide distrust of confessions and a disincentive for torture; He argues that as a result, punitive spectacles were rare in Jewish penology, as was the use of physical coercion to leverage political, interrogative, or judicial goals. He further concludes that even in interrogations where rabbis were inclined to accept a coerced confession, the law prohibiting confessions had a restraining impact (Kirschenbaum 1991, 2005; BT Hulin 141b; Kiddushin 12; Shvuot 41).

In practice, communities used physical coercion and rabbis debated the admissibility of confessions given under duress.[3] The position that such admissions should be accepted as truthful is supported by the rule that allows the enforcement of compliance to religious law using physical duress (*Kofin al HaMitsvot*—BT Ktubot 86a; Shochatman 2008). The classic case is of a man who refuses to abide by a rabbinic court ruling to willfully divorce his wife. Maimonides rules that the husband should be flogged "until he says: 'I want to (divorce her)'" (Maimonides, Gerushin, 2, 20). By validating the husband's declaration of wanting a divorce, Maimonides rules that the recalcitrant husband retains his free will under physical duress. This supports the notion that confessions under duress could be truthful.

7.3.3 Corporal Punishment

Rereading the complex laws on flogging, following Améry, revealed approaches to pain, the mind-body interface and authority in Jewish jurisprudence, even though flogging is not torture, as punishment has explicitly been excepted from the CAT convention (UN, Art. 1).

7.3.3.1 The Twisted Logic of the Positive Approach to Corporal Punishment

Many Jewish sources portray pain, inflicted by authority, as necessary and positive. Jewish penology uses pain and shame to punish disobedience and to physically coerce obedience. Flogging is an educational rehabilitation technique, using pain and shame (Kirschenbaum 2013, Chap. 13). Capital punishment, where no rehabilitation is intended, was designed by the rabbis to limit the duration and extent of pain, and limit disfiguring of the body—"choose for him a 'good' death" (BT, Sanhedrin 45A; Kirschenbaum 2013).[4]

Recognizing hazards in using corporal punishment, rabbinic law set out to control and monitor the severity of the pain and for how long it could be inflicted. Punishments are carried out in the presence of judges, and the number of lashes is predetermined, restricted to the perceived ability of the accused, not to exceed 39. Designed to wound the skin and flesh, not the bones, the punishment explicitly seeks to return the reformed convict to society as quick as possible, with a structured reintegration process.

Améry treated religiously based torture, in which the tortured and the torturer share the belief in the punishment, as being just and effective in principle: Pain has meaning, since it is theoretically accepted voluntarily.

> *Theological complicity [...] in the Inquisition joined both sides; faith united them even in the delight of tormenting and the pain of being tormented. The torturer believed he was exercising God's justice, since he was, after all, purifying the offender's soul; the tortured heretic or witch did not at all deny him this right. There was a horrible and perverted togetherness.* (Améry 1980, p. 34)

In Jewish law, corporal punishment is couched in a similar cultural construction of shared belief in a common system. The punishment was restricted to offenses in which the perpetrator publicly and voluntarily accepted liability for the offense and accepted the punishment before committing the deed (Kirschenbaum 2013, pp. 341–438). One can easily escape corporal punishment by not accepting the punishment upon oneself before committing the offense. The lashing is thus reserved for those who want atonement and identify with the system. In such situations (which were very rare), the chance of the punished individual to maintain his dignity and free will is higher (see Sect. 7.3.1).

7.3.3.2 Torture Beyond Pain: The Mental Transformations

Améry reminds us that even for a perpetrator seeking atonement through pain, wanting or expecting pain can never prepare a person from the terror of the torture.

> *I thought there could be nothing new for me in this area. [...] Prison, interrogation, blows, torture; [...] Thus it was written and thus it would happen. [...] Only in rare moments of life do we truly stand face to face with the event and, with it, reality.* (Améry 1980, pp. 25–29)

Indeed, the presumed rehabilitative power of flogging doesn't depend only on the deterrent effect of agonizing pain and its powerful memory. No less important are the mental transformations inherent in the experience of unescapable pain and lack of control over the body (Crane 2011, pp. 474, 493). Améry describes:

> *Only in torture does the transformation of the person into flesh become complete. Frail in the face of violence, yelling out in pain, awaiting no help, capable of no resistance, the tortured person is only a body, and nothing else. [...] the more hopelessly man's body is subjected to suffering, the more physical he is, then of all physical celebrations torture is the most terrible.* (Améry 1980, pp. 27, 33)

It is this transformation that leaves its lasting impression, with the accompanying shame and humiliation (the Hebrew word *Nikla*), more than the pain and wounds. This is incomprehensible from afar, but "*for the person who suffers them they are still experiences that leave deep marks*" (Améry 1980, p. 27).

Jewish corporal punishment isn't bent on pain but on the transformation. It dictates that if the convict soils himself by urinating or excreting on himself, even after only one lash, the punishment is fulfilled (Deut. 25:3; Mishnah Makkot 3:14; Maimonides, Sanhedrin 17), no more infliction of pain is allowed. An intervention of law and courts stops subsequent lashes, reconstructing the experience of painful humiliating violation into the realm of lawful, limited, controlled, and rehabilitation-directed punishment.

7.3.3.3 Rehabilitation

Jewish law recognizes the hazard of experiencing a total irrevocable alienation from society and distrust of its institutions. The verse links the humiliating transformation "*nikla*" to the command to see the punished person "as your brother," immediately after the lashing is over. The duty to rebuild the lost trust, a concept completely foreign to the logic of torture, rests on the community, because for the condemned:

> *[I]f from the experience of torture any knowledge at all remains that goes beyond the plain nightmarish, it is that of a great amazement and a foreignness in the world that cannot be compensated by any sort of subsequent human communication.* (Améry 1980, p. 39)

As opposed to the torture described by Améry, the controlling mechanisms of flogging as designed by the rabbis keeps the experience within ("civilized") society, and limits the adverse effects of full-fledged torture:

> *With the first blow from a policeman's fist [...] which no helping hand will ward off, a part of our life ends and it can never again be revived.* (Améry 1980, p. 29)

This is the difference between torture and punishment, the latter reduces the loss of trust. Still, any rehabilitation can only start from others seeing the convict as "brother," not "other."

7.3.3.4 Between Legitimate Punishment and Criminalized Torture

The Jewish prohibition on interpersonal violence is learned by *a fortiori* from a peculiar law regarding flogging. Even though the flogging is carried out by a public servant obeying a legitimate court of law in punishing a guilty criminal, an explicit law prohibits any excess. If the stipulated punishment is exceeded by even one lash, the person carrying it out is liable to be subject to flogging himself, as a criminal (Lichtenstein 1998). Combining the law of pursuer with this criminalization of excessive use of force crystalizes two important insights that make it very difficult to justify torture. These insights crystallized only after linking Améry's contemplations to the law of the pursuer.

First, in extreme perceived need like the "ticking bomb" scenario, some rabbis permit require or excuse torture. Wygoda (2000) argues that this is based on the private obligation of *rodef*. Namely: if a private citizen can or should torture to save people, then *a fortiori*, members of the security forces can and should do so. However, the *a fortiori* argument does not hold due to two mitigating considerations: the protective role of security forces vis-à-vis all civilians (Crane 2011, p. 501) and the greater tendency of officials to excessive violence (Améry 1980, pp. 30–32, 35, 39–40). These are both reasons to prohibit torture that do not hold for individuals.

Second, Wygoda concurs with the Israeli attorney-general, who published ex-ante guidelines defining conditions and organizational procedure for justification of torturous "special measures" ex-ante. This profoundly changes the reality of torture in Israel, creating some inescapable torture that is condoned by the state—those who torture aren't accountable but are commended for their "by-the-book" actions (Améry 1980, pp. 30–31, 34–36). Wygoda's reliance on the law of the pursuer in this argument doesn't hold. In Jewish law, the act of every *rodef* and his perception of reality are to be scrutinized by a rabbinical court. Due to the severity of allowing killing to save, together with the chaotic circumstances discussed earlier, internalization of risk is very important. The ex-post judgment serves as a threat, making the ex-ante choice more difficult and responsible. If one is sure that his unlawful actions are justified, he should be prepared to personally account for his actions and bear the risk of being wrong. Benvenisti (1997, pp. 610–611) argues convincingly that this judicial accounting should always be done retrospectively, not through ex-ante systemic decisions (Compare Warhaftig 2000; Bleich 2006; Crane 2011, pp. 482–483). Israeli law could also consider adopting the criminalization of the mistaken pursuer-torturer, without requiring (the full) punishment (see Sect. 7.3.1), like senator McCain suggested that American officials be held accountable for torture, without punishing them (Welch 2018).

7.3.4 *Categorical and Universal Prohibition*

The biblical God hears the cry of all oppressed, weak people, who are exploited by those in power—not just Jewish victims and victims of Jewish perpetrators (see, e.g., Gen. 18:21; Amos Chap. 2). As Prof. Rabbi Isaac Breuer said, the biblical Jewish god is universal, requiring a universal response to human cries (Israel-Vleeschhouwer 2016b, p. 12). The biblical god's vows for retribution against abusing kings and strongmen echo

Améry universalist rage—*"Hear O World" is requesting to burst from me in rage* (Améry 1980, p. 100).

The preamble of the CAT convention (UN 1984) evokes the universalist "equal and inalienable rights of all members of the human family" derived "from the inherent dignity of the human person." These principles, far from being redundant or ceremonial, preempt an us-them normative paradigm (Berreby 2008). The temptation to use torture arises in its strongest form when seemingly inhuman and easily demonized "others" hurt cherished in-group members. Améry's urgent universalist need for social reform and his existential sensitivity to injustice is based on the six-digit number on his forearm. Trust in humanity and society requires the categorical and non-conditional prohibition of torture, based on an appreciation for human dignity, limitation of institutional abuse of power and recognition of the unique harm of torture. It does not allow for a local prohibition, while allowing torture by proxy abroad, as the CIA did (US senate 2014). It does not allow the torture of "others," while prohibiting torturing people from your in-group (compare Bleich 2006, discussed in Crane 2011, p. 481). Rabbi HaCohen of Gerba, Tunisia; Rabbi Haim Halevi of Tel Aviv, ultra-Orthodox Rabbi Dr. Isaac Breuer and other rabbis have argued that only universal international law can stop atrocities in war (Israel-Vleeschhouwer 2012, part I). The same holds for international crimes, like torture.

None of the four legal interpretations offered in this section is a game breaker in the tension between the opposing positions in Jewish law. However, the impact of reading Améry accentuated considerations in the legal debates, shed new perspectives on legal sources and legitimized important interpretational options. There also seems to be some congruence between the two last sections, revealing narrative foundations of legal insights and legal expressions of cultural fundamentals.

7.4 War and Necessity and the Utilitarian Debate

Rabbi Prof. Broyde (2006a) argues that the state of emergency in war supersedes certain regular laws.[5] Goals such as victory in a just war and protecting civilians (and combatants) justify acts otherwise abhorred, like killing and according to him—torture. The Israeli Supreme Court ruled that although torture is totally and categorically prohibited, the defense of necessity may be invoked when relevant (HCJ 1999; see Ballas 2019). Article 2 of the anti-torture convention flatly rejects such justification of torture: "No exceptional circumstances whatsoever, whether a state of war or a threat of war, internal political instability or any other public emergency, may be invoked as a justification of torture" (CAT, Art. 2(2), emphasis mine, A.I.).

7.4.1 *Short-Term Versus Long-Term Framing*

While in concrete cases some argue for torture's ad hoc utility, it seems that using torture as policy is ineffective (US senate 2014; Welch 2018). Restrictions on torture in Britain and Israel arguably had no notable long-term adverse effects on national security. Security services who testified under oath that torture was indispensable, found other legal ways to fulfill their mission to protect. True, when torture is permitted, hopefully very restrictedly, some lives, pain and anguish may be spared, which would maybe be endangered in a regime where no torture is allowed. However, the opposite may also come to pass: backlash may occur in the form of revenge and the reduced chance for reconciliation, such that where torture is not allowed, more lives might be saved in the long run.

The costs of torture are far-reaching. Torture has a lasting effect on the relationship between the tortured human, the torturing authorities and the society in which it was perpetrated (Améry 1980, "Resentment," pp. 62–81). Reading Améry and Nachmanides emphasizes that torture doesn't stay in the torture rooms, but continues to reverberate, with potential negative impacts on institutions of authority, the society, and its individual members. Warhaftig (2000) discusses the corrupting dangers of spillover, from the torturing of "others" to torturing of citizens, and from use in extreme cases only, to broader applications (see also Lichtenstein 1998).

7.4.2 *Beyond Simple Utility: Who We Are and What Are We Willing to Pay for It*

Even assuming a "net" efficacy, where the total costs would be "worth" the benefit torture brings, this kind of "utility" is a narrow framing, as one should consider the utility of the costs and benefits according to their worth in the relevant culture and human preferences.

Counterintuitively, the exceptional nature of war and emergencies can justify the categorical prohibition of torture. Exceptional conditions like war, justify sacrifice and suffering for national and cultural values and interests. For example, America made grave sacrifices to eradicate slavery;

America's and England's decision to fight evil in World War II (WWII) came at a great compromise to the immediate well-being of soldiers and civilians.

In Jewish law, there are goals deemed worthy enough to justify or even require the sacrificing of life—saving other people's lives, not committing hideous acts like raping your mother (or idolatry), fighting for the existence of your people and sanctifying god's name. Martyrdom to sanctify God's name and preserving God's image (tselem Elohim), are considered worthy goals justifying endangering human lives (Israel-Vleeschhouwer 2014). If one could justify going to war (with its costs) to eradicate torture, a government could legitimately consider prohibiting torture and bearing the possible non-negligible and even terrible costs of this decision.[6]

This choice is arguably equivalent to preferring institutional integrity and justice over innocent lives and prevention of suffering. This exact preference is evident in Maimonides' rejection of circumstantial evidence in criminal procedures, arguing: "It is better and more moral to release/acquit a thousand criminals, than [the possibility that we may] one day kill a single innocent person" (Book of Commandments, prohibition 290). Releasing 999 criminals into society has severe potential costs in terms of human suffering and innocent lives, but Maimonides prefers a perfect record of zero false convictions. He acknowledges that this policy choice may be perceived as "cruel," but holds that just institutions are worth the price. Rather than getting dragged into individual cases, where judges would find it difficult to set a suspect free because the evidence was "only" circumstantial, Maimonides takes the long view of preferring the policy that better preserves the integrity of the courts.[7]

A comment within the utilitarian analysis: Broyde (2006b) argues that because killing is allowed in war, even required—permitting killing *a fortiori* allows the lesser evil of torture. This *a fortiori* reasoning is flawed. Jewish law recognizes that those tortured might rationally seek death (BT Ketuboth 33). Similarly, international law categorically prohibits torture, while accepting the legitimacy of killing in war and self-defense. This is of course clear to readers of Améry (1980, e.g., pp. 22, 34, 36).

7.5 Conclusion: An Urgent Call for Action

People are conditioned to believe in the justification of their behavior (Feldman 2018), including the evidence supporting their approach to torture. Executors of state violence see themselves—and are seen by members of society—as heroes in the war against crime and terrorism, invested in protecting civilians and public safety.

Religion can be a detrimental factor, dehumanizing "others," exempting religiously justified actions by special "chosen" people and by framing the violence as a divinely justified retaliation (Warhaftig 2000; compare Kahn 2008; Lincoln 2010). Religious beliefs can demand resilience to suffering, especially of "others," and even endorse rejoicing in committing atrocities (Israel-Vleeschhouwer 2014, Chap. 3a; compare Améry 1980, pp. 31–33).[8]

Considering past religious acceptance of torture (Crane 2011), an explicit religious prohibition is important. However, Jewish law seems to be reluctant to religiously criminalize formerly condoned behaviors, like rape, genocide (Israel-Vleeschhouwer 2016a), or torture. Other religions and some states, including Israel, are also reluctant to follow through. This article attempts to influence the Jewish religious discourse about torture, not by discovering neglected sources or by introducing new values or norms.

Améry's combination of personal testimony with conscious and far-reaching contemplations can place policymakers in the shoes of potential torture-victims in a very alert and reflective state. This experience won't necessarily change their previous knowledge, convictions, and ideology but will rarely leave them untouched. At least, reading Améry impresses vivid images of the atrocity of torture into the reader's cognition. These images can offset the impact of competing vivid images, social pressures and norms that serve to endorse torture (Israel-Vleeschhouwer 2016c).

Finally, reading Améry moves the debate from theory to practice and from the philosophical, historical, and literary spheres to the legal and political ones. Realizing that *somewhere, someone is crying out under torture. Perhaps in this hour, this second* (Améry 1980, p. 24), injects urgency into the need to discuss our policy and awakens the passion to change it (ibid., xi). We owe it to the victims of torture; we owe it to ourselves.

Notes

1. Linking the prohibition in Exodus against abusing the *ger* (stranger/other, also: convert) to Egyptians' torture of Israelites, positions the injunction against torture as a universal prohibition. The historical link also delegitimizes the justification of torturous oppression by supposed subversive actions, because the Egyptians justified the oppressive security measures by casting the Jews as a potential threat (Ex. 1).
2. Nachmanides criminalizes an act by culturally august figures, despite the matriarch's status and Sarah's ready excuse, the need to protect her position.

The act is also is divinely sanctioned, since the angel commands Hagar to return to her "mistress and be tortured under her hands" (Gen. 16: 9).

3. A de jure prohibition of torture could enable and even facilitate the de facto use of excessive violence, whenever those in power wanted. Brundage (2018) documents this duality in the history of the United States, while Améry (1980, pp. 22–24) argued this is true for almost all states and societies.
4. One exception is a rabbinic form of extremely painful execution called "*kipa*" (BT Sanhedrin 71; Crane 2011, p. 491).
5. The extreme version of this argument—namely, the total suspension of law in state of emergency (Schmitt 1998)—is untenable from a Jewish legal perspective, certainly since WWII, and is not held by Broyde (see 2006b, p. 4).
6. Often, society is selective regarding what values merit inordinate efforts to save lives. In Israel, deaths from terrorism are significantly less than from car accidents, lack of preventive medicine or even accidents at workplaces (Israel-Vleeschhouwer 1998). Saving lives should be a systemic policy, not a single-agenda justification.
7. Under the Jewish Laws of Kings or the ancient rabbinical court's emergency powers, torture was a legitimate practice in Jewish history (Kirschenbaum 1991, 2013; Crane 2011). However, these practices have no normative power (Kirschenbaum 2013; Israel-Vleeschhouwer 2014).
8. Police officers tend to justify violence against certain groups or kinds of people as part of their profession (Wahl 2017, Chap. 2, 5). Carver and Handley (2016) stress that it is actual practice in police stations and detention centers that matters, not ratified treaties or laws in books (even religious ones), which only have minor effect on practice.

References

Améry, J. (1980). *At the Mind's Limits: Contemplations by a Survivor on Auschwitz and Its Realities* (S. Rosenfeld & S. P. Rosenfeld, Trans.). Bloomington: Indiana University Press.

Ballas, I. (2019). Fracturing the "Exception": The Legal Sanctioning of Violent Interrogation Methods in Israel Since 1987. *Law and Social Inquiry.* Forthcoming.

Benvenisti, E. (1997). The Role of National Courts in Preventing Torture of Suspected Terrorists. *European Journal of International Law, 8*, 596–612.

Berreby, D. (2008). *Us and Them: The Science of Identity.* Chicago: University of Chicago Press.

Biale, D. (1986). *Power and Powerlessness in Jewish History.* New York: Schoken Books.

Bleich, D. J. (2006). Survey of Recent Halachic Literature: Torture and the Ticking Bomb. *Tradition, 39*, 89–121.

Broyde, M. J. (2006a, July 7). Jewish Law and Torture. *N.Y. Jewish Week*. Retrieved from http://www.broydeblog.net/uploads/8/0/4/0/80408218/jewish_law_and_torture.pdf.

Broyde, M. J. (2006b). Only the Good Die Young? *Meorot*, 6/1 (Shevat 5767), 19. Retrieved from http://www.edah.org/backend/JournalArticle/Conversation%20-%20Final.pdf.

Broyde, M. J. (2007). Just Wars, Just Battles and Just Conduct in Jewish Law: Jewish Law Is Not a Suicide Pact! In L. Schiffman & J. B. Wolowelsky (Eds.), *War and Peace in the Jewish Tradition* (pp. 1–44). New York: Yeshiva University Press.

Brundage, W. F. (2018). *Civilizing Torture: An American Tradition*. Boston: Harvard University Press.

Carver, R., & Handley, L. (2016). *Does Torture Prevention Work?* Liverpool: Liverpool University Press.

Cover, R. (1983). The Supreme Court, 1982 Term – Foreword: Nomos and Narrative. *Harvard Law Review, 97*, 4–68.

Crane, J. K. (2011). Torture: Judaic Twists. *Journal of Law and Religion, 26*, 469–504.

Feldman, Y. (2018). *The Law of Good People*. Cambridge: Cambridge University Press.

Habermas, J. (2005). Religion in the Public Sphere. *Philosophia Africana, 8*(2), 99–109.

Harrison B. W. (2005). *Torture and Corporal Punishment as a Problem in Catholic Theology*. Retrieved from http://www.rtforum.org/lt/lt119.html.

HCJ. (1999). HCJ 5100/94, *Public Committee Against Torture in Israel* V. Government. Retrieved November 10, 2018, from http://elyon1.court.gov.il/files/94/000/051/09a/94051000.09a.htm, decided September 6, 1999. Translation: http://versa.cardozo.yu.edu/opinions/public-committee-against-torture-v-israel.

Henkin, Y. H. (2000). Hearot al HaHalacha VeHaMetoda HaAkademit, Al A, Ravitski, Harut Al HaLuhot. On Jewish law and the Academic Method. *Akdamot*, 8, 179–182 (Hebrew).

Israel-Vleeschhouwer, A. (1998). *Fear from Terrorism: Social Identity as a Mediating Factor*. MA thesis, Department of Psychology, Tel Aviv University (not published, on file with author).

Israel-Vleeschhouwer, A. (2012). *The Attitudes of Jewish Law Towards International Law: An Analysis of Jewish Legal Materials and Processes*. PhD dissertation, Tel Aviv University (not published, on file with author).

Israel-Vleeschhouwer, A. (2014). Endangering Soldiers and Protecting Innocents in Battle: An Analysis of Jewish Legal Attitudes and a Process Oriented View. *Law and Business, 17*, 605–662.

Israel-Vleeschhouwer, A. (2016a). Introducing *Jews' Laws* Through the Study of Genocide and Rape. *Jewish Law Association Studies, 26*, 70–108.

Israel-Vleeschhouwer, A. (2016b). The Mandate System as a Messianic Alternative in the Ultra-Religious Jurisprudence of Rabbi Dr. Isaac Breuer. *Israel Law Review, 49*(3), 339–363.

Israel-Vleeschhouwer, A. (2016c). Psikat Halacha (Jewish Legal Decision Making) as a Cognitive Event. In A. Roznak (Ed.), *Halakha as an Event* (pp. 96–133). Jerusalem: Magnes Press, Van Leer Institute. (Hebrew).

Kahn, P. W. (2008). *Sacred Violence: Torture, Terror, and Sovereignty*. Ann Arbor: University of Michigan Press.

Kirschenbaum, A. (1991). *Torture, Confession and the American Plea-Bargaining: A Jewish Legal Perspective*. Cincinnati, OH: University Cincinnati Judaic Studies Program.

Kirschenbaum, A. (2005). *Harsha'a Atsmit BaMishpat HaIvri*. Self-Incrimination in Jewish Law, Hebrew. Jerusalem: Magness Press.

Kirschenbaum, A. (2013). *Beit Din Makin VeOnshin: Ha'anisha HaPlilit BeAm Yisrael – Torata VeToldoteha*. Jewish Penology, Hebrew. Jerusalem: Magness Press.

Lichtenstein, A. (1998). Lo Yosif. *Ki Tetse*. Retrieved November 10, 2018, from https://www.etzion.org.il/he/%D7%9C%D7%90%D7%99%D7%95%D7%A1%D7%99%D7%A3 (Hebrew).

Lincoln, B. (2010). *Religion, Empire, and Torture: The Case of Achaemenian Persia, with a Postscript on Abu Ghraib*. Chicago: University of Chicago Press.

Nowak, M. (2017). Powerlessness as a Defining Characteristic of Torture: Comments on Basoglus Definition of Torture in US Law. In M. Başoğlu (Ed.), *Torture and Its Definition In International Law: An Interdisciplinary Approach* (pp. 433–444). Oxford: Oxford University Press.

Rechnitz, I. (2016). Torturing Suspects in Jewish law. *Makor Rishon*, Shabbat section, 1.1.2006. Retrieved from https://musaf-shabbat.com/2016/01/01/%D7%A2%D7%99%D7%A0%D7%95%D7%99-%D7%97%D7%A9%D7%95%D7%93%D7%99%D7%9D-%D7%91%D7%9E%D7%A9%D7%A4%D7%98-,%D7%94%D7%A2%D7%91%D7%A8%D7%99-%D7%A2%D7%99%D7%93%D7%95-%D7%A8%D7%9B%D7%A0%D7%99%D7%A5/ [Inui Hashudim BePehsa, *Tehumin* 36, 371–380].

Reza, S. (2007). Torture and Islamic Law. *Chicago Journal of International Law, 8*, 21–41. Retrieved from http://chicagounbound.uchicago.edu/cjil/vol8/iss1/4.

Salcioglu, E. & Başoğlu, M. (2017). Domestic Violence and Torture: A Theoretical and Empirical Comparison. In M. Başoğlu (Ed.), *Torture and Its Definition in International Law: An Interdisciplinary Approach* (pp. 107–138). Oxford: Oxford University Press.

Schmitt, C. (1998). *Political Theology: Four Chapters on the Concept of Sovereignty* (G. Schwab, Trans.). Cambridge, MA: MIT Press.

Shochatman, E. (2008). Al HaKefia LeKayem Mitsvot, 311 Weekly Parasha: Yitro. Retrieved from http://www.daat.ac.il/mishpat-ivri/skirot/311-2.htm (Hebrew).

Simon, T. W. (2016). *Genocide, Torture, and Terrorism: Ranking International Crimes and Justifying Humanitarian Intervention.* London: Palgrave Macmillan.

UN, United Nations. (1984). Convention Against Torture and Other Cruel, Inhuman or Degrading Treatment or Punishment. G.A. Res. 39/46, Annex, 39 U.N. GAOR Supp. No. 51, U.N. Doc. A/39/51.

Unger, Y. (2004). Zchut Hashtika. The Right to Remain Silent. *Techumin, 24,* 22–36 (Hebrew).

US Senate. (2014, December 9). *Committee Study of the Central Intelligence Agency's Detention and Interrogation Program together with Foreword by Chairman Feinstein and Additional and Minority Views.* S. Rpt. 113–288. Retrieved from https://www.intelligence.senate.gov/sites/default/files/documents/CRPT-113srpt288.pdf.

Wahl, R. (2017). *Just Violence: Torture and Human Rights in the Eyes of the Police.* Stanford: Stanford University Press.

Warhaftig, I. (2000). Hakirot HashaBak LeOr HaHalacha. *Tehumin, 20,* 145–150.

Welch, M. (2018, August 27). What John McCain Taught Us About Torture. *NY Times.* Retrieved from https://www.nytimes.com/2018/08/27/opinion/john-mccain-torture-.html.

Wygoda, M. (2000). Hakirot HashaBak Mekorot Hamashpat HaIvri, Opinion of Head of Jewish Law Department, Ministry of Justice. Retrieved from www.Justice.gov.il/MOJHeb/MishpatIvri/HavotDaat (Heb.).

Zakheim, D. S. (2007). Confronting Evil: Terrorists, Torture, the Military and Halakhah, *Meorot,* 6/1. Retrieved from https://library.yctorah.org/files/2016/07/zakheim_-_final.pdf.

CHAPTER 8

Total Destruction: The Case of Jean Améry

Yochai Ataria

8.1 Introduction

The term torture requires no introduction. However, for the purpose of clarity, it can be defined as a process during which one human being uses various physical and/or mental techniques to break another. This definition applies even if some define torture as a radical interrogation technique which is utilized to acquire intelligence in "justifiable" cases.[1] The techniques employed during torture are well known. Furthermore, it is quite obvious that, at the end of this process, most tortured individuals will break down. In a theoretical sense, then, there is nothing surprising about this process; we know everything there is to know. However, once this knowledge ceases to be theoretical and becomes knowledge-in-the-flesh, we are completely shocked and stunned—nothing in a person's previous life can serve as preparation for this situation:

> Nothing really happens as we hope it will, nor as we fear it will. But not because the occurrence, as one says, perhaps "goes beyond the imagination" (it is not a quantitative question), but *because it is reality and not phantasy.* (Améry 1980, pp. 25–26, emphasis added)

I would like to thank Shaun Gallagher and Eli Pitcovski for their helpful comments on earlier drafts.

Y. Ataria (✉)
Tel-Hai Academic College, Upper Galilee, Israel

Y. Ataria et al. (eds.), *Jean Améry*,
https://doi.org/10.1007/978-3-030-28095-6_8

This paper suggests that, as Jean Améry argued based on his own experience, torture is indeed "the most horrible event a human being can retain within himself" (p. 22). Further, it attempts to pin down this notion by demonstrating that torture breaks the most basic structure of the human being. Considering Améry's own words, this breakdown can be explicated in terms of the following five phenomena (presented in greater detail below, in this order):

(a) Torture can lead to a severe sense of helplessness which, in extreme cases, may develop into an *existential consummation of total destruction*.
(b) It reduces a person to the body-as-object and, eventually, to pure pain. The individual eventually identifies the body, rather than the torturer, as the source of pain and suffering: this leads, in radical instances, to attempts to dispose of one's own body.
(c) It can result in the collapse of the shared social world.
(d) Extended torture causes the victim to accept the logic of the oppressor, who holds all the power. Tragically, the tortured individual subsequently internalizes this logic, feeling obliged to follow through with it—even after the torture has ceased. In that sense, torture does not end until the tortured victim *finishes the job*.
(e) Finally, during torture the sense of trust in the world collapses; in turn, the victim loses any ability to feel *at-home* within the world.

8.2 Helplessness

From the very first blow, the prisoner realizes that he[2] is totally and absolutely helpless: "The first blow brings home to the prisoner that he is helpless, and thus it already contains in the bud everything that is to come" (Améry 1980, p. 27). This first blow profoundly changes the tortured person's field of possibilities—torture is no longer something that *might happen* but rather becomes the only possible reality, the only thing about which one can be certain: "Upon the first blow they are anticipated as real possibilities, yes, as certainties" (p. 27). Let us elaborate on this notion further, with the first blow, the sense of possessing various kinds of possibilities (and possibilities for possibilities) collapses into one determinative reality. In this new situation, one can no longer be-in-the-world; rather, one is being-tortured and, eventually, not only the world vanishes but the very possibility of just "being" collapses altogether. Therefore, only torture remains: "You could be hungry, be tired, be sick. *To say that one purely and simply is, made no sense.* And existence as such, to top it off, became definitively a totally abstract and thus empty concept" (pp. 18–19, emphasis added).

Once torture begins, one no longer possesses one's own life: "They are permitted to punch me in the face, the victim feels in numb surprise and concludes in just as numb certainty: *they will do with me what they want*" (p. 27, emphasis added). The tortured person is completely alone in this situation, knowing that no one will come to his rescue: "Whoever would rush to the prisoner's aid—a wife, a mother, a brother, or friend—he won't get this far" (p. 27). Under these conditions, it is clear why torture and isolation lead to a sense of helplessness.

The Merriam-Webster dictionary defines helplessness as a situation in which one is incapable of defense. Similarly, the Cambridge English Dictionary characterizes helplessness as being "unable to do anything to help your[one]self or anyone else." Other dictionaries define this as a feeling of being "powerless or incompetent" or "deprived of strength or power; powerless; incapacitated." In addition, in such circumstances the individual finds it "impossible to control." However, the sense of helplessness can also be understood in terms of radical changes in one's field of affordances.

According to Gibson (1979), the notion of affordance refers to an ecological relation between the animal and the environment: affordances are "properties of the environment relative to an animal" (Gibson 1982, pp. 403–404) Affordance can also be described in terms of potential for action: "Different layouts afford different behaviors for different animals, and different mechanical encounters" (Gibson 1979, p. 128). Gallagher and Lindgren (2015) maintain that "we perceive the world in terms of what we can do, that is, in terms of its pragmatic meaning" (p. 393). When we perceive something, we perceive it as actionable even if we are not planning to take action (Merleau-Ponty 1968). Note, however, that for Gibson (1979) affordance cannot be reduced merely to perception. Rather, it is a concept that refers to "the whole spectrum of social significance" (p. 128).

In our daily life, we feel *at-home* within the world: we feel that we belong to the world. In terms of affordance, this feeling of belonging is the sense that things are within our reach—we can act in the world in order to change the situation, or, better put, our situation, at least to some degree. To feel *at-home*, then, is to *know-how* to act in the world (pre-reflectively) in order to achieve our goals. This sense of *knowing-how* is so basic that in our daily life we simply do not have the ability to grasp it (Dreyfus 2017): the *knowing-how* is part of the intentional structure and hence cannot be perceived directly like any other object. Indeed, as long as one *knows-how*, one forgets oneself within the world. For instance, while writing this text my fingers and the keyboard are (almost completely) forgotten in favor of the actual text. Ideas simply appear in front of me on the screen, yet my body, the chair I am sitting on, the keyboard, even the screen and the words, are all in the background. Likewise, in order for a pianist to play well she must forget not only her hands but also the piano. When the writing or playing is fluent, the world, or my world, is charged with meaning—once again, this is simply because I *know-how* to manipulate, pre-reflectively, the environment in which I am absorbed (Dreyfus 1992). Essentially, in this situation one is being held by the world (Heidegger 1996). To feel at-home within the world, then, is to be absorbed within a world which is already full of meaning (Dreyfus 1991), one in which each sign is part of a whole structure that can be defined as a referential totality (Dreyfus 2017). When one is thrown out of the world, one is no longer part of this referential totality and hence signs become meaningless—"I staggered through a world whose signs remained as inscrutable to me as Etruscan script" (Améry 1980, p. 47).

With this in mind, we may say that during torture the victim develops a sense of nonbelonging to the world so that the range of possibilities decreases and the pragmatic phenomenal field of affordances representing the I-Can shrinks. This results in a feeling that almost everything is beyond the victim's reach (Arieli and Ataria 2018). The phenomenal field becomes an I-Can-Not kind of field and the world no longer calls for actions—what was once part of the field of affordances is now unreachable; the world of the living becomes inaccessible and unapproachable (Ataria 2019a).

Using the notion of affordance to describe the sense of helplessness enables us to redefine torture as a situation in *which the world is no longer within our reach*—one in which the *knowing-how* structure has collapsed (Arieli and Ataria 2018; Ataria 2015b, 2018). In terms of perception, we may say that a world that is not within reach is a disorganized world, one in which our expectations are repeatedly unfulfilled: "There was no order for me in this world" (Améry 1980, p. 47).

The story, however, does not end here. Helplessness is not a yes/no phenomenon but rather can be located on a spectrum. During torture, the sense of helplessness escalates to the extreme, at which point, as Améry suggests, total helplessness leads to total destruction: "If no help can be expected, this physical overwhelming by the other then becomes an *existential consummation of destruction altogether*" (p. 28, emphasis added).

8.3 Body = Pain = Death

This destruction can be understood in terms of the body. A phenomenological investigation of the body reveals that "there are two extreme poles between which my attitude towards the body oscillates: total separation, on the one hand, and total immersion, on the other" (Dorfman 2014, p. 69). While at the pole of total separation the body becomes "a thing in the world: an external and rather hostile object," at the other extreme of total immersion, "Objectivity disappears and I feel an inseparable and mutual belonging between myself and my body, as well as between my body and the world" (Dorfman 2014, p. 69). Essentially, whereas in the first case the body-as-object shapes the structure of our experience—one feels dissociated from the world—in the second case, the body-as-subject shapes the structure of our experience—one feels more unified with the world (Ratcliffe 2015). This notion can be further developed. Ordinarily, the body-as-subject and the body-as-object are in steady equilibrium. Any change in this equilibrium marks a change in our way of being-in-the-world: this "appears as an object of conscious attention, particularly when it is inadequate for a task to be performed, be it by a lack of capacity, fatigue, illness or numbness, and whenever it becomes an object for others to whom I feel exposed." Under such circumstances, the lived-body ceases to be implicit; instead, "[T]he body's performance is made explicit and may often be disturbed" (Fuchs and Schlimme 2009, p. 571).

In light of this, we may say that when one's field of affordance shrinks and becomes an I-Cannot kind of field, the equilibrium between the body-as-object and the body-as-subject tends toward the former. Ratcliffe (2008) stresses that "when one feels 'at home' in the world, 'absorbed' in it or 'at one with life,' the body often drifts into the background" (p. 113). Yet, when we can no longer feel at-home within the world, the entire body becomes increasingly salient: "The body is no longer a medium of experience and activity, an opening onto a significant world filled with potential activities." Instead, "[I]t is thing-like, conspicuous, an object... an entity to be acted upon" (ibid.). For instance, "[A]t times of illness one may experience one's body as more or less 'unuseable.' It can no longer do what it once could." Hence, "[T]he sick body may be experienced as that which 'stands in the way,' an obstinate force interfering with our project" (Leder 1990, p. 84). When the body becomes an obstacle, the equilibrium between the lived-subjective body and the dead-objective body is disrupted, tipping toward the body-as-object.

The life of the tortured individual is reduced not merely to the body-as-object but specifically to one point of maximum pain. During this process, one dwindles to a singular point of pure suffering. This singular point is not abstract but rather manifests itself in a certain location in the body:

> In the bunker there hung from the vaulted ceiling a chain that above ran into a roll. At its bottom end it bore a heavy, broadly curved iron hook. I was led to the instrument. The hook gripped into the shackle that held my hands together behind my back. Then I was raised with the chain until I hung about a meter over the floor. In such a position, or rather, when hanging this way, with your hands behind your back, for a short time you can hold at a half-oblique through muscular force.... *All your life is gathered in a single, limited area of the body*, the shoulder joints, and it does not react; for it exhausts itself completely in the expenditure of energy. But this cannot last long... I had to give up rather quickly. And now *there was a crackling and splintering in my shoulders that my body has not forgotten until this hour.* The balls sprang from their sockets. *My own body weight caused luxation*; I fell into a void and now hung by my dislocated arms, which had been torn high from behind and were now twisted over my head. (p. 32, emphasis added)

When the tortured individual cannot separate the sense of self from the body, that individual undergoes a process of absolute reduction to the body-as-object, ultimately resulting in a negation of the self. This is the critical breaking point, at which the tortured individual begins to relate to his own body as the enemy (Ataria 2016a, 2016b; Ataria and Gallagher 2015; Ataria and Somer 2013). The tormentor is no longer responsible for the victim's pain; rather the victim's own body is responsible for this agony:

> Whoever is overcome by pain through *torture experiences his body as never before. In self negation, his flesh becomes a total reality.* Partially, torture is one of those life experiences that in a milder form present themselves also to the consciousness of the patient who is awaiting help, and the popular saying according to which we feel well as long as we do not feel our body does indeed express an undeniable truth. *But only in torture does the transformation of the person into flesh become complete.* (p. 33, emphasis added)

When unable to disconnect from the body during torture, the sense of self is reduced to the body-as-object. Jorge Semprún, who was arrested in 1943 by the Gestapo and deported to the Buchenwald concentration camp, describes this process as follows:

> My body was suffocating, becoming mad, begging for mercy, ignobly. My body asserted its independent presence in an uprising from my gut that pretended to reset me as a moral entity. It beseeched me to give in to the torture, it demanded that. *To come out a winner in this battle with my body, I had to give in, to control it, while abandoning it to the threats of pain and humiliation.* (Semprún 1998, p. 148, emphasis added)

To understand the logic leading individuals to treat themselves as their own enemy, let us return to Améry's statement: *those who are unable to separate from their body, experience the body in a way they never experienced it before.* The tortured individual is reduced to this shattered body and unable to separate from it. The victim is nothing more than a body-as-object which has become the cruelest enemy—a tool that creates pain. Dissociation is one method of coping (Ataria 2015a, 2015c). However, if dissociation fails, the only remaining alternative (or better put, a dominant one) is to attacking the body (Ataria 2018). This process begins when the sense of self is completely reduced to the body-as-object: "Frail in the face of violence, yelling out in pain, awaiting no help, capable of no resistance, *the tortured person is only a body, and nothing else beside that*" (Améry 1980, p. 33, emphasis added).

At this stage, one could rightly point out that the entire story appears dualistic in nature. I believe that Merleau-Ponty's phenomenology of the body clarifies this issue. According to Merleau-Ponty (2002), the body is a unique instrument which possesses particular capabilities and limitations—indeed we are thrown into the world through our body: "[I]t is through my body that I understand other people, just as it is through my body that I perceive 'things'" (p. 216). In fact, "I could not grasp the unity of the object without the mediation of bodily experience" (p. 235). However, it is not the body-as-object that enables us to engage with the world. Rather, we understand the world around us through the living-body; the lived-body, or the body-as-subject, shapes and is shaped by the environment in which it acts. Indeed, as we saw, when things are fluent in our lives we forget we that have a body; more precisely, we forget that we are our body and simply do what needs to be done. Theoretically speaking, in such situations, the equilibrium between the body-as-subject and the body-as-object tends toward the former. In other cases (such as depression, sickness, disabilities, etc.), however, this equilibrium tends toward the latter (Ataria 2019b). Torture is a radical situation in which not only does the equilibrium tend toward the body-as-object, but the body-as-subject is reduced to the body-as-object. Fundamentally, torture destroys the lived-body. One can no longer be thrown into the world: rather, the body-as-object occupies the entire space. Yet, given that the victim fails to disconnect from the body-as-object, he is reduced to this body-as-object, the outcomes are quite severe:

> In the end, we would be faced with the equation: *Body* = *Pain* = *Death*, and in our case this could be reduced to the hypothesis that torture, through *which we are turned into body by the other*, blots out the contradiction of death and allows us to experience it personally. (p. 34, emphasis added)

It is well known (Heidelberger-Leonard 2010) that Améry was deeply inspired by Sartre, and hence it seems only natural to bear this in mind when reading his description. According to Sartre (1956), "My fundamental connection with the Other-as-subject must be able to be referred back to my permanent possibility of being seen by the Other" (p. 256). Sartre further continues, saying that "the person is presented to consciousness in so far as the person is an object for the Other" (p. 260), and stressing that "I grasp the Other's look at the very center of my act as the solidification and alienation of my own possibilities. In fear or in anxious or prudent anticipation" (p. 263). Essentially, when the Other's gaze totally objectifies me, I completely lose my freedom: "Being-seen constitutes me as a defenseless being for a freedom which is not my freedom. It is in this sense that we can consider ourselves as 'slaves' in so far as we appear to the Other" (p. 267). Thus, according to Sartre:

> *The Other reveals to me the impossibility of my being an object except for another freedom*… I experience the Other's infinite freedom. It is for and by means of a freedom and only for and by means of it that my possibles can be limited and fixed… This is because the order and the prohibition cause us to experience the Other's freedom across our own slavery. Thus in the look the death of my possibilities causes me to experience the Other's freedom. *This death is realized only at the heart of that freedom; I am inaccessible to myself and yet myself, thrown, abandoned at the heart of the Other's freedom.* (pp. 270–271, emphasis added)

Returning to Améry, we may say that torture is a situation in which the gaze of the Other (the tormentor) completely nullifies the tortured individual—note that it is erroneous even to use a word such as *individual*. Thus, from the victim's perspective, during torture the victim experiences in-flesh *the Other's infinite freedom*, becoming a pure slave—a *defenseless being for a freedom which is not my freedom*. The victim does not have even the slightest opportunity to objectify his tormentor and is therefore reduced to pure object; more precisely, to his body, which becomes nothing but stone—*abandoned at the heart of the Other's freedom*. Thus, given that the subject has been completely destroyed, the victim loses any ability to dissociate from his painful body: by being reduced to his body, he is in fact reduced to pure pain. With this in mind, the last part of the equation (*Body = Pain = Death*) remains unexplained. Let us return once again to Sartre, who wrote:

> I grasp simply the death of my possibility... *The Other is the hidden death of my possibilities* in so far as I live that death as hidden in the midst of the world.... the shock which seizes me when I apprehend the Other's look, this happens-that suddenly *I experience a subtle alienation of all my possibilities*, which are now associated with objects of the world, far from me in the midst of the world. (pp. 264–265, emphasis added)

When the Other implements his abilities fully, he thus cancels my own possibility to BE. In so doing, the tormentor becomes a God—as Sartre put it, "God here is only the concept of the Other pushed to the limit" (p. 266). Interestingly, Améry presents the exact same idea or, better put, those exact feelings—confronting a god:

> There were moments when I felt a kind of *wretched admiration for the agonizing sovereignty they exercised over me*. For is not the one who can reduce a person so entirely to a body and a whimpering prey of death *a god or, at least, a demigod*? (p. 36, emphasis added)

Under these conditions, the victim has no alternative—this is the *death of my possibilities*. Death in the Sartrian world can be understood as the loss of one's alternatives, which, in turn, can be defined as a reduction to pure object.

Let us close this section with Schilder's (1935) words: "When the whole body is filled with pain, we try to get rid of the whole body" (p. 104). Indeed, when *Body = Pain = Death*, the body becomes one's worst enemy, one's curse:

> There are situations in life in which *our body is our entire self and our entire fate. I was my body and nothing else*: in hunger, in the blow that I suffered, in the blow that I dealt. *My body, debilitated and crusted with filth, was my calamity.* (Améry 1980, pp. 90–91, emphasis added)

8.4 Cast out of the Shared World

As we saw, during torture the victim is reduced to the body, to pain. Essentially, pain negates any ability to communicate: "The pain was what it was. Beyond that there is nothing to say. Qualities of feeling are as incomparable as they are indescribable. *They mark the limit of the capacity of language to communicate*" (p. 33, emphasis added). Pain is not something that one can share with others, because "if someone wanted to impart his physical pain, he would be forced to inflict it and thereby become a torturer himself" (p. 33). With this in mind, it becomes clear why torture can potentially destroy the foundations of the social world:

> Torture becomes the *total inversion of the social world*, in which we can live only if we grant our fellow man life, ease his suffering, bridle the desire of our Ego to expand: *But in the world of torture man exists only by ruining the other person who stands before him.* (p. 35, emphasis added)

During torture, the victim is cast out of the shared world, and he is no longer part of a WE: "I was no longer an I and did not live within a We" (p. 44). Once rejected and thrown out of society, not only does one's existence in the present become meaningless, but one's past existence likewise disappears: "In order to be one or the other we need the consent of society. But if society repudiates that we ever were that, then we have also never been it" (p. 60).

In a sense, despite the presence of others, the prisoner in the death camp remains isolated—one may say that in the death camp there are no gazes. Thus, relying on Levinas' philosophy (2006) we may say that, when the gaze is diminished, the very notion of subjectivity collapses. Indeed, the structure of the death camp is enforced isolation, broken solidarity—as in the Kafkian world, each one stands trial completely alone. Therefore, once one is being starved to death and has no possibility of release (even while trying to sleep), once one discovers that it is impossible to trust anyone, once one internalizes the notion that in the death camps *the survival of the fittest* is the only applicable rule, once one has lost any dignity and been reduced to the number tattooed on one's hand, a shared social world is no longer possible.

Essentially, one cannot easily shift from this existential sense of isolation to a shared world. The tortured person cannot forget the fact that (almost) no-one helped him: "But we also lost the people: the schoolmate from the same bench, the neighbor, the teacher. They had become informers or bullies, at best, embarrassed opportunists" (p. 42). By saying that he has *lost the people*, Améry means that he lost his trust in the very notion of a shared community, and thus he has yet more reason to believe that when the time will come, he will be abandoned once again. In this situation, the tortured individual feels alone and isolated even when he returns to society outside the camps. The prisoner has learned something about the nature of human beings and the fragility of the shared world, and this insight cannot be easily wiped out: "The experience of persecution was, at the very bottom, that of an extreme loneliness. At stake for me is the release from the abandonment that has persisted from that time until today" (p. 70).

8.5 Remaining Logical Until the End

One of the most important processes that the tortured person undergoes involves abandoning his old logic in favor of a new one, one that can be defined in terms of self-destruction. In the beginning, he may try to reject this logic, yet as time passes the tortured individual learns to accept it as the only possible solution. Essentially, in order to accept this, he needs to embrace a set of presumptions which includes the assumption that *everything is possible*, meaning that "the unimaginable became reality" (p. 13), as well as certain values, for example, *the stronger you are, the more right you are*—"were not those who were preparing to destroy him in the right, owing to the undeniable fact that they were the stronger ones?" (p. 11). Thus, as time goes by, the victim accepts not merely the victimizers' logic but also their values:

> The rejection of the SS logic, the revolt that turned inward, the muted murmuring of such incantations as: *"But that is not possible," did not last long.* After a certain time there inevitably appeared something that was more than mere resignation and that we may designate as an *acceptance not only of the SS logic but also of the SS system of values*… (pp. 10–11, emphasis added)

This logic is not out of context but is situated as part of a complete master-slave structure:

> With that the torturer and murderer realizes his own destructive being, without having to lose himself in it entirely, like his martyred victim. *He can, after all, cease the torture when it suits him.* He has control of the other's scream of pain and death; *he is master over flesh and spirit, life and death.* (p. 35, emphasis added)

Once the tortured individual, situated within the master-slave structure, accepts the torturers' presumptions and values, the next rational step is to follow this new logic. For example, if everything is possible, and *the stronger you are, the more right you are*, the prisoner's belief that he did nothing wrong, that he is innocent, is probably mistaken: hence, he should pay the price.

Essentially, this kind of logic forces the prisoner to internalize the notion that he should be, and must be, annihilated: "[Those] who experienced the logic of the SS as a reality that proved itself by the hour, *now took a few fateful steps further in his thinking*" (p. 11, emphasis added). Sadly, however, this is not the most tragic part of the story. Indeed, the prisoner accepts and internalizes this logic so deeply that, even when released from the camps, he cannot reject it, leading "straight into a tragic dialectic of self-destruction" (p. 10). Upon returning *home*, not only does the victim feel completely unnecessary and that he does not belong, but also (rightly) feels himself to be a nuisance that should be disposed of—"toothless ghosts with shaven heads, just about *useful enough to give testimony quickly and then to clear out to where they really belonged*" (p. 64, emphasis added).

Once the tortured subject has internalized the torture-tortured structure, logically not only should the tortured subject accept the notion that he deserved to die but, if the oppressor did not complete the mission, he believes it his own responsibility to do so. It is not, at least not only, about identifying with the aggressor, but rather adopting the aggressor's presumptions and logic, and following it through completely: "The temptation to reject ourselves has survived within us" (p. 68).

8.6 Loss of Trust

Torture goes beyond damage to tissue; to describe torture in terms of harm, injury, and the like misses the main point. Torture is a process via which one learns something new about oneself and about society (Ataria 2017). Similarly to the situation described in Kafka's *Panel Colony* (2007), the tortured subject learns in his flesh what the notion of humanity truly means. This is not intellectual knowledge, but rather facts burned deeply onto the lived-body. Following such a shift there is no way back—something has been broken and cannot be restored—"a part of our life ends and it can never again be revived" (Améry 1980, p. 29).

This kind of knowledge-in-flesh is, at least to some extent, immune to change. Torture not only breaks the very notion of communication: in that case the possibility of restoring the communicative ability could remain, at least to some degree. Rather, in addition to destroying our ability to communicate, torture rebuilds it anew in terms of masters and slaves, blocking (almost) any possibility for regular human communication to influence the tortured individual. As a result of this new structure-in-flesh, the tortured subject becomes a complete stranger to the world. Eventually during torture one becomes a stranger to oneself: "From other places the screams penetrated as little into the world as did once *my own strange and uncanny howls* from the vault of Breendonk" (p. 23, emphasis added). The tortured individual loses the ability to feel *at-home* within the world. Essentially, these are not simply feelings that can be overcome, but an existential situation which changes the entire background, the very structure of being-thrown-into-the world, not once, but for good. In the long term, this sense of homelessness blocks the ability to exist in a shared world and hence negates the very notion of communication with others:

> If from the experience of torture any knowledge at all remains that goes beyond the plain nightmarish, it is that of a great amazement and a *foreignness in the world that cannot be compensated by any sort of subsequent human communication.* (p. 39, emphasis added)

The victim of torture loses the ability to be part of this world: the very notion of humanity has collapsed, and he understands, not theoretically but rather in his flesh and bones, that "there is no document of civilization which is not at the same time a document of barbarism" (Benjamin 1969, p. 256). Consequently, whenever the tortured individual thinks about the notion of humanity, he is filled with fear and brute horror:

> Whoever has succumbed to torture *can no longer feel at home in the world.* The *shame of destruction cannot be erased.* Trust in the world, which already collapsed in part at the first blow, but in the end, under torture, fully, will not be regained. That one's fellow man was experienced as the antiman remains in the tortured person as accumulated horror. It blocks the view into a world in which the principle of hope rules. One who was martyred is a defenseless prisoner of fear. (Améry 1980, p. 40, emphasis added)

For the tortured person, the other is no longer someone who can be trusted:

> I am certain that with the very first blow that descends on him *he loses something we will perhaps temporarily call "trust in the world"*... [I]n our context what is solely relevant, is the certainty that by reason of written or unwritten social contracts the other person will spare me—more precisely stated, that he will respect my physical, and with it also my metaphysical, being. (p. 28, emphasis added)

The tortured individual not only loses the ability to trust others but develops a new kind of belief, according to which the Other's goal is destruction: "Amazed, the tortured person experienced that *in this world there can be the other as absolute sovereign, and sovereignty revealed itself as the power to inflict suffering and to destroy*" (p. 39, emphasis added).

Following severe torture, the victim can no longer understand the meaning of the word "human." Better put, following severe torture, the victim understands precisely what being human means—indeed, for this reason Primo Levi's first book (first published in 1947) was entitled *If This Is a Man* (Levi 1959) and Robert Antelme's first book (first published in 1947) was given the title *The Human Race* (1992). This is, in fact, the victim's catastrophe—knowing the human race too well. Thus, this knowledge is not theoretical but rather knowledge-in-flesh—it is imprinted on the victim's body and cannot be erased or removed, *the shame of destruction cannot be erased*. As time passes, even after the victim's release, this knowledge does not dissipate. Quite the opposite: the knowledge which has accumulated in the body becomes the basis upon which the victim rebuilds himself. Consequently, the theories that a torture victim constructs to explain the surrounding world are rooted in his experiences during the torture—all other sources of information are no longer valid. As time passes, his entire phenomenal field becomes saturated with the insights that he acquired during torture. This is not a process of healing but one of deterioration, a fatal process that only continues to worsen as long as the survivor digests the various meanings of the torture he endured in the past:

> In a time span that now already runs into decades, [he] has had to learn that it was not a wound that was inflicted upon him, one that will scar over with the ticking of time, but rather that he *is suffering from an insidious disease that is growing worse with the years*. (Améry 1980, p. 57, emphasis added)

8.7 Concluding Remarks

Based on Améry's writings (1980), this article has investigated the notion that torture is "the most horrible event a human being can retain within himself" (p. 22), seeking to give it a phenomenological and cognitive basis. During torture, the victim develops a severe sense of helplessness: the world is no longer in the victim's reach. In radical cases, the sense of helplessness becomes so severe that it is converted into an *existential consummation of complete destruction.* In the long term, if the tortured individual loses the ability to dissociate, he is reduced to his body-as-object, and his own body becomes nothing but pain. Being reduced to the body-as-object-as-pain, the victim's freedom declines to zero—the outcome is the actual death of possibilities. Essentially, *when the whole body is filled with pain, we try to dispose of the whole body.* Moreover, during torture, the victim becomes completely isolated, he is alone in the world in the most profound way—communication is no longer possible because signs themselves lose all context and cannot be understood. In this process, the victim begins to embrace the tormentor's logic, a new kind of logic that ends only when the victim internalizes the most basic principle of torture—he no longer belongs to the world. To be more accurate, from the very outset his life has been nothing more than an accident; in truth, he was never part of this world: in that sense, he simply gets what he deserved. Finally, torture breaks the very ability to trust the world. Indeed, during torture the victim learns something new about the structure of humanity: his new motto becomes "Trust-no-one."

Note

1. For the sake of the argument, let us assume that such cases exist.
2. The discussion uses the masculine form because it is based on Améry's writings and experiences.

References

Améry, J. (1980). *At the Mind's Limits* (S. Rosenfeld & S. P. Rosenfeld, Trans.). Bloomington: Indiana University Press.

Antelme, R. (1992). *The Human Race* (J. Haight & A. Mahler, Trans.). Marlboro: Marlboro Press.

Arieli, A., & Ataria, Y. (2018). Helplessness: The Inability to Know-That You Don't Know-How. *Philosophical Psychology, 31*, 1–18.

Ataria, Y. (2015a). Dissociation During Trauma: The Ownership-Agency Tradeoff Model. *Phenomenology and the Cognitive Sciences, 14*(4), 1037–1053. https://doi.org/10.1007/s11097-014-9392-9.

Ataria, Y. (2015b). Trauma from an Enactive Perspective: The Collapse of the Knowing-How Structure. *Adaptive Behavior, 23*(3), 143–154. https://doi.org/10.1177/1059712314578542.

Ataria, Y. (2015c). Sense of Ownership and Sense of Agency During Trauma. *Phenomenology and the Cognitive Sciences, 14*(1), 199–212. https://doi.org/10.1007/s11097-013-9334-y.

Ataria, Y. (2016a). I Am Not My Body, This Is Not My Body. *Human Studies, 39*(2), 217–229. https://doi.org/10.1007/s10746-015-9366-0.

Ataria, Y. (2016b). When the Body Becomes the Enemy: Disownership Toward the Body. *Philosophy, Psychiatry & Psychology, 23*(1), 1–15. https://doi.org/10.1353/ppp.2016.0002.

Ataria, Y. (2017). *The Structural Trauma of Western Culture: Toward the End of Humanity*. New York: Palgrave Macmillan.

Ataria, Y. (2018). *Body Disownership in Complex Post-Traumatic Stress Disorder*. New York: Palgrave Macmillan.

Ataria, Y. (2019a). Becoming Nonhuman: The Case Study of the Gulag. *Genealogy, 3*(2), 27.

Ataria, Y. (2019b). When the Body Stands in the Way – Complex Posttraumatic Stress Disorder, Depersonalization and Schizophrenia. *Philosophy, Psychiatry, & Psychology, 26*, 19–31.

Ataria, Y., & Gallagher, S. (2015). Somatic Apathy: Body Disownership in the Context of Torture. *Journal of Phenomenological Psychology, 46*(1), 105–122. https://doi.org/10.1163/15691624-12341286.

Ataria, Y., & Somer, E. (2013). Total Otherness in Dissociative Identity Disorder. *Journal for Otherness, 4*(1), 1–25.

Benjamin, W. (1969). Theses on the Philosophy of History. In H. Arendt & H. Zohn (Eds.), *Illuminations*. New York: Schocken.

Dorfman, E. (2014). *Foundations of the Everyday: Shock, Deferral, Repetition*. London, New York: Rowman & Littlefield International.

Dreyfus, H. L. (1991). *Being-in-the-World: A Commentary on Heidegger's Being and Time, Division I*. Massachusetts and London: MIT Press.

Dreyfus, H. L. (1992). *What Computers Still Can't Do: A Critique of Artificial Reason*. Cambridge, MA and London: MIT Press.

Dreyfus, H. L. (2017). *Background Practices*. Oxford: Oxford University Press.

Fuchs, T., & Schlimme, J. E. (2009). Embodiment and Psychopathology: A Phenomenological Perspective. *Current Opinion in Psychiatry, 22*(6), 570–575. https://doi.org/10.1097/YCO.0b013e3283318e5c.

Gallagher, S., & Lindgren, R. (2015). Enactive Metaphors: Learning Through Full-Body Engagement. *Educational Psychology Review, 27*(3), 391–404. https://doi.org/10.1007/s10648-015-9327-1.

Gibson, J. (1979). *The Ecological Approach to Visual Perception*. Hillsdale, New Jersey: Lawrence Erlbaum Associates.
Gibson, J. (1982). *Reasons for Realism: Selected Essays of James J. Gibson* (E. Reed & R. Jones, Eds.). Hillsdale, NJ: Lawrence Erlbaum.
Heidegger, M. (1996). *Being and Time* (J. Stambaugh, Trans.). Albany: New York Press.
Heidelberger-Leonard, I. (2010). *The Philosopher of Auschwitz*. London and New York: IB Tauris.
Kafka, F. (2007). In the Penal Colony. In *Kafka's Selected Stories, Norton Critical Edition* (S. Corngold, Trans., pp. 35–59). New York: Norton.
Leder, D. (1990). *The Absent Body*. Chicago: The University of Chicago Press.
Levi, P. (1959). *If This Is a Man* (S. Woolf, Trans.). New York: The Orion Press.
Levinas, E. (2006). *Humanism of the Other* (N. Poller, Trans.). Urbana; Chicago: University of Illinois Press.
Merleau-Ponty, M. (1968). *The Visible and the Invisible* (C. Lefort, Ed., & A. Lingis, Trans.). Evanston: Northwestern University Press.
Merleau-Ponty, M. (2002). *Phenomenology of Perception* (C. Smith, Trans.). London: Routledge and Kegan Paul.
Ratcliffe, M. (2008). *Feelings of Being*. Oxford: Oxford University Press.
Ratcliffe, M. (2015). *Experiences of Depression*. Oxford: Oxford University Press.
Sartre, J.-P. (1956). *Being and Nothingness* (H. Barnes, Trans.). New York: Philosophical Library.
Schilder, P. (1935). *The Image and Appearance of the Human Body*. New York: International Universities Press.
Semprún, J. (1998). *Literature or Life* (L. Coverdale, Trans.). New York, NY: Penguin Books.

CHAPTER 9

Language in Exile, Exile in Language

Dana Amir

The psychoanalytic literature on trauma refers extensively to the major role of the other in bearing witness to a trauma the victim often has not, and could not have, witnessed him or herself. Authors from various theoretical fields (Laub and Auerhahn 1993; Oliner 1996) describe trauma as something that has taken place "over there, far away", an event that does not belong to the experiencing "I". At the heart of the traumatic experience there is an experience of excess that escapes representation and leaves a lacuna within consciousness (LaCapra 2001). Caruth (1996, pp. 91–92) writes about the traumatic paradox in which the most direct contact with the violent event may occur only through the very inability to know it. Trauma is not only an experience, but also the failure to experience that experience: not merely the threat itself, but the fact that the threat was recognized as such only a moment too late. As it was not experienced in time, the event is condemned not to be fully known (Caruth 1996, p. 62). As such, it returns to claim its presence, trying to cover an experiential void through compulsive repetition. Van der Kolk et al. (1996) argue that while terrifying events may be remembered extremely vividly, they may equally resist any kind of integration. These memories remain powerful

D. Amir (✉)
University of Haifa, Haifa, Israel

The Israel Psychoanalytic Society, Jerusalem, Israel

Y. Ataria et al. (eds.), *Jean Améry*,
https://doi.org/10.1007/978-3-030-28095-6_9

but frozen, un-transformable by either circumstantial processes or the passing of time (ibid., pp. 282, 296). As Modell (2006) suggests, trauma tends to freeze the past and therefore "deprives it of the plasticity it needs if it is to connect to the present" (Stern 2012, p. 56). Traumatic memories are not only rigid and concrete—but unmentalized. As such, they remain "things-in-themselves", neither adaptable nor generative (ibid.).

Dori Laub (2005) quotes Moore (1999) who argued that the traumatized subject cannot know that the traumatic event has taken place until an other supplies it with a narrative. A person can know his or her story only when he or she tells it to what Laub calls "the inner thou" (internal other). But since trauma critically injures both the internal and external other, namely the addressee of any dialogical relationship—it ruins the possibility of an empathic dyad in the inner representation of the world, leaving the subject with nobody to address, either inside or outside him or herself:

> To understand it one has to conceive of the world of the Holocaust as a world in which the very imagination of the Other was no longer possible. There was no longer an other to which one could say "Thou" in the hope of being heard, of being recognized as a subject, of being answered. The historical reality of the Holocaust became, thus, a reality which extinguished philosophically the very possibility of address, the possibility of appealing, or of turning to, an-other. But when one cannot turn to a "you" one cannot say "thou" even to oneself. (Felman and Laub 1992, pp. 81–82)

Laub further argues that the fragmenting effects of the traumatic experience can be better understood if we postulate the presence of unbound, un-neutralized death instinct derivatives.[1] Conscious memory is the first casualty of these unbound death instinct derivatives. Furthermore, erasure of traumatically lost objects and of the traumatic experience itself may lead the survivor to complete oblivion, or to doubt the veracity and authenticity of his or her own experiences, compromising his or her entire sense of identity and continuity:

> How to attest to the way things were from within the very situation of delusion and illusion—from inside the utter blindness to what in reality things were? How to bear witness to historic truth from inside the radical deception (amplified by self-deception) by which one was separated from historic truth at the very moment one was most involved in it? … It is impossible to testify from the inside because the inside has no voice … Who would be in a position, then, to tell? The truth of the inside is even less accessible to the

> outsider. If it is indeed impossible to bear witness to the Holocaust from inside, it is even more impossible to testify to it from the outside. (Felman and Laub 1992, pp. 231–232)

Thus, traumatic experiences often activate a process of psychic self-annihilation. Their toxicity creates a type of psychic holes which absorb the unbearable traumatic substances along with the subject who contains them, to the point of a total collapse of inner barriers. This collapse of barriers leaves the subject imprisoned in a territory of *negative possession* (Amir 2012, 2018), where the traumatic contents are neither digested nor worked through. The only chance of recovery from this condition lies in the possibility of depositing the traumatic substances in another subject who cannot be annihilated by them. This is the core of bearing witness (Felman and Laub 1992; Laub 2005; Amir 2012; Roth 2019).

In his *Remnants of Auschwitz* (2002), Giorgio Agamben mentions that there are two Latin words for the English word *witness*. The first of these is *testis*, whose etymology points at one who puts himself in the position of the mediator or arbitrator, the third party in a conflict between two sides. The other word is *superstes*: the one who has experienced something to its ultimate end—and thereby can testify to it. Based on the movement between the first and the third person of experience, the function of the inner witness as I defined it (Amir 2012) encapsulates both these meanings. It refers to the ability to shift between being a *superstes*—who has undergone the full experience—and being a *testis* who mediates between the ultimate experience and language (Amir 2018).

Agamben (2002) writes:

> To bear witness is to place oneself in one's own language in the position of those who have lost it, to establish oneself in a living language as if it were dead, or in a dead language as if it were living. [...] What cannot be stated, what cannot be archived is the language in which the author succeeds in bearing witness to the incapacity to speak. In this language, a language that survives the subjects who spoke it coincides with a speaker who remains beyond it. (pp. 161–162)

Since every testimony is an intersection between "what cannot be stated" and what is actually spoken, every act of testimony is simultaneously a collapse and a formation of language: a collapse of language—since bearing witness to what cannot be testified renders testimony a meaningless event, or one that conveys "archival meaning" (ibid.) only; and a formation of language—since where language succeeds to speak not in spite of the lacuna but in its name, not beyond it but through it, it becomes a real event of testimony, one that constitutes the subject of witnessing as such. In other words, in order to render account of himself, a person has to cross the abyss and simultaneously dwell in it; he must hold, within language, the unbridgeable gap between what can be said and what, exactly in being said, is elided. Agamben argues in this context that the act of witnessing is always a struggle between the one who has a voice, yet has nothing to say, and the one who does have something to say but has no voice. The witness is thus an exile by definition: either from himself or from language.

9.1 The Witness' Second Exile

What happens when another exile, namely the exile from one language to another, is added to the exile that is already inherently structured into the act of witnessing? It is this type of "second exile" that constitutes the subject of the essay "How Much Home Does a Man Need?" by Jean Améry (1980).

Améry writes:

> For the exiled person who came to the new country already as an adult, penetrating the signs will be not a spontaneous but rather an intellectual act, one combined with a certain expenditure of mental effort. Only those signals that we absorbed very early, that we learned to interpret at the same time that we were gaining possession of our external world, become constitutional elements and constants of our personality. Just as one learns one's mother tongue without knowing its grammar, one experiences one's native surroundings. Mother tongue and native world grow with us, grow into us [...]. (ibid., p. 48)

The greatest rupture for the exile involves, according to Améry, the lost sensual link to language. This is not merely an inability to grasp certain nuances in the new language, or the fact that to the exile the new language presents its surface rather than its more profound strata. It is the irreversible caesura language poses for the person in exile, one that touches on his ability to relate to himself as one continuous entity: "To live in one's homeland means that what is already known to us occurs before our eyes again and again, in slight variants", Améry writes (ibid., p. 47). Being at home somewhere implies, in other words, an accumulation of versions of existential experience whose unconscious link produces a sequence of meaning. This meaning, moreover, is not rationally elicited from language but forms in a manner that predates any knowledge of its grammar. This is exactly the rupture Améry refers to: the necessity to acquire in an intentional and structured manner what should have been a given for the speaker prior to any act of learning; the necessity to replace the mother-tongue, the language of one's home, with a language that receives the exile in a "reserved manner", as he puts it, and for "brief formal visits" only (ibid., p. 53).

In his article "Mourning and Melancholia" (1917), Freud draws one of the most crucial distinctions for the understanding of the human psyche, the one between the state of mourning and the state of melancholia. His key argument in this article is that in contrast with mourning—which directs itself at a concrete loss of a concrete object—the melancholic state is one where the loss is of a more ideal kind. Here it is not necessarily the object itself that has been lost but the meaning the subject associated with it: "he knows whom he has lost but not what he has lost in him. This would suggest that melancholia is in some way related to an object-loss which is withdrawn from consciousness, in contradistinction to mourning, in which there is nothing about the loss that is unconscious" (ibid., p. 245).

And since in contrast to mourning—which is always conscious and of a real, concrete object—melancholia is an unconscious mourning of an inner, ideal object—melancholic loss is always more extensive and comprehensive than mourning, its implications extending not only toward the future but also harking back to the past. Coping with the loss of an internal object, a person not only confronts the loss of the future (which would be typical of the condition of mourning) but also that of the past, because melancholy paints the past in different colors than those in which it appeared before. Freud moreover argues that melancholia, unlike mourning, does not aim at the world but at the ego: "in mourning it is the world which has become poor and empty; in melancholia it is the ego itself" (ibid., p. 246).

In my book *On the Lyricism of the Mind* (2016) I suggested the difference between mourning over an actual object and mourning over a possible (Gilead 1999, 2003) one. While mourning—however extreme—is always over an actual (even when symbolic) object, as Freud put it, melancholia relates to the death of a possible object, that is, to the death of the possibility it represented within the subject. It is not the person whom one loved that died, but love as a possibility. And worse than that: Love is experienced, in the melancholic state, as never having existed in the first place, that is to say, even when it seemed to exist, it was nothing but an illusion. Often a kind of "confusion of tongues" marks the state of melancholia: while the person ostensibly mourns an actual object, he does not in fact distinguish between the actual object (a specific loved one, a specific homeland) and the possible one (the very possibility of love, the very possibility of being at home). It is, in fact, this collapse of barriers between the actual and the possible that turns mourning into melancholia (ibid.).

To revert to Améry: The loss of homeland he deplores is not the loss of the actual home but the loss of the possible one: "We, however, had not lost our country, but had to realize that it had never been ours", he writes (p. 50). Since this is not a mourning state of mind but a melancholic one, addressing the possible rather than the actual lost object, it focuses not on the specific loss of the specific country, but on the loss of the very possibility of being at home anywhere. The internal experience of "being at home" is deeply linked to the capacity to bear witness. The melancholic collapse of the inner witness is not the collapse of the capacity to bear witness to a specific actual catastrophe—but of the very possibility of being a witness to oneself. Thus, it extends itself toward the speaker, not only toward what is spoken about. Not only the possibility to lament the specific home is attacked but the very possibility of being a lamenting (witnessing) subject, namely a subject of language and within language.

Améry has a unique formulation for this attack of language in the melancholic subject:

> Instead of a "crumbling away of the mother tongue, I would rather speak of its shrinking. We moved about not only in the foreign language, but also, when we did make use of German, in the narrowing confines of a vocabulary that constantly repeated itself. By necessity, conversations with our comrades in misfortune revolved about the same topics [...]. Those who spoke with us did not supply our language with any new substance; they only mirrored our own. [...] There, in the hostile homeland, the evolution of the language took its course. Not that it was a beautiful language that emerged there, not that. But it was—along with enemy bomber, enemy action, front control station, indeed even along with all the actual Nazi slang—a language of *reality*. All developed speech is figurative, whether it tells us of a tree that defiantly stretches a bare branch toward the sky, or of the Jew who infuses Near Eastern poison into the German national body. (p. 52)

By means of these probing sentences Améry points at the catastrophic rupture between the language of the homeland and the language of exile. While the language of the perpetrator, the language of the homeland, continues its process of natural production, yielding new expressions and new images day by day—the language of exile, that of the victim, grows steadily reduced. Having been detached from its roots, it now resembles a plant which has been put into a pot. It stays alive but does not unfold as plentifully or deeply as it might have done had it remained attached to its patch of ground. It survives in terms of surface but loses its deeper layers, that is, the sources of its vitality.

Julia Kristeva, In *Strangers to Ourselves* (1991), writes:

> Bearing within oneself like a secret vault, or like a handicapped child—cherished and useless—that language of the past that withers without ever leaving you. You improve your ability with another instrument, as one expresses oneself with algebra or the violin [...]. You have a feeling that the new language is a resurrection: new skin, new sex. But the illusion bursts [...]. Thus, between two languages, your realm is silence. [...] Silence has not only been forced upon you, it is within you: a refusal to speak, a fitful sleep riven to an anguish that wants to remain mute [...]. Saying nothing, nothing needs to be said, nothing can be said. At first, it was a cold war with those of the new idiom, desired and rejecting; then the new language covered you as might a slow tide, a neap tide. (pp. 15–16)

The language of exile, the language of the "neap tide" as Kristeva puts it, is a language that sticks to what one may call "a secure mode": a limited, barren mode allowing for the survival of basic functions at the cost of all other, more complex ones. In this sense the caesura of exile is catastrophic: the continuation of life depends on amputation, but this amputation demands nothing less than life itself as its price. However, the traumatic rupture of language does not relate only to the exiled person's detachment from his concrete roots. It is also related to his experience of these roots as tainted, an experience which causes him to resist any contact with them: "Finally, whether we resisted or not, our mother tongue became just as inimical as the one they spoke around us" writes Améry (p. 53). This is the unbearable paradox of the forced exile: though isolation from his deepest origins seems to enable his survival as a speaker, it malignantly and irreversibly impoverishes his position as a subject in and of language. Being isolated from his mother tongue leads to a situation in which all speech acts simultaneously link and attack linking (Bion 1959), enable and disable continuity: "The hostile home was destroyed by us, and at the same time we obliterated the part of our life that was associated with it", writes Améry (p. 51). Since he experiences his yearning for home and mother tongue as emotional manipulation, "Journeys home with falsified papers and stolen pedigree" (Ibid.), he turns his back on it. But denying this homesickness turns out to be a denial of his own self: "He looks back—[...] and he doesn't detect himself anywhere" (p. 59). Améry can be seen to describe here two types of "alienation from the self" (p. 43): one is reflected in a type of yearning for something that never belonged to him in the first place; the other is the alienation associated with his turning away from this yearning. It is between these two types of alienation that Améry finds himself dangling as between two abysses.

In *Black Sun* (1987), Julia Kristeva proposes a fascinating distinction between what she calls "objectal depression" and "pre-objectal depression". For the one who suffers from pre-objectal depression, namely the child who never had a mother whose absence can be mourned—sadness is the only object. Taking the place of the lost (or never present) object, it becomes itself the object of attachment to which the deepest yearning goes out. Sadness, in such cases, may be understood as a defense against fragmentation, a mechanism which restores, albeit in pathological ways, the affective coherence which was lost to the self or never created. Reading Améry in Kristeva's terms enables us to think of this double alienation as the most profound lamentation about what he has lost. No longer existent as an object, the homeland language takes on the status of a "pre-object"—whose presence can only be marked or preserved through the obsessive clinging to its absence.

9.2 The Collaboration of the Exile

Towards the end of this essay, Améry mentions the poet Alfred Mombert, a fellow prisoner in the camp in southern France. Mombert concludes a letter in which he tells a friend what has befallen him, with the question: "Has anything similar ever happened to a German poet?" (Améry, p. 59). Améry writes: "[...] Only someone who writes poetry not merely *in* German but also *for* Germans, upon their express wish, can be a German poet" (ibid., p. 60). Further on he writes: "His readers of yesterday, who did not protest against his deportation, had undone his verses" (ibid.). In order to be a German poet it doesn't suffice just to write in German; one must supply for the needs of the German nation, that is, to satisfy the needs of the perpetrator, to identify with the aggressor's needs, in Sandor Ferenczi's (1988) terms.

According to Ferenczi, a subject threatened by someone who terrorizes him will do his utmost to obey the latter's every wish and desire. This is not a mere external form of obedience, but an introjection of the aggressor, becoming one and the same with him. In this way the subject stops being himself and assumes the image of the other's desire. Writing in German, Améry argues in this context, is nothing but the introjection of the German nation and its needs into the subject's language, in fact erasing the subject himself from that language. And thus the reason why Mombert was robbed of his identity as a German poet was not only related to the German nation's silence regarding his being expelled, a silence that erased both his future and his past as a poet, as Améry observed. It was rather related to the fact that writing in German became an ambiguous act. Its being rooted in the perpetrator's language sentenced this poetry to the dubious status whereby pretending to reclaim the German language it actually repeats the speaker's very expulsion from it.

The tragic paradox of the exile from language is associated with the fact that both agreeing with and refusal of exile are types of collaboration with the erasure of the speaking subject. In the exile of language, or in the exile from language, what saves from death is simultaneously what threatens life. The tragic nature of this psychic territory is related to the fact that in it, the exiled is ordained to eternally pursue a past which on the one hand must not be looked at, and on the other hand will forever be the primal condition for every gaze.

Note

1. The link between trauma and the unleashing of the death instinct derivatives can be found in Freud's reference to the negative effects of trauma leading to "an inhibition—even an inability to deal with life" (Freud, quoted in Kirshner 1994, p. 238).

References

Agamben, G. (2002). *Remnants of Auschwitz: The Witness and the Archive* (D. Heller-Roazen, Trans). New York, NY: Zone Books.

Amir, D. (2012). The Inner Witness. *International Journal of Psycho-Analysis, 93*, 879–896.

Amir, D. (2016). *On the Lyricism of the Mind: Psychoanalysis and Literature*. London and New York: Routledge.
Amir, D. (2018). *Bearing Witness to the Witness: Four Modes of Traumatic Testimony*. London and New York: Routledge.
Améry, J. (1980). How Much Home Does a Man Need? In *At the Mind's Limits* (S. Rosenfeld & S. P. Rosenfeld, Trans.). Indiana: Indiana University Press.
Bion, W. (1959). Attacks on Linking. *International Journal of Psycho-Analysis, 40*, 308–315.
Caruth, C. (1996). *Unclaimed Experience: Trauma Narrative and History*. Baltimore, MD: Johns Hopkins University Press.
Felman, S., & Laub, D. (Eds.). (1992). *Testimony: Crises of Witnessing in Literature, Psychoanalysis, and History* (pp. 93–119). New York, NY: Routledge.
Ferenczi, S. (1988). Confusion of Tongues Between Adults and the Child—The Language of Tenderness and of Passion. *Contemporary Psychoanalysis, 24*, 196–206.
Freud, S. (1917). Mourning and Melancholia. The Standard Edition of the Complete Psychological Works of Sigmund Freud, Volume XIV (1914–1916): *On the History of the Psycho-Analytic Movement, Papers on Metapsychology and Other Works*, 237–258.
Gilead, A. (1999). *Saving Possibilities: A Study in Philosophical Psychology*. Amsterdam: Rodopi.
Gilead, A. (2003). How Does Love Make the Ugly Beautiful? *Philosophy and Literature, 27*(2), 436–443.
Kirshner, L. A. (1994). Trauma, the Good Object, and the Symbolic: A Theoretical Integration. *International Journal of Psycho-Analysis, 75*, 235–242.
Kristeva, J. (1987). *Black Sun: Depression and Melancholia* (Leon S. Roudiez, Trans.). New York: Columbia University Press.
Kristeva, J. (1991). *Strangers to Ourselves* (Leon S. Roudiez, Trans.). Columbia: Columbia University Press.
LaCapra, D. (2001). *Writing History, Writing Trauma*. Baltimore, MD: Johns Hopkins University Press.
Laub, D., & Auerhahn, N. (1993). Knowing and Not Knowing: Forms of Traumatic Memory. *International Journal of Psycho-Analysis, 74*, 287–302.
Laub, D. (2005). Traumatic Shutdown of Narrative and Symbolization. *Contemporary Psychoanalysis, 41*, 307–326.
Modell, A. (2006). *Imagination and the Meaningful Brain*. Cambridge, MA: MIT Press.
Moore, R. (1999). *The Creation of Reality in psychoanalysis*. Hillsdale, NJ: The Analytic Press.
Oliner, M. (1996). External Reality: The Elusive Dimensions of Psychoanalysis. *Psychoanalytic Quarterly, 65*, 267–300.

Roth, M. (2019). *Reading the Reader: A Psychoanalytic Perspective on Reading Literature*. London and New York: Routledge.

Stern, D. B. (2012). Witnessing Across Time: Accessing the Present from the Past and the Past from the Present. *Psychoanalytic Quarterly, 81*, 53–81.

Van der Kolk, B., McFarlane, A., & Weisaeth, L. (1996). *Traumatic Stress: The Effects of Overwhelming Experience on Mind, Body, and Society*. New York, NY: The Guilford Press.

CHAPTER 10

The Healing Power of Imagination: Playfulness in Impossible Situations

Mooli Lahad

10.1 Prologue

The fact that Améry was "playing" with suicide as a solution to his troubling life, years before he committed suicide, is documented in the books and stories he wrote well before the war (Heidelberger-Leonard 2010). But despite the temptation for a simple interpretation of the artist's writings as an inner desire or wish, this type of "solution" or reaction in nineteenth-century writing was rather common. In Russia, for example, Turgenev's novelettes (*L'Antchar*, *An Unhappy Girl*, and *Klara Milich*) describe the suicide of his main female character. In his book Suicide Century, which investigates suicide as a prominent theme in twentieth-century contemporary literature, Bennett (2017) argues that the literature responds to the act and idea in an increasingly normalized manner.

However, when we connect Améry's suicide to his tortured Auschwitz experience and look at it as an act of protest, we need to look at the wider picture of the Holocaust, survivors' reactions during and following the

M. Lahad (✉)
Tel-Hai Academic College, Upper Galilee, Israel

Community Stress Prevention Center, Qiryat Shemona, Israel
e-mail: mooli.lahad@icspc.org

Y. Ataria et al. (eds.), *Jean Améry*,
https://doi.org/10.1007/978-3-030-28095-6_10

Holocaust and mostly to the question of whether Améry was aware of other ways of coping with the horrendous experiences during and after the war. Can we look at Améry's writings and contentions from a psychological perspective of Post-traumatic Stress Disorder (PTSD) or Complex Grief, and in contemporary post factum argue that there was an alternative to Améry's continuous self-torture and torment, an alternative that was available, known to him, and in today's methods of treatment may have given him the tools to go on living?

Based on my own and others' research into the phenomena of trauma, we are of the opinion that people who have been exposed to traumatic experiences and were able to use positive or playful imagination and humor, could withstand the trauma. I called this phenomenon "transcendence into Fantastic Reality," a term that I will elaborate on later. This is a perspective that sees the psychiatric manifestation of dissociation as a spontaneous means of the mind to survive the impossible human cruelty.

This chapter will argue that Améry spontaneously used "transcendence into Fantastic Reality," and was aware of its positive potential for coping, as he observed others benefiting from it. But due to his philosophy of intellectualism, he could not and perhaps didn't want to exercise any other options of coping with the trauma of Auschwitz.

Let me briefly explore some aspects of twenty-first-century psychology thinking on trauma, PTSD, and traumatic grief, pointing out the very few studies on Holocaust survivors' use of playful imagination and humor. I will then extensively describe the use of imagination in Impossible Situations and illustrate my observations of Améry by using quotes from his book *At the Mind's Limits*. This chapter brings forth a new approach of helping the at-risk group of those exposed to severe traumatic events that helps them regain mental control over their suffering by using imagination and playfulness in impossible situations.

I will put my arguments in a dialog format, so every part will start with a question I posed to myself and to you, the reader.

10.2 What Is PTSD?

The history of post-trauma is as old as human existence on this planet. I will briefly explain some of its most profound aspects concerning the case at hand and will not attempt to expand too much or too deeply on it.

PTSD is a mental health condition that is triggered by a terrifying event—whether we experience it or witness it. The exposed person may feel immense fear, terror, horror, and helplessness. PTSD symptoms may include flashbacks, nightmares, severe anxiety, as well as uncontrollable thoughts about the event. Symptoms include intrusive memories, avoidance, negative changes in thinking and mood, as well as changes in physical and emotional reactions, and suicidal thoughts. Some of the symptoms may include negative thoughts about the future, memory problems, including failure to remember important aspects of the traumatic event. In the social aspect, we see difficulty to maintain close relationships, detachment from family and friends markedly diminished interest in activities that used to be enjoyable. Persistent inability to experience positive emotions, such as happiness, love, and joy. Emotional numbness, affecting the ability to be playful (Waldman-Levi et al. 2015).

Important aspects of PTSD that emerge in Améry's writing relate to arousal reaction, such as being easily startled or frightened, always being on guard for looming danger or from flood of memory and emotions, self-destructive behavior, including suicidal ideations and suicidal attempts, trouble sleeping, irritability, angry outbursts or aggressive behavior, overwhelming guilt or shame. This shame and guilt are at the core of the post-traumatic reaction. It is a tormenting idea that one should be ashamed of one's behavior during and after the events, the shame and guilt experienced as a result of one's behavior toward loved ones that are expressed by avoidance behavior, outbursts of anger, or withdrawal from life. There is also guilt for not fighting back, and a sense of responsibility for what has happened. This deep sense of shame and guilt, including the notion that they deserve to suffer or they don't deserve to feel better, prevents many PTSD sufferers from getting professional help (for detailed description please refer to DSM 5) (2013).

10.3 Are There References in Améry's Writing to Support a Full or Partial Diagnosis of PTSD?

Let's examine a few examples.

Let us look at the following statement:

> *Whoever was tortured, stays tortured. Torture is ineradicably burned into him, even when no clinically objective traces can be detected.* (1980, p. 34)

One may argue that Améry described here the sense of trauma that is bodily imbedded and the idea of what is sometimes called the "transparent wound" (Tanielian et al. 2008). This is so confusing, as on the outside the person suffering from PTSD looks intact, but inside they are burned.

Another phenomenon of PTSD is the haunting memories that retain the original pain as they were either not processed or repressed. Améry says: "*Twenty-two years later, I am still dangling over the ground by dislocated arms, panting, and accusing myself. In such an instance there is no 'repression'*" (ibid., p. 36).

Self-accusation, the feeling that he is to be blamed for his present behavior, for his past inability to act, or even worse, the self-tormenting idea that victims blame themselves by the belief that they somehow contributed to their misfortune is obvious when he says: "*accusing myself*."

The estrangement from life, the feeling that there is no place in this world that is safe (Foa and Rothbaum 2001), when emotional processing is stymied, survivors develop two "erroneous cognitions" that together create and maintain PTSD: The world is an entirely dangerous place, followed by helplessness. In Améry's words: "*Whoever has succumbed to torture can no longer feel at home in the world*" (p. 40). And he adds another very central sentiment of mistrust and inability to regain any of it: "*Trust in the world, which already collapsed in part at the first blow, but in the end, under torture, fully, will not be regained*" (p. 40).

The following paragraph with highlighted words indicates the sense of helplessness and confusion as to good or bad signs and a sense of hopelessness that are at the basis of so many people suffering from chronic PTSD. In their book about the treatment of trauma, Foa and Rothbaum (2001) clearly state that these negative cognitions are at the core of the trauma schema of the victim: "I'm not good enough," "The world isn't safe," "No one can be trusted." In Améry's words, "*There was* ***no order for me in this world...*** *Was the* ***smile*** *of the police official who checked our papers* ***good-natured, indifferent, or mocking****? Was his deep* ***Voice resentful or full of goodwill? I didn't know****. Did the old bearded Jew, whose gurgling sounds I nevertheless grasped as sentences,* ***mean it well with us or did he hate us****... I staggered through a* ***world*** *whose signs* ***remained*** *as* ***scrutable to me as Etruscan script***" (p. 47).

This profound reflective account is akin to what we often come across in trauma literature (Herman 1992). The destruction of basic trust and confusion leads victims to stick to the known, even if the "known" is their perpetrator. "***At times I felt more vulnerable before them [the gurgling Jew and the policeman] than before the SS man at home****, because of him I* *had at least known with certainty that he was stupid and mean and that he was after my life*" (p. 47).

But suppose it is not PTSD. Perhaps we are dealing with a more complex combination of PTSD and Traumatic Grief. Let's examine Traumatic Grief and see if that can also explain the emotional state that governs Améry.

10.4 What Is Traumatic Grief?

Prigerson et al. (1997) describe Traumatic Grief as encompassing the following:

1. Symptoms of **separation distress**, such as **preoccupation** with thoughts of the deceased to the point of functional impairment, upsetting memories, **longing, searching, and loneliness** following the loss.
2. Disbelief, **mistrust**, anger, **detachment** from others, shock, and experiencing somatic symptoms similar to those of the person who died.

It seems to me that Améry was caught in what the literature calls traumatic grief, as he was constantly reliving the past: "*Absurdly, it demands that the irreversible be turned around, that the event be undone. Resentment blocks the exit to the genuine human dimension, the future. I know... that the time-sense of the person trapped in resentment is twisted around, dis-ordered, if you wish, for it desires two impossible things: regression into the past and* ***nullification of what happened***" (p. 68).

So far, I was trying to assure my reader that Améry's writings allude to manifestations of PTSD and Traumatic Grief. But was Améry so different from his fellow Holocaust Survivors?

The evidence I bring herewith suggests that this is common amongst the survivors of the Holocaust. Trappler et al. (2007) found that the prevalence of depression and PTSD symptoms were very high among survivors. Oquendo et al. (2003) in a study on PTSD, depression, and suicidality support the idea that more depressed patients, with PTSD, than depressed patients without PTSD, had attempted suicide. Suicidal ideation was most severe in the depressed patients who had current PTSD and, therefore, more symptoms, suggesting that suicidal ideation lessens in major depressive episodes once PTSD subsides.

I dare suggest that the suicidal ideations and attempts are known amongst the aging survivors. Barak et al. (2005), who investigated the risk of attempted suicide among aging holocaust survivors, indicated that aging of survivors is frequently associated with depression, reactivation of traumatic syndromes, physical disorders, loss, and psychological distress, increasing the risk of suicide. In fact, this is the combination of PTSD and traumatic grief.

As I mentioned earlier, this is the easy path to understand Améry's reaction to his horrible experience. May I suggest that we now consider his inclination to and interpretation of intellectualism as a more profound hindrance to his ability to cope during and following the Auschwitz experience?

10.5 Was There Another Solution and Did Améry Know About It: If So, Why Didn't He Opt for That Solution?

Let's start this inquiry by examining the option of "diverting attention," or as it is often described, "dissociation."

Dissociation, Imagination, and Playfulness as impossible situations in coping with trauma.

The linking of trauma and dissociation dates to the works of Janet on hysteria (1887), as well as Freud and Breuer (1892) and that of Morton Prince (1906) on multiple personality and dissociation—all put forward the notion that **dissociative symptoms** frequently develop in response to subjectively perceived traumatic events. Some may argue that these dissociative symptoms are related to and stem from an underlying (structural) dissociation of the personality (Van der Hart and Dorahy 2009).

In clinical psychology and psychiatry, "Imagination" has many pathogenic aliases: Fantasy, delusion, hallucination, illusion, dissociation, fiction, denial; all carry a pathological perspective, except one positive word—"creativity."

Van der Hart and Dorahy (2009) discuss the difference between a narrow and a broad conceptualization of dissociation (pp. 20–21). The "narrow" approach calls dissociative only to the phenomena produced by a divided consciousness, or a divided personality. The broad conceptualization defines dissociation as a "breakdown" in integrated function. Thus, any psychological experience, which is characterized by a "breakdown" in integrated function, is "dissociative." That may be due to (1) parallel streams of consciousness, (2) a narrowing of the field of consciousness, (3) alterations in conscious experience, or (4) a post-traumatic, divided personality structure.

In Psychology, we witness a wide array of experiences, from mild detachment from immediate surroundings to more severe detachment from physical and emotional experiences. The major characteristic of all "dissociative phenomena" involves detachment from reality, rather than a loss of reality, as in Psychosis. Dissociation is commonly displayed on a continuum. On the mild end, dissociation is regarded as a coping mechanism or a way of seeking to gain mastery, minimize, or tolerate stress. On the extreme end, pathological dissociation involves PTSD and dissociative disorders, dissociative fugue, depersonalization disorder. Due to their unexpected and largely inexplicable nature, these symptoms tend to be quite unsettling. Başoĝlu (2009) says that regular dissociation is more common in response to interpersonal trauma (such as sexual assault, trauma in combat) than non-interpersonal trauma (such as natural disasters, car accidents, etc.). When referring to dissociation in warlike situations, continuous captivity is considered a severe interpersonal trauma. The reason for it is that the captives undergo a deliberate and continuous traumatization by their captors, who use psychological tactics designed to break the prisoner's mind, thus making the captors seem to have endless power.

In the absence of other means of escape, prisoners of war use dissociation as a coping mechanism that distorts their perception of reality, allows them to deny, repress, and limit their thoughts.

Other common experiences of dissociation such as depersonalization and derealization were associated with positive effects, as they allow individuals to protect themselves from the extreme emotions and arousal activated by a traumatic event. In some cases, individuals are protected even from memories of the event, when psychogenic amnesia is produced (Williams et al. 2003; Kihlstrom 2005). Assessment of dissociative experiences in nonclinical populations proposes that not only are such experiences not inherently distressing, but that they may often be associated with pleasurable or playful recreational or creative activities, and that they exhibit good adaptation in everyday life (Lynn and Rhue 1986; Rhue and Lynn 1987; Merckelbach et al. 1999).

Améry describes this coping style in detail, when he refers to the "unintellectual":

> *Our religiously or politically committed comrades were not at all, or only a little, astonished that in the camp the unimaginable became reality... their belief or their ideology gave them that firm foothold in the world from which they spiritually unhinged the SS state.... Their kingdom, in any event, was not the Here and Now, but the Tomorrow and Someplace, the very distant Tomorrow of the Christian, glowing in chiliastic light, or the utopian worldly Tomorrow of the Marxists. The grip of the horror reality was weaker where from the start reality had been placed in the framework of an unalterable idea.* (p. 13)
>
> *For the unintellectual had never a universal humane logic, rather only a consistent system of self-preservation.* (p. 12)

And Améry concludes (my highlighting ML):"*One way or the other, in the decisive moments their political or religious belief was* ***an inestimable help*** *to them,* ***while we skeptical and humanistic intellectuals took recourse, in vain, to our literary, philosophical,*** *and artistic household gods*" (p. 12).

Let's examine in depth the "*glowing in chiliastic light*" or in my terms the benefits of imagination and playfulness in traumatic situations.

We can argue that these were the ones who used their imagination and perhaps playfulness. Here are two concepts that I have studied in reference to sufferers of PTSD and I wish to discuss herein.

According to the Oxford English dictionary (2005), imagination is "the faculty or action of forming new ideas, or images or concepts of external objects not present to the senses." Duffy (1998): "Detach oneself from the tangible world and move beyond concrete situations, not be restricted to the immediate perceived world, internalize perception separate action and object from their meaning in the real world and give them new meaning, contemplate what is not but might be and pretend" (p. 21).

Imagination is a known method of coping with stress. The imaginary world provides a means for assessing and coping with different stress-inducing situations, until the solution that can be applied is found (Singer and Singer 1990). The individual imagines situations and occurrences, through which he develops an internal dialogue and experiments with the emotions evoked in the process. Imaginal preparedness, with all the possibilities and emotions it evokes, is a coping resource that prepares the individual for a harsh reality that may await him. This way, imagination may help soothe during times of stress, provide a sense of control, and enable one to take flight from reality. In emotion-focused coping situations, the individual reassesses the situation and assigns a less threatening meaning to it (Lazarus and Lazarus 2001). Many researchers (Cohen

1996; Singer 1975; Singer and Singer 1990) claim imagination is a necessary state of awareness for a healthy emotional life. The research literature has many references to the advantages of imagination in assisting in problem solving, mental flexibility, coping with stressful situations, crises, and difficult situations (Clark 1998; Kaufman 2009; Taylor et al. 1998). The use of imagination in severely stressful situations is mentioned by Hilgard (1977), who describes how during times of crisis and great danger the individual has at his disposal a coping strategy that enables him to temporarily detach from the life-threatening event. Rape victims, survivors of traumatic disasters, torture victims, prisoners, and hostages report this detachment from reality, which we discussed earlier as dissociation. Lloyd (1998) views this detachment as one of nature's small graces that shields against unbearable pain and enables subjective distancing, sensory numbness, and analgesia in these situations.

Klinger (1990) and Butler (2006) describe normative dissociation as typically involving experiences of absorption, narrowing, or attentiveness and focused utilization of cognitive resources; the absorbed individual becomes unaware of the external environment, self-awareness, and critical thought are adjourned and time perception may become faint.

Playfulness referring to style or attitude. A person with playful attributes is governed by internal motivation, internal orientation, is unbound to external rules, and is actively involved in his environment (Barnett 2007).

Play and coping are linked in terms of adaptability to the demands of the environment, exploration of options, creative problem solving, social competence, and internally driven motivation (Saunders et al. 1998).

Research suggests that playfulness facilitates healing, improves morale, and increases motivation. Thus, it can be speculated that playfulness relates to other indicators of well-being, including the psychological, cognitive, and physical aspects.

Tegano (1990) found significant relationships between adults' creativity, playfulness, and what she called "tolerance of ambiguity," defined as how predisposed an individual is to handle ambiguous situations.

Gordon (2014) builds upon research in attachment theory that correlates secure attachment in infancy with an adult's well-being, to demonstrate how playfulness might be a lifelong outcome of secure attachment, and a primary factor in well-being among adults aged 28–63 years old. According to the interpretation of this study's findings, playfulness allows adults to approach activities with the same openness of mind with which the child approaches play; the beginning is known, and a precise end is anticipated, but the nature of its unfolding may vary. With playfulness, difficult situations are perceived as challenges, opportunities to learn, and possibilities to increase one's competence and skills. Furthermore, mistakes are no longer considered a failure, rather a possibility to learn and to grow (Proyer 2012). Monahan and Lurie (2015) suggest that "in order to play, an individual has to allow him or herself the freedom of self-expression and imagination. In this context, vulnerability and hypervigilance, two states of feelings frequently experienced by trauma survivors, can dampen freedom of expression, thus hampering play" (p. 21).

Further support of the possible adaptive function that playfulness may serve in adulthood is found in Magnuson and Barnett's (2011) cross-sectional study. They investigated the interrelationship between playfulness in 898 young adult students, as well as perceived stress, and styles of coping. Their findings revealed that playful individuals reported lower levels of perceived stress than their less playful counterparts and that these individuals more frequently utilized adaptive, stressor-focused coping strategies; they were also less likely to employ negative, avoidant, and escape-oriented strategies. The results suggested that playfulness served as a strong adaptive function with university students, providing them with specific cognitive resources from which they could incorporate effective coping behaviors in the face of stressful situations.

The paucity of research on older adult playfulness is unfortunate; the majority of research on Americans' health is "negative or disease oriented," particularly in studies of older adults. There is compelling evidence that positive factors in individual's lives, such as favorable emotions, happiness, life satisfaction, and quality of life, relate intimately to healthy aging. Playfulness might be an important characteristic of cognitive functioning and emotional growth, both of which are important components of healthy aging. In the Proyer et al. (2010) study in a sample of elderly people, a positive relationship is reported between playfulness and various indicators of quality of life that supports these notions.

According to Waldman-Levi et al. (2015), there are no published data regarding the possible relationships between well-being, participation, and playfulness with cognitive-emotional functioning among the elderly. Playfulness is a personal disposition that taps into cognitive and emotional factors, and it is manifested in many important behaviors in one's adaptability and resilience in life, especially in later life. As Proyer (2011) reported of the positive relation between playfulness and various indicators of quality of life in a sample of elderly people, this concept should be included in studies aiming to explore healthy aging, well-being, and participation of the elderly.

Before resuming our investigation of Améry, we ought to look into the question whether inmates of the Nazi camps used humor, playfulness, imagination, and positive dissociation.

For a long time, this was a difficult subject for research, as it seems inappropriate to associate humor with such a tragic event. "Laughing about massive human destruction betrays every rule of etiquette..." (Carpenter 2010, p. 12). However, more and more evidence has been collected. And Carpenter (2010) suggests that "Laughter was useful in response to the Holocaust's tragedy, because it provided an alternative way of internalizing abnormality, it was a defense mechanism and established a type of revolt, and for many of the prisoners, it provided a link for sustaining their faith tradition" (p. 12). Laughter did not allow the prisoner an easy escape. However, it provided another perspective to their world. Then it became a matter of making a conscious choice to live in the other perspective.

Carpenter (2010) writes: "Each day that they woke up, they had to make the decision to laugh at their imprisonment or become consumed by it" (p. 17) and he quotes Bussie (2007), saying: "*We were looking underground for things to laugh at, even when there weren't any*" (p. 43).

Sanders (1995) says that their search for comedy was not in vain. This kind of attitude was restorative for the prisoners.

But when Améry mentions a joke or humor (just once, I must admit) it is only in reference to his Jewish identity, and so he immediately states that "*I cited it here not because of its humorous value, but only because of its usefulness as an illustration*" (p. 43).

That is, as I will demonstrate later, a moment of inability to suppress the distancing that humor allows us. "*The novelist Erich Maria Remarque it is told, was repeatedly visited after 1933 at his home in Ticino by emissaries of Goebbel's ministry, because they wanted to induce the emigre writers who were 'aryan' and thus never completely dominated by evil to return, to convert. When Remarque remained aloof, the envoy of the Reich finally asked him: For God's sake, man, aren't you homesick? Homesick, what do you mean? Remarque is said to have replied. Am I a Jew?*"

Ostrower (2009) classifies the types of humor and jokes and studies their respective functions in the ghettos, concentration camps, and death camps. She categorizes their purpose and suggests the following: self-humor, gallows humor, humor connected with food, humor stemming from superiority, humor stemming from frustration, aggressive humor, and sexual humor. One of her interviewees said: "... *Look, without humor we would all have committed suicide. We made fun of everything. What I'm actually saying is that, that helped us remain human, even under hard conditions*" (p. 17).

When Viktor Frankl discusses this exact experience, he suggests that in grave circumstances, "*what alone remains is the last of human freedoms; the ability to choose one's attitude in a given set of circumstances*" (p. 4). For the victims, this type of humor functioned as a spiritual weapon to turn the situation upside down and feel equal or even superior to their oppressor. "Resistance was expressed in the constant effort to maintain inner freedom while outwardly adapting" (Pawelczynska 1979, p. 127).

Now, we established that Améry observed these reactions and noticed how helpful they were "*One way or the other, in the decisive moments their political or religious belief was* ***an inestimable help*** *to them,* ***while we skeptical and humanistic intellectuals took recourse, in vain, to our literary, philosophical****, and artistic household gods*" (p. 12).

10.6 Why Then Didn't Améry Use Transcendence?

Despite his statement that once the intellectual's first resistance had flagged, he still clung to his armors of knowledge and analysis, even though these efforts left him with less ordnances with which to oppose his destroyers, compared to the unintellectual. In my view, this is where Améry's inability to play, to make belief and to revert and become an *unintellectual* interferes. The unintellectual option of coping was too threatening. He could not or did not want to abandon his intellectual convictions; what else would he lean on to withstand the horrific experiences, but his firm, and perhaps rigid stand, and so he says:

> *I did not want to be one with my believing comrades, [who transcended themselves and projected themselves into the future. They were no windowless monads; they stood open, wide open onto a world that was not the world of Auschwitz.]* (p. 14)

Being ***trained*** to use reflection, observation, and contemplation he couldn't discard his insights altogether and so with ambivalence he says:

> *But I would have wished to be like them: unshakable, calm, strong.* (p. 14)

Améry couldn't betray his intellectual conviction, though he was fully aware of its disadvantages. He said he was convinced that as an intellectual he couldn't make use of what the commoners could: "the intellectual did not so easily acknowledge the unimaginable conditions as a given fact as did the nonintellectual. Long practice in questioning the phenomena of everyday reality prevented him from simply adjusting to the realities of the camp, because these stood in all too sharp a contrast to everything that he had regarded until then as possible and humanly acceptable" (p. 10).

His contemplation is reflected in the following statement where he admits to the limits of his coping mechanisms: "... In the beginning, the defiant wisdom of folly held true for him: what surely may not be, cannot be. But only in the beginning" (p. 10).

Still there was a time that, according to my understanding of traumatic conditions, even Améry "surrendered" to imagination, or as will be explained below, "transcended into Fantastic Reality." But he immediately criticized it, calling it intoxication combined with emptiness and shame.

> *Now there were, to be sure, exceptions, which arose in certain conditions of mental intoxication.... And suddenly my consciousness was chaotically packed to the brim with the content of books, fragments of music I had heard, and—as I could 'not help but imagine -original philosophic thoughts. A wild longing for things of the spirit took possession of me, accompanied by a penetrating self-pity that brought tears to my eyes. At the same time, in a layer of my consciousness that had remained clear I was fully aware of the pseudo quality of this short-lived mental exaltation. It was a genuine state of intoxication, evoked by physical influences.* (p. 9)
>
> *Like all intoxications, they left behind a dreary, hangover-like feeling of emptiness and shame.* (p. 10)

I am not sure whether his contention with hope started in the camp. I am aware that philosophically he was influenced by Schopenhauer and Nietzsche, both critical about "Hope." For Schopenhauer's "hope" was problematic in respect to its influence on the intellect, because it presented what we wish for as probable (Schopenhauer 1958, pp. 216, 218). He claims that Hope distorts cognition in a problematic way because it hinders the intellect to grasp the truth. And Nietzsche, perhaps the most famous critic of Hope, who wrote "Zeus did not want man to throw his life away, no matter how much the other evil that fled from the box might torment him, but rather to go on letting himself be tormented anew. To that end, he gives man hope. But in reality, it is the worst of all evils, because it prolongs the torments of Man" (*Human, All Too Human*, 1986, p. 71).

I dare add that it is a combination of the above, but also Améry's resentment of fantasy, imagination, and playfulness. Indeed, when we examine Moulton and Kosslyn's (2009) definition of hope we can see it clearly. Hope is based on the imagining of a better future and fantasizing positive possible outcomes. Hope is the emotional state which promotes the belief in a positive outcome related to events and circumstances in one's life. Some claim that the ability to imagine is intended to anticipate the future, based on past experiences. Taylor and her colleagues (Taylor et al. 1998) argue that the ability to imagine the future is a strategy for emotional regulation. But Améry refused to use imagination and thus lost hope.

Améry's ambivalence is creeping out for a moment when it seems that he wishes to have *a "view into a world in which the principle of hope rules*" (p. 40).

Based on my earlier argument that Améry suffered from the combination of PTSD and traumatic grief, his inclination toward intellectualism as an unfortunate and firm identity meant that he was indeed governed by it, as he stated: "*Whoever has succumbed to torture* **(himself and others like him)** *can no longer feel at home in the world. The shame of destruction cannot be erased... Trust in the world, which already collapsed in part at the first blow, but in the end, under torture, fully, will not be regained... It blocks the view into a world in which the principle of hope rules*" (p. 40).

Before I continue any further, I feel it is important to say that there are researchers that will support Améry's refrain from the use of imagination. Rauschenberger and Lynn (1995) agree with Améry. They claim that a tendency to daydream and fantasize is correlated with psychological dysfunction and impaired adjustment. This opinion is based on Freud's (1963) position that links fantasy with neurosis, psychosis, and organic illnesses. Rauschenberger and Lynn (1995) claim that people with a tendency to fantasize have flexible boundaries between reality and imagination and between internal and external experiences, which make them more susceptible to emotional pathologies. They suggested that people with a high tendency to fantasize reported, significantly more episodes of major depression in their past, compared to people with a lower tendency to fantasize. Peritraumatic dissociation (PD) has been consistently found to be associated with PTSD in a diversity of trauma populations

(Lensvelt-Mulders et al. 2008). PD is defined as an immediate reaction to overwhelmingly stressful events, consisting of disturbances in memory, depersonalization and derealization, alterations in time perception, and a sense of detachment from others and one's surroundings (Marmar et al. 1994). Though PD may protect an individual from immediate devastating emotions (Van der Hart et al. 2004), it may also preclude long-term recovery by preventing emotional processing of the event (Marmar et al. 1994; Ehlers and Clark 2000). Still, there is no general consensus across prospective Type I trauma studies (a single incident trauma) that PD qualifies as an important independent predictor of PTSD symptomatology (Van der Velden and Wittmann 2008).

So, with this disagreement amongst scholars, I tend to come back to my understanding of Améry and suggest that in my view he confirms what Kaplansky (2009) and my own studies (Lahad and Doron 2010) show that those with severe PTSD lose their ability to transcend into Fantastic Reality.

10.7 "Fantastic Reality," or the Healing Power of Imagination

This space of **"Fantastic Reality"** is a temporary safe place from the pain experienced in reality. In this space, an alternate narrative can be created, and can thus serve as a healing space in which mental resilience may be built in the midst of a harsh reality, thus enabling one to cope with situations that are otherwise hard to bear (Lahad and Leykin 2012).

"Fantastic Reality" allows the psyche to play again as it did in early childhood, in a space where laws of reality do not govern, where one can invent stories as part of the quest for answers and insights for real life situations, for which logical solutions are no longer satisfactory. Often, the journey to fantastic reality and back brings relief, even when there is no practical application of the "insights" or "lessons" experienced. This relief may stem from the principle of "distancing for the sake of getting near." Being in fantastic reality is often experienced as a trance-like state. The resulting relief is perhaps comprised of the sensorial experience of childhood omnipotence that enables the adult to experience what Winnicott calls "creating a world". This experience parallels the empowerment process whereby the individual feels competent and influential, has self-respect and feels others respect him as well.

The link between the ability to transcend to fantastic reality and PTSD was examined by Kaplansky (2009) in her doctoral research, following the findings of Ozer et al. (2003), which indicate that PD that occurs in close proximity to the event predicts a higher risk of developing PTSD. According to them, 70 percent of those who have experienced PD at the acute stage (ASR) will develop PTSD (Ozer et al. 2003).

Later, Brooks and his colleagues (Brooks et al. 2009) suggested two causes of peritraumatic dissociation: an alternative awareness and derealization (disturbances in subjective and objective perception). They found that the derealization factor alone predicted a severe stress reaction as well as symptoms of anxiety and depression among trauma victims.

Kaplansky (2009) examined a group of participants who underwent a near-death experience (NDE) (Greyson and Stevenson 1980). Participants in this group were exposed to an extreme life-threatening event and gave an account of the event, including elements such as floating, a tunnel with light, an encounter with spiritual beings, an "out of body" sensation, and a sense that "life flashed before my eyes like a movie." Greyson (2000, in Nathan and Gorman 2002) suggested that NDE is a non-pathological type of dissociative response to a stressor. This phenomenon, occurring during the Peri Traumatic dissociation (PTDIS) stage, may place this group at a higher risk for developing PTSD. In a review article from 2007, Greyson notes that all of the hypotheses regarding NDE phenomena as resulting from hypoxia/anoxia were not supported by research as was the possibility that these phenomena resulted from drugs or medication (the later findings were similar to Kaplansky 2009). Greyson (2001) attributes the lack of connection, to the positive affect associated with an NDE experience during the unfolding of NDE dissociative features at the time of the trauma. Kaplansky's (2009) research replicated Greyson's findings from 2000 that the NDE group not only did not suffer from PTSD but its scores on the anxiety and dissociation scales were low in comparison to both the general population and to clients diagnosed as suffering from PTSD. An essential and significant difference between those who experienced NDE and those who suffered from PTSD and experienced symptoms of NDE was the category of "seeing my life flash before my eyes." The PTSD patients experienced these ten times more than those who underwent NDE. Kaplansky (2009) believes this category of NDE is the closest to reality, as it is a kind of "life review" process that most probably includes anxiety, guilt, remorse, and perhaps a deep sorrow at a life ending, but certainly not the joy of floating, or encountering light or spiritual beings. When looking at what might have encouraged the development of these abilities in childhood, Kaplansky's study demonstrates a clear distinction between the NDE group, the control group and the group suffering from PTSD, in their childhood pastime and recreational activities. These are described as playfulness, e.g., playing musical instruments, dancing, painting and art, sports and most of all, telling stories and tales. Those who reported experiencing NDE surpassed the rest in the length of time and the intensity of their stay in playfulness mode, yet maintained their ability to move back and forth between fantastic reality, such as telling stories and tales, and reality. In addition, the study suggests the possibility that children, who "practiced" transcending into fantastic reality and whose parents encouraged such activity, may have developed resilience to extremely threatening situations. In fact, Kaplansky's conclusions support the findings of Council and Greyson (1985) who found that the tendency to fantasize and use the imagination in both childhood and adulthood among people who experienced NDE was significantly higher, compared to people who never had such an experience. Which further supports the idea that dissociation enables the individual to escape the traumatic stressful event which overwhelms the sufferer and does not allow physical escape (Megged 2001; Van der Kolk et al. 1996; Van der Kolk et al. 2005).

While playfulness has been linked to positive attributes, a more comprehensive understanding of exactly what playfulness provides to an individual is needed.

The findings of Magnuson and Barnett's (2011) clearly indicate that playful adults have a propensity to attack stressors directly and that they more infrequently utilized less adaptive coping styles, such as self-blame. This implies that playful individuals correctly believed that they have the inner resources necessary to overcome their stressors and are successful in their utilization of coping strategies.

Perhaps most notable is that adult playfulness seems to contribute to an individual's resilience through its unique dissemination of coping styles in the face of stressful situations, as playful adults seem to see stressors as non-debilitating and attack them directly and readily.

Although the direct relationship between creativity and PTSD was rarely tested in literature, there is evidence that creativity could assist as a protective factor and could facilitate resiliency (Metzl and Morrell 2008). Overall, evidence of creativity and mental flexibility as protective factors were found to indices of overall psychological difficulties, but not for specific symptom measures, and as significant predictors of resilience (Tol et al. 2013; Metzl 2009).

In light of the considerable benefits of playfulness, another natural question regarding future implications is whether it is possible to teach individuals how to be playful. With the conceptualization of playfulness holding that it is an aspect of personality, which is largely stable across time, it seems that enhancing playfulness in an individual would be a challenging endeavor. At the same time, it does not seem accurate to view playfulness as dichotomy; it should not be viewed as an all-or-nothing construct. Rather, playfulness seems to range along a continuum from low to high (Glynn and Webster 1992). If every individual possesses at least some amount of playfulness, it follows that the adaptive functions of playfulness can be enhanced to benefit everyone. Unfortunately, many times latent playfulness is mistaken for a lack of playfulness, and it is subsequently not further developed, encouraged, or given credence. Playfulness in all people, however, should be nurtured so that its benefits can be realized.

I wish to reexamine Améry's following statement and suggest that in my view the result of Améry's rejection of the potential for healing imbedded in imagination and fantastic reality deterred him from a potential or partial recovery. He describes his postwar experience in a terrifying and somewhat dissociative manner. He describes his worldly experiences as a haunted world full of encounters with "monstrous" beings, "*Tile man with the square skull, the police agent with the resentful voice, the gurgling Jew were my lords and masters*" (p. 40). He lost his home but was it a real home or an introjected hopeful memory of the past? "*There was no order for me in this world.*" He lost his confidence in his ability to discriminate between good and threatening signals. "*Was the smile of the police official who checked our papers good-natured, indifferent, or mocking? Was his deep Voice resentful or full of goodwill? I didn't know. Did the old bearded Jew, whose gurgling sounds I nevertheless grasped as sentences, mean it well with us or did he hate us...*" He lost his basic trust in his ability to understand the world after the war, as if he is still psychologically incarcerated in the past, but confused, as this was the same past that haunts him, yet the most "certain" past he had to rely on. "*I staggered through a world whose signs remained as scrutable to me as an Etruscan script. Unlike the tourist, however, for whom such things may be a piquant form of alienation, I was dependent on this. World full of riddles....*"

And he preferred the known hell to uncompressible and alienating present. "*At times, I felt more vulnerable before them than before the SS man at home, because of him I had at least known with certainty that he was stupid and mean and that he was after my life*" (p. 47).

This, to me, portrays the long-term effects of the traumatic experience in Auschwitz.

10.8 Treatment of PTSD Using Imagination, Creativity, and Playfulness

In a solo article we found on "Play and Playfulness in Holocaust Survivors," Auerhahn and Laub (1987) describe three cases of analytical treatments focusing on "the ability of a survivor to play, or to be playful, as one important index of the severity of the Holocaust trauma and of the potential for its healing" (p. 56).

Recuperative psychological processes such as fantasy, reflection, dreams, artistic productions, and play were shuttered or annihilated in the concentration camps, where every type of human form including that of the human body was under constant assault, created disruptions in survivors' abilities to narrate, symbolize, and integrate abilities that, for children, are manifested in play.

They claim that the link with the therapist meant for the patient a relinking with his own inner world, "and it was this that allowed the play of his memory and imagination, as well as his return to playing. Only then could proper healing begin" (p. 57).

In the clinical world different therapeutic methods have used imagination as an effective tool (Holmes 2014). Recalling past memories and retrieving episodic, as well as autobiographical memory is one common supplementary therapeutic technique used in the treatment of anxiety and stress related disorders (Cooper and Clum 1989), including Cognitive Behavior Therapy (CBT), Prolonged Exposure therapy (PE), Imaginal Flooding (IF), Virtual Reality Exposure (VRE), Imagery Rescripting, Systematic Desensitization, Eye Movement Desensitization and Reprocessing (EMDR), SEE FAR CBT and creative arts.

SEE FAR CBT is a relatively new protocol (Lahad and Doron 2007, 2009; Lahad et al. 2011, 2016) for the treatment of anxiety disorders and PTSD, using a creative form treatment based on empowerment through imagination and the Fantastic Reality. The model emphasizes the role of Fantastic Reality (FR) and the use of imaginal re-narration of the traumatic event with the use of metaphoric cards as a means of externalization or distancing. In practice, FR uses playfulness methods as part of the healing process. It is introduced by the use of metaphoric therapeutic cards (TC) (Ayalon 2007) to represent both "a pleasant/safe place," a subjective feeling of comfort and security, and the re-narrating process of the traumatic story. The use of cards as an "externalization" of the otherwise internally haunting images or as "distancing," allows the clients to take the position of the observer in their own drama, thus giving them a sense of control and mastery over the incident. Moreover, FR allows the client to make use of the "as if space," an imaginative space where all the IFs are possible and where the impossible becomes possible. This practice reintroduces the client to his/her ability to play and to experience empowerment (Lahad et al. 2010). The treatment protocol incorporates methods of somatic memory reduction as well as CBT elements. It is a mental state and a function of our imagination, in which the individual experiences an alter awareness mode. Using FR allows us to possess an "in between" mental state in which we are experiencing reality and an imaginative representation, at the same time. Individuals suffering from PTSD may use this function of imagination to control arousal, change, suppression, and inhibition of their traumatic memory or intrusive content (for a full review see: Lahad 2000, 2005; Lahad and Doron 2010). SEE FAR CBT was found to be associated with effective alleviation of traumatic symptoms, showing statistically significant decreases in their trauma symptoms over time (Lahad et al. 2010, 2011).

10.9 Epilogue

I hope that my reading through Améry's writings has been useful clarifying my perception that he wasn't playful or optimistic, nor did he give "imagination" a chance to sooth the dreads of the Holocaust experience, or his own aging.

So, all he has been left with was resentment.

> *Resentment blocks the exit to the genuine human dimension, the future.* ***I know… that the time-sense of the person trapped in resentment is twisted around****, dis-ordered, if you wish, for it desires two impossible things: regression, into the past and nullification of what happened.* (p. 68)

It is not surprising that his messages are depressive, disillusioned, and demonstrate grieving and despair. "*Whoever was tortured, stays tortured.*

Torture is ineradicably burned into him, even when no clinically objective traces can be detected" (p. 34).

And the outcome for him was "*whoever has succumbed to torture can no longer feel at home in the world. The shame of destruction cannot be erased. Trust in the world, which already collapsed in part at the first blow, but in the end, under torture, fully, will not be regained...It blocks the view into a world in which the principle of hope rules*" (p. 40).

I have tried to convince the reader that he was aware of the option that the "*believer is not a captive of his individuality; rather he is part of a spiritual continuity that is interrupted nowhere, not even in Auschwitz...*" Both of them transcended themselves and projected themselves into the future. "*They were no windowless monads; they stood open, wide open onto a world that was not the world of Auschwitz*" (p. 14).

And despite momentary succumbing to transcendence and relief in "*fragments of music I had heard, and—as I could not help but imagine-original philosophic thoughts. A wild longing for things of the spirit took possession of me*" (p. 10). He resented it by calling it "*a genuine state of intoxication, evoked by physical influences*" (p. 9). *Like all intoxications they left behind a dreary, hangover-like feeling of emptiness shame* (p. 10).

And so, he reverted to his intellectual position, or to the philosophy of intellectualism, and could not and perhaps didn't want to exercise other options of coping with the trauma of Auschwitz, despite his observations and reflections on the options of the nonintellectual.

Could it have stopped him from committing suicide, or cured his depression? I am not sure but I do think that careful reading of his final letters written by him just before his suicide, suggest that it wasn't only his wish to protest and make a statement but also his realization that "he has aged and, in a time span that now already runs into decades, has had to learn that it was not a wound that was inflicted upon him, one that will scar over with the ticking of time, but rather that he is suffering from an insidious disease that is growing worse with the years" (p. 57) or even stronger "he lies unrecognizable in the ruins of the years 1933 to 1945" (p. 59).

And from this human perspective his only "hope" was suicide which he called "a glimmer, the barest inkling of inner peace."

And so, he writes to his wife probably minutes before the act: "*I am on the road to open. It is not easy, but it is deliverance all the same. You already know everything I have to say to you: that I loved you eternally and that you are the last image that stands before my eyes. You see, my heart's beloved, I am at the end of my powers and cannot look on at my physical, mental, and intellectual decline*" (Peng-Keller and Mauz 2018, p. 147).

It seems to me that this letter shed a very humane light on Améry's final words, leading me to use Nietzsche's book, title as a paraphrase for Améry's departure from his misery: **Human, all too human**.

References

Auerhahn, N. C., & Laub, D. (1987). Play and Playfulness in Holocaust Survivors. *Psychoanalytical Study Child, 42*, 45–58.

Ayalon, O. (2007). Healing Trauma with Metaphoric Cards. *Therapy Today, 18*, 22–24.

Barak, Y., Aizenberg, D., Szor, H., Swartz, M., Maor, R., & Knobler, H. Y. (2005). Increased Risk of Attempted Suicide Among Aging Holocaust Survivors. *American Journal of Geriatric Psychiatry, 13*(8), 701–704.

Barnett, L. A. (2007). The Nature of Playfulness in Young Adults. *Personality and Individual Differences, 43*, 949–958.

Başoğlu, M. (2009). A Multivariate Contextual Analysis of Torture and Cruel, Inhuman, and Degrading Treatments: Implications for an Evidence-Based Definition of Torture. *American Journal of Orthopsychiatry, 79*(2), 135–145.

Bennett, A. (2017). *Suicide Century: Literature and Suicide from James Joyce to David Foster Wallace*. Cambridge: Cambridge University Press.

Brooks, R., Bryant, R. A., Silove, D., Creamer, M., O'Donnell, M., McFarlane, A. C., & Marmar, C. R. (2009). The Latent Structure of the Peritraumatic Dissociative Experiences Questionnaire. *Journal of Trauma Stress, 22*(2), 153–157.

Bussie, J. A. (2007). *The Laughter of the Oppressed: Ethical and Theological Resistance in Wiesel, Morrison, and Endo*. New York: T&T Clark International.

Butler, L. (2006). Normative Dissociation. *Psychiatric Clinics of North America, 29*, 45–62.

Carpenter, W. (2010). Laughter in a Time of Tragedy: Examining Humor During the Holocaust. *Denison Journal of Religion, 9*(3), 11–25.

Clark, C. D. (1998). Childhood Imagination in the Face of Chronic Illness. In J. Sarbin & J. De Rivera (Eds.), *Believed-in Imaginings: The Narrative Construction of Reality* (pp. 87–100). Washington, DC: American Psychological Association.

Cohen, A. (1996). *The Dream of the Soul: Imagination, Fantasy and Daydreaming*. Haifa: Amatzia (Hebrew).

Cooper, N. A., & Clum, G. A. (1989). Imaginal Flooding as a Supplementary Treatment for PTSD in Combat Veterans: A Controlled Study. *Behavior Therapy, 20*(3), 381–391.

Council, J. R., & Greyson, B. (1985). *Near-Death Experiences and the "Fantasy-Prone" Personality: Preliminary Findings*. 93rd Annual Convention of the American Psychological Association, Los Angeles, CA, 23–27.

Duffy, B. (1998). *Supporting Creativity and Imagination in the Early Years*. Buckingham, UK: Open University Press.

Ehlers, A., & Clark, D. M. (2000). A Cognitive Model of Posttraumatic Stress Disorder. *Behaviour Research and Therapy, 38*, 319–345.

Foa, E. B., & Rothbaum, B. O. (2001). *Treating the Trauma of Rape: Cognitive-Behavioral Therapy for PTSD*. New York: Guilford Press.

Freud, S., & Breuer, J. [1892] (2004). *Studies in Hysteria* (N. Luckhurst, Trans.). London: Penguin Books.

Freud, A. (1963). The Concept of Developmental Lines. *The Psychoanalytic Study of the Child, 18*(1), 245–265.

Glynn, M., & Webster, J. (1992). The Adult Playfulness Scale: An Initial Assessment. *Psychological Reports, 71*, 83–103.

Gordon, G. (2014). Well Played: The Origins and Future of Playfulness. *American Journal of Play, 6*, 234–266.

Greyson, B., & Stevenson, I. (1980). The Phenomenology of Near-Death Experiences. *American Journal of Psychiatry, 137*, 1193–1196.

Greyson, B. (2001). Posttraumatic Stress Symptoms Following Near-Death Experiences. *American Journal of Orthopsychiatry, 71*, 368–373.

Holmes, J. (2014). *The Therapeutic Imagination: Using Literature to Deepen Psychodynamic Understanding and Enhance Empathy*. London: Routledge.

Heidelberger-Leonard, I. (2010). *The Philosopher of Auschwitz: Jean Améry and Living with the Holocaust*. London and New York: IB Tauris.

Herman, J. L. (1992). Complex PTSD: A Syndrome in Survivors of Prolonged and Repeated Trauma. *Journal of Traumatic Stress, 5*(3), 377–391.

Hilgard, E. R. (1977). The Problem of Divided Consciousness: A Neodissociation Interpretation. *Annals of the NY Academy of Science, 296*, 48–59.

Janet, P. (1887). L'Anesthésie Systematisée el la Dissociation des Phénomenes Psychologiques. *Review of Philosophy, 23*(1), 449–472.

Kaplansky, N. (2009). *Dissociating from Death: An Investigation into the Resilience Potential of Transcendence into Fantastic Reality During Near-Death Experiences* (Unpublished doctoral dissertation). Anglia Ruskin University, Chelmsford, UK.

Kaufman, J. C. (2009). *Creativity 101*. New York: Springer.

Kihlstrom, J. (2005). Dissociative Disorders. *Annual Review of Clinical Psychology, 1*, 227–253.

Klinger, E. (1990). *Daydreaming*. Los Angeles, CA: Tarcher (Putnam).

Lahad, M., Baruch, Y., Shacham, Y., Niv, S., Rogel, R., Nacasch, N., & Leykin, D. (2011). Cultural Sensitivity in Psychosocial Interventions Following a Disaster: A Tri-National Collaboration in Sri Lanka. In R. Kaufman, R. L. Edwards, J. Mirsky, & A. Avgar (Eds.), *Crisis as an Opportunity: Organizational and*

Professional Responses to Disaster (pp. 129–154). Lanham, MD: University Press of America.

Lahad, M., & Doron, M. (2009). *SEE FAR CBT.* Kiryat Shmona: CSPC (Hebrew).

Lahad, M., & Doron, M. (2010). *Protocol for Treatment of Post-Traumatic Stress Disorder: See Far CBT Model: Beyond Cognitive Behavior Therapy.* Amsterdam: IOS Press.

Lahad, M. (2000). *Creative Supervision.* London: Jessica Kingsley Publication.

Lahad, M. (2005). Transcending into Fantastic Reality: Story Making with Adolescents in Crisis. In C. Schaefer, J. Mccormick, & A. Ohnogi (Eds.), *International Handbook of Play Therapy: Advances in Assessment, Theory, Research and Practice* (p. 133). Lanham, MD: Jason Aronson.

Lahad, M., & Doron, M. (2007). *Beyond CBT, SEE FAR CBT Post-Traumatic Stress Disorder Treatment Protocol.* Kiryat Shmona: CSPC.

Lahad, M., Farchi, M., Leykin, D., & Kaplansky, N. (2010). Preliminary Study of a New Integrative Approach in Treating Posttraumatic Stress Disorder: SEE FAR CBT. *The Arts in Psychotherapy, 37*, 391–399.

Lahad, M., & Leykin, D. (2012). The Healing Potential of Imagination in the Treatment of Psychotrauma: An Alternative Explanation for the Effectiveness of the Treatment of PTSD Using Fantastic Reality. In S. A. Lee & D. M. Edget (Eds.), *Cognitive Behavioral Therapy, Application Methods and Outcomes* (pp. 71–93). New York: Nova.

Lahad, M., Leykin, D., Farchi, M., Doron, M., Gidron, Y., Rozenblat, O., & Fajerman, Z. (2016). SEE FAR CBT Therapy for Children with Post-Traumatic Stress Disorder Under Prolonged Political Conflict. *Journal of Psychology and Psychotherapy Research, 3*, 1–12.

Lazarus, R., & Lazarus, B. (2001). *Emotion and Logic.* Haifa: University of Haifa and Zemora Bitan Pub. [Hebrew].

Lensvelt-Mulders, G., van der Hart, O., van Ochten, J. M., Van Son, M. J. M., Steele, K., & Breeman, L. (2008). Relations Among Peritraumatic Dissociation and Posttraumatic Stress: A Meta-Analysis. *Clinical Psychology Review, 28*, 1138–1151.

Lloyd, D. (1998). The Fables of Lucy R.: Association and Dissociation in Neural Networks. In D. Stein (Ed.), *Connectionism and Psychopathology* (pp. 247–272). Cambridge: Cambridge University Press.

Lynn, S. J., & Rhue, J. W. (1986). The Fantasy-Prone Person: Hypnosis, Imagination, and Creativity. *Journal of Personality and Social Psychology, 51*(2), 404–408.

Magnuson, C. D., & Barnett, L. A. (2011). The Playful Advantage: How Playfulness Enhances Coping with Stress. *Leisure and Science: An Interdisciplinary Journal, 35*, 129–144.

Marmar, C. R., Weiss, D. S., Schlenger, W. E., Fairbank, J. A., Jordan, B. K., Kulka, R. A., & Hough, R. L. (1994). Peritraumatic Dissociation and

Posttraumatic Stress in Male Vietnam Theater Veterans. *American Journal of Psychiatry, 151*, 902–907.

Megged, A. (2001). *Fairies and Witches: Metaphoric Stories in Caring for Children at Risk*. Haifa: Nord Publication [Hebrew].

Merckelbach, H., Muris, P., & Rassin, E. (1999). Fantasy Proneness and Cognitive Failures as Correlates of Dissociative Experiences. *Personality and Individual Differences, 26*(5), 961–967.

Metzl, E. S. (2009). The Role of Creative Thinking in Resilience After Hurricane Katrina. *Psychology of Aesthetics, Creativity, and the Arts, 3*(2), 112.

Metzl, E. S., & Morrell, M. A. (2008). The Role of Creativity in Models of Resilience: Theoretical Exploration and Practical Applications. *Journal of Creativity in Mental Health, 3*(3), 303–318.

Monahan, K., & Lurie, A. (2015). The Use of Humor with Older Adults Aging in Place. *Journal of Social Work and Mental Health, 13*, 61–69.

Moulton, S. T., & Kosslyn, S. M. (2009). Imagining Predictions: Mental Imagery as Mental Emulation. *Philosophical Transaction of the Royal Society B, 364*(1521), 1273–1280.

Nathan, P. E., & Gorman, J. M. (Eds.). (2002). *A Guide to Treatments That Work* (2nd ed.). New York, NY: Oxford University Press.

Nietzsche, F. W. (1986). *Human, All Too Human* (R.J. Hollingdale, Trans.). Oxford University Press (Original work published in 1878).

Oquendo, M. A., Friend, J. M., Halberstam, B., Brodsky, B. S., Burke, A. K., Grunebaum, M. F., Malone, K. M., & Mann, J. J. (2003). Association of Comorbid Posttraumatic Stress Disorder and Major Depression with Greater Risk for Suicidal Behavior. *American Journal of Psychiatry, 160*(3), 580–582.

Ostrower, H. (2009). *It Kept Us Alive: Humor in the Holocaust*. Jerusalem: Yad Va Shem Hebrew Edition.

Oxford English Dictionary: Single User Version. (2005). (Vols. 1–3). Oxford: Oxford University Press.

Ozer, E. J., Best, S. R., Lipsey, T. L., & Weiss, D. S. (2003). Predictors of Posttraumatic Stress Disorder and Symptoms in Adults: A Meta-Analysis. *Psychological Bulletin, 129*(1), 52–73.

Pawelczynska, A. (1979). *Values and Violence in Auschwitz: A Sociological Analysis*. Berkley, CA: University of California Press.

Peng-Keller, S., & Mauz, A. (Eds.). (2018). *Sterbenarrative: Hermeneutische Erkundungen des Erzählens am und vom Lebensende*. Berlin: Walter de Gruyter GmbH & Co.

Prigerson, H. G., Bierhals, A. J., Kasl, S. V., Reynolds, C. F., Shear, M. K., Day, N., Beery, L. C., Newsom, J. T., & Jacobs, S. (1997). Traumatic Grief as a Risk Factor for Mental and Physical Morbidity. *American Journal of Psychiatry, 154*(5), 616–623.

Prince, M. (1906). *The Dissociation of a Personality.* New York: Longmans, Green, & Co.
Proyer, R. T., Ruch, W., & Müller, L. (2010). Sense of Humor Among the Elderly: Findings Using the German Version of the SHS. *Z Gerontology Geriatric, 43*, 19–24.
Proyer, R. T. (2011). Being Playful and Smart? The Relations of Adult Playfulness with Psychometric and Self-Estimated Intelligence and Academic Performance. *Learning and Individual Differences, 21*, 463–467.
Proyer, R. T. (2012). Development and Initial Assessment of a Short Measure for Adult Playfulness: The SMAP. *Personality and Individual Differences, 53*, 989–994.
Rauschenberger, S. L., & Lynn, S. J. (1995). Fantasy Proneness, DSM-III-R Axis I Psychopathology and Dissociation. *Journal of Abnormal Psychology, 104*(2), 373–380.
Rhue, J. W., & Lynn, S. J. (1987). Fantasy Proneness and Psychopathology. *Journal of Personality and Social Psychology, 53*(2), 327–336.
Sanders, B. (1995). *Sudden Glory: Laughter as Subversive History.* Boston, MA: Beacon Press.
Saunders, I., Sayer, M., & Goodale, A. (1998). The Relationship Between Playfulness and Coping in Preschool Children: A Pilot Study. *American Journal of Occupational Therapy, 53*, 221–224.
Schopenhauer, A. (1958). *The World as Will and Representation* (p. 216). New York: Dover Publications.
Singer, D. G., & Singer, J. L. (1990). *The House of Make-Believe: Children's Play and the Developing Imagination.* Cambridge, MA: Harvard University Press.
Singer, J. L. (1975). Navigating the Stream of Consciousness: Research in Day-Dreaming and Related Inner Experience. *American Psychologist, 30*, 727–738.
Tanielian, T., Haycox, L. H., Schell, T. L., Marshall, G. N., Burnam, M. A., Eibner, C., Karney, B. R., Meredith, L. S., Ringel, J. S., & Vaiana, M. E. (2008). *Invisible Wounds of War: Summary and Recommendations for Addressing Psychological and Cognitive Injuries.* Santa Monica, CA: Rand Corp.
Taylor, S. E., Pham, L. B., Rivkin, I. D., & Armor, D. A. (1998). Harnessing the Imagination. Mental Simulation, Self-Regulation, and Coping. *American Psychologist, 53*(4), 429–439.
Tegano, D. W. (1990). Relationship of Tolerance of Ambiguity and Playfulness to Creativity. *Psychological Reports, 66*(3), 1047–1056.
Tol, W. A., Song, S., & Jordans, M. J. (2013). Annual Research Review: Resilience and Mental Health in Children and Adolescents Living in Areas of Armed Conflict – A Systematic Review of Findings in Low- and Middle-Income Countries. *J Child Psychology Psychiatry, 54*(4), 445–460.

Trappler, B., Cohen, C. I., & Tulloo, R. (2007). Impact of Early Lifetime Trauma in Later Life: Depression Among Holocaust Survivors 60 Years After the Liberation of Auschwitz. *American Journal of Geriatric Psychiatry, 15*(1), 79–83.

Van der Hart, O., Nijenhuis, E., Steele, K., & Brown, D. (2004). Trauma-Related Dissociation: Conceptual Clarity Lost and Found. *Australian and New Zealand Journal of Psychiatry, 38*, 906–914.

Van der Hart, O., & Dorahy, M. J. (2009). History of the Concept of Dissociation. In P. F. Dell & J. A. O'Neil (Eds.), *Dissociation and the Dissociative Disorders: DSM-V and Beyond* (pp. 3–26). New York, NY: Routledge/Taylor & Francis Group.

Van der Kolk, B. A., Roth, S., Pelcovitz, D., Sunday, S., & Spinazzola, J. (2005). Disorders of Extreme Stress: The Empirical Foundation of a Complex Adaptation to Trauma. *Journal of Traumatic Stress, 18*, 389–399.

Van der Kolk, B., Van der Hart, O., & Marmar, C. R. (1996). Dissociation and Information Processing in Posttraumatic Stress Disorder. In B. Van der Kolk, A. C. McFarlane, & L. Weisaeth (Eds.), *Traumatic Stress: The Effects of Overwhelming Experience on Mind, Body and Society* (pp. 303–327). New York: Guilford Press.

Van der Velden, P. G., & Wittmann, L. (2008). The Independent Predictive Value of Peritraumatic Dissociation for PTSD Symptomatology After Type I Trauma: A Systematic Review of Prospective Studies. *Clinical Psychology Review, 28*(6), 1009–1020.

Waldman-Levi, A., Bar-Haim Erez, A., & Katz, N. (2015). Healthy Aging Is Reflected in Well-Being, Participation, Playfulness, and Cognitive-Emotional Functioning. *Healthy Aging Research, 4*, 8.

Williams, C., Haines, J., & Sale, I. (2003). Psychophysiological and Psychological Correlates of Dissociation in a Case of Dissociative Identity Disorder. *Journal of Trauma and Dissociation, 4*(1), 101–118.

PART III

Beyond: Philosophy and Literature

CHAPTER 11

Without Love or Wisdom: On Jean Améry's Reluctant Philosophy

Roy Ben-Shai

In the following pages, I sketch a profile of Améry's intellectual persona. Améry is now often regarded as a philosopher; "the philosopher of Auschwitz" has become something of an epithet (cf. Heidelberger-Leonard 2010; Zolkos 2011a). As my remarks will indicate, I do believe there is merit in viewing his work in philosophical light, and, no less importantly, in viewing philosophy itself in the twilight generated by his work. But it is equally important for me to explain that Améry's unique mode, and method, of philosophizing challenges the very meaning of the Greek word "philosophy," and with it, our understanding of why and how it might be practiced.

Philosophia means the Love of Wisdom. In his intellectual persona at least, Améry was too sad and hurt to love, and too overwhelmed by his experiences to admit, or even aspire, to wisdom. In his life and in his work, he presents a profoundly different image of the philosopher and of the contemplative life: the philosopher as not a particularly *good* thinker (or a particularly good person for that matter), and the contemplative life as not a *good* one at all. Instead of love, one finds in Améry a very nuanced

R. Ben-Shai (✉)
Department of Philosophy, Sarah Lawrence College, Bronxville, NY, USA
e-mail: rbenshai@sarahlawrence.edu

Y. Ataria et al. (eds.), *Jean Améry*,
https://doi.org/10.1007/978-3-030-28095-6_11

conception of empathy, and the cultivation of human relationships precisely in those regions in which affinity and fondness are lacking. Instead of wisdom, we find in him a devotion to honesty and the cultivation of thoughtfulness, especially in those "twilight" regions that seem most difficult and unrewarding to thought.

I draw on methodological passages in some of his most accomplished original works: *Jenseits von Schuld und Sühne* (2002 [1966])—*At the Mind's Limits* in the English edition (1980)—*Über das Altern* (2005a [1968]) or *On Aging* (1994), and *Hand an sich legen* (2005b [1976]) or *On Suicide* (1999). These are books, and passages, I find particularly representative of Améry's intellectual personality and method.[1] Through their analysis, I wish to paint the picture that I have come to form of him and of his work; a picture and an intellectual relationship that has had, and perhaps was meant to have, a transformative impact on my self-understanding and on my understanding of the vocation—philosophy—that I have chosen.

* * *

The nature of Jean Améry's work in its mature phase (from the mid-1960s until his death in 1978) is difficult to pin down and categorize. For the most part comprised of series of essays, originally conceived for the radio and later published in print, his work combines intimate autobiographical reflections with critical engagement with scientific, philosophical, and literary sources. It oscillates between philosophy and fiction, between personal testimony and political address. Each series of essays not only takes on a different topic but also a different mode of presentation suitable to it. As a result, Améry's books are scattered across different library shelves—under sociology, autobiography, critical studies, German literature. The reception of *At the Mind's Limits*—the work to which his renown owed most—has largely been restricted to Holocaust Studies. The nonsystematic manner of his expositions, the diversity of style and subject matter, and the fact that Améry's books and essays were often read in isolation, all helped to keep the methodological and substantive guiding thread of his project hidden from sight.

In recent years, there has been a growing interest in Améry among philosophers (e.g., Bernstein 2015, 2016; Brudholm 2008; Stauffer 2015; Zolkos 2011a, 2011b), accompanied by a renewed acknowledgment of the depth, rigor, and force of his insight. I say "renewed" because such acknowledgment was there at the very beginning. Adorno was captivated by "Torture," one of Améry's first essays to appear in the intellectual magazine *Merkur*; it is difficult to overstate the extent of Améry's (under-acknowledged) influence on *Negative Dialectics*, the book on which Adorno was working at the time. Another intellectual to be struck by Améry was Alfred Andersch, who, with some foresight, wrote to him in a letter (1967): "It will be some time before political and philosophical thinking understands the importance of your book... but it is unthinkable that it will not be understood..." (Heidelberger-Leonard 2010, p. 171).

The reasons for which it took some time for philosophical thinking to understand Améry's importance are multiple. Not least among them is the fact that Améry himself was reluctant to identify as a philosopher. In *On Aging*—perhaps the most methodologically self-conscious of his books—he asks to distance himself from literature and philosophy alike:

> One's intellectual ambition must be surrendered... to the investigation of time. One may be contented even if whatever comes out of it is bad as long as it is right, where "right" [*recht*] cannot mean "correct" [*richtig*], only "honest"... This bad, right thinking [*Das schlechte, rechte Denken*] should only describe its own path. All else would be literature or philosophy, and they are absolutely good for nothing in this matter. (Améry 1994, p. 12; 2005a, p. 32, translation modified)

I count at least three closely related reasons for Améry's aversion to the term philosophy. The first is that he associates it with "sophisticated speculations" (e.g., Améry 1980, p. viii), the sort that are traditionally garbed in dense prose and an air of near-magical profundity. In *At the Mind's Limits*, after stating that his experience in Auschwitz made him neither wiser nor deeper, he seconds the words of Arthur Schnitzler: "Profundity has never clarified the world. Clarity looks more profoundly into its depths" (Améry 1980, p. 20). And elsewhere: "Reality is always more clever than the philosophy that impotently wishes to reflect it" (Améry 1984, p. 141).

A second problem was philosophy's traditional assumption of a universal or impersonal stance. Améry's own thinking, by contrast, as conveyed in the passage just cited from *On Aging*, means "only [to] describe *its own path*" (Améry 1994, p. 12, italics added). Doing so was particularly important in "an era when intelligence is turning away not only from what is immediately given by consciousness but from *the person* altogether

[*Menschen überhaupt*]—in whose place systems and codes appear as the subject of inquiry." To counter this neglect of the person, he chooses to keep "entirely to what has been lived: *le vécu*" (Améry 1994, p. xxi; translation modified).

Lastly, "philosophy" is also taken by him to name the professional discipline and self-enclosed discourse, with which he had, and wanted, little to do. As he notes in *On Aging*, he perceives of his thought as treading the thin line between "two danger zones, both of each are equally fatal":

> On the one hand, we are threatened by dull ruminations and dilettantish brooding. On the other, we have the technical language of the specialist in the discipline of philosophy, which, in sounding learned, strives to prove its own significance more than the value of its knowledge. (Améry 1994, p. 4)

It matters, in this respect, that Améry's major essays were originally conceived and delivered as radio talks. The audience he had in mind was not a select group of the initiated but a broader public of thoughtful listeners with whom he could speak, and whom he could impact, directly.[2]

Now, what concerns me in this essay is a fundamental point of contention between Améry's mode of reflection and traditional philosophy, which can be gleaned from the general spirit of his work and his personality as a thinker.

From its inception, philosophy has associated itself with the mythical figure of Eros, or Love. Plato, in his *Symposium*, offered a memorable account of Eros—the bastard son of the divine Poros (literally, resource, or wealth) and the human Penia (literally, poverty). Taking after his mother, Eros is

> always poor, and he's far from being delicate or beautiful (as ordinary people think he is), instead, he is tough and shriveled and shoeless and homeless, always lying on the dirt without a bed… always living with Need. But on his father's side he is a schemer after the beautiful and the good; he is brave, impetuous, and intense, an awesome hunter… intense in his pursuit of intelligence, a lover of wisdom…. (Plato 1997, p. 486)

Thus, "by nature neither immortal nor mortal," Eros

> now springs to life… [and] now he dies—all in the very same day. Because he is his father's son, however, he keeps coming back to life, but then anything he finds his way to always slips away, and for this reason Love is never completely without resources, nor is he ever rich. He is between wisdom and ignorance as well… (Ibid.)

I take this as a reflection about the human condition, similarly caught in in-betweenness (*metaxy*) and, while always grounded in this place and in this time, is always driven by the Erotic desire for self-transcendence: toward the absolute, the unconditional, the divine. The epitome of this erotic drive is the Love of Wisdom, philosophy.

As unrequited as this Love of Wisdom may be, it is not without *hubris*. Aristotle famously recommended it—philosophy, the contemplative life—as the happiest kind of life, and also the most divine. If "reason is divine in comparison with man," he wrote,

> ...[then] the life according to it is divine in comparison with human life. [And] we ought not to follow those who advise us, being men, to think of human things, and, being mortal, of mortal things, but must, so far as we can, make ourselves immortal, and strain every nerve to live in accordance with the best thing in us; for even if it be small in bulk, much more does it in power and worth surpass everything... (Aristotle 2001, p. 1105)

It is precisely here that the example set forth by Améry is so unique and defiant. For it is, I believe, in direct contrast to such amorous and self-rewarding labor, that he professed the need to *surrender* "[o]ne's intellectual ambition," to dedicate oneself instead to the investigation of *time* (Améry 1994, p. 4). Time—especially in the context of a study of aging—connotes all that distinctly pertains to the finitude, and indeed poverty, of human existence.

From Améry's *At the Mind's Limits*, his first major book—which studied the conditions of victimhood and forced exile—to his last book on Charles Bovary (1997 [1978])—subtitled "Portrait of a *Simple* Man"—Améry remained utterly devoted to Eros's human mother Penia (poverty). Never the "manly" hero, the protagonist of his philosophy is characteristically "shriveled and shoeless and homeless," helpless and "living with Need..." (Plato 1997, p. 486). If philosophy traditionally drives us upwards, Améry's brand of thinking *methodically pulls us down*.

Looking more closely at the passage from *On Aging* cited earlier, Améry tells us there that, when thinking forfeits its intellectual ambition (*Ehrgeiz*), it becomes *impoverished, weak*, even *bad* (*schlecht*). What motivates thinking to take up a task that weakens it so is not the pursuit of honor (*Ehre*) but a commitment to its less assuming relative, honesty (*Ehrlichkeit*). Thinking here does not aspire to the self-fulfilling Wisdom (or to being "correct"). In fact, it is content with being "bad." When the subject is the poorest, and at times the worst facets of the human condition, it is fitting (*recht*) that thinking should be poor or bad as well. When thinking, for example, about the condition of a person undergoing torture, there is a limit to how clear-sighted one can be.

Now, I maintain that his personal reservations notwithstanding, Améry is nonetheless (if not all the more) a *philosopher*, insofar as we understand by it a person whose vocation is thinking or contemplation (the term *geistiger Mensch*—person of mind—is ordinarily translated with the more high-sounding "intellectual"). Although he never finished high school (not because he was a rebel, but because he routinely caved under the stress of taking exams), Améry was not only a self-taught polymath but doggedly devoted to reflection and study. Even in Auschwitz, as he attested, "only rarely did thinking grant itself respite. [Although] it nullified itself when at almost every step it ran into its uncrossable borders" (Améry 1980, p. 19).

This mental determinant of his existence is most explicit at the beginning of *On Aging*, where Améry notes that what compels and drives him in writing the book is "nothing more than an inclination to be contemplative, and perhaps to practice being so" (Améry 1994, p. xxi). As I see it, it is precisely this fact that accounts for his need to distance himself from "philosophy." If his vocation were not so inherently close to philosophy, he would never have regarded it as one of two "danger zones" into which he runs the risk of straying (Améry 1994, p. 4).

It is equally important to recall, however, that watching for the other "danger zone," the risk of falling into "dilettantish brooding," keeps him also from straying *too far* from the philosophical pole. His hope therefore remains that, despite "every self-restriction," and despite being limited to the description of its own path, the results of his investigation could nevertheless "be transformed into something universally binding" (Améry 1994, p. xxiii).

Améry's cautionary notes-to-self about the hazards of philosophical *hubris* are something that philosophy itself might do well to pay heed to, especially because of its concern for truth, universality, and even wisdom. As long as Eros has his back turned toward his mother side, his origin, his urgings may end up perpetuating, rather than negating, our state of ignorance and immaturity.

* * *

I have suggested that one of the benefits to reading Améry philosophically is that it can help bring to view the unity of his project and method, against the reduction of his work to a variety of "specialized disciplines" and its consequent fragmentation. And I have just hinted at what I perceive to be the main thrust of Améry's "philosophy," namely, the methodical effort to pull the intellectual gaze "*downward*"—below the human condition, or toward its underbelly, so to speak—rather than "upward." I will now elaborate a bit more about the kind of method involved, and about the significance of this "downward" movement.

At the Mind's Limits is perhaps the first work to fully display Améry's distinctive philosophical approach. Right at the beginning of the first essay, he announces to his readers: "My subject is: At the Mind's Limits. That these limits happen to run alongside the so unpopular horrors is not my fault…" (Améry 1980, p. 1). This statement makes the order of his priorities unequivocal: what is essential to him is "At the Mind's Limits," *not* "the horrors" ("The Holocaust," as we refer to it today). It is important that we bear this in mind, since a proximity to horror is pervasive in Améry's intellectual work, making it is easy to mistake it for the thing itself. Nevertheless, the appeal to the horrors is certainly not arbitrary or incidental. Hannah Arendt once wrote, very suggestively, that "the speechless horror at what man may do and what the world may become is in many ways related to the speechless wonder of gratitude from which the questions of philosophy spring" (Arendt 1994, p. 445). I do not know whether the questions of philosophy "*spring*" from speechless horror, but the point, for Améry, seems to me that, at the mind's limits, these questions, and the answers to them, are significantly modified. It is this kind of exigent engagement with, or testing of, philosophical questions, rather than the horrors themselves, that occupies Améry.

One of the consequences of the failure to understand the philosophical nature of Améry's project is that this crucial fact about it has often been overlooked or misunderstood. Even Primo Levi (2017) scoffed at Améry for choosing (as if arbitrarily) to focus on the figure of the "intellectual" in his study of Auschwitz. Addressing such a calamity through such a lofty lens seems almost inappropriate, and certainly irrelevant to the vast majority of the victims. This objection fails to heed two things: first, that the intention is precisely to *deflate* (or rather, to honestly record the deflation of) the intellectual *hubris* that Améry considered his prewar self to be guilty of, and rightly supposed some of his readers might be as well, and not to reify or to reenact it. More importantly, Levi's objection fails to heed Améry's express proclamation that Auschwitz is *not* the main subject of inquiry, whereas the "intellectual," as he defined this figure, *is*. In other words, Améry has something to tell his readers—the philosophically minded among them, especially—about *themselves*, calling their own self-understanding and the understanding of their vocation into question.

Auschwitz, and the intellectual's experience in it, thus stands as a radical counterpoint—a contrasting gravitational center—to the mind's erotic flight to the divine. And while "it was not the case that the intellectual—if he had not already been destroyed physically—had now become unintellectual" (Améry 1980, p. 19), it was no longer clear what it meant to *be* an "intellectual." "The axes of its [the intellect's] traditional frames of reference [were] shattered. Beauty: that was an illusion. Knowledge: that turned out to be a game with ideas..." (ibid.; Améry 2002, pp. 51–52, translation modified). Even the Good, which marks the indisputable horizon of all human activities for Plato and Aristotle, no longer appeared relevant. The questions are thus beckoned: What now is thinking to be? How should it respond? And why?

Approximating the limits of the mind is essentially a matter of incurring self-awareness and self-examination. To be sure, self-examination has always been regarded as the primary philosophical task, and self-consciousness as the goal, and achievement, of every enlightenment. And Améry, indeed, was always a staunch advocate of the enlightenment and an equally fierce opponent of the anti-enlightenment sentiments which he anxiously saw emerging in postwar German Left and more markedly in the French Left of the 1960s and 1970s (in thinkers like Barthes, Deleuze, Guattari, and Foucault). In what he bleakly described as "the modishly gesticulating, arrogant, but wholly unsound argument that [the enlightenment] is 'outdated'" (Améry 1984, p. 141), he detected a growing tendency toward irrationalism, which he feared would up end up serving neofascist impulses. The "enlightenment," as he wrote against this tendency, "was no seamless doctrinary construct but rather the constant illuminating dialogue we are obliged to conduct with ourselves and with others..." (ibid.). He thus maintained that "it was not the Enlightenment that failed, as we have been assured ever since the first wave of the Romantic counter-enlightenment, but rather those who were appointed its guardians..." (Améry 1984, p. 136).

These general proclamations notwithstanding, in his original work Améry did suggest an effort to *revise* the self-understanding of the original architects of the "enlightenment," especially in Germany. Thus, in his call to approximate of the mind's limits, we are looking at a very different type of self-awareness, and a very different sense and sensibility for rational thinking. In one of the most revealing, and striking, methodological statements in his oeuvre, in the second preface to *At the Mind's Limits*, he explains that "the concept of the enlightenment," as he understands it,

> [embraces] the will and the ability to speculate phenomenologically, to empathize, to approach the limits of reason. Only when we fulfill the law of the enlightenment and at the same time transcend it do we reach intellectual realms in which *ratio* does not lead to shallow rationalism. *This is why* I always proceed from the concrete event, but never become lost in it; rather I always take it *as an occasion* for reflections that extend beyond reasoning and the pleasure in logical argument to areas of thought that lie in an uncertain twilight and will remain therein, no matter how much I strive to attain the clarity necessary in order to lend them contour. However—and in this I must persist—enlightenment is not the same as clarification [*Aufklärung is nicht gleich Abklärung*]. I had no clarity when I was writing this little book, I do not have it today, and I hope that I never will. Clarification would also amount to disposal, settlement of the case, which can then be placed in the files of history. My book is meant to aid in preventing precisely [that].… (Améry 1980, p. xi, italics added)

The refrain about "clarity" (*Licht*) is a recurring theme in Améry's work and among the most decisive features of his thought. It conflicts not only with the most obvious connotation of the term "enlightenment," but with the entire tradition that, at least since Plato, equates reason to *light*: the bright light of the sun. For Améry, such brightness is not the most conducive to a reflection concerned with the human condition and human relations. Between the full light of knowledge and the darkness of ignorance lies the twilight of reflectiveness. "Day and night," as he puts it in *On Aging*, "cancel each other out [*heben einander auf*] in twilight" (Améry 1994, p. 52; 2005a, p. 80).

Along the same line, he warns his readers in *On Suicide*: "one can't get through this [subject] *with clear thinking*" (Améry 1999, p. 23, italics added). With an eye to Wittgenstein, who once declared against mystical thinking that "the riddle does not exist," Améry insists that, when it comes to the phenomenon of suicide, it *does*: "It is imperative to reflect upon this mystery in talk that is circular—or, more exactly, half-circular—repetitious, struggling constantly for precision though never attaining it. One may talk without clarity about that to which the light of clear language…

does not shine. And [yes,] the riddle exists" (Améry 1999, p. 24).[3] The premise of *At the Mind's Limits* is similar: "Evil really is singular and irreducible in its total inner logic and its accursed rationality," he wrote; "For this reason, all of us are still faced with a dark riddle..." (Améry 1980, p. viii).

It is important to stress that what concerns Améry as a philosopher is not simply this or that event (he does not wish to "become lost in it"), but whatever in human experience and history pushes the mind to its limits, disabling its habitual activity and casting doubt on its habitual assumptions and frames of reference. This concern with the mind's limits, and with the mode of reflection and self-awareness they occasion, remains the constant in later books—most notably in his treatises on aging and suicide—whereas the Holocaust no longer plays an explicit part.

To read Améry as a philosopher is thus to have an eye, beyond particular essays and themes (the Holocaust, torture, resentments, aging, suicide), to the guiding principles of his thought—his *method*.

I have identified three methodological principles:

1. *Always proceed from the concrete event but never become lost in it.*

   When an event is painful or horrific, the mind (*Geist*) prompts us to transcend it in various ways and directions—causal explication, symptomatic or symbolic analysis, prevention, solution, redemption, forgiveness, and so on. Remaining grounded in the concrete event *itself*, and keeping to it as a standard, is a manner of *countering* this prompting; resisting transcendence; remaining close to the edge of the immanence of the event and of its experience. Thus, resisting both the call of the heavens and a complete descent into hell, thinking remains in the twilight.
2. *Keep to, or gravitate toward, the lived-experience* (le vécu) *and its description.*

   Wherever there is an experience there is a person. Gravitating toward lived-experience is not only a matter of "keeping it real," but also a matter of maintaining the interpersonal context of reflection. Being as honest, nonsentimental, and nonjudgmental about the experience as one can be, renders its inner features available to the reader in a way that—although the experience is not *appropriable*—it can nonetheless become *binding*; somehow indicative of the human condition more generally.

3. *Strive toward and approximate the limits of your mind.*
   Experientially approximating the mind's limits involves an *increasing* hardship and impoverishment of thought. This hardship is partly the result of resistance, or pushback, from two sides. The first resistance is from the subject matter itself; when the experience (e.g., torture) is of a sort that is not already mediated by the categories of perception and understanding, it defies the possibility of thought; it deprives the mind of its most "basic quality," which Améry, following the French existentialists, called "transcendence" (Améry 1980, p. 7). It becomes very difficult to think clearly. The second resistance is from the mind's own desire (Eros) to *resume* or *reclaim* this transcendence, for example, through the search for redemptive meaning.[4] The mind, as Spinoza once argued, "endeavors to think only of the things that *affirm its power of activity*" (Spinoza 1992, p. 135). It certainly does not endeavor to think of things that impoverish it, and, indeed, why would it?

What, then, accounts for this concern with the impoverishment of the mind? The simple answer has already been alluded to. It belongs to what Améry calls "the law of the enlightenment" (Améry 1980, p. xi). Thinking at the limits is quintessential to the kind of activity that Immanuel Kant called a "*critique* of reason," and thus to the courage to know and the fight against dogmatism, ignorance, and superstition. But there is also another, more specific, merit to thinking at the limits, a *phenomenological* one, of which I now want to expand: it seems to serve the goal of describing *essences*.

Thus, for example, while grounded in his personal experience, *At the Mind's Limits*, and especially the investigation of torture, brings us to reflect on the essence of *victimhood*. "Confessing and meditating," as he writes in the preface, "I arrived at an examination or, if you will, an *essential description* [*Wesensbeschreibung*] of the existence of the victim [*Opfer-Existenz*]" (Améry 1980, p. xiii; Améry 2002, p. 21; italics added, translation modified). Similarly, *On Aging*, while commencing with his personal experience, is, as already noted, an attempt to inquire into the essence of *time*. Finally, *On Suicide*, again revolving around his own and others' personal experiences, reaches for the essence of what Améry calls, "the logic of life" (perhaps rationality itself). Put together, these three books, and others by Améry, join in a sustained reflection about what it means to be human.

But why is it that asking philosophical questions of essence must go through an interrogation of limit-situations and experiences that are so *extraordinary* and difficult to generalize from? Why does one need to think of aging or dying in order to think about time? Why must one think of suicide in order to think about rationality? And how do lived experiences as extreme as Nazi torture and extermination camps—which Améry himself regards as a *conditio inhumana* (Améry 1994, p. vii)—tell us something essential about victimhood, let alone about the human condition?

Améry's texts suggest two answers to these questions. First, as he notes in *On Aging*, "it's a rather cheap truth to say that our condition [*Befinden*] generally gets noticed only when we are out of condition [*Misbefinden*]" (Améry 1994, p. 34). Améry's approach, in this respect, can be regarded as a kind of extroverted phenomenology: interrogating a condition *from without*, or more precisely, through the *experience* of being out of it.[5] This approach is nowhere more patent than in the third essay of *At the Mind's Limits*, where Améry interrogates the significance of *Heimat* (homeland) via the peculiar *Heimweh* (homesickness) of German-Jews like him, who were not only permanently exiled from the *Heimat*, but at the same time were forced to realize that they never really had one to begin with (Améry 1980, p. 48).

The "cheap truth" that being out of condition tells us something about the condition itself seems to coincide with the common saying that "the exception proves the rule." But this is not, in my view, what Améry has in mind. The exception here does not serve to *prove* the rule but, on the contrary, to *limit* its application, to call it into question and doubt. Unlike ordinary phenomenological work, in which the reader is always called upon to appropriate the position of the author/investigator (the transcendental subject, or Dasein), in Améry's work, an insurmountable fence is established between reader and author, and between both of them and the experience or event discussed. In the preface to *At the Mind's Limits* he calls it an "unbridgeable chasm" (Améry 1980, ix).

Thus, the experience of the German-Jew serves as an inverted mirror for the German audience, insofar as the members of this audience do have, and are secure in, their *Heimat*. It brings the security and comfort of their *Heimat*, which some of them would sooner deny or understate, into awareness, *together* with some vague consciousness about its precarity and limits. The experience of the intellectual in Auschwitz similarly serves to de-mirror the condition of his readers, who, while reading, are well within their element, enjoying that very same transcendence whose loss is being attested to.

Améry had an operative name for this type of reflection-through-contrast: *Widersprüchlichkeit* (contradictoriness). In *On Aging* he explained:

> ... we have to take... contradictoriness upon ourselves, have to take upon ourselves absurdity and the risk of every thought-contortion [*Gedankenverwirrung*] when we meditate on our condition [*Befindlichkeit*]. *It is aging that exposes us to that kind of consciousness and makes us capable of it.* (Améry 1994, p. 51; 2005a, p. 79; italics added, translation modified)

In other words, what is otherwise a horrible experience is what enables a particular mode of reflection at the limits, whereby one gets to think of oneself, as it were, from or through the outside. The "enlightenment" suggested here is neither in the pursuit of knowledge nor a matter of securing room for rational faith. It is, rather, the cultivation of what Améry elsewhere called *self-mistrust* (Améry 1980, p. 77), a significantly modified ("contorted") form of self-consciousness that is mediated not by transcendental subjectivity or reason, but by the experience of people living in profoundly different conditions than one's own. This mediation/contradiction increases awareness not only to the essential features of one's condition but also to their essential precariousness, to their limits and outer edges.

The last point brings me to the second significance of thinking at (or approximating of) the mind's limits. By persistently focusing his studies on the experience of the underdog, the oppressed, the dehumanized, the fatally ill, Améry problematizes the possibility of *relation* and *trust* between author and reader. In this vein, the epigraph of *On Suicide* (taken from Wittgenstein's *Tractatus*), reads: "The world of the happy person is a different world than the one of the unhappy person. Just as with death the world does not change, but stops." Do they even share a world? Can they meaningfully communicate at all? Améry's readers often find themselves sharing (or demanded to share) intellectual space with someone who refuses to either help them or to be helped by them. The victim of torture, Améry tells us, not only lost all trust in the world, but, moreover, resents all those who would try to regain or reestablish that trust for him. The subject of *On Suicide* is not only resolved to take his own life, but resents all attempts to dissuade him or even make sense of his decision.

And yet, despite all that, in the conclusion to the original preface of *At the Mind's Limits*, he insists that, if only his study should meet its aim, then it would "concern all those who wish to live together as fellow human beings [*die einander Mitmenschen sein wollen*]" (Améry 1980, p. xiv). How so?

When relations are experienced with difficulty, when they are all but impossible, they are experienced as a problem that is *lived*; they are experienced *in person*. In a revealing passage in *On Aging*, he notes to this effect:

> time is not a personal problem for anyone who is living for the world—until, of course, the moment when one realizes, 'Alas, where have all my years gone'. Only then, when one becomes aware of what has disappeared and gone beyond recall... settling down by the wayside, does one understand time as a question *directed at oneself*. (Améry 1994, p. 13)

Améry wants his audience to experience relationality, *Mitmenschlichkeit* (being with other humans) and the existence of trust, as a question directed at themselves, which he aims to achieve through withdrawal, resistance, and refusal. This, I believe, brings us to the very crux of his work: its aspiration to cultivate care, and meaningful relations, beyond love, friendship, affinity, and mutual benefit. This is the aspect that he finds most lacking in traditional enlightenment: "Where is it decreed that enlightenment must be free of emotion? To me, the opposite seems to be true..." (Améry 1980, p. xi).

The theme of relationality helps explain why he seems to regard the notion of approximating the mind's limits as almost synonymous with *empathy*. To recall, his understanding of the enlightenment, as he puts it, embraces "the will and the ability to speculate phenomenologically, to empathize, to approach the limits of reason..." (Améry 1980, p. xi).

A couple of passages in *On Suicide* may provide us better insight into the nature of this link between empathy and limit. Under "certain impossible conditions," he writes there, "it is necessary to think 'toward' things that are... unthinkable." (Améry 1999, p. 28) Here, the phrase "to think toward" suggests the now familiar task of approximating the mind's limit. But earlier in the book we find a similar expression. We are "on our way," Améry tells us, "*not away* from persons annihilating themselves, but *toward* them" (Améry 1999, p. 4). Thus, thinking "toward" the mind's limits is at the same time thinking toward another person, another experience, perhaps another world. What is added here is the thought that a limit is not necessarily an *end* but, just like a twilight, an in-between. Like a fence, it is both a separation, even a chasm, and a point of meeting.

* * *

Life of Bryan, Monty Python's parody of the life of Jesus, ends with a song sung in choir by a group of people hanging from crosses: "Always look on the bright side of life...." The parody hits at something essential to the Christian ethos, with which Améry was intimately familiar from his childhood and upbringing. Looking on the bright side goes hand in hand with the emphasis on the redemptive power of Love. As noted in the beginning of this essay, the union between love as a communion of souls, and love as the flight-upward to the divine is already embedded in the figure of Eros as described by Plato. And, as also suggested, while Love is intimately associated with thinking-up, the kind of thinking toward espoused by Améry is always a thinking-*down*. By way of conclusion, I would like now to return to this theme.

I have mentioned Aristotle, but it is not only in him that the concern for happiness furnishes the horizon for thinking as a whole. This tradition is alive in Stoic philosophy, Judeo-Christian Theology (as well as in Buddhism), early modern rationalism, in psychotherapy (including Viktor Frankl's), and, in a more popular form, self-help literature. The potential problem with the philosophical, and even the political, quest for the good or happy life and community is that this quest may discourage honest attention to whatever undermines or stands in the way of such prospects, as, for instance, the experience of past victims who refuse to reconcile, heal, or be rehabilitated. There is a tendency in such cases to pathologize damaged life and resentments or to reduce them to weakness of character.

Hegel, for example, attributed the dire circumstances of European Jews to their refusal to assimilate, and more generally, to a stubborn attachment to finitude (or, rather, a resistance to infinitude) which he found emblematic of their religion and "fate." The "circumstances of the Jewish people," he wrote,

> up to the mean, abject, wretched circumstances in which they still are today, have all of them been simply consequences and elaborations of their original fate. By this fate—an infinite power that *they set against themselves* and could never conquer—they have been maltreated and will be continually maltreated

until they appease it by the spirit of beauty and so annul it by reconciliation. (Hegel 1996, pp. 199–200, italics added)

We are to gather from this that the Jews' refusal to reconcile to the (Christian) spirit of beauty—in other words, to renounce their unique experience—ensues, like self-punishment almost, in their being maltreated. It might be said that Nazism put the seal on this hypothesis, since, as far as it was concerned, it mattered little whether a Jew was willing or unwilling to assimilate. Moreover, it was perhaps the self-same "spirit of beauty" that, in Nazism, sought to actualize itself, not only by getting rid of the Jews, but ultimately of *all* things that are abject, unhealthy, and unbeautiful. If Améry entertained any illusions or aspirations of assimilation prior to the war, the conflicted Jewish identity he ended up adopting in its aftermath—that of "the Catastrophe Jew," as he called it (Améry 1980, p. 94)—along with his categorical refusal to forego his resentments and reconcile, was at least in part a matter of defending victimhood (abjection, wretchedness) *as such* against all endeavors and pretenses—however well-intentioned—to "cure" it.

A revolt against the happiness and health-oriented tradition can hardly become as popular or seductive as that which it rebels against. It is not only unpopular but non-popularizable. Améry therefore apologizes to his readers that he must impose upon them a reflection on all those "unpopular horrors" they perhaps would rather leave in the past because they can. But philosophy has always, and again from its earliest days, pitted itself *against* the popular. If philosophers do not take upon themselves the task of inquiring into the abject facets of the human condition—a task which impoverishes the mind, and which the mind is therefore naturally inclined to reject—then who would?

For Socrates, who was notoriously unhandsome and uncompromisingly agnostic, philosophy was a matter of self-examination, and education for self-examination, in the name of social justice rather than authentic individualism or altruistic love. His publicly oriented and essentially relational practice annoyed and disturbed the public more than it seduced it; provoked its fears and aversions more than it catered to its desires, fantasies, and aims.

In line with this Socratic tradition, Améry's mode of thinking consisted, as seen, in a methodical defiance of and revolt against natural and conventional impulses.[6] This is why I see in him an exemplary image of the philosopher and the contemplative life; exemplary not for being attractive, happy, virtuous, or wise (in all these respects he deemed it a "failure"), but for having the courage to methodically suspend all such considerations in the interest of honesty and empathy. He thus decoupled the true from the good, being thoughtful from being well.

Améry's voluntary death some 40 years ago was clearly less an act of revolt than of resignation, less a matter of cultivating relations than of simply renouncing them. But the fact that he put to voice and paper his experience "in the moment before the leap" (Améry 1999, p. 13) is more representative of his intellectual personality. Like Améry's other major works, *On Suicide* marks his resolve to remain at the mind's limits, challenging us—those more fortunate than him—to approximate them.

Notes

1. In the context of this essay I do not engage comprehensively with Améry's many writings about figures or movements of the philosophical canon (the sixth volume of Améry's *Werke* [2017] contains the bulk of his essays on philosophy, some of which have been translated and compiled in *Radical Humanism* [1984]). I have done more in-depth comparative studies of Améry and various philosophers in my dissertation (2012), and more specifically on his relation to the enlightenment in Ben-Shai 2014a and 2016; to Heidegger, Kant, and Wittgenstein in Ben-Shai 2010, 2011, and 2016; to Nietzsche in Ben-Shai 2014b, and to Arendt in Ben-Shai 2007.
2. In "Jean Améry takes his life," Susan Neiman 1997 comments on the affinity between Améry's variant of rationalism and writing style and that of French Enlightenment thinkers. It can be added in the context that Améry endorsed that enduring image of the public intellectual in France, as a social critic especially in support of the oppressed groups—a figure or function he found woefully lacking in Germany, especially during the war. This image was epitomized for him in Emile Zola's "*J'accuse!*" which he echoed in his *Charles Bovary* (1978), a book in which he defends the "simple man," and in general the petite bourgeoisie, this too in the spirit of the enlightenment. It is for the same reasons that he particularly admired the French existentialists Jean Paul Sartre and Simone De Beauvoir, whose efforts to balance between philosophy and literature on the one hand, and between individualism and political resistance on the other, he aspired to reproduce in his own life and work.
3. Améry's relationship to Wittgenstein, I should note, is complex, and by no means as oppositional as this citation makes it sound. The "neopositivism inspired by Wittgenstein," he admits, "is always simultaneously right and wrong" (Améry 1999, p. 24). Améry had a personal relationship to this brand of "positivism," since during the 1920s he attended some of the

meetings of the Vienna Circle. The group's commitment to public, and informal venues of study accorded with its social democratic ethos, which Améry held in favor, just as he was suspicious, as I noted above, of some of the anti-positivist channels of continental thought. The type of thinking Améry espouses, in any case, while it challenges the absolute dominion of ordinary rationality—what he calls "the logic *of life*"—does not for all that undermine, or purport to ground, the logic of life or logic itself, nor does it venture into a "beyond."

4. It is useful in this context to observe that Améry's approach to Auschwitz, as his general intellectual ethos, is diametrically opposed to that of another famous survivor, Viktor Frankl (2006 [1946]). Whereas Frankl insists on the capacity to establish meaning (and "optimism") even in the most adverse or "tragic" of conditions, Améry insisted, and fought to show, that this capacity is *limited*, and better so. Since the premises of Frankl's work are very much in tune with French existentialism (the decisive common influence on both being Nietzsche), the contrast to Frankl is also an opportunity to observe the decisive limits of Améry's indebtedness to Sartre. His emphasis in *At the Mind's Limits* on victimhood runs counter to the almost exclusive valorization in French existentialism of action and freedom.
5. The idea that something about the human condition only gets noticed in an *inhuman* condition is echoed by South-African novelist, J.M. Coetzee, who, in his fictional narrative of torture in *Waiting for the Barbarians*, wrote: "My torturers were not interested in degrees of pain. They were interested only in demonstrating to me what it meant to live in a body, as a body, a body that can entertain notions of justice only as long as it is whole and well … They did not come to force [a] story out of me … They came to my cell to show me the meaning of humanity, and in the space of an hour they showed me a great deal …" (Coetzee 1982, p. 113).
6. For example, "suicides tear to pieces a prescription of nature…" (Améry 1999, p. 13).

References

Améry, J. (1980). *At the Mind's Limits: Contemplations by a Survivor on Auschwitz and Its Realities*. Bloomington, IN: Indiana University Press.

Améry, J. (1984). *Radical Humanism: Selected Essays*. Bloomington, IN: Indiana University Press.

Améry, J. (1994). *On Aging: Revolt and Resignation*. Bloomington, IN: Indiana University Press.

Améry, J. (1997 [1978]). *Charles Bovary, Landarzt. Portrait eines einfachen Mannes*. Stuttgart, BW: Klett-Cotta.

Améry, J. (1999). *On Suicide: A Discourse on Voluntary Death*. Bloomington, IN: Indiana University Press.
Améry, J. (2002 [1966]). Jenseits von Schuld und Sühne: Bewältigungsversuche eines Überwältigten. In G. Scheit (Ed.), *Werke, Bd. II*. Stuttgart, BW: Klett-Cotta.
Améry, J. (2005a [1968]). Über das Altern: Revolte und Resignation. In M. Bossart (Ed.), *Werke, Bd. III*. Stuttgart, BW: Klett-Cotta.
Améry, J. (2005b [1976]). Hand an Sich Legen: Diskurs über den Freitod. In M. Boussart (Ed.), *Werke, Bd. III*. Stuttgart, BW: Klett-Cotta.
Améry, J. (2017). Aufsätze zur Philosophie. In G. Scheit (Ed.), *Werke, Bd. VI*. Stuttgart, BW: Klett-Cotta.
Arendt, H. (1994). *Essays in Understanding, 1930–1954: Formation, Exile, and Totalitarianism*. New York, NY: Harcourt, Brace &Co.
Aristotle. (2001). Nicomachean Ethics. In R. McKeon (Ed.), *The Basic Works of Aristotle* (pp. 935–1126). New York, NY: Modern Library.
Ben-Shai, R. (2007). *Reductio ad Moralem*: On Victim-Morality in the Work of Jean Améry. *The European Legacy, 12*(7), 835–851.
Ben-Shai, R. (2010). To Reverse the Irreversible: On Time Disorder in the Work of Jean Améry. In J. Watson (Ed.), *Metacide: In the Pursuit of Excellence* (pp. 73–92). Amsterdam, NL: Rodopi.
Ben-Shai, R. (2011). Imposition, or Writing from the Void: Pathos and Pathology in Améry. In M. Zolkos (Ed.), *On Jean Améry: Philosophy of the Catastrophe* (pp. 109–134). Lanham, MD: Lexington Books.
Ben-Shai, R. (2014a). Jean Améry (1912–1978): The Homesickness and Enlightenment of a Catastrophe-Jew. In Z. Mankowitz, D. Weinberg, & S. Kangisser Cohen (Eds.), *Europe in the Eyes of Survivors of the Holocaust* (pp. 11–35). Jerusalem, IL: Yad Vashem.
Ben-Shai, R. (2014b). In Sickness and in Health: Nietzsche, Améry, and "the Moral Difference". In R. Ben-Shai & N. Lebovic (Eds.), *The Politics of Nihilism* (pp. 125–150). New York, NY: Bloomsbury.
Ben-Shai, R. (2016). The Fifth Antinomy: A Reading of Torture for a Post-Kantian Moral Philosophy. *Journal of French and Francophone Philosophy, XXIV*(3), 17–37.
Bernstein, J. M. (2015). *Torture and Dignity: An Essay on Moral Injury*. Chicago, IL: University of Chicago Press.
Bernstein, J. (Ed.). (2016). Jean Améry, Commemoration and Comparative Engagement. *Journal of French and Francophone Philosophy, 24*(3), 1–2.
Brudholm, T. (2008). *Resentment's Virtue: Jean Améry and the Refusal to Forgive*. Philadelphia, PA: Temple University Press.
Coetzee, J. M. (1982). *Waiting for the Barbarians*. New York, NY: Penguin Books.
Plato. (1997). Symposium. In J. M. Cooper (Ed.), *Plato: Complete Works* (pp. 457–505). Indianapolis, IN: Hackett Publishing Company.

Frankl, V. E. (2006 [1946]). *Man's Search for Meaning*. Boston, MA: Beacon Press.
Hegel, G. W. F. (1996). *Early Theological Writings*. Philadelphia, PA: University of Pennsylvania Press.
Heidelberger-Leonard, I. (2010). *The Philosopher of Auschwitz: Jean Améry and Living with the Holocaust*. New York, NY: I.B. Tauris.
Levi, P. (2017). The Intellectual in Auschwitz. In *The Drowned and the Saved* (pp. 113–134). New York, NY: Simon & Schuster.
Neiman, S. (1997). Jean Améry Takes His Life. In S. L. Gilman & J. Zipes (Eds.), *Yale Companion to Jewish Writing and Thought in German Culture 1096–1996* (pp. 775–784). New Haven: Yale University Press.
Spinoza, B. (1992). *Ethics and Treatise on the Emendation of the Intellect*. Indianapolis, IN: Hackett Publishing Company.
Stauffer, J. (2015). *Ethical Loneliness: The Injustice of Not Being Heard*. New York, NY: Columbia University Press.
Zolkos, M. (Ed.). (2011a). *On Jean Améry: Philosophy of Catastrophe*. Lanham, MD: Lexington Books.
Zolkos, M. (2011b). *Reconciling Community and Subjective Life: Trauma Testimony as Political Theorizing in the Work of Jean Améry and Imre Kertész*. London: Continuum.

CHAPTER 12

Jean Améry on the Value of Death and Dying

Eli Pitcovski

12.1 Introduction

The notion of death has received ongoing philosophical attention. The question about the value of death, the degree to which death is good or bad[1] for its subject, is particularly notable for preoccupying philosophers of different eras and traditions. Epicurus is famous for nullifying the value of death on account that whenever death is there, the subject is no longer there to be harmed, let alone benefitted. German romanticists, like Novalis[2] or Schopenhauer, have glorified death, taking it to be the ultimate way out of the miserable human condition; the ultimate transcendence from the mundane. For Heidegger, death underlies all other human possibilities; without going into detail: authenticity, for Heidegger, depends on the recognition of this dramatic role of death. Contemporary analytic philosophers standardly consider the value of some particular death and take it to depend upon the value of the portion of life that this particular death deprives from its subject: the better that portion of life, the worse it is for the subject to die[3] (more on this later). Unlike their predecessors, contemporary philosophers do not provide any categorical answer regarding the value of death in general.

E. Pitcovski (✉)
Tel-Hai Academic College, Upper Galilee, Israel

Y. Ataria et al. (eds.), *Jean Améry*,
https://doi.org/10.1007/978-3-030-28095-6_12

Given the vast philosophical interest in death, one may be surprised by the scarcity of philosophical attention directed to dying, that is, the occurrence of death and the process by which it is brought about.[4] Despite so greatly differing with respect to the value of death, Epicurus, German romanticists, and contemporary analytic philosophers all consider death in complete abstraction from dying. Epicurus explicitly restricts his insights to the time in which the subject no longer exists; romanticist aspirations are definitely not directed to the often miserable and hideous process of dying; and to quote one characteristic analytic philosopher dealing with death: "The question is not whether one death can be worse than another in the manner of its occurrence... Our question is instead whether... one person may suffer a greater harm in simply ceasing to exist than another... It is essential to be able to determine how bad death is for the victim [in the relevant sense specified]" (McMahan 2002, p. 95).

Given this background, Améry's approach to death and dying is strikingly unique. The two essential ideas, that together form Améry's alternative to traditional philosophical thinking about death, can be extracted from just a few passages at the end of his essay "At the Mind's Limits" (the first essay of his main book, which is also named after it) (Améry 1980). In outline, the two ideas are the following: (1) the degree to which some death is good/bad cannot be assessed in abstraction from the causal background of that death. (2) 'The harm of dying' is categorically more basic than 'the harm of death'. Where, as I clarify below, 'dying', in the sense employed by Améry, refers to (roughly) everything that is caused to the subject by the cause of death. This includes death, of course, but it also includes an important part of the process preceding death.

These two deeply related points (viz. (1) and (2)) seem to underlie Améry's more comprehensive writings about death, namely *On Suicide: A Discourse on Voluntary Death* (Améry 1999) and the fifth section of *On Aging* (Améry 1994), titled "To Live with Dying". Indeed, Améry's (1999) assessment of voluntary death is essentially linked to the causes of that death (in this case: oneself) as advised by (1). And Améry's (1994) reflections on aging are primarily focused on the process of dying, as advised by (2). Be that as it may, fully establishing this point will take me too far from my plan. The goals of this chapter are somewhat modest, especially as far as Améry exegesis goes. To be clear, I will not be providing a systematic study of Améry's reflections about particular manifestations of death and dying, or about how they relate to his experience in Auschwitz (a study that is worth carrying out independently). Rather, I will restrict myself to extracting (1) and (2), arguing in their favor, and explaining their implications for the philosophical debate about the value of death. In terms of structure: the next section is closer to the text, and its main goal is to locate (1) and (2) and, along the way, discuss their straightforward implications for the romanticist conception of death. The following section employs (1) and (2) to defend a viable response to Epicurus' view on the value of death, that is at the same time opposed to standard contemporary views on the value of death.

12.2 Death in Auschwitz Versus Death in Venice

Concluding his essay on intellectuals in Auschwitz ("At the Mind's Limits"), Améry writes: "We didn't leave Auschwitz wiser [...] but we were no doubt smarter" (p. 20).[5] In other words, according to Améry, although the camp did not provide intellectuals with any profound realizations, it did provide them with clarity, or a sense of reality.[6] This should not be underestimated: it is often exactly clarity of this sort that is so rare in intellectual discourse. And albeit somewhat associative and unpolished, Améry's remarks on death in this essay have a great deal of smartness in the sense just specified.

Methodologically, one may question the general applicability of Améry's notes on death. After all, Améry begins his remarks on death by clarifying how unique and incomparable was the camp inmates' encounter with death. I would agree that some remarks are indeed context-specific (outside the camp, it is definitely not the case that death has "no sting" (p. 18) for instance). Nevertheless, the general scheme describes the stages required for the intellectual to earn measures of what we have just called 'smartness' about death in general. To gain clarity that was not accessible for him outside the camp. If this is the case, context-specific remarks about the encounter with death concern the way to revelation on the subject matter. Even so, we should be methodologically cautious and distinguish cases in which these bits of testimony appear in the context of discovery from cases in which they appear in the context of justification. In other words, although they are sometimes intertwined, I will do my best to put aside remarks that can only be read as a biographic explanation for the formation of Améry's view about death, and focus my attention to remarks that serve as a ground for that view. Having that said, let me address the two main elements of Améry's attitude toward death.

The first element is the result of a thorough elimination of sensory (or pseudo-sensory) predication with respect to death. So, for example, death, according to Améry, cannot be a mystery (in the sense of something that the dead can discover or explore), and it cannot be a release (in the sense of offering ongoing comfort for the dead). These sensory-based metaphors cross the line between abstraction and illusion.[7] When push comes to shove, that is, when one cannot employ the formative nature of language to escape or deny reality, all that we are left with, in the realm of experience, is dying. Hence, "just like his nonintellectual comrade, the intellectual inmate did not occupy himself with death, but with dying" (p. 17). "To reach out beyond concrete reality with words", an option that in other contexts was open for the intellectual, "became, before our very eyes, a game, that was not only worthless […] but mocking" (p. 19). Whenever one tried "to establish an intellectual, and metaphysical relationship to [death], he ran up against the reality of the camp which doomed such an attempt to failure" (p. 17). In light of this, while dying "was omnipresent", death "vanished from sight" (p. 17), or was "totally absorbed into the torment of dying" (p. 18).

Améry takes his insights about death and dying to have a general application. To be sure, "if one is free it is possible to entertain thoughts of death that at the same time are not also thoughts of dying, fears of dying" (p. 17). But according to Améry, thoughts of this kind "lead nowhere" for "no matter where you are, the fear of death is essentially the fear of dying" (p. 18). But his experience does play a justificatory role because 'the reality of the camp' (which prevents the establishment of an intellectual attitude to death) is special, in comparison to other realities, only in the sense that this reality prohibits the sort of illusions in question. The reality of the camp is not surreal or outlandish. On the contrary, "nowhere in the world was reality so real" (p. 19). But it is first and foremost an inescapable reality. And the fact that it is inescapable serves to expose the illusory nature of the pseudo-sensory conception of death altogether.

A straightforward implication of this (first) element, which Améry explicitly writes about, is "the total collapse of the esthetic view of death", a view which was for the German intellectual, his legacy at least "…from the time of German romanticism". Améry mentions Schopenhauer, Novalis, Hesse, Rilke, and Wagner as representatives of the view. He also refers to Mann while writing that "for death in its literary, philosophic, or musical form there was no place in Auschwitz. No bridge led from death in Auschwitz to Death in Venice" (p. 16). In this context, 'Death in Venice' signifies not only the beautiful death but death as a means to transcend reality. For Améry, the loss of this view of death (i.e. of death as transcendence) consists in the loss of an illusion. Talk of transcendence is a futile attempt to "reach beyond reality with words".

At this point, an uncareful reading would suggest that Améry's view comes down to Epicurean skepticism, that is, that according to Améry, while the process of dying can be extremely harmful, death itself cannot be good or bad for the dying subject. But this reading fails to take into account a second major component of Améry's view about death. Améry stresses the point that death in the battle and death in the camp "are two incommensurables" (p. 16) with respect to value (with the latter being incomparably worse).[8] For while the death of the frontline soldier was "a hero's or victim's death", that is, a somewhat respectable death, the prisoner could only try "in vain, to say it straight off, to exemplify its dignity". This implies that somewhat like many contemporary analytic philosophers, Améry thought that some deaths can be much worse than others. In light of this, Améry clearly thought that some deaths are (at least partly) harmful for their subjects.[9]

There is a felt tension between the view that death is sometimes extremely bad and the view that, even when it is terribly bad, that is, in the camp, death itself is an abstraction that deserves no direct attention. To resolve the tension, we can read Améry's approach as consisting of two perfectly compatible ideas, earlier mentioned in the introduction:

1. The degree to which some death is good/bad for its subject cannot be assessed in abstraction from the causal background of that death.

Améry does not offer any systematic method to determine the overall value of specific deaths. But as we have seen, he certainly held the view that some circumstances can make death much worse than an otherwise similar death: the difference of causal background, broadly conceived, is what makes the difference between the frontline soldier's death and the camp prisoner's death so grave. It is essential for Améry that with respect to the soldier "the state did not order him to die, but to survive", whereas "the final duty of the prisoner was death" (p. 16). If death itself does have some value; if, according to Améry, some deaths can be worse than others, it seems that he doesn't share the Epicurean view that only the process preceding death can be bad. But given his above remarks (about the pointlessness of considering death in abstraction from dying) it seems safe to say that he held the following view:

2. 'The harm of dying' is categorically more basic than 'the harm of death'.

Where, on the reading I propose, 'dying', for Améry, is not merely the process preceding death but rather: that process and death itself taken conjointly; everything that is caused to the subject by the cause of death.[10]

To justify this reading let me emphasize two points: first, it is clear that according to Améry, death itself can be more or less harmful depending on the causal circumstances leading to it. Reading 'the torments of dying' to refer only to the suffering in the portion of time preceding death, and concentrating first and foremost on the value of dying, is in clear tension with this view. Second, especially in the camp, there is nothing particularly special in the period immediately preceding death, and special attention to it would call for explanation.[11] What (2) means is that although theoretically possible, specifying the value of death is (practically) futile. But thinking of the process preceding death in complete abstraction from death, as just another part of life, is equally uninteresting as a candidate for evaluation. This is how I understand Améry's (1994, p. 107) contention that "Death is empty without dying; but the latter, too, has no content without empty death". In light of this, the basic unit for assessment of value in practical contexts ought to be dying: the harm of death and the rest of the harm associated with the causal circumstances leading to death, taken as a whole.

If (1) and (2) can be justified, this would mean that the rest of the views we have so far considered stem from asking the wrong question and providing the wrong answer to it.

12.3 Death and Its Causes

How can death harm its subject? And just how harmful is death for its subject?

According to Epicurus, death cannot harm its subject.

According to the contemporarily received view, "death, when bad for someone, is bad in virtue of the goodness it keeps that person from having" (Bradley 2004, p. 2), viz. in virtue of what it deprives from its subject. Call this view 'the deprivation theory'. Versions of the deprivation theory have been defended by Nagel (1970), Feldman (1991), Feit (2002), Broome (2004), Bradley (2009), and many others.[12] According to this view, pace Epicurus, death is overall bad for its subject in case it deprives her of more good than bad, that is, in case her life was overall better if it was not for that death.[13]

Aside from providing a reply to Epicurus, the deprivation theory is typically taken to provide the key to determine the degree to which death is bad. Along the same lines, the harm resulting from some particular death is measured by "comparing the actual world, in which [the subject] just died, to the closest possible world in which [they] live longer" (Luper 2009, p. 240): the degree to which that world is better for the subject is the degree to which the particular death in question is bad for them.

Both Epicurus and deprivation theorists deny that death can be intrinsically good or bad. They equally agree, that is, that death does not involve harm or benefit in and of itself. Deprivation theorists, however, think that death can be extrinsically good or bad. Unlike Epicurus, they think that events in general, and death in particular, can be extrinsically harmful or beneficial by preventing[14] something that is intrinsically good or bad (respectively), in the case of death: some life time that would have been overall intrinsically beneficial or harmful. Where does Améry fit in?

As we have seen, Améry would definitely not apply hedonistic properties to death itself: not only is death neither pleasurable nor painful according to Améry. Every hint of the sensory realm (the use of metaphors like 'release' or 'sleep', that we cannot grasp unless via some sort of imagined sensation) seems inappropriate on his conception of death. Moreover, Améry shares the basic insight of deprivation theory, according to which death can be good or bad in virtue of depriving the subject from a portion of life that is harmful or beneficial (respectively).[15] However, as opposed both to Epicurus and to deprivation theorists, Améry did think that death can sometimes be intrinsically good or bad. This is because he was not committed to a hedonistic conception of intrinsic value. What the comparison between the prisoner's death and the soldier's death teaches us is that (1) when death exhibits ultimate helplessness, and killing exhibits ultimate domination, death itself (not just the process leading to it, or whatever death brings about) can be humiliating. And when this occurs, death itself, not only the fact that death prevents the subject from enjoying later benefits, can be intrinsically bad. (2) Though I will not dwell on this, death can also be (at least partly) intrinsically good. The death of a hero, for instance, contributes to the subject's dignity.[16,17]

To add some intuitive oomph to the idea that death can be bad by virtue of being humiliating, consider also the following cases:

EXECUTION-I: Rachel is sentenced to death, and is supposed to be electrified to death. Just at the set time of the execution, the prison guards decide to play a cruel and perverse practical joke on her expense. At the most dehumanizing moment, she is electrified to death by a huge mosquito-electric-trap to the guards' amusement.

EXECUTION-II: Rachel is sentenced to death and is electrified by all regulations at the time set by the judge.

EUTHANASIA-I: Rachel was in great pain and was expected to die within two weeks. She has no friends or relatives. Following her own will, the doctors decide to stop respirating her. A careless nurse reads the decision letter, and since she is already near Rachel's bed, she takes out the chewing gum she happened to be chewing, she sticks it into the respiratory machine's tube, and leaves the room. As a result, Rachel dies.

EUTHANASIA-II: Rachel was in great pain and was expected to die within two weeks. She has no friends or relatives. Following her own will, the doctors decide to stop respirating her. This decision is carried out with deep respect, and following all regulations for this sort of cases.

Supposing that the cases are otherwise similar, the two forms of death deprive the subject of just the same portion of life.[18] Nevertheless, the death in EXECUTION-I and in EUTHANASIA-I seemed more humiliating than the death in EXECUTION-II and EUTHANASIA-II (respectively), and in this respect, worse for the dying subject.

One may suspect that this is just a case of a moralistic fallacy; that is, that although the harm suffered directly by death is identical in both cases, we are misled to judge it differently because of the bad character and blameworthiness of the culprit.[19] I would agree that we are sometimes liable to this sort of fallacy, and that despite initial appearances, not every case of killing is worse for the subject than some otherwise similar natural death. However, I think that the difference between the cases is relevant for assessing the value of death for the subject. This is because humiliation directly harms the subject, and is fundamentally opposed to their interest.[20] In fact examples that were used to support deprivation theory also support this basic insight: Nagel (1970, p. 76) has famously argued against the view that one has to suffer in order to be harmed by giving the example of someone who is intuitively misfortunate for being ridiculed behind his back by everyone he knows, despite being completely unaware of his misfortune due to the polite treatment he receives to his face.

One may argue that humiliation, in the cases discussed above, should be attributed to the cause of death rather than to death itself. It is, of course, important to keep in mind the distinction between the badness of the cause of death, and the badness of death. However, note that the causes in questions lose much of their humiliating punch in case they are not followed by death. Crucially, sticking a bubble gum on a breathing tube is not all that humiliating in and of itself. It is being dead as a result of this act that is humiliating. (And the degree to which it is more humiliating to be dead than to survive this independently humiliating act contributes to the degree to which death itself is otherwise bad.) Besides, when comparing Rachel's death to other humiliating events, this line of reasoning seems ad hoc. Tripping over, for instance, can be humiliating. It can surely be more humiliating when it is a result of one thing rather than another. But, eventually, being in the state of 'tripped over' is often humiliating in and of itself; we would not attribute this feature strictly to whatever caused it. Likewise, a humiliating way of dying often contributes to the badness of being dead; it is sometimes intrinsically against the subject's interest to be dead (i.e. in the state of death) for this reason.

If the above considerations are correct, the question whether one person suffers a greater harm in simply ceasing to exist than another is sometimes tightly related to the manner of its occurrence. In some causal circumstances ceasing to exist is humiliating whereas, in other circumstances, it is not. Hence, the degree to which some death is bad cannot be assessed in complete abstraction from the causes of that death (1). But as the tripping over example suggests, it seems that often, what we should in fact be evaluating is the event and the relevant causal background as a whole. This supports the idea that dying is a more natural candidate for evaluation than death (2). Estimating the overall harm caused by the cause of death[21] will pinpoint both the relevant torments having to do with the process preceding death, and the degree to which death itself is bad, in terms of what it deprives of its subject and in terms of factors like humiliation and pointlessness.[22] Realizing (1) and (2) has further prospects.

Realizing (1) opens the way for explaining other ways in which death is intuitively intrinsically bad. Aside from being humiliating, death can be bad for other reasons that depend on its causes (broadly construed). Consider, for example, the following cases, meant to support the view that death can be intrinsically bad by virtue of being tragically pointless:

> ROMEO: Romeo thinks his life is worthless without Juliette. He has the false (albeit justified) impression that Juliette is dead, so he commits suicide. But Juliette is actually alive when he dies.

> ABRAHAM: Abraham loves Sarah, and would enjoy the rest of his life with her. But he suffers from a heart condition of which he knows nothing about and which eventually causes his inevitable death.

Supposing that ROMEO and ABRAHAM are otherwise similar (Romeo and Abraham die at the same age, they love their beloved ones to the same degree, they happen to suffer the same degree of anxiety near the end of life, etc.) Romeo's death and Abraham's death seem to deprive them from leading very similar lives. Nevertheless, Romeo's death seems pointless in a way that makes it more tragic than Abraham's death, and in this respect, worse. Note, had Romeo's intentional action not resulted in death, but in a short sleep, it would not be all that tragic for him. The fact that Romeo is dead is what makes the situation so tragic. It is in this sense bad for him to be dead over and above whatever is deprived of him due to death.

Realizing (2) explains why when not doing philosophy, it is often the harm of dying that is at center stage. In practical contexts, when discussing healthcare policy, security regulations, or criminal law, we do not assess the value of death (for the dying subject) in isolation. For instance, in case of healthcare policy, when we have to choose between vaccinating all the population from X-disease, or saving a few patients from Y-disease, among other things, we ought to take into account the degree to which dying of Y is bad for the people who are sick; not to isolate the degree to which their death is bad for them. Likewise, in criminal law, the degree to which dying of hunger is bad for a certain victim plays a role (among other factors that we may be interested in), but isolating the degree to which the situation of being dead is bad for the victim, rarely gets to play any role in those contexts. We identify particular deaths by their causes and evaluate particular deaths along with their cause. It is somewhat curious that philosophers addressing the ethics of killing insist on keeping apart death and its causes and providing independent means for assessing the value of death.

Let us close with two technical remarks about death and its causes. First, there are some widely discussed complications concerning the way in which we ought to pick out the cause of death. The main problem concerns both deprivation theory and the view I have been defending on behalf of Améry. Consider the following case:

> DEATH-CAGE: Joe is thrown into a locked cage containing various deadly threats. The cage is designed such that if one escapes the crocodile, they will likely die of some explosive device. If they safely escape the explosives, they will most-definitely be electrified to death after two minutes. Joe is in fact drowned to death by the crocodile.

How should we specify the cause of Joe's death? If we focus strictly on the drowning, when assessing the value of death, deprivation theory will be comparing the actual world (in which Joe dies at t) to a world in which Joe dies of some explosive device very shortly after t. On this perspective, his death will seem to deprive him of very little good life, and not to be very bad for him. But if we focus on the fact that Joe was thrown to the death-cage and take that to be the cause of his death, assuming that Joe will have led a prosperous life if he wasn't thrown into the death-cage, Joe's death will seem tragic. Likewise, on the theory I have been defending: if the cause of death contributes to the value of death, different ways to pick out the cause of death will often deliver different results in this respect.

In order to bypass this difficulty, we can follow the strategy embraced by many deprivation theorists (most straightforwardly Bradley (2009, Chap. 2)). To deliver the intuitive result that Joe's death was extremely bad for him, deprivation theorists will sometimes take the cause of death to be more than just the direct cause, before consulting nearby possible worlds. They will generally be pluralist about 'particular death', and let context decide which particular death (and which particular cause) is being picked.[23] But we can also follow suit with various monistic views of 'the cause of death', and continue to insist that however 'the cause of death' is picked out, it sometimes contributes to the value of death. As far as the main argument goes, we can safely remain neutral on this issue.

A second remark: it is the context in which death occurs, not merely the cause of death that determines the degree to which death is bad. To wit: it seems that contextual factors other than the cause of death may also contribute to the degree to which some particular death is humiliating, and thereby intrinsically bad.

In response: I would be happy to take this on board. The view I have been defending can be extended to include other components of context. The main argument still entitles dying as the basic category for assessment, whether we understand 'dying' to be restricted to death and its causes, or to designate death and the manner of its occurrence more broadly.

12.4 Conclusion

Looking backward, Améry's conception of death and dying seems to match our everyday conception. When saying of some death that it was particularly bad in an everyday context, we normally, and by default, refer to dying as a whole viz. to death and the circumstances leading to it conjointly. Note also that the examples discussed in the previous section are not all that exotic or sophisticated, but rather trivial, especially compared to other examples in the philosophical literature. This raises the question of why the connection between the value of death and the causes of death is so broadly overlooked. I suspect that the reasons for that have to do with two philosophical prejudices.

First, the challenge set forth by Epicurus, concerning whether death can harm its subject in the first place, still dominates much of the philosophical discourse. Departing from the assumption that this is the central question, focusing on dying may be conceived as too close to begging it. However, supposing that the Epicurean challenge has been settled by deprivation theory, and focusing on the question about which factors are relevant for determining the degree to which death is bad, makes factors having to do with the cause of death worth considering. It also licenses the pursuit for the most natural candidate for evaluation.

Second, philosophers often conflate question regarding the value of life with the question regarding the badness of death. To quote just one example, due to Broome (2008, p. 49): "When I asked what your life is worth to you, I meant, more precisely: … what harm would be done to you by not continuing to live?" Deprivation theorists explicitly embrace this[24]: the badness of death on their view is measured by the value of the life it deprives. The cases discussed above suggest that the badness death ought to be distinguished from the value of life. There are factors affecting the degree to which death is bad for its subject independently of the degree to which their life is worth to them.[25]

Notes

1. I will use 'bad' and 'harmful' interchangeably throughout. When not explicitly stated, context will make it easy to follow whether 'harm' refers to overall (all things considered) harm or partial, prima facie, harm (like the pain involved in an overall beneficial injection).
2. For example, the poem "Longing for death" appearing in Hymns to the Night (Novalis 1998).

3. Versions of this view have been defended by Nagel (1970), Feldman (1991), Feit (2002), Broome (2004), Bradley (2009) and many others.
4. An important exception is the bioethical literature addressing questions about end of life processes.
5. Page numbers appearing alone will henceforth refer to this text.
6. With respect to not being any wiser, Améry writes: "We perceived nothing that we would not already have been able to perceive on the outside. Not a bit of [...] practical guidance" (pp. 19–20) With respect to being smarter, he quotes Schnitzler: "Profundity has never clarified the world. Clarity looks more profoundly into its depth" and adds: "Nowhere was it easier than in the camp, and particularly in Auschwitz, to assimilate this clever thought" (pp. 19–20).
7. This is the sense in which Améry often refers to death as unthinkable (e.g. 1994, p. 104).
8. This is, perhaps, not the best choice of words on behalf of Améry. Strictly speaking, if two things are incommensurable, it is impossible to say that one of them is worse. But Améry definitely thinks that death in the camp is, other things equal, much worse than death at the frontline. I take him to be using an informal way of speech, meant to express how grave the difference of degree is.
9. As clear from Améry (1999, especially Chaps. 2 and 5), in unfortunate conditions, voluntary death is better, more dignified, than death that is waited for. (see e.g. pp. 48, 49, 93, 149, 152).
10. Although perhaps not every particular part of that process. If the process is worsened by something that has nothing to do with the degree to which the cause of death is bad (e.g. if one is stung by a bee in the midst of the process preceding death) we would intuitively not wish to count it as affecting the badness of dying. (More on this later.)
11. Améry thinks of dying as a distinctive category (essentially different from other forms of suffering, or other portions of life). Although torture, for instance, is perhaps categorically worse than dying (p. 22), dying receives special attention, due to its unique structure, having to do with its being bound with death.
12. For some noteworthy versions: Williams (1993) limits the badness of death to the deprivation of fulfilling categorical desires, desires that are not conditional on whether the subject continues to live (see also Belshaw 2009; Draper 1999) limits his account to deprivation of what was reasonable to expect.
13. Although it is definitely the most popular view, deprivation theory is not agreed across the board. Notably, McMahan (1988, 2002) argues that death is at least sometimes worse for a subject in virtue of that subject being more psychologically connected to their projects (this is meant to

explain the sense in which it is worse to die as a young adult than to die at the age of 1 month). See also Dworkin (1993), for a view that is similarly oriented. To note some other examples: following McMahan (2002), Milum (2015) suggest that factors like cognitive development also contribute to the badness of death. Blatti (2012) suggests that death is bad for delimiting autonomy.

14. Or, with respects to events other than death, by bringing about something that is intrinsically good or bad.
15. This nicely explains why death did not have much sting for camp inmates: given the expected benefit of their continuing to live, death was mainly conceived as preventing harm. This also explains why Améry thinks of suicide as a natural option when the life ahead of the person committing it is expected to be overall harmful (1999, Chap. 2).
16. Améry also takes death that is a result of suicide to often be dignified (1999, Chap. 4).
17. This could explain our tendency to save special praise to heroic actions that ended in death, and pay more attention to those actions than to similar heroic actions that did not end in death. To the extent that this ought to be so, death itself sometimes contributes to the hero's dignity.
18. Assuming she is equally cognitively developed, and psychologically connected to her projects, both cases are similar also with respect to other accounts as well.
19. Consider Bradley (2009, p. 68), D'Arms and Jacobson (2000), and Norcross (2015, p. 171).
20. If we have a hedonistic criterion of 'interest' this may not be so of course. But on many accounts of dignity, humiliation is intrinsically bad for the subject independently of whether one is aware of it. Likewise, dignity can be intrinsically good independently of whether one enjoys it (see, for instance, Waldron 2012).
21. As noted above, some factors that have nothing to do with the cause of death also affect the process preceding death: that process can be eased, if I have painkillers, or worsened, if I am stung by a bee. But focusing on the harm resulting from the cause of death takes into account exactly what we intuitively should: dying of a gunshot is intuitively not as bad when I have access to painkillers. But it is not in any way worse when I get stung by a bee. This is because the harm caused by the cause of death is lessened in the first case, and stays intact in the second. There may be some intuitive price to pay in case part of what the cause brings about has nothing to do with the process of death. But I think that the price is not very high: when noting that dying of a certain cause is terrible, we normally do not really draw a line between harms having to do directly with the process of dying and the rest (I thank Berit Braun for discussion on the last point).

22. In some contexts, we may wish to distinguish the badness of the process of death (was it painful, was it slow) from the badness having to do with the nature of the cause itself (was it humiliating). This distinction will always be available, but in terms of priority, dying seems to me like a more basic category. In any event, it is most important for me to stress that it is more basic than death itself (I thank David Heyd for illuminating this point).
23. See Feit (2015) for discussion of further complications.
24. But other theorists equally share it. If (as some philosophers following McMahan (2002) hold) death at the age of 30 is, other things equal, worse than death at the age of 1 month, death is not only bad due the life it deprives; but it is nonetheless bad due to the fact that one's life is worth more to them when they are 30 than when they are 1 month of age.
25. I wish to thank Dan Baras, Berit Braun, Eran Fish, Moshe Halbertal, Arden Kohler, Amit Kravitz, Iddo Landau, Andrew Peet, an anonymous referee for Palgrave Macmillan Publishers, the audience of 'The Israeli Philosophical Association Conference, 2018' (Haifa), and the audience of 'The IAPDD conference 2018' (Uppsala), for comments on an earlier draft and an abstract, in which some of the major themes have appeared. Very special thanks to David Heyd and to Magnus Jedenheim-Edling for comments and discussion that have greatly contributed to the current version of the chapter.

References

Améry, J. (1980). *At the Mind's Limits* (S. Rosenfeld & S. P. Rosenfeld, Trans.). Bloomington: Indiana University Press.

Améry, J. (1994). *On Aging*. Bloomington: Indiana University Press.

Améry, J. (1999). *On Suicide*. Bloomington: Indiana University Press.

Belshaw, C. (2009). *Annihilation*. McGill-Queen's University Press.

Blatti, S. (2012). Death's Distinctive Harm. *American Philosophical Quarterly, 49*(4), 317–330.

Bradley, B. (2004). When Is Death Bad for the One Who Dies? *Noûs, 38*, 1–28.

Bradley, B. (2009). *Well Being and Death*. Oxford: Oxford University Press.

Broome, J. (2004). *Weighing Lives*. New York: Oxford University Press.

Broome, J. (2008). Retrieved from https://www.jstor.org/stable/20028164?seq=1#page_scan_tab_contents.

D'Arms, J., & Jacobson, D. (2000). The Moralistic Fallacy: On the "Appropriateness" of Emotions. *Philosophy and Phenomenological Research, 61*, 65–90.

Draper, K. (1999). Disappointment, Sadness, and Death. *The Philosophical Review, 108*, 387–414.

Dworkin. (1993). Retrieved from https://www.penguinrandomhouse.com/books/44340/lifes-dominion-by-ronald-dworkin/9780679733195/.
Feit, N. (2002). The Time of Death's Misfortune. *Noûs, 36*, 359–383.
Feit, N. (2015). Plural Harm. *Philosophy and Phenomenological Research, 90*(2), 361–388.
Feldman, F. (1991). Some Puzzles About the Evil of Death. *The Philosophical Review, 100*, 205–227.
Luper, S. (2009). *The Philosophy of Death*. Cambridge: Cambridge University Press.
McMahan, J. (1988). Death and the Value of Life. *Ethics, 99*(1), 32–36.
McMahan, J. (2002). *The Ethics of Killing: Problems at the Margins of Life*. New York: Oxford University Press.
Milum, J. (2015). Age and Death: A Defence of Gradualism. *Utilitas, 27*(3), 279–297.
Nagel, T. (1970). Death. *Noûs, 4*(1), 73–80.
Norcross, A. (2015). Harming in Context. *Philosophical Studies, 123*, 149–173.
Novalis. (1998). *Hymns to the Night* (D. Higgins, Trans.). McPherson & Co Publishers.
Waldron, J. (2012). *Dignity, Rank and Rights*. Oxford University Press.
Williams, B. (1993). The Makropulos Case: Reflections on the Tedium of Immortality. In Fischer (Ed.), *The Metaphysics of Death* (pp. 73–92). (First published 1973).

CHAPTER 13

Jean Améry: Suicide, the Refusal to Heal, and Humanistic Freedom

Grace Campbell

13.1 The importance of Améry's *On Suicide*

On Suicide [*Hand an sich Legen. Diskurs über den Freitod* (1977)] is Améry's penultimate work. While there has recently been a renewed interest in Améry's defense of suicide, the essay collection is given comparably less serious philosophical contemplation than his work on resentment. I argue that his examination of *échec*, his challenge to the "logic of life", and his defense of suicide, represent a culmination of Améry's philosophical project. Améry's commitment to privileging autonomy and freedom over well-being is introduced in his writings on resentment and further exemplified in his defense of suicide. This conception of a radically free human subject who is able to reject coercion toward well-being even to the point of self-annihilation, in turn, illuminates the tensions in Améry's ambiguous relationship with Enlightenment thinking.

Améry wrote *On Suicide* after an unsuccessful suicide attempt and before his successful suicide in 1978. In the essays, he eschews attempts to

G. Campbell (✉)
School of Historical and Philosophical Enquiry, The University of Queensland, Brisbane, QLD, Australia
e-mail: g.campbell5@uq.edu.au

Y. Ataria et al. (eds.), *Jean Améry*,
https://doi.org/10.1007/978-3-030-28095-6_13

examine the phenomenon through psychological or quantitative sociological methods and instead attempts to elucidate the lived phenomenon of suicide. This in turn positions suicide as both an assertion of individual freedom and as an act brings freedom. As such, discussions of suicide cannot be fully contained within the discourses of psychology and sociology or more generally within what he referred to as the domain of the "logic of life". The "logic of life" refers to a collection of often unexamined sociological, psychological, and biological pressures and inertias that encourage and coerce continued living and well-being (Améry 1999b).

On Suicide also represents the culmination of Améry's pessimism in his writing and philosophy.[1] His defense of suicide expands on the pessimism of *At the Mind's Limits* (1999a) and *On Aging* (1994). He continues to confront problematic "common sense" schemas that coerce well-being at the expense of human freedom. In these prior projects, Améry rejects what he views as clichéd platitudes such as "time will heal all wounds" and "forgive and forget". He also rejects the sentiment that aging is an unavoidable part of life that nonetheless brings wisdom and contentment. In contrast to what he defines as this common-sense view, Améry privileges the experiences that the logic of life marginalizes. This pessimism results in an ambiguous relationship with the future and temporality. Despite a commitment to progress, Améry fundamentally critiques the notion of time as a positive healing process and instead frames the passage of time in primarily negative and alienating terms.

Améry's defense of suicide builds on his defense of resentment and his refusal to accept healing and forgiveness in the aftermath of World War II. The ability to reject forgiveness is framed as the right and privilege of a free human subject. Améry acknowledges both that forgiveness may bring a sense of psychological healing for the victims of atrocities and that the passage of time will inevitably historicize the Holocaust. However, people can and ought to rebel against these natural processes and push against the forces of inertia that encourage healing. This key concept that people are not determined by the biological, sociological, and temporal inertias which naturally guide them toward healing and well-being provides a basis from which people can examine and ultimately reject the logic of life through committing suicide.

A serious examination of *On Suicide* highlights and elucidates several tensions within Améry's philosophy. Améry's defense of suicide exemplifies his ambiguous defense of the Enlightenment as well as his condemnation of what he saw as "anti-Enlightenment thinkers" such as Foucault and members of the Frankfurt school. Améry criticized what he saw as the rejection of subjectivity and progress in postmodernism. However, Améry's defense of suicide and resentment also challenge what he defines as the "logic of life" and Enlightenment norms of well-being, flourishing, and the inevitability of the future. As such, Améry simultaneously defends a humanistic conception of the autonomist subject, while rejecting notions of that this subject must promote and extend their lives and well-being.

In *On Suicide* (1999b), Améry continues to frame himself as an existentialist and borrows heavily from Sartre's opus, while acknowledging his different conclusions from Sartre's existentialism. Améry places greater emphasis on the role of the body than Sartre. This is demonstrated both when discussing the phenomenon of torture and self-destruction (Améry 1999a, b). Améry also criticizes Sartre's political work, particularly his later work (Améry 1984c). However, he continues to recognize his debt to Sartrean radical freedom and free will (Améry 1984c). He utilizes the conception of Sartrean freedom to provide a conception of subjectivity that allows for individuals to challenge the inertia of the logic of life through suicide and challenge historical entropy through resentment. As such, *On Suicide* represents the culmination of Améry's project and reliance on a radically undetermined subject. For him, the notion that "everyone has to live" represents the ultimate example of social, biological, and physical pressure to continue living. It is only via an absolute and uniquely human freedom that people are not determined by this and are able to challenge the "natural" status quo and instead chose death.

13.2 Rejecting the Logic of Life and Embracing *Échec*

In *On Suicide* Améry focuses on the phenomenon of the person "before the leap". That is, Améry is interested in examining the individual parasuicidal subject on the precipice of suicide. He does not reject sociological studies of suicidology. However, for the suicidal person, these general population based and quantitative studies are "empty". He writes:

> Suicidology is right. Except that for suicides and potential suicides what it says is empty. For what it comes to for them is the total is the total and unmistakable singularity of their lived situation, their *situation vécue*. (Améry 1999b, p. 8)

As such, what is of value for Améry is a philosophical investigation of the lived experience of the suicide or the potential suicide on a personal and subjective level.

The lived situation of the suicidal person fundamentally challenges the logic of life and is marked by a deep sense of *échec*. The term *échec* is taken from the French word for failure as Améry claims the term aesthetically denotes failure's shattering nature. *Échec* is not a literal failure to achieve a specific goal. Rather, it refers to a more general inability to retain faith in the world. "*Échec* means something like a failure, a defeat [...] Basically, one can live in *échec* but only in a disgraceful almost 'unnatural' way" (Améry 1999b, p. 41). Society compels individuals to move beyond and defeat their sense of *échec*. He states, "to be normal is to overcome *échec*, and society applauds the brave man who is not frightened". However, in the case of the suicidal person, this failure moves from an experience of *échec* in life and becomes an ***échec* of life** or a feeling of disgust in the world. Rather than overcome their failure, the suicidal person instead chooses to escape *échec* through rejecting the logic of life and life itself.

This *échec* can take many forms and affect many situations. Améry compares a litany of historical, contemporary, and fictional suicides to examine how *échec* can operate equally powerfully in both seemingly serious and trivial situations. He gives a supposedly trivial example of a woman who had "thrown herself out of a window 'because of her unhappy love for a radio lover'" (Améry 1999b, p. 6). This supposedly "foolish" suicide is contrasted to the less controversial case of Freud's euthanasia. Améry writes:

> [T]ake Sigmund Freud. The old man's cancer of the gums was in its final stage. The patient's mouth produced a pestilential odor so obnoxious that his favorite dog wouldn't go near him anymore. He said to his personal physician that everything was just torture and more torture and demanded the injection that would liberate him—which his old friend did not deny him. (Améry 1999b, p. 6)

In addition, Améry describes the fictitious Lt. Gustl who claims he will commit suicide as he feels that he disgraced the honor of his army uniform by failing to retaliate against a physically imposing baker who insulted him.[2] These examples serve to expand discourses on suicide beyond discussions about when suicide is acceptable or can be considered morally justifiable euthanasia.

Améry rejects any attempt to divide suicides into so-called acceptable suicides in the face of insurmountable physical pain, terminal illness, or certain torture, and "frivolous" suicides which are committed or attempted for supposedly spurious reasons. What unites these cases is that the suicidal or parasuicidal person finds continuing to exist intolerable. The person before the leap feels a deep sense of *échec* or failure in the world. This marks a sharp departure from ethical and political debates on the permissibility of suicide and euthanasia.

The fact that the suicidal person has lost this faith in the world means that they are no longer operating within the logic of life. The logic of life refers to everyday functioning of continued existence. For Améry the logic of life has a societal, biological, and even atomistic or quantum dimension.

> Anyone who wants to commit suicide is breaking out, out of the logic of life, as I've already indicated. This logic of life is given to us, the biologist knows it just as well as the behavioral scientist, and perhaps also the physicist, because recent works of theoretical physics seem to allow the conclusion that bios [the domain of life] and human beings are perhaps more than "chance hits" as Jacques Monod thought. The logic of life is prescribed for us, or "programmed" if you wish, in every daily reaction. (Améry 1999b, p. 13)

Rejecting or moving beyond the logic of life represents a rupture with the status quo and a fundamental challenge to the most basic norms of social and biological existence. The taboo of suicide is not merely socially imposed but is instead formed by the natural underpinning state of all life and matter. As previously discussed, Améry states that the "common sense" approach to life is that "everyone has to live". However, the potential suicide moves beyond this common sense dictum and questions "does one have to live?" before answering with a defiant "no". The lived situation of the suicidal person is one in which life is intolerable and voluntary death becomes a way of reclaiming one's dignity. This is exemplified in the supposedly absurd case of Lt. Gustl. Lt. Gustl disgraces his military code of honor when he is insulted by the physically imposing local baker. Gustl is unable to retaliate due to the baker's size. Furthermore, he cannot regain his sense of dignity through dueling as the baker does not have sufficient social standing. From this, he fears public humiliation and loses his sense of pride and dignity. For Gustl, it is irrelevant that his actions could be generally considered reasonable and easily sanctioned. Rather, his supposed cowardice and then inability to reclaim his honor marked him with a deep sense of *échec*.

However, by rejecting the natural inertia of continued existence the suicidal or parasuicidal person exhibits their uniquely human capacity for genuine freedom and dignity. In this sense, Lt. Gustl can reclaim his sense of honor and autonomy through his affirmation that he will reject the logic of life and commit suicide, even if he does not ultimately act on his decision. Consequently, the suicidal person's defiant "no" to the necessity of continued existence and their rejection of the logic of life is an assertion of human autonomy.

When the act of suicide challenges the logic of life, the suicidal person moves into the "anti-logic of death". This logic is described as the following:

> The *logic of death* is not a logic in the usual sense, upholding reason alone, for it allows no conclusion other than just one, again and again and again: not is the same as not with which the statement of every logical (that is, analytic) judgement, already in itself containing no reality, loses its last tie to reality; that tie above all in which the equation of two categories of being that are symbolically recorded as in mathematics, or are rooted in everyday language, is now related to something that is nothing and is not—a pure negation and an accursed inconceivability. (Améry 1999b, p. 19)

Subsequently, the logic of life cannot be considered a logic in the traditional sense. Rather death is rooted in negation and violently rejects the physical and biological inertia that determines the logic of life. As such, suicide exists in a kind of anti-logic. For Améry, suicide is a unique situation as the parasuicidal person has remaining attachments to the logic of life while also reaching into the anti-logic of death.

Améry positions both the anti-logic of death and the suicidal person's ambiguous positioning between the logic of life and the anti-logic of death as disturbing. As the logic of life represents the everyday continuation of existence it is "natural" and in step with the continuation of the positive existence of a sensible universe.[3] Suicide's rupture with the logic of life is a confronting revolt against this natural logic.

These ruptures also highlight a key tension in Améry's philosophy in regards to the passage of time. There is a potential conflict between his support of progress and his reticence to frame the passage of time in positive terms. Améry repeatedly states that he believes in progress. In his address after receiving the Hamburg Lessing Prize, he laments: "What sad aberration has brought us to the point where modern thinkers do not dare to employ concepts such as progress, humanization, and reason except within damning quotation marks?" (Améry 1984b, p. 135). He is highly critical of what he saw as popular poststructuralist, postmodernist, and Frankfurt School thinkers' critiques of the enlightenment. He dismissed these schools and characterized them as believing: "Progress? The frenzied obsession with production and profit of a bourgeoisie that has subjugated the proletarian and with him the earth" before strongly rejecting this suggestion (Améry 1984b, p. 135).

However, this belief in progress and the positive potential of continuing to move forward is tempered by an acknowledgment of and respect for the human potential to fight against the passage of time. This is performed both in the ultimately futile but autonomously chosen action to fight against historical entropy and the decision to reject life itself. This represents Améry's multifaceted but humanistic commitment to respect for autonomy. I will elaborate further on the discomforting nature of this action in my next sections.

13.3 Suicide, Autonomy, and Améry's Humanism

Améry focuses on the uniquely human aspect of suicide. In his essay, he goes beyond the statement that people ought to have the right to commit suicide. Rather, suicide is an action that brings human freedom. Améry quotes the suicidologist Jean Baechler who claims that "suicide is specifically and universally human" (1999b, p. 43). Améry argues that suicide is not reducible to a mistake or a symptom of mental illness. Rather it represents a freely chosen rejection of the natural inertia of continued existence.

Saying "no" to the logic of life represents a revolt and rebellion against the "natural" order and demonstrates that people are not determined by the logic of life. Committing suicide is an example of autonomous action as it is the most explicit exemplar of the capacity to act freely against a status quo or preexisting momentum. The uniquely human capacity to reject the logic of life relies on Améry's indebtedness to Sartre's notions of radical ontological freedom. However, crucially this subject remains a humanist subject in contrast to poststructuralism of counter-enlightenment thinking.

The suicidal person has a historical, sociological, biological, and even subatomic facticity which predisposes them to the inertia of the logic of life. However, by virtue of human free will, they can reject being determined by this facticity and instead spontaneously act against it. As such, suicide is an action that is based in dignity and freedom. Améry's conception of suicide goes beyond the right to die to avoid pain and instead asserts suicide as an act of human freedom that can challenge both society and biology itself. He writes that the decision to kill oneself is a decision "not only made in freedom but also brings real freedom to us" (Améry 1999b, p. 132). This freedom does not come purely from the act of dying as society often condones "unnecessary" death such as dying in wars. What is unique about suicide is that death is freely chosen and embraced. It is through suicide's voluntary nature that Améry is able to retain his notion of a radically autonomous, humanist subject while simultaneously critiquing norms that coerce well-being.

Other holocaust writers such as Hannah Arendt and Primo Levi reach similar conclusions about autonomy and suicide from a different perspective. In the *Origins of Totalitarianism* (1967), Arendt examines the complete extinguishing of spontaneity in the concentration camps to the point where people were unable to even commit suicide.

> For to destroy individuality is to destroy spontaneity, man's power to begin something new out of his own resources, something that cannot be explained on the basis of reactions to environment and events [...] In this context also belongs the astonishing rarity of suicides in the camps. Suicide occurred far more often before arrest and deportation that in the camp itself, which is of course partly explained by the fact that every attempt was made to prevent suicides which are, after all, spontaneous acts. (Arendt 1967, p. 455)[4]

Levi also writes about how Auschwitz prisoners were reduced to the status of animals and subsequently generally cut off from the human activity of suicide (Levi 2000). Writing about his hunger and exhaustion he states "I am not even alive enough to know how to kill myself" (Levi 2000, p. 121).[5] Both these writers demonstrate that the ability to resist and revolt is a key component of human freedom. The reduction of this capacity for freedom represents a severe injury to the human subject.

The freedom to kill oneself may be disturbing; however, the decision to "throw one's life away" represents a pure and overwhelming experience of freedom which ultimately negates the value of the logic of life. The ability to reject inertia and act in a spontaneous manner has value on an ontological, psychological, and moral-political level.

The assertion of the value of suicide builds on Améry's defense of the value of resentment. Améry steadfastly clings to his feelings of resentment toward the Germans after his liberation from Auschwitz. In his writing, he highlights how he fundamentally identifies himself as a victim and when he speaks of the atrocities of Nazi Germany he does so from this position. He explicitly dismisses Hannah Arendt's political polemics to instead focus on his personal anger and subjective experience as a victim. In *The Human Condition,* Arendt explores the restorative potential of forgiveness. She states:

> [W]ithout being forgiven, released from the consequences of what we have done, our capacity to act would, as it were, be confined to one single deed from which we could never recover; we would remain the victims of its consequences forever. (Arendt 1958, p. 237)

This forgiveness is framed as being beneficial for both the victim and the perpetrator of the acts. The performance of forgiveness is what allows people to move beyond actions committed in the past in order to permit the future performance of pluralistic actions in the political sphere.

Améry in contrast wholeheartedly rejects the notion that people should be encouraged or pressured to forgive. He describes other Jewish intellectuals who "were trembling in the pathos of forgiveness and reconciliation", as distasteful (Améry 1999a, p. 64). For Améry, refusing to forgive and surrender to the healing process of time represents a free and autonomous action. The coercion of victims to engage in forgiveness or the pathologization of the refusal to forgive is a reprehensible act of victimization and dehumanization.

To demonstrate this, Améry engages with Nietzsche and psychological accounts of "concentration camp syndrome" (Améry 1999a, p. 64). He represents "Nietzsche as morally condemning resentment and modern psychology ... [is] only able to view it as a disturbing conflict". Améry rejects this dismissal of resentment and attempts to philosophically elaborate on what it means to be a resenting victim. He states that "a forgiving and forgetting induced by society is immoral" (Améry 1999a, p. 60). He rails against the idea that he ought to be pressured or forced to forgive, from both a moral and psychological point of view. Rather, he extols the value of our ability to resist healing and hold on to our injuries.

Again, Améry's defense of resentment is both political and personal. In *Ethical Loneliness* (2012), Jill Stauffer highlights the importance of the political situation in which Améry was writing. She highlights how, at the time of writing, the discipline of Holocaust scholarship was in its infancy.

> It was not widely known that there had been a concerted effort to eliminate a group of people from the earth … This puts Améry's struggle in a wider context: his resistance to forgiveness was in part a way to demand a wider recognition of the specific harms he had suffered, since no preexisting general term would capture adequately the horror of what he survived. (Stauffer 2012, p. 12)

Therefore, Améry wrote in a context where there was real political pressure to underplay the importance of the Holocaust and to engage in the political process of forgiveness; which often entailed Amnesty and desisting prosecutions due to statutes of limitations. Améry's sense of both resentment and *ressentiment* act as a political locus of resistance against this forced forgiveness and to call for, at least partial justice to be served against the purveyors of the Holocaust. When discussing the execution of his Auschwitz torturer, the SS-man Wajs, Améry writes:

> The experience of persecution was, at its very bottom, that of an extreme *loneliness* … When SS-man Wajs stood before the firing squad, he experienced the moral truth of his crimes. At that moment he was with *me*—and I was no longer alone with the shovel handle. I would like to believe that at the moment of his execution he wanted exactly as much as I do to turn back time, to undo what had been done. When they led him to the place of execution the antiman had again become a fellow man. (Améry 1999a, p. 72)

From this, the clinging to resentment functions politically as it stands as testament to the atrocities of the Third Reich and resists an unearned and forced forgetting.

Thomas Brudholm also engages with the political dimension of Améry's thought when discussing his use of the term resentment. Brudholm discusses how Améry's use of the term "resentments" encompasses the feeling of resentment, Nietzschean *ressentiment*, and the notion of a grudge (Brudholm 2010). These terms are multifaceted and often shift throughout Améry's writings. Brudholm argues that Améry attempts to rehabilitate a morally justifiable form of *ressentiment* which goes beyond Nietzsche's dismissal of the phenomenon. A dimension of Améry's *ressentiments* is the political ability of the resentful victim to stand as testament to the horrors of the Holocaust. Brudholm argues that Améry's *ressentiment* is therefore partially focused on the attitudes of forgiveness which developed in the postwar period. However, these sentiments are not reducible to Martha Nussbaum's notions of anger in the face of evil nor a simple understanding of justified resentment. Rather, "Améry conceptualizes *ressentiment* as something 'monstrous'—a special kind indeed"; however, this monstrous *ressentiment* continues to be valuable (Brudholm 2010, p. 102).

This monstrous *ressentiment* refers to a tortured attachment to past injustices. However, despite the testimonial and ethical significance of *ressentiment*, Améry's defense goes beyond its capacity for restitution and change in the political sphere. Clinging to *ressentiment* also represents autonomy and dignity for the resentful victim. It is fundamentally important to acknowledge that, for Améry, the Holocaust can never be reversed nor can it adequately be made amends for. Améry continues to argue against the push for amnesties and broad-scale Arendtian forgiveness. However, he also acknowledges that any kind of complete justice or punishment for the Holocaust is both impossible and undesirable. Writing about the possibility of revenge against those responsible for the Holocaust, Améry claims:

> They cannot consist in a revenge dealt out in proportion to what was suffered. I cannot prove it, but I am certain that there is no victim who would even have considered hanging the man Bogner, of the Auschwitz trial, in the Bogner swing. Even less would any sane person among us ever venture the morally impossible thought that four to six million Germans be taken away to their death ... It can be a matter neither of revenge of one side or of a problematic atonement [on the other]. (Améry 1999a, p. 81)

As such, the Holocaust can never be undone, avenged, or completely atoned for in the political sphere. This renders Améry's relationship with both the Holocaust and the passage of time complex and personal. His status as a resentful or ressentiment-ful victim cannot be ameliorated in a practical or moral sense or naturally by the passage of time. Resentment instead represents the victim's choice to resist the power of historical entropy and forgiveness in a way that allows them to assert their autonomy against the inertia of time.

Améry expands the importance of this ability in his prior essay *The Time of Rehabilitation* (1984d). In the essay, Améry examines the inevitable historicization of the Holocaust. He refers to this process as "historical entropy". He argues that societal memories of atrocities dissipate and that eventually the outrage of Nazism cannot be felt as strongly as it was at the conclusion of World War II. While this process is unavoidable, Améry claims that historical entropy should not be encouraged and should be fought against as strongly as possible. This represents a defiance against nature and against healing. While this defiance may be futile, it remains a victim's prerogative and right to act in this manner.

What is pertinent from this is the value of choosing to cling to past injury; even if this is absurd. Améry highlights how the nature of linear time means that it is impossible to avoid the process of the historicization of the Holocaust. Similarly, Améry admits that his rejection of forgiveness and demand the irreversible be reversed are absurd. By clinging to resentment he rejects the "natural" account of time which privileges self-betterment and well-being to instead embrace a disordered time sense which is not future oriented (Ben-Shai 2010). However, it is this inevitability and absurdity of historical entropy that renders clinging to resentment and combating the inertia of time free, autonomous, and moral.

Améry dismisses forced forgiveness or overly permissive forgiveness by stating

> Whoever lazily and cheaply forgives, subjugates himself to the social and biological time-sense, which is also called the 'natural' one. Natural consciousness of time actually is rooted in the physiological process of wound-healing and became part of the social conception of reality. But precisely for this reason it is not only extramoral, but also *anti*moral in character. **Man has the right and privilege to declare himself to be in disagreement with every natural occurrence, including the biological healing that time brings about**. (Améry 1999a, p. 92, emphasis mine)

Therefore, despite the inherent absurdity of the refusal to forgive, pushing against the natural inertia of forgiveness and the natural conception of time is an autonomous action that in turn brings human dignity. It is this human capacity to push against the tendency toward sociological and natural healing which allows for ultimate freedom.

This rationale is then extended to view suicide as the ultimate example of the free choice to reject well-being. Just as it is necessary to move beyond discussions of so-called Concentration Camp Syndrome to properly understand resentment, it is necessary to avoid pathologization of the suicidal person. Like clinging to resentment, suicide represents a choice to operate pessimistically. As such, *On Suicide* represents an expansion and culmination of Améry's defense of autonomy and the right to reject healing. By embracing resentment and suicide, Améry rejects the claim that certain seemingly negative phenomena are merely side effects that should be minimized as much as possible. Rather, he highlights how they can have value in their own right and in some situations ought to be sought.

13.4 Rejecting Condemnation and Pathologization

Throughout *On Suicide*, Améry argues against both secular and religious condemnations of suicide as immoral. However, he also rejects attempts to pathologize suicide as purely the result of diagnosable mental illness. Both these schemas demonize suicide and undermine its status as a valid and freely made choice. The former condemns suicide and undermines the right of a person to challenge the logic of life. The latter undermines the respect for the autonomy and capacity to freely make decisions of a person in the instance when they do challenge the logic of life. These rejections again demonstrate the measured nature of Améry's defense of Enlightenment thinking. Améry embraces an account of progress that criticizes unwarranted condemnation of free human actions while also rejecting conceptions of progress which privilege diagnosis and healing over autonomy.[6]

Suicide is presented a valid choice that should not be morally condemned. Améry's critique of the moral condemnation of suicide is built into his linguistic choices. He uses the term *Freitod*, or voluntary death, over the more commonly used term *Selbstmord* which literally translates as self-murder (Améry 1999b).[7] This phrasing highlights the importance Améry places on freedom as the phrase *Freitod* avoids the moralistic tones of *Selbstmord* while still highlighting the intentional nature of the act. Similarly, Améry repeatedly uses the phrase "to lay hands on oneself". This phrase highlights the free character of suicide while also placing the act suicide in the domain of one's own reasonable action.

By championing suicide as a freely chosen action, Améry is also highly critical of attempts to render the act of suicide as a symptom of a diagnosable mental disorder. He is especially critical in the cases in which there are no other diagnosable symptoms aside from an attempted or completed suicide.

Attempts to view suicide as a symptom of mental health reduce *échec* and disgust in the world to symptoms of an illness. He claims that "both phenomena... have been robbed of their dignity by the sciences of psychology and psychiatry" (Améry 1999b, p. 56). He claims that sickness carries a stigma of disgrace and by rendering these phenomena as sicknesses psychiatry erases a dimension of human experience.

Viewing suicide as a symptom of mental illness destigmatizes the suicidal person as they are no longer considered blameworthy for their actions. However, this paradigm restigmatizes the suicidal person as mentally ill or mad. The suicidal person is no longer considered an autonomous agent and their prior autonomy is transferred to psychiatric doctors.

Lisa Lieberman highlights that after Améry's first suicide attempt he was reduced to the status of a thing. She highlights how his resuscitation and hospitalization robbed him of his freedom and how Améry described the process as the worst occurrence of his life (Lieberman 2003). She reluctantly admits that Améry's eventual successful suicide functioned as a statement of his self-ownership despite her discomfort over his coldness in the face of his voluntary death. However, this acceptance is difficult for her and pathologization and medicalization allow for depersonalization of the suicidal person and act as shields against the confronting nature of the act (Lieberman 2003). This depersonalizing tendency is mirrored in the history of discourses surrounding suicide. Lieberman highlights how Christian prohibitions against suicide, starting with St Augustine and extended by Thomas Aquinas, were loosened in the eighteenth century and were then supplanted by appeals to broad-scale sociological factors and mental health outcomes (Lieberman 2003). While these schemas remove blame from the suicidal person, they also remove the dignity associated with being an autonomous subject.

This stigmatization continues in contemporary times. The critical psychiatrist Thomas Szasz argues that societal and psychiatric understandings of suicide mask the phenomenon. He writes:

> We deny suicide by attributing its cause to nearly everything—from rock music to natural disasters and, above all else, to mental illness—except the subject's own decision. We are willing to *accuse* people and drugs and songs of causing suicide; we are willing to *excuse* suicide by blaming it on several of the causes listed and, above all, on mental illness; but we are not will to *accept* suicide as suicide. (Szasz 2002, pp. 22–23)

Like Améry, Szasz argues against this paradigm and views suicide as a phenomenon within its own right. I argue that Améry's writing provides this conception of suicide as a radical and freely chosen action.

13.5 The Unsettling Duality of Suicide

While it is not as significant a focus as autonomy, Améry also briefly touches upon the unsettling duality of suicide. Positioning self-destruction as a chosen and autonomous act raises contradictions and tensions. The logic of life gives way to the anti-logic of death in which "logic and dialectic fail in tragicomic agreement" (Améry 1999b, p. 153). Voluntary death is a person acting as a subject in order to attack themselves as an object. It is a person acting in order to limit their capacity for action. Suicide reveals the "road to the open", in as much as it is a radically free action, but this road leads nowhere (Améry 1999b, p. 152). A person engaging in self-destructive behavior also presents as having an ambiguous relationship between the mind/ego and the body as self-destruction represents an action performed on the body to obliterate the ego. These tensions highlight disquieting dualities within self-destruction.

Améry argues that suicide is an example of a person "de-selfing their self themselves" (Améry 1999b). Améry suggests that this is a double contradiction. The first contradiction is centered on the fact that people live their lives and engage in their projects with the knowledge that they will die. However, suicide has a secondary element of contradiction. Suicide is *prima facie* voluntary. However, suicide simultaneously serves to annihilate the subject that performs the act and is a project that cuts its performer off from any potential for future action.

Améry's description of his torture by the Nazis provides a basis for this tension. Améry writes about the fundamental difference between the tortured and non-tortured person. After being arrested as part of the Belgian resistance, Améry was taken to a Nazi facility to be interrogated. He recalls awaiting his torture and attempting to imagine what he would experience. During his interrogation, he realizes "nothing [torture] happens as we imagine because there is a difference between phantasy and reality" (Améry 1999a, p. 25). This is because torture is inflicted on the lived body and consequently is always personal and can never be entirely rendered theoretical or imagined.

Améry begins to understand the true nature of torture as the interrogation begins. He realizes that his "ability to feel at-home-in-the-world is as much physical as epistemological" (Améry 1999a, p. 48). With the "first blow" from his torturer's fist strikes him, Améry loses his "trust in the world" (Améry 1999a). The person under torture is reduced to pain and flesh. They are reduced to a profane and obscene body. Furthermore, the tortured person loses their sense of self and boundaries. Their body is no longer theirs but instead belongs to the torturer, who is rendered a sovereign. He describes this process saying

> I have not forgotten that there were moments when I felt a kind of wretched admiration for the agonizing sovereignty they exercised over me. For is not the one who can reduce a person so entirely to a body and a whimpering prey of death a God, or at least, a Demigod? (Améry 1999a, p. 25)

However, this relationship between the Godly torturer and the reduced-to-flesh tortured becomes contradictory when both the torturer and the tortured are the same person. In the case of torture, the sovereign torturer inflicts pain on the lived body and flesh of the tortured. However, the self-destructive person is both sovereign and flesh simultaneously. Torture happens *to* the victim. As flesh, the tortured victim does not consent or consciously act; the victim is acted upon by the torturer. This is why the reality of torture cannot be theoretical or imagined. Torture *is* and *exists* simpliciter in its performance (Améry 1999a). However, in the case of self-destruction, this dynamic is more complicated. The self-destructing person must exist as the wholly transcendent torturer and the tortured flesh. Améry writes in detail about the meticulous and sometimes painful methods chosen to commit suicide. He describes the careful planning involved in procuring sleeping pills or fashioning a noose, the technical difficulty of severing one's throat, as well as the extreme case of blacksmith who excruciatingly crushes his head in his vice despite the sound of his own skull shattering. In these cases, the suicidal person simultaneously occupies the *Being* simpliciter of experiencing pain and the higher order process of inflicting it. This results in the self-destructive person relating to themselves as both subject and Other.

This relation to the self is further both self-obsessed and depersonalizing. Suicide highlights tensions between the body and ego. Améry focuses on the fact that suicide is an act performed on the body in order to obliterate the ego and the subjective self. He borrows Sartrean terminology to explain this phenomenon. He claims that there is normally both a singularity and a duality between the body and the ego. Bodies exist "and they are part of the outside world" while our inner psychic life is not readily available to others (Améry 1999a, p. 63). However, the two aspects permeate each other in a complex and protean manner. Améry writes, "we are not aware of our bodies during everyday existence" (Améry 1999a, p. 63).

By this, he means that we do not think of our bodies as being-in-the-world and tangible objects for others. Instead, if we become aware of our bodies, it is generally from the ego-tinged perspective of how our bodies feel for us. However, in the case of suicide, the body must be destroyed, which entails being able to view the body as a tangible object. Again, this body as a tangible object is attacked by the ego as a *subject*. This, in turn, means the suicidal person has a "peculiar relationship to the manifestations of unity and duality" (Améry 1999b, p. 63). The blurring of these boundaries is unsettling.

Further elaborations on this ambiguous duality are beyond the scope of this chapter. However, these tensions highlight that within *On Suicide*, Améry demonstrates a complex and ambiguous conception of subjectivity and freedom that in turn allows for the freedom to destroy one's freedom.

13.6 The Relationship Between Suicide and Améry's Measured Defense of the Enlightenment

I argue that Améry's defense of suicide epitomizes Améry's protean relationship with the general Enlightenment project. It shows an embrace of the notion of progress in as much as progress represents a further respect for a complex humanistic subject and their freely made decisions. However, he can reject the "guardians of the Enlightenment" who attempt to limit human subjectivity in the name of healing and well-being.

This same reasoning lies behind Améry's suspicion of medicalization of suicide and resentment while also rejecting his contemporary anti-psychiatrists. Améry defends what he sees as rationally chosen action. As such, he simultaneously critiques what he sees as the threat of both Enlightenment-inspired pathologization from schemas which do not view the decision to reject healing as valid and postmodern conceptions which do not embrace the idea of the human subject.

Throughout his popular publishing, Améry openly defended the thinking of the Enlightenment. He writes:

> And still, I profess loyalty to enlightenment, specifically to the *classical* enlightenment—as a *philosohpia perennis* that contains all of its own correctives, so that it is an idle game dialectically to dissect it. I stand up for analytical reason and its language, which is logic […] I believe that even today, as in the days of the Encyclopedists, knowledge leads to recognition and recognition to morality. And I maintain that it was not the Enlightenment

> that failed, as we have been assured ever since the first wave of the romantic counter-Enlightenment, **but rather those who were appointed its guardians**. (Améry 1984b, p. 136, emphasis mine)

For Améry, critique is embedded within the ideals of Enlightenment rationality. As such, he can defend what he sees as the positive development of bourgeois humanism while still challenging the supremacy of psychiatric discourse.[8]

However, there remains a contradiction between Améry's defense of humanism and his defense of suicide and refusing to heal. Embedded in Enlightenment rationality is a schema that privileges healing, well-being, and flourishing. Popular discourses in the seventeenth and eighteenth centuries moved away from notions of original sin and positioned people as naturally acting toward their own well-being. This well-being in some cases allowed for euthanasia in the face of illness or pain. However, this conception of well-being also implies a natural avoidance of pain as well as voluntary death which is not the consequence of illness or the greater good. While Améry defends the greater focus on human rationality—he lies in tension with how actions that were deemed as failures in rationality were dealt with and movements toward pathologization.

Améry's arguments reassert and surpass David Hume's defense of suicide.[9] In his 1777 essay, Hume attempts to provide a defense of suicide that will restore mankind to their "natural liberty"—that is, allow people their natural determination over their life and when to end it (Hume 2007). He first argues that suicide is not a dereliction of duty one has toward either others or God. He preempts this argument with the claim "men are entrusted to their own judgment and discretion in the various shocks of matter, and may employ every faculty, with which they are endowed, in order to provide for their ease, happiness, or preservation" (Hume 2007, p. 185). Similarly for Améry suicide, or failure to heal after trauma, is not a culpable moral sin or a dereliction of duty.

However, Hume does not allow for the possibility that a person in possession of their rational faculties would ever commit suicide for so-called frivolous reasons. He asserts that humans have a natural horror of death and therefore would not "throw one's life away if it was worth keeping" (Hume 2007, p. 185). In contrast, Améry views supposedly frivolous suicides as emblematic of the power of disgust in the world and the human capacity to reject the logic of life. Furthermore, Améry goes beyond Hume to state that suicide is not merely a capacity and right of the autonomous person, but it is an action that *brings* autonomy and freedom in itself. As a result, Améry expresses a conception of autonomy and freedom that allows for a far greater degree of self-destruction than even the most permissive of Enlightenment thought.

Similarly, Améry praises the "sanity of Cartesianism" over the "sophisticated twaddle" of Deleuze and Guattari (Améry 1984c). However, he lies in tension with Descartes' conjecture that humans have a natural capacity to avoid mental discomfort, physical pain, and death. Descartes associates the feeling of pain with the experience of sadness (Descartes 1985). He positions pain as a God-given homeostatic mechanism to prevent injury to the body. He writes, "Nature teaches me nothing more explicitly, however, than that I have a body which is hurt when I feel pain, which needs food or drink when I experience hunger or thirst, and so on" (Descartes 1985, p. 142). This fundamentally conflicts with a conscious desire to reject healing and reject the logic of life.

Consequently, Améry's defense of the Enlightenment is complex and he does not explicitly acknowledge many of the tensions that are implicit within his defense of suicide. He is in conflict with one of the major revolutions in Enlightenment thinking—the notion that humans psychologically have a tendency toward well-being, and that a deviation from this tendency is symptomatic of madness or correctable ignorance. Améry offers a radical expansion of the Enlightenment project in which the humanistic respect for autonomy trumps all other values including well-being. This is exemplified in the respect for the pain of resentment as well as the decision to "throw one's life away" in the case of suicide. However, these critiques and rejections are always framed within a search for truth and based upon an understanding of a humanistic subject.

13.7 Améry's Rejection of "Anti-intellectualism"

Despite the complex relationship Améry displayed with the Enlightenment, he unambiguously dismisses what he viewed as the anti-intellectualism of contemporary anti-Enlightenment thinkers. Améry dismisses the schools of Critical Theory, poststructuralism, postmodernism, and what he viewed as the latter corruption of Sartre's existentialism. While these schools of thought critique oppressive norms of compulsory well-being, they also critique the notion of the autonomous subject that Améry champions and promotes as a necessary condition for challenging the logic of life. I will limit my discussion to his rejection of Horkheimer, Adorno, and Foucault.

Améry was originally sympathetic to *The Dialectic of Enlightenment*. Even after ultimately disagreeing with its conclusion, he continued to hold it in charitably high esteem (Améry 1984d). Treitler (2011) highlights how Améry rejected the notion that the Enlightenment developed dangerous elements in an attempt to make people "safer" which ultimately lead to the horrors of totalitarianism. Rather, Améry asserts that the Holocaust was the ultimate betrayal of Enlightenment values. What is needed is a return to the humaneness of humanism (Treitler 2011). This, in turn, is exemplified in the case of the suicide. Despite structural issues in the pathologization of the suicidal person, what is needed is a greater respect for the subjective decisions of the suicidal person and a philosophical acceptance of the illogic of death not a wholesale rejection of Enlightenment values.

Despite his critiques of the medicalization of suicide, Améry is explicit in his rejection of Foucault's critiques of psychiatry. Améry writes "[f]or years, Foucault has been using high quality, idealistic zeal for what he saw as good, and which was often de facto good: for 'the madmen and the convicts'" (Améry 1978, online, translation mine). However, Améry entirely rejects Foucault's critique of the "episteme" of humanity. He claims that Foucault's assertions that the human subject is an oppressive artifact of Enlightenment thinking are unfounded and based on faith. Améry accuses Foucault of "mesmerizing" rather than debating and rendering rational argument, the cornerstone of academic endeavors, impossible (Améry 1978). This dogmatic rejection of reason, for Améry, seeps into Foucault's analysis of the oppressive regime of psychiatry. Améry states that Foucault's analysis of psychiatry is "bizarre and unfounded" with little evidence to its credit (Améry 1978). In *Enlightenment as Philosophia Perennis*, he writes:

> And what is one to say about the intentions of the anti-psychiatrists, for whom reason is nothing but bourgeois alienation of man, and who celebrate insanity as the free inner space of people who they claim are permanently manipulated by society? Subjectively, their intentions are good, that is certain; but objectively they are a menace to culture. (Améry 1984b, p. 138)

The statements demonstrate how Améry argues against placing the reasoned and autonomous decision to remain resentful or to kill oneself in the domain of psychiatry. He does not argue against the domain of psychiatry itself but rather its zealous overreach. Therefore, it is not necessary to critique the notions of madness and rationality or sanity. Rather, it is necessary to develop a conception of rationality in which a sane person can be understood to freely choose to reject healing, well-being, and life.

These key differences between the thinkers are exemplified in their different approaches to suicide. In his essay *The Simplest of Pleasures* (Foucault 1996 [1979]), Foucault positions suicide as an aesthetic act of self-care. He provocatively writes:

> So let's see what there is to say in favor of suicide. Not so much in support of legalizing it or making it 'moral'. Too many people have already belabored these lofty things. Instead, let's say something against the shady affairs, humiliations, and hypocrisies that its detractors usually surround it with: hastily getting boxes of pills together, finding a solid, old-fashioned razor, or licking gun store windows and entering some place pretending to be on the verge of death. In my opinion a person should have the right not to be rushed, which is very bothersome. (Foucault 1996, p. 262)

Foucault's article was published after Améry's death and therefore it is speculative how he would have commented. However, the difference in attitude demonstrates the vast disagreements between the two defenses of suicide. For Améry, limits and deficiencies in Enlightenment thinking can be remedied by a greater commitment to humanism rather than a deconstruction of the human. Suicide functions as the ultimate example of this. The act should not be reduced to churlish hyperbole and, while there are aesthetic considerations of suicide, suicide cannot be reduced to a vanity project. Instead suicide functions as the ultimate example of a freely made human decision.

13.8 Conclusions

Améry philosophy contains ambiguous tensions and confronting challenges of taboos. Throughout his work, he demonstrated a commitment to rejecting what he saw as oppressive "common sense" schemas which coerced well-being over autonomy. In rejecting these schemas he defended the right and ability for autonomous subjects to freely choose to reject life and healing. It is from this position that he defends suicide not as a failure of rationality but as an exemplar of human freedom and spontaneity in contrast to the natural inertia of continued existence. In this chapter, I have argued for the philosophical importance of this position. Améry's views on suicide represent the continuation of his respect for autonomy even when confronted with the logic of life itself. There are deep ambiguities in Améry's defense of suicide. These ambiguities mirror the tension between Améry's rejection of the healing nature of time and his belief in progress. Taking Améry's philosophical work on suicide seriously contextualizes these tensions and demonstrates his overall commitment to the value of human freedom.

Notes

1. This term is somewhat contentious. Améry had a fraught relationship with pessimism, hope, and historicity. I will examine how there is a tension between these aspects of Améry's writings in the second half of this chapter. I will also examine how these tensions can be best understood in light of Améry's conclusions about suicide.
2. Lt. Gustl does not ultimately commit suicide as he is released from his obligation and fears by the death of the baker. Relieved, Gustl regains his sense of dignity and is confident he will succeed in his afternoon duel. However, Améry continues to associate Gustl's former parasuicidal behavior with the loss of his sense of dignity and autonomy after compromising his military duties. As such, for most of the novel he represents an example of a parasuicidal person "before the leap" when he professes his decision to kill himself.
3. The coming of death is also natural for Améry. I will examine these tensions further in my subsequent section on tensions and dualities within suicide.
4. Améry was highly critical of *Eichmann in Jerusalem* and what he saw as Arendt's condoning of oppressive forgiveness. However, there remain parallels between their conceptions of freedom and spontaneity.
5. This lament was both practical and psychological. For Levi resistance to the dehumanization of the camps through rituals such as cleaning oneself, friendship, and the potential for spontaneous action was what was crushed before a person was reduced to the status of the walking dead *Mussalman*.
6. Améry controversially compares the destigmitization of suicide with the decriminalization of homosexuality.
7. The linguistic shift occurred considerably earlier in English. The term "self-murder" was commonly used in the sixteenth century but was mostly replaced by the less value laden "suicide" by 1650 (Bahr 2013).
8. Améry distinguishes himself from his contemporary anti-psychiatrists. He does not think madness represents a social construct and is dismissive of attempts to valorize irrationality.
9. Améry does not directly reference Hume's *Of Suicide* throughout his *On Suicide*. However, the English title is a direct reference to the prior work. Similarly, given Améry speaks at length of his study of his reading of the British empiricists it is highly likely he was familiar with the work.

References

Améry, J. (1978, March 31). Archeology of Knowledge – Michel Foucault and His Discourse of Counter-Enlightenment [Archäologie des Wissens – Michel Foucault und sein Diskurs der Gegenaufklärung]. Republished in *Zeit Online*. Retrieved from https://www.zeit.de/1978/14/archaeologie-des-wissens/komplettansicht.

Améry, J. (1984a). *Radical Humanism* (S. Rosenfeld & S. Rosenfeld, Trans.). Indiana Press.

Améry, J. (1984b). Enlightenment as Philosophia Perennis. Originally Published 1977.

Améry, J. (1984c). Sartre: Greatness and Failure. Originally Published 1974.

Améry, J. (1984d). The Time of Rehabilitation. Originally Published 1981.

Améry, J. (1994). *On Aging: Revolt and Resignation*. Bloomington: Indiana University Press.

Améry, J. (1999a). *At the Mind's Limits: Contemplations by a Survivor on Auschwitz and Its Realities*. Bloomington: Indiana University Press.

Améry, J. (1999b). *On Suicide* (J. Barlow, Trans.). Indiana University Press.

Arendt, H. (1958). *The Human Condition*. Chicago: University of Chicago Press.

Arendt, H. (1967). *The Origins of Totalitarianism* (Rev. ed.). London: Allen & Unwin.

Bahr, A. (2013). Between "Self-Murder" and "Suicide": The Modern Etymology of Self-Killing. *Journal of Social History, 46*(3, Spring), 620–632.

Ben-Shai, R. (2010). To Reverse the Irreversible: On Time Disorder in the Work of Jean Améry. In J. R. Watson (Ed.), *Metacide: In the Pursuit of Excellence* (pp. 73–92). Amsterdam, Netherlands: Rodopi.

Brudholm, T. (2010). *Resentment's Virtue: Jean Améry and the Refusal to Forgive. Paperback*. Philadelphia: Temple University Press.

Descartes, R. (1985). *Meditations on First Philosophy* (Ronald Rubin, Trans.). Arete Press.

Foucault, M. (1996). The Simplest of Pleasures. In *Foucault Live: (Interviews, 1961–1984)* (Hochroth and Johnson, Trans.) (pp. 295–297). New York: Semiotexte.

Hume, D. (2007). Of Suicide. In S. Buckle (Ed.), *An Enquiry Concerning Human Understanding and Other Writings* (pp. 181–189). Cambridge: Cambridge University Press.

Levi, P. (2000). *If This Is a Man: The Truce* (Vol. 222). London: Everyman Publishers.

Lieberman, L. (2003). *Leaving You*. Ivan R. Dee Chicago.

Stauffer, J. (2012). *Ethical Loneliness*. Columbia University Press.

Szasz, T. (2002). *Fatal Freedom – The Ethics and Politics of Suicide*. Syracuse University Press Edition.

Treitler, W. (2011). Saying No and Fleeing Nowhere. In M. Zolkos (Ed.), *On Jean Améry – Philosophy of Catastrophe*. Lexington Books.

CHAPTER 14

Between the *Logic of Life* and the *Anti-logic of Death*: Reflections on Suicidality in the Wake of Jean Améry

Yael Lavi

14.1 Introduction

For the most part, suicidology literature of the last century views suicidality as a pathological phenomenon of misjudgment or failure of judgmental abilities. Jean Améry challenges this view in his text *On Suicide: A Discourse on Voluntary Death* (1999).[1,2]

Améry, who was educated in philosophy and literature in Vienna in the early 1930s, was deeply influenced by the Enlightenment notions of reason, freedom, and autonomy (Améry 1980, 1984; Heidelberger-Leonard 2010). Later, he learned their limitations in Auschwitz, where he acquired an intimate acquaintance with death, pain, and humiliation (ibid.). For Améry, voluntary exile following World War II proved to be not only from his homeland, language, and name but eventually from his own life. According to his final account, voluntary death (*Den Freitod*) is the radical and fatal conclusion of the *anti-logic of death.*

Y. Lavi (✉)
School of Philosophy, Linguistics and Science Studies, The Lester and Sally Entin Faculty of Humanities, Tel Aviv University, Tel Aviv, Israel

Y. Ataria et al. (eds.), *Jean Améry*,
https://doi.org/10.1007/978-3-030-28095-6_14

The phrase ‘anti-logic of death’ seems to enclose an implicit assumption according to which the ‘inference’ of its ‘conclusion’ (i.e., voluntary death), has a logical structure to some extent. Nonetheless, this assumption raises two questions: (1) what does *anti-logic* mean, and (2) what is the nature of its relation to death? A hint may be found in Améry’s account of the suicidal position as an epistemological state, which I refer to as *loss of trust in the world*, rather than a psychological one. However, I wish to argue that according to Améry, the practical response resulting from this epistemological stance cannot be justified by the anti-logic of death alone. Another question is, therefore, (3) what is the role of the anti-logic of death in Améry’s argument.

My chapter aims to answer these questions through a critical, yet sympathetic analysis. The first section provides a short conceptual clarification focused on the ‘anti-logic of death’ compared to the ‘logic of life’. This clarification will then be employed to address questions (1) and (2). The second section will explain the role of the anti-logic of death in Améry’s argument and its close proximity to the absurd (3). Subsequently, I will articulate in the third section, some reservations regarding Améry’s seemingly dialectical argumentation, and some insights in respect to possible value of Améry’s anti-logic of death.[3]

14.2 I

Prima facie, there is nothing that can be said about the anti-logic of death in constructive terms by any means, for in its essence, according to Améry, it denies any possibility of conceptualization. Nonetheless, in order to explain it, let us turn first to the positive side of Améry’s equation—the logic of life, or the ‘logic of being’. The logic of life refers to ‘all logical conclusions that we draw in statements about life [which] are constantly bound to the fact of this life’ (p. 18). In other words, Améry’s logic of life is based on an unmediated ontological notion of being that drives an epistemological framework, which in turn, enables the establishment of an (implicit or explicit) ethical approach. Paraphrasing his well-known equation ‘*Body=Pain=Death*’, taken from the memoir *Torture* (1980, pp. 33–34), the logic of life can be encapsulated with the equation *Body=Sensation=Life*.

At the basis of this three-part structure lies the brute fact of being alive and experiencing a fundamental spontaneous sense of vitality. In terms of contemporary phenomenology, it can be defined as the *minimal self*, which is 'a consciousness of oneself as an immediate subject of experience, unextended in time' (Gallagher 2000, p. 15).[4] What follows, according to Améry, from the mere sense of being, is the second layer of the logic of life, which reflects life and its preserving instinct as valuable. It is a thin, almost invisible layer, yet it is an entailment that constitutes the affirmation of life as more than a biological fact. That is to say, the initial sensory impression is perceived as a valuable truth, whereas the affirmation of 'Life' and its approval becomes associated with existence and its preservation. While at the first level—the minimal self—the social dimensions are questionable, at the second level, the reference to others is a condition of possibility as well as the necessary outcome of the human ontological vulnerable existence.[5] For it is not only a basic survival mechanism or blind reproduction instinct that constitutes human mutuality but an implicit and unconscious reflection of a positive value as intentionality toward a future. This intentionality and valuation are forced upon us by nature; it is, as Améry argues: 'prescribe[d] for us or "programmed" [...] in every daily reaction' (p. 13). Thus, at the third layer of Améry's logic of life, it is not surprising to find what he calls an 'abstraction of higher order':

> Because we mean by the logic of life not only the immanent logic of behavior that preserves the self and the species, to which we are tributary, but also the logic gained from this logic as an abstraction of higher order, one that weighs being against being, sets one against the other, and therefore can come to the knowledge of the logical 'true' and 'false,' whereby true as much as false are tacitly accepted as categories of being because there is no bridge from being to nonbeing. (pp. 19–20)

To use phenomenological terms again, the third level is that of the *narrative self*—that is, a fairly coherent self-image that is constituted by integrating and internalizing life experiences into intelligible accountable stories or narratives (Macintyre 1985; Ricoeur 1985; Gallagher 2000). It is a *logic* of *life* because 'true' and 'false' are taken as categories of being, of 'human being' to be more precise. Thus, according to the law of contradiction, it is impossible to exist and not exist at the same time (so long as you are not Schrödinger's cat). It follows that there is no logical way to bridge being and nonbeing; therefore, what is *not being* can be considered by the logic of life only as the negation of existence (absence, emptiness, no-thing, etc.) or as a contradiction ('there is nothing'). Similarly, the law of identity already contains the 'being' of *a*, which is not *b*—an *I*, which is not *you* (e.g., p. 11). Thus, the 'logic' of life refers not only to formal language as an argumentative deductive system but also to an informal language. Put differently, it is the *logos* (λόγος) itself as an (implicit or explicit) expression of proportion, opinion, expectation, or plea in relation to time (Liddell, H. G., & Scott, R. 1889). It follows that the sense of agency, that is, the notion 'I am the one who is causing or generating an action; I can choose; I bear responsibility' appears as a construct of the logic of life, and so are hope and trust.[6,7]

We are now in a better position to delve into Améry's anti-logic of death, namely through its negation of life and its logic. Yet, as mentioned above, it would be too simplistic to settle for a definition of contrast. First, because while the connection between life (as a fact, an experience, or as a concept) and the logic of life can be described using a causal explanation, it is not clear whether and how this is possible in the case of death and anti-logic. Second, because it is not clear how far we should take Améry's conception of anti-logic as negation. Is it really possible to accept *Nothingness* as a reference point in the first place? If it is, then how does it bridge between being (body, pain) and nonbeing (death)? In order to answer this, let us take a closer look at Améry's words:

> The logic of death is not a logic in the usual sense, upholding reason alone, for it allows no conclusions other than just one, again and again, and again: not is the same as not, with which the statement of every logical (that is, analytic) judgment, already in itself containing no reality, loses its last tie to reality; that tie above all in which the equation of two categories of being that are symbolically recorded as in mathematics, or are rooted in everyday language, is now related to something that is nothing and is not—a pure negation, an accursed inconceivability (p. 19, emphasis by the current author).

It seems plausible to assume that 'something that is nothing and is not' is the essence of the anti-logic of death, while 'pure negation' is its praxis, and that with the notion 'not is the same as not' Améry remains somewhat loyal to the law of identity in its negative form (whatever that means when the subject is 'not'). As praxis, the anti-logic of death is a negation of the values that have been produced by the logic of life. So, it might be useful to think of it as an extreme skepticism that is directed at *logos* itself, undermining the sufficiency of all reasons, expressions of proportion, opinion, expectation, and pleas. It undermines all 'abstraction of a higher order' by rejecting the basic categories such 'Time' and 'True' as its categories of being, whereas in the face of nonentity (not being), any ultimate, grounded distinction becomes meaningless.

By its essence, the anti-logic of death negates human reality as a multiplicity that can be converged under a certain principle or be interpreted as some kind of unity. It is a *logic* insofar as it has a tautological structure according to which its conclusion is equivalent to its *axiom*: death. In its nothingness, death is an indistinguishable, incomprehensible, monolithic, and motionless. Its logic in accordance is 'something that is nothing and is not'.

Death is the only certainty in human life, yet it is completely external to it. Death is senseless. It is senseless for if it is not a state of being but rather of nonexistence; it is a priori located out of the range of the logic of life. It is 'nothing' to us, as Epicurus stated, since while we are, death has not come, and when death comes, we are not (1966).[8] That is to say, death is not an object of human experience, nor of human perception as it is 'not the *noema* of a *noesis*', to use Critchley's words (2004, p. 83). Because death cannot be bound to any categories of being through which human perception understands the world (Space, Time, True, False, Cause, Effect, Good, Bad, etc.), it cannot bear any content for human intentionality; therefore, any representation of it will be 'misrepresentations, or rather [...] representation of absences' (ibid., p. 16). As such, death is the point at which language and logical discourse disconnect. Informal language espouses the 'naturalness' of death because abstraction, ambiguity, and vagueness allow it to provide an apparent explanation of what cannot be explained and to include what cannot be generalized, for formal logic. Yet, death is not only beyond logic but also out of reach of any habitual thought and act sheltered by informal language. It is therefore 'offensive to reason and to life' (p. 10).[9]

However, if death is incomprehensible, how can it function as a conclusion or an axiom? Furthermore, can negation exist not as an expression of logos? And does the praxis of negation stand in contradiction to its essences, that is, the anti-logical mode of emptiness? In order to provide a feasible explanation, I wish to argue that the anti-logic of death is not *all* about nothingness, but rather about the *possibility* of nothingness, about the relation between reality (human reality) and death (the absolute nothingness). Death, as what deviates from life and its logic, and therefore, from language, is the absence which shows itself in the logic of life. Anti-logic of death in this sense is the horizon of logic life that will forever be out of reach, whose presence exposes an absence. The *absence* is fundamental for Améry's anti-logic of death. It is not only the absence *of* life but also an absence *in* life. It is an absence that quite often cannot be subordinated to explanation or reasoning, but only recognized by negation: despair as an absence of hope, madness as an absence of sanity, illness as an absence of health, and so on. The absence presents itself via epistemological, physical, and emotional doubts, to put it better, via an existential *Loss of Trust*. The last articulation is more than a semantic distinction per se: *loss* of trust and not pure skepticism, as it is not an *a priori lack* of trust, but rather the *loss* of it.[10] As will be clarified in the next section, the (emotional and physical) pain associated with the loss is essential for Améry, in order to understand the living experience of the anti-logic of death. Losing trust in the world in this sense is losing trust in all three levels of the logic of life. It undermines the connection Logos-body and therefore the capacity of agency, it incites a deep sense of estrangement which jeopardizes the inner sense of vitality, that is, it is a loss of trust in life itself.

Yet, if indeed death is the *conclusion* of anti-logic as much as its *axiom*, then the anti-logic of death appears to be nothing but a paralyzing emptiness that destroys all structure of meaning and all intentional act. If that is so, how can Améry assign a positive meaning to the choice of voluntary death? In order to answer this question, it is important to keep in mind Améry's main goal, which is to recognize the suicidal judgment as valid (p. 17). Accordingly, the anti-logic of death is not a standalone argument in relation to life, but rather it is more like a premise in an argument or a dialectical moment. The immediate implication of this insight is that voluntary death is an intersection between the logic of life and the anti-logic of death and should not be taken as the conclusion of the logic of death per se.

Given this proposed analysis, it is plausible to think of the relationship between the logic of life and the anti-logic of death in terms of *the absurd*. The Absurd is the unsolvable tension between the lack of a priori meaning on the one hand, and the irreducible urge for such on the other, to use Albert Camus definition (1955).[11] Or rather, as Thomas Nagel describes, a collision between 'two inescapable viewpoints' inside one's self (1971, pp. 718–722): between the internal aimed and engaged agent's perspective which is necessarily partial relative on the one hand and on the other, the detached, indifferent spectator (i.e., the perspective of the absolute). The absurd is revealed through a sense of mismatch, of inadequacy with the world, or as Nagel analyzed, through the 'discrepancy between [...]

aspiration and reality' (p. 118). Thus, if we take Améry's logic of life to stand for the inner pole (the pole of meaning), death is according to this analysis, the absolute pole (the pole of indifference). The anti-logic of death is the way death (which cannot be perceived), marks the boundaries of meaning, language, and being, by presenting their relativity, arbitrariness, and contingency, without offering any positive horizon. It is an empty horizon that exposes itself through the negation of any relational point of view. As it is impossible to reconcile the logic of life and the anti-logic of death on the one hand, and on the other, to deny any of them, the result is an endless and inevitable 'rabbit-duck' flip between the two points of view, which could never converge or mediate.[12] This constant movement leads to an existential instability which involves absence, foreignness, and doubt. Alienation, Vertigo, and Anxiety may describe this experience. And while for Nagel some sense of humility and irony could reduce this anxiety and for Camus alienation could be converted back into solidarity (Camus 1991), for Améry, the range of possibilities of the absurd is more limited. It is limited because, on his account, one cannot reduce or ignore anti-logic of death once it has been recognized, nor to reject logic of life as long as one still breathes, and so, it is impossible to reduce the absurdity of life in life.

Recapitulating: The anti-logic of death is the negation of what the logic of life affirms (sensation, intelligibility, mutuality). It is related to death in two ways: (1) the non-actuality of death, which is the void associated with loss of trust in the world, generates the anti-logic of death; (2) combined with the logic of life (and only so), it gives rise to absurdity, which in turn, grounds voluntary death. In order to better explain the role of the anti-logic of death in this context, the next section will review Améry's complete argument, according to which voluntary death—the absurdist revolt—constitutes freedom as the affirmation of subjectivity, through negation.

14.3 II

Améry's formulation of the anti-logic of death situates his argument outside the scientific and the moral discourse on voluntary death. Améry rejects any type of apologetics on behalf of the suicidal subject through reference to psychiatric categories, psychological pathologies, or sociological explanations (pp. xxiv–xxv). Similarly, he does not conduct any moral-normative debate (p. 12). By restricting himself to bear witness in the name of one for whom the thought of voluntary death is constantly present in life as an inseparable part of his subjective existence (1999, pp. xxiv–xxv), Améry calls for recognition in voluntary death as a realization of human freedom. Based on Améry's testimony, this section aims to describe the relation between the anti-logic of death and voluntary death as it unfolds into an argument, according to which voluntary death is an *absurd résistance* (p. 151). In order to understand what this *résistance* means for Améry, and why it is absurdist, a short detour to the realm of the absurd is essential.

As stated above, Armey's inquiry sprouts from the swampy soil of the absurd, which is embodied in the vulnerability of human existence. Humans are vulnerable to injury, sickness, and death, and this vulnerability creates mutual dependency. Humans are also vulnerable due to their awareness of their vulnerability and dependency; it seems plausible to argue then, that human's physical and mental vulnerability constitutes the *desire* for meaning (i.e., the need to explain loss, pain, and suffering which are immanent to human existence), as well as the practical *need* for meaning as a social tool. It also seems plausible to argue that human coexistence (as an array of habits, language, types of social relationships, regulations, and institutions) is what enables and establishes the capacities of autonomy and agency. Insofar as this is so, autonomy and agency, conditioned (as a necessary condition even if not as a sufficient condition) by interpersonal relationships and a shared form of life (underlying meaning, values, beliefs, etc.), are also vulnerable.[13] What follows is that human vulnerability, as much as it belongs to the logic of life, might also lead to the notion anti-logic of death and therefore to the absurd.

Death in this manner is the ultimate threat to the individual existence, as well as to coexistence. As death itself is insurmountable, its anti-logic in its utter inexplicability is opposed to language itself. Therefore, it disavows not only bodily existence, but also coexistence, values, and meanings without nullifying the *need* and the *desire* for it. Hence, Vulnerability might lead to an experience of (to use absurdist terms) a fundamental alienation. This alienation is reflected in the structure of intentionality toward the world and others as much as toward one's self. The Body itself and thereby the world (or vice versa: the world and thereby the body) becomes strange, distant, and threatening. The fundamental otherness intensifies the sense of vulnerability as it permeates into the self, revealing the various layers of the self and the different narratives through which beliefs and conventions are established. The result is an undermining of the seemingly necessary connection between the first and second levels of the logic of life, so that the validation of any 'abstraction of a higher order' becomes questionable, to say the least. In this sense, alienation plays a major role in the phenomenological account of the experience of losing trust in the world.

The broken trust appears when one's existential balance is disrupted—'with the very first blow that descends on him' (Améry 1980, p. 18). While, for Améry, this 'first blow' could be directly related to torture, in other cases, it can result from other forms of physical or mental violence, from illness or a loss and even from a strong sense of failure. It is an experience of significant harm to the agency which explicitly threatens one's sense of life, and often distorts the consciousness of the relation time-body. The brute vulnerability is being exposed, and with it exposes the notion of death and the possibility according to which existence is not inescapable. The pain (physical or mental, usually both) caused by the 'blow' changes the basic equation of the logic of life. The body becomes strange and hostile. Bodily sensations converted into pure senseless pain and incompetency. It is an experience of being as pain and nothing but a pain, the only abstraction of which is death. It is an experience that sabotages the sense of *being* whether by willing *not to be* (in order to cease pain) or whether by the feeling of *not being* (as a kind of a dissociative response).

The proximity of being and not being (i.e., the experience of the contradiction) reveals the logic of life as it is: a *logic of* life—that is to say, as merely a cognitive framework that aims toward the affirmation of being. Death Inclination in this manner is an expression of a notion according to which, to use Joshua F. Dienstag's words, 'time is a burden; [...] the course of history is in some sense ironic; [...] freedom and happiness are incompatible' (Dienstag 2009, p. 19).[14] That insight establishes a Pessimist epistemology that challenges trust in the world as a place of progress, reason, and rational hope. Anti-logic of death 'turns the Socratic idea that rational thought would lead to human flourishing on its head' (ibid., pp. 33–34). It undermines the intuitive trust in the world that 'including the irrational and logically unjustifiable belief in absolute causality perhaps, or the likewise blind belief in the validity of the inductive inference' (Améry 1980, p. 28). The consolation of social existence is being lost when the logic of life begins to crumble and crack beneath, and while the anti-logic of death cannot offer any positive alternative but the echo of nothingness.

The 'first blow' is not necessarily terminal, yet it contradicts the implicit and explicit verdicts of the logic of life. This indicates the possibility that the same structure of the logic of life which enables trust in the first place inflicts its disruption by unveiling the anti-logic of death. Thus, it seems plausible that it is not a specific kind of pain, loss, or humiliation that is important to Améry's argument, but rather the way in which it cracks the self and diminishes the sense of agency. In fact, Améry goes further by adding two more factors to the pessimist's equation of 'broken trust in the world'. First is the concept of '*Échec*'—a sense of defeat or complete ruin which is in 'opposition to dignity and to the right to happiness' (1980, p. 45).[15] In its extreme form, '*Échec*' is the experiencing of one's failed existence.[16] Whether the experience of failure is associated with an error in understanding reality or poor performance, the result is a deep sense of inability to cope with what is required in order to continue to live, and/or a reluctance to agree with what is needed to continue to live. For when agency failed, there is no 'can', nor an 'ought implies can' maxim. Accordingly, the structure of intentionality toward the world becomes fundamentally different. As it is shaped by a lack of confidence and by a strong sense of uselessness and incompetence it is an intentionality structure which is not supported by any repression mechanism that could enable the needed optimistic cognitive bias toward reality.[17]

Aside from the anti-logic of death and the *Échec* there is another ingredient in Améry's formula—the affect of *Disgust (La nausée)*. Disgust is a basic and primal emotion; according to Robert Plutchik's (2001) *Emotion Wheel*, Disgust, is the opposite of Trust. While Trust creates intimacy (= Eros)[18] and therefore is directly identified and embraced by the logic of life, Disgust creates repulsion and distance. This is not surprising, considering that its evolutionary role was to avoid contamination by visceral autonomic responses such as lowered heart rate and reduced blood pressure, nausea, and so on, that elicit behavioral reactions of withdrawal. Consequently, says Améry, Disgust has been 'denied by civilization's howling rabble set on preserving the species' (p. 47).[19] Disgust in its full inexorability is only experienced, when existential balance has already been violated and given a critical mass of failures. To some extent it is the sensory experience of the anti-logic of death insofar as it is a strong corporal and mental repulsion from one's body, from being a mass of flesh, from being conditioned by others and reality, from being lonely, from being oneself.[20]

The combination of broken trust, *Échec*, and Disgust, is by itself a bent beyond the limits of the logic of life, or, as Améry calls it, an inclination toward death (pp. 73–79).[21] Death inclination excludes one, not only from one's self as a vital, reasoning animal and therefore from values and meanings, but also from relational space with its vastness of possibilities, and therefore from any future goals or projects.[22] The fracture in the epistemological and emotional structure of the self goes deeper, while the logic of life as the source of meaning, values, and habits through which one knows oneself in the world, loses its autocracy (e.g., pp. 18–19).

Nonetheless, the fact that the logic of life is not exclusive and well-founded does not mean that it is necessarily wrong. Furthermore, and maybe more crucial, as long as one still breathes, one submits to some aspects of the logic of life; that is, any mental or physical action takes part in a certain project of living and as such it is a projecting of oneself into the world. Projecting into the world contains (implicitly or explicitly) some degree of future-oriented intentionality. However, is intention without an object is possible (as future is nothingness according to the anti-logic of death)? What follows is that an 'inclination toward death' should not be taken as a suicidal instinct per se, but rather as a turn of the Logos 'toward nothingness' and 'toward nowhere' (pp. 149, 78). This experience of existential disorientation and imbalance validate the fact that although humans are usually bound to an implicit mindset that is driven from the unmediated notion of 'being', it does not warrant that *life is good* or that *life is worth living*.

Obviously, the premise that *life is not the highest good of all* is not equivalent to *life is not worth living*, nor does it imply it. Hence, voluntary death is not an imperative of the pessimist mindset (note Rousseau, Leopardi Schopenhauer),[23] and it is not a necessary reaction to the absurd (note Camus 1955 and Nagel 1971) to Échec or to Disgust. However, in some cases, it is the only fitting reaction. In this respect, it is important to note Jean Baechler's definition, according to which suicidal ideation refers to 'all behavior that seeks and finds the solution to an existential problem' (1979, p. 11).[24] 'Existential problems' refer to difficulties that arise from the structure of human existence, first and foremost a relational existence which requires a minimal degree of trust.[25] When trust in the world brakes down, these existential problems can affect (actively or passively) all levels of experience, causing misery and anguish. That is to say, it is not a philosophical exercise or some abstract way of thinking, nor is it a purely emotional state or 'mood'. It is a multi-system reaction that brings fundamental change to basic concepts, presumptions, and evaluation systems, which in turn leads to a paradigm shift of one's life-world perception. That shift is accomplished when trust in the world is no longer accessible, when life is experienced as an irreparable failure, when disgust is overflowing.[26]

These aspects of the suicidal mental life are widely addressed by psychiatric and psychological models supported by empirical evidence, according to which this paradigm shift often implicates different evaluation styles ('negativistic', 'narrowing', 'hopelessness', 'helplessness', and 'psychache') of the experienced behavioral options and meanings (Ringel 1976; Beck et al. 1979; Shneidman 2001; Schlimme 2013).[27] Nevertheless, as Améry points out, these accounts are missing the lived experience of the suicidal subject, not only because of their generalization and abstraction but also because they are exclusively committed to the logic of life. As such, these disciplines already subscribe to an implicit, particular notion of '*being in the world*' that stems from a premise according to which life *is the highest good*. Hence, their terms, sets of values, and calculations comprise a bias toward life and its logic (pp. 3, 5, 14, 59, 102). Similarly, it seems that the philosophical account of suicide permissibility as well as the deprivation discourse is pointless and nonsensical from the suicidal standpoint. Nonsense not only because of the enigmatic nature of death, but also and more importantly, because the concepts used to describe life are radically different between the two worldviews.[28]

This fundamental discrepancy constitutes a singular experience of *being torn between the logic of life and the anti-logic of death*. De facto, it is an engagement in an unprecedented debate with one's own body, logos, and ego (p. 74), which never really comes to an end. Paradoxically, to decide that life is 'worthwhile' requires the repression of distrust; that is, the elimination of the fractured self. However, banishing it yields annihilation on the one hand or epistemic ignorance on the other.[29] Thus, when *Échec* and *Disgust* become unbearable, time and space converge into an intolerable critical mass (p. 88) so that the range of possibilities is seemingly reduced to a binary choice: 'to be or not to be'. Nonetheless, this exclusive disjunction, insists Améry, must be rephrasing in order to break 'out of the order of things' (p. 119). Outside the order of things, the contradiction can exist: not to be in order to be. It is intentionality toward nothingness: consciousness 'aims at death but [is] not subservient to [its] anti-logic' (p. 132); that is to say, logic of life seeks to manifest itself via death inclination, by wavering the *logos* as secondary to the *deed*. Judgment is therefore 'set in motion' (p. 92), while one decides to 'snatch death' for one's self in the name of humanity and dignity (p. 149): 'I die therefore I am'.[30]

While Camus is quick to get the Socratic idea back up on its feet and take a stand against suicide as a flight from the absurd, For Améry, choosing voluntary death *is* the ***absurd résistance*** (p. 151) as it is the ultimate manifestation of human freedom (p. 140). More than re-claiming humanity, and dignity, deciding in favor voluntary death is actually to reaffirm human subjectivity *as freedom*.[31] Choosing suicide, in this sense, does not function as a borderline that one crosses toward freedom, but rather as an actualization of freedom. Hence, it is not death or dying that stands at the heart of Améry's account but rather the *leap* that seeks to leave contingency behind. That leap requires, as stated, a suspension of the Logos on the one hand, and active conscious intentionality on the other, hence the act itself is absurdist. The leap sets up the inversion points in which 'nothing is valid anymore' (p. 133) so that 'negation all at once become something positive' (pp. 152–153). Voluntary death is an absurdist answer triggered by an unbearably absurd reality; '*it is absurd but not foolish because it is clear that its absurdity does not increase the absurdity of life but decreases it*' (p. 133).

14.4 III

The previous section followed Améry`s analysis of the cognitive and mental leap toward voluntary death, as a process of negation stemming from the structure of the absurd, namely, from the relation between the logic of life and the anti-logic of death. According to this analysis, voluntary death encloses a tension between practicing subjectivity as freedom ('voluntary') and the absolute lack of subjectivity ('death').

Nonetheless, this conclusion is puzzling: is it possible to reconcile this tension? If this tension can be resolved in any way then 'voluntary death' will not cohere with Améry's characterization of anti-logic of death (Améry takes the tension of this phrase to be inherent). On the other hand, if the tension cannot be resolved, then seemingly, we need some way to prevent it from making Améry's reasoning contradictory and fallacious. Otherwise, Améry's dialectical structure collapses, and with it the claim for recognition of the absurd rebellion. In the third and last part, I will argue (1) that any attempt to resolve the tension is doomed to failure as it leaves us in the realm of the absurd. Thus, (2) the anti-logic is not unnecessary since it is a condition of the absurd. In addition, I will suggest that (3) the very attempt to reduce Améry's insights to a logical argument, is necessarily subjected to the logic of life. Therefore, it a priori falls short of fully grasping the experience that Améry wishes to bring to light, that is, the experience of being torn between the logic of life and the anti-logic of death, that is, the absurdist inclination toward death.

As we have seen, according to Améry, the anti-logic of death is a necessary condition for the formation of the absurd, as well as for its reduction. However, it is not a sufficient condition. The logic of life is also necessary both for the absurd and for the rebellion against it. Since the anti-logic of death and the logic of life are two contradictory moments, which ostensibly their mutual negativity manifests freedom, it seems at first glance, that Améry`s equation is of a dialectical nature. Not dialectic in its classical use since, as anti-logic of death is empty and cannot provide any counter-arguments, there is no basis for a dialogue, but rather, Hegelian dialectically negation.[32] The sublated [*Aufgehoben*] achieved through coming-to-be and ceasing-to-be of subjectivity. The dialectical move from subjectivity to objectivity embodied in the choice of voluntary death, suggests that Améry invites us to think of experiencing suicidal ideation as a 'performance of freedom'. It is important to note that the choice and not its outcome is what manifests freedom for Améry. It is the very act of deviation of subjectivity from itself, deviation that will lead eventually to annihilation. Therefore, Améry insists that 'a precondition of one's decision as an act of liberation is that one is *serious* about it' (133).

Nonetheless, given that any decision that promotes death cannot be made from an exclusive perspective of the logic of life, nor can it be understood by it, it is plausible to assume that it is anti-logic of death that drives it. But death is inaccessible as long as one is alive. Anti-logic of death, as it turned toward nothingness cannot take a positive shape, but only question, doubt and negate any state of affairs and any explanation provided by the logic of life.[33] In this situation it is not clear how any decision can be made, nor how anything can be justified at the first place, as there is only a vacuum.

It is not only a technical issue, it is substantial: Améry himself was well aware that this sublated is 'good for nothing' (p. 153) because eventually there is only annihilation, oblivion, and nothingness—'An equation whose sum is zero' (p. 152). Furthermore, 'freedom' is only a word (p. 149) and thereby already belongs to the logic of life, just like 'experience' and 'absolute'.[34] Even seriousness itself seems a requirement which is consistent with the logic of life. For if indeed anti-logic of death negates all meaning and possibility of evaluation, Améry's dialectical argument seems refuted, for what does freedom mean and how can it be valued given that affirmation of values is grounded in the value of life qua life? Under the anti-logic of death there is no rule of causality or a measure that can be valid.[35] Under the anti-logic of death, all values are senseless and so is the value of humanity, dignity, and freedom which Améry attributes to the act/thought. Therefore, the dialectical move itself turns out to be empty and hence senseless.

Senseless, and yet, Améry still insists to use criterions such as Truth, and attribution of values, such as Freedom. That may indicate that eventually, Améry does not really negate the value of life, but rather affirms it as a 'life worth to live under certain conditional values'. That, of course, is far from 'pure negation' which embodied in voluntary death, but again, it is the *act of decision* that we are talking about and not death itself (e.g., p. 132). It is an act that as much as it aimed toward death is not subservient to its anti-logic (ibid.). If that is so, there is a place to wonder whether the whole function of the anti-logic of death in Améry's argument, therefore, reduced to a mere point of reference?

I think not. I think that anti-logic of death is fundamental to Améry's lived experience in the contradiction that establishes the absurd (and not just his). Even more so, it is the anti-logic of death that paradoxically allows a paused interval within which a subjectivity that has been overcome by reality can reflect herself. In this respect, it seems to me that Améry would have insisted on remaining with the contradiction, as he insisted on the validity of an objective truth that is beyond determinism and indeterminism:

> The fact is that we only fully arrive at ourselves in a freely chosen death. It and only it is 'la minute de la verité' (the moment of truth). [...] I die therefore I will no longer be: that is unassailable; it is the rock of our subjective truth that becomes objective when we are dashed to pieces on impact. (p. 149)

At this puzzling deadlock, I want to suggest that the main function of the anti-logic of death in Améry's argument is the creation of the possibility of a space, which is not a priori explained in accordance to any claim and therefore it can produce a margin for a critical delay. The infinite nonentity of the anti-logic of death is space without time. The absence of temporality enables a different perspective, not only with respect to the structure of human action but also to the criteria by which it valued. As such, it functions as a part of an alternative mode of being, which undercuts any 'regime of truth',[36] and challenges language boundaries. The decision in favor of death is a leap *out* of the realm of explanations and reasoning toward nothingness, an act of refusal to preserve and maintain the absurd tension.

Contemplating one`s own death according to this line of thought, in the minutes, hours, days, or years before the leap, is practicing subjectivity throughout improvising on the thin rope of the absurd, stretched between the logic of life and the anti-logic of death. Suicidal thinking on this account is a state of being 'torn between the logic of life and the logic of death: That consists of the ontically murky singularity' of subjectivity (p. 20). Accordingly, what I find crucial here is that the 'broken trust in the world' is not mercenarily a denial of the possibility of meaning altogether, but rather it is the rejection of a priori objectives and a universal meaning in the world. This difference is essential because it leaves room for reverberation. It leaves room for another system of processing that may allow access to a wider range of the lived experience, which seems to support the validity of Améry's claim: to 'recognize the suicidal judgment, insofar as it does not call into question the totality of all experience' (p. 57). Considering, speculating, imagining, and planning our own death is a way to scathe the limits of life. By exploring these limits, one is creating oneself. One is becoming oneself. One is making and unmaking meaning.

As Améry identified, this individual stance bares some uncomfortable and disruptive implications with regard to social as well as political structures. The establishment of the self as a deviation from the normative framework has an undeniable influence on the normative field itself, which leads me to another lesson I am taking from Améry with respect to the importance of expanding the boundaries of philosophizing. For it becomes clear, the fact that the first task is not to determine whether suicide is morally right or wrong but rather the opposite: to undertake a nonjudgmental inquiry into the field of the phenomena wherein we can explore the relationship between the beliefs we hold, our human evaluation apparatus, and the modes of choice. Thus, mapping the space in which the logic of life and the anti-logic of death are intertwined could help us examine life in the face of death as space within which the subject emerges. In doing so, we might gain an alternative understanding of what it means to be a human being—a vulnerable and yet open and dynamic entity. This insight might not only raise additional philosophical questions, but it also demands different medical-scientific definitions as well as different modes of therapeutic work.

Notes

1. All references refer to the above text unless otherwise stated.
2. The book form of *On Suicide*, based on a series of radio broadcasts which was delivered by Améry in 1976, after an unsuccessful suicide attempt two years earlier (1974). Two years later (1978), Améry succeeded to accomplish his Voluntary death.
3. As much as my offered exegetic might indicate the need for a re-examination of some liberal beliefs in regard to freedom, autonomy, and rationality, I will not address these issues directly here, for my aim in this chapter is to clarify Améry's anti-logic of death and indicate its applicability to the current philosophical study of suicidality.
4. As Gallagher points out, "one does not have to know or be aware of this brain processes and an ecologically embedded body, in order to have an experience that still counts as a self-experience" (2000, p. 15). I am aware of the fact that I am using Gallagher's terms (minimal and narrative self) quite tolerantly, yet I think it could be useful for the sake of the argument that I am attempting to posit. As far as it might turn out to be a valuable question later on, I am not getting to the question of whether the minimal self is bound (still implicitly perhaps) in the most basic sense with interpersonal relations or not (see for example: Zahavi, D. 2007, 2017; Brinck, I., Reddy, V., & Zahavi, D. 2017), for it seems that Améry himself is undecided on the matter (e.g., pp. 59–122 regarding the question of undeniable belonging vs. existential loneliness).
5. By *Ontological Vulnerability*, I refer namely to the first of the three sources in the taxonomy developed by Mackenzie et al. (2014): inherent vulnerability, which is 'intrinsic to the human condition'; situational vulnerability, which is 'context specific'; and finally, pathogenic vulnerability, which stems from abuse, oppression, and injustice. These sources may appear according to Mackenzie et al. in two states: dispositional vulnerability and occurrent vulnerability (pp. 7–9).
6. See Baier (1991, 1995), Ratcliffe, M., (2009, 2013) and Bernstein (2011).
7. By using the word *Construct*, I refer to the sense of agency as a conceptual entity, an explanatory variable, which is not directly observable and whose existence depends upon the subject's mind. In other words, it is a psycho-subjective (personal as well as collective) interpretation of physical objects in the world.
8. This superficial definition will suffice at the moment for the sake of my argument, but it is important to note that there is a rich field of writing that seeks to philosophically analyze and define death. For further reading, see Bradley, Feldman, and Johansson (eds., 2013) and Luper (2009). It is also needless to say that there are of course philosophical traditions that

undermine this assumption (for example, Buddhist reincarnation, or to a certain extent, the religious concept of paradise).

9. Death as such, in its inaccessibility, is an anonymous death and, therefore, it opposes the Heideggerian concept of death as one's own possibility or as Dasein's authentic existence. To some extent, it mirrors Maurice Blanchot's conception of death as it appears in *The Space of Literature* (1982).
10. See: Baier (1991) and Bernstein (2011).
11. Although there are different definitions and interpretations of the absurd, I will refer here the to the absurd mostly as it characterized by Camus (1955) and Nagel (1971)—a kind of necessary relationship between people and the world resulting from the 'act of attention' (Camus 1955, p. 43) or intentionality.
12. See Wittgenstein, L. (1958 Part II, §xi).
13. That is why 'reality', for Améry, is always a human reality that is dynamic and influenced by the relationship of interdependence between the subject and the other. It follows that any self-determination regarding 'being' is impossible: 'It is what it is not and is not what it is' (Sartre 1992, p. 112).
14. However, there are two reservations that should be noted in this context: (1) the vast majority of Pessimists aim to eventually find reasons to oppose suicide. Some, like Schopenhauer and Rousseau, come to a solution of celibacy and reduction, while others like Camus offer more involved solutions, sometimes even political (see Dienstag 2009, p. 103); and (2) for the most part, Améry's own voluntary death is attributable more to his notion of human freedom and less to pessimism. Nonetheless, as my analysis suggests, it seems plausible that it is the latter that produces the former.
15. *Échec* is the French equivalent of "check" in the game of Chess. That is the declaration of a defeat that can put an end to the game. However, in the context that Améry uses it, this is a declaration of self-defeat. Therefore, Améry's emphasis of *Échec* is decided upon by the subject and not by society, although it is the second authority that may 'Define the condition under which person's vital situation can be designated as *Échec*' (p. 45).
16. As Améry himself was well aware, *Échec* is a more common and conspicuous threat than death (p. 42), whether as a failure *in* life (e.g., bankruptcy, dismissal, or divorce), or whether as a failure *of* life (because eventually all lives are submissions to death, or because fundamental loneliness is irrefutable [pp. 114–115]). Thus, For the most part, the *Échec* does not lead to extreme conclusions such as voluntary death, and even if it does, it is usually a momentary, fleeting notion. It is only the 'affected person [who] experiences in its full inexorability' (ibid.). What then does 'affected' refer to here? My guess is that Améry refers here to the affect of the anti-logic of death which was activated by the 'first blow'.

17. Ratcliffe refers to a traumatic experience, which was certainly present in Améry's life (although Améry refuses to refer to himself as 'traumatized', but rather as having experienced a 'spiritual and psychic condition [which] corresponds completely to reality' (Améry, 1980, p. 99)), as well as to victims of all kinds of abuse, which according to many studies on the subject, constitute a large percentage of suicides. However, the criterion for traumatic experience can be as broad as it can be narrow and limited. Here, I am applying it broadly. Further exploration should address Ratcliffe's notion that modification occurs at the pre-intentioned structure as well. Clarifying this issue can potentially support the thesis that death inclination is deeply involved in life instincts.
18. Plutchik R (2001). To be honest, for Plutchik and his successors, *Eros* does not constitute an 'emotion'. However, for the sake of my argument, the distinction is not important.
19. As with *Eros*, words fail to fully capture it, yet, it is interesting to note though that the functions of both *Eros* and *Disgust* are to preserve life; nonetheless, in extreme cases, they act against the organism itself in a kind of autoimmune attack. Should we conclude that such cases indicate pathology? I would like to argue that they do not, and the explanation for this is closely related to how one might think of death inclinations.
20. Self-disgust is a fairly common matter in Western society, and, to a certain extent, everyone is likely to have experienced some level of it (whether from binge eating, from an unnecessary cigarette, or from the image staring at us from the mirror).
21. Inclination toward death [*Todesneigung*] is the term that Améry uses to distinguish his exegetics from Freud`s *Todestrieb*. Nevertheless, it seems to me that the analysis suggested by Améry is somewhat problematic and insufficient. First, because although Améry quotes Freud using the term *Todestrieb* as 'Death instinct' (pp. 73–75), it is important to notice that Freud himself insists that it is a drive [*der Trieb*], and not an instinct [*der Instinkt*]. The second reason is that, to some extent, his interpretive proposal seems to already exist in Freud scripts.
22. See Bernstein (2011, pp. 398–399). It is worth noticing here that through an analysis of psychosis and interpersonally induced trauma, Ratcliffe conceives a disruption of the pre-reflective 'trust' that guides everyday perceptions. If interpersonal relations affect the integrity of intentionality (i.e., the basic experience of being in one kind of intentional state rather than in another), then it is not only significance that undergoes a change, but also the affective bodily and interpersonal expectations that tacitly guide our own encounters of others and the world. Therefore, the experiential precondition itself is claimed to be relational.
23. See Dienstag (2009).

24. I find Windt's definition for suicidality very useful here: suicidality as an 'open texture' event with a 'weak' family-resemblance criterion (1981, p. 40).
25. For example, 'It is not Being that oppresses me, or Nothingness, or God, or the Absence of God, only society. For it and only it caused the disturbance in my existential balance, which I am trying to oppose with an upright gait. It and only it robbed me of my trust in the world' (Améry 1980, p. 100).
26. In this sense, Wittgenstein's distinction seems accurate—indeed, 'the world of the happy man is a different one from that of the unhappy man' (2018, §6.43).
27. For an updated comprehensive and clear review of psychological and sociological approaches to suicide and suicidality, see Gunn III JF and Lester D (2014).
28. This difference is more than a difference between two language games, to use Wittgenstein's notion (1958), because the anti-logic of death opposes any common practices, regulation and rules altogether, and as a result it denies the possibility of a game, let alone participation in it. Therefore, to quote Clements, 'In a real sense, an individual who does not value existence does not value anything at all, and to apply tools of cognitive values to this primary effect is to deny him his validity in a totally arbitrary fashion' (1980, p. 107).
29. 'Epistemic Ignorance' is not a lack of knowledge but a lack of utilizing it. Yet, it is not a wholly conscious choice or a 'not caring', but rather, it is closer to denial than exclusion or repression. The more it is used, the more it becomes deeper and comprehensive. This is because ignorance as a substantive epistemic practice is not only a 'defect' on the part of the 'knower' but a structural problem. (For further reading: Tuana 2004; Gilson 2011, 2014).
30. It is important to clarify that the structure of an act/thought in no way implies that it is impulsive. There are, of course, suicides that can be characterized as impulsive (usually among teenagers), but these are not at the heart of the analysis proposed here.
31. Be that as it may, I will not get into the rich, complex discussion over the question of free will that Améry refers to, nor shall I try to explain his position and defend it. I will just mention that, for Améry, freedom is not existential (p. 125). That is, freedom is not a state of pure objective being (as opposed to truth or reason) but an individual, endless process of constant change that is 'subject to a multi causality that is almost infinite' (p. 137). That is, one is conditioned (by the logic of life, whether you call it biologics, physics, or neurochemistry facts, or as 'unity of consciousness

and the categories', or as speaking animal), and yet one experiences one's self as free (p. 137).

32. Hegel, G.W.F. (1977) *Phenomenology of Spirit.*
33. To some extent, Améry's anti-logic of death can be analogous to Blanchot's *Other Night* (1982, pp. 162–163), as it refuses any possibility of positive conceptualization. This movement, as Blanchot points out, 'makes us sense not only its discretion and its essential intimacy but also its profound unreality: death as abyss, not that which founds but the absence and the loss of all foundation' (1982, p. 153). The endless reflections that reverberate the absolute reveal the non-exclusivity of the logic of life; yet, at the same time, it resists dialectical negation by shattering any possibility of meaning. This superficial comparison to Blanchot raises an important question in regard to Améry's positive reversal that is embodied in voluntary death.
34. This point, used and articulated by the 'Two States View' advocates, as Cowley argued, contends that the concept of rationality is essentially future-oriented; since the suicidal subject has no future after suicide, it makes no sense to call suicide rational or irrational (2006, p. 497) or, as Devine claimed: 'We are dealing, that is, not with a situation concerning which rational men will exhibit a range of estimates, but with a situation in which one man's estimate is as good as another, because what is being done is a comparison with an unknown quality' (1980, p. 139).
35. It is more likely that facing the anti-logic of death may lead one to 'feel no impulse to oppose or stand for anything at all' (Kulp 2014, p. 126), not even to die. Therefore, Kulp's own conclusion according to which 'the ultimate outcome of this logic of death is the lack of the need to do or be anything, is suicide' (ibid.) seem to be a contradiction. For further discussion on the issue of temporality, narrative and intention in Améry's writing see: Ben-Shai (2010, 2011).
36. Or 'The production and maintenance of a compulsory ontology of pathology' (Marsh 2013, p. 747). See also Marsh (2010).

References

Améry, J. (1980). *At the Mind's Limits* (Translated from German by S. Rosenfeld and S. P. Rosenfeld). Bloomington: Indiana University Press.

Améry, J. (1984). *Radical Humanism: Selected Essays* (Translated from German by S. Rosenfeld and S. P. Rosenfeld). Bloomington: Indiana University Press.

Améry, J. (1999). *On Suicide: A Discourse on Voluntary Death* (Translated from German by J. D. Barlow). Bloomington: Indiana University Press.

Baechler, J. (1979). *Suicides.* New York: Basic Books, Inc.

Baier, A. C. (1991). "Trust and Its Vulnerabilities" and "Sustaining Trust". In *Tanner Lectures on Human Values* (Vol. 13). Salt Lake City: University of Utah Press.

Baier, A. C. (1995). *Moral Prejudices: Essays on Ethics*. Cambridge, MA: Harvard University Press.

Beck, A. T., Kovacs, M., & Weissman, A. (1979). Assessment of Suicidal Ideation: The Scale for Suicidal Ideation. *Journal of Consulting and Clinical Psychology, 47*(2), 343–352.

Ben-Shai, R. (2010). To Reverse the Irreversible: On Time Disorder in the Work of Jean Améry. In J. R. Watson (Ed.), *Metacide* (pp. 73–92). Leiden, The Netherlands: Brill | Rodopi.

Ben-Shai, R. (2011). Imposition, or Writing from the Void: Pathos and Pathology in Améry. In M. Zolkos (Ed.), *On Jean Améry: Philosophy of the Catastrophe* (pp. 109–134). Lanham: Lexington Books.

Bernstein, J. M. (2011). Trust: On the Real But Almost Always Unnoticed, Ever-Changing Foundation of Ethical Life. *Metaphilosophy, 42*(4), 395–416.

Blanchot, M. (1982). *The Space of Literature* (Translated from [language] by A. Smock). London: University of Nebraska Press Lincoln.

Bradley, B., Feldman, F., & Johansson, J. (2013). *The Oxford Handbook of Philosophy of Death*. Oxford: Oxford University Press.

Brinck, I., Reddy, V., & Zahavi, D. (2017). The Primacy of the We? In C. Durt, T. Fuchs, & C. Tewes (Eds.), *Embodiment, Enaction, and Culture* (pp. 131–148). Cambridge, MA and London: MIT Press.

Camus, A. (1955). *The Myth of Sisyphus, and Other Essays*. New York: Knopf.

Camus, A. (1991). *The Rebel an Essay on Man in Revolt* (With a Foreword by Sir Herbert Read A Revised and Complete Translation from French by Anthony Bower). New York: Vintage Books.

Clements, C. (1980). The Ethics of Not-Being. In M. Pabst Battin & D. Mayo (Eds.), *Suicide: The Philosophical Issues* (pp. 104–114). New York: St. Martin's Press.

Cowley, C. (2006). Suicide is Neither Rational nor Irrational. *Ethical Theory and Moral Practice, 9*(5), 495–504.

Critchley, S. (2004). *Very Little – Almost Nothing: Death, Philosophy, Literature*. London and New York: Routledge.

Devine, P. E. (1980). On Choosing Death. In M. Pabst Battin & D. Mayo (Eds.), *Suicide: The Philosophical Issues* (pp. 138–142). New York: St. Martin's Press.

Dienstag, J. F. (2009). *Pessimism: Philosophy, Ethic, Spirit*. Princeton, NJ: Princeton University Press.

Epicurus. (1966). Principal Doctrines. In J. Saunders (Ed.), *Greek and Roman Philosophy After Aristotle*. New York: Free Press.

Gallagher, S. (2000). Philosophical Conceptions of the Self: Implications for Cognitive Science. *Trends in Cognitive Sciences, 4*(1), 14–21.

Gilson, E. (2011). Vulnerability, Ignorance, and Oppression. *Hypatia, 26*(2), 308–332.

Gilson, E. (2014). *The Ethics of Vulnerability: A Feminist Analysis of Social Life and Practice*. New York: Routledge.

Gunn, J. F., III, & Lester, D. (2014). *Theories of Suicide: Past, Present and Future*. Springfield, IL: Charles C Thomas.

Hegel, G. W. F. (1977). *Phenomenology of Spirit* (Translated from German by A. V. Miller with Analysis of the Text and Foreword by J. N. Findlay). Oxford: Clarendon Press.

Heidelberger-Leonard, I. (2010). *The Philosopher of Auschwitz: Jean Améry and Living with the Holocaust*. London and New York: I. B. Tauris.

Kulp, M. J. (2014). *The Limits of Rationality: Suicidality, Affectivity, and the Rational*. PhD. Dissertations. Retrieved from http://ecommons.luc.edu/luc_diss/1277.

Liddell, H. G., & Scott, R. (1889). 'Logos'. *An Intermediate Greek–English Lexicon*. Retrieved from http://www.perseus.tufts.edu.

Luper, S. (2009). *Philosophy of Death*. Cambridge: Cambridge University Press.

Macintyre, A. (1985). *After Virtue: A Study in Moral Theory* (2nd ed.). London: Duckworth.

Mackenzie, C., Rogers, W., & Doods, S. (Eds.). (2014). *Vulnerability: New Essays in Ethics and Feminist Philosophy*. New York: Oxford University.

Marsh, I. (2010). *Suicide: Foucault, History and Truth*. Cambridge, UK: Cambridge University Press.

Marsh, I. (2013). The Uses of History in the Unmaking of Modern Suicide. *Journal of Social History, 46*(3), 744–756.

Nagel, T. (1971). The Absurd. *The Journal of Philosophy, 68*(20), 716–727.

Plutchik, R. (2001). The Nature of Emotions. *American Scientist; Research Triangle Park, 89*(4), 344–350.

Ratcliffe, M. (2009). Existential Feeling and Psychopathology. *Philosophy, Psychiatry, & Psychology, 16*(2), 179–194.

Ratcliffe, M. (2013). What Is It to Lose Hope? *Phenomenology and the Cognitive Sciences, 12*(4), 597–614.

Ricoeur, P. (1985). *Time and Narrative* (Translated from French by K. McLaughlin & D. Pellauer). Chicago: University of Chicago Press.

Ringel, E. (1976). The Presuicidal Syndrome. *Suicide and Life-Threatening Behaviour, 6*(3), 131–149.

Sartre, J. P. (1992). *Being and Nothingness* (Translated from French by H. Barnes). New York: Washington Square Press.

Schlimme, J. E. (2013). Sense of Self-Determination and the Suicidal Experience. A Phenomenological Approach. *Medicine, Health Care and Philosophy, 16*(2), 211–223.

Shneidman, E. S. (2001). *Comprehending Suicide: Landmarks in 20th-Century Suicidology*. Washington, DC: American Psychological Association.

Tuana, N. (2004). Coming to Understand: Orgasm and the Epistemology of Ignorance. *Hypatia, 19*(1), 194–232.

Windt, P. (1981). The Concept of Suicide. In M. Pabst Battin & D. J. Mayo (Eds.), *Suicide: The Philosophical Issues*. London: Peter Owen.

Wittgenstein, L. (1958) *Philosophical Investigations* (Translated from German by Anscombe GEM) (2nd ed.). Oxford: Basil Blackwell Ltd.

Wittgenstein, L. (2018). *Tractatus Logico-Philosophicus Logisch-Philosophische* Side by Side Edition v. 0.53. Retrieved from http://people.umass.edu/klement/tlp/.

Zahavi, D. (2007). Self and Other: The Limits of Narrative Understanding. In D. Hutto (Ed.), *Narrative and Understanding Persons* (pp. 179–201). Cambridge: Cambridge University Press.

Zahavi, D. (2017). Thin, Thinner, Thinnest: Defining the Minimal Self. In D. Christoph, T. Fuchs, & C. Tewes (Eds.), *Embodiment, Enaction, and Culture: Investigating the Constitution of the Shared World* (pp. 193–199). Cambridge, MA: MIT Press.

CHAPTER 15

"The Nonsense that You Cannot Write Poetry After Auschwitz": Jean Améry, the Interrupted Writer

Oshrat C. Silberbusch

15.1 Opening

In 1949, while Jean Améry was scraping by as a freelance journalist in Brussels, trying to pick up the pieces of a life that Auschwitz had brutally interrupted, the Frankfurt School philosopher Theodor W. Adorno penned the phrase he is to this day most widely remembered by: "Writing a poem after Auschwitz is barbaric". Dubbed "Adorno's *Diktum*", this fraction of a sentence plucked from the end of a twenty-page essay quickly became famous, stirring incomprehension and outrage from critics and writers alike. Jean Améry was no exception. Even though he only mentions the *Diktum* itself once, almost thirty years after it was put to paper, his wording doesn't seem to leave much room for debate: "The nonsense that you cannot write poetry after Auschwitz…" (Améry 2005c, p. 99). *Unsinn*—the verdict is damning. Améry drops it in passing and does not linger on it. The (im)possibilities of art and literature after Auschwitz don't seem to be foremost on his mind.

O. C. Silberbusch (✉)
Independent Scholar, Brooklyn, NY, USA

Y. Ataria et al. (eds.), *Jean Améry*,
https://doi.org/10.1007/978-3-030-28095-6_15

15.2 The Obsession to Tell a Story

Objectively speaking, he would have had good reasons to react to the *Diktum*. Not only was he an Auschwitz survivor who had repeatedly made clear that he didn't like to be spoken for by armchair philosophers (particularly Adorno[1]), he was also one of those very *Dichters*[2] that Adorno seemed to want to silence. Indeed, when Améry made his laconic statement on Adorno's nonsense, he wasn't only speaking as the critic and essayist most of us know him to be, but as a writer of fiction himself. Three years earlier, Améry had published *Lefeu or The Demolition*, his first substantial piece of fiction since the 1935 novel *Die Schiffbrüchigen [the shipwrecked]* (which remained unpublished until recently). Much more than a simple whim of an accomplished essayist trying his luck at another genre, this late return to literature was, as Améry himself put it, the realization of a "very old desire anchored in the far depths of my life" (Améry 1982, p. 172). He speaks of his "*obsession* to tell a story [erzählen zu wollen]" (Améry 1982, p. 172) and calls the book "a *summa*, one that takes stock of my own existence, my own thinking" (Améry 1982, p. 184), "a kind of life work [*Lebenswerk*] in small format".[3] For him, this novel-essay, as he called it, was not a side project, but quite possibly his most important work of all. Let us say right away that the critics and readers of his time did, for the most part, not agree with him. As Améry himself noted, the reactions ranged from "half-hearted approval to vicious hatchet job", while "thousands of unsold copies languish[ed] like bricks"[4] on the shelves of his publisher Klett. The largely indifferent to negative reception was a heavy blow for Améry. Not only because he considered Lefeu "the best thing [he had] ever written" (Améry 1992, p. 100), but because the critically acclaimed essayist had never gotten over the *Dichter* he had not become, as he makes quite clear in a letter to his friend Ernst Mayer:

> Why is this book [*Lefeu*] so important to me? Because in it, for the first time after so many years, I attempt something like *Dichtung* [literature]. Do you remember how in our youth, we jokingly called each other '*Dichter*'? Obviously, I have been more attached to this self-assessment than I have been willing to admit in these past decades as I built myself some reputation as an essayist.[5]

In another letter, he speaks of the "nagging feeling to have done it all wrong": "I think I know now that I was meant to be not a pure thinker, but a thinking novelist [*denkender Erzähler*]".[6] Why then was *Lefeu* a failure—or was it? And, if Améry really wanted to be a *Dichter* more than anything else, why did he wait almost forty years after *Die Schiffbrüchigen* to write a novel again? Examining these questions will not only present Améry's work in a new light but also gradually lead us back to where we started off: to Adorno's *Diktum*. What, if anything, does Améry's "failure" as a *Dichter* have to do with the impossibility of writing a poem after Auschwitz? Can Adorno's meaning illuminate Améry's struggle—and vice versa?

Let us begin at the beginning. Why did Améry not return to fiction after he came back from the camps? The simple answer to this question is that in fact, he did—or at least, he tried. For the first few years after the war, while he was making a meager living as a journalist, Améry filled page after page with fragments of fiction, apparently attempting to pick up where he left off—quite literally. Indeed, the dozens of fragments, which appear at times only loosely connected, all feature as their protagonist the very same Eugen Althager that Améry killed off at the end of his 1935 novel *Die Schiffbrüchigen*. The fact that he not only took up fiction again but even resuscitated his prewar hero, is a striking testimony to the strength of his desire to reconnect with the past, to throw a bridge across the gulf that separated the Auschwitz survivor from the young, aspiring writer in Vienna. The manuscripts are almost all variations on the same theme: the story of a man who grieves the loss of two women—his dead wife, alternately named Agathe or Beate,[7] and his lover Odette, who left him for someone else. Irene Heidelberger-Leonard sees the fragments as remnants of an abandoned attempt at a novel (Heidelberger-Leonard, 2008), a theory that seems buttressed by the few traces the manuscripts left in Améry's correspondence. In an undated letter draft to his childhood friend Ernst Mayer, he writes that he is working on "a novel, whose skeleton is the recent, unfortunate story [die eben geschehene, unselige Geschichte]" (Améry 2008a, p. 544). Those tempted to believe that the "unfortunate story" in question must be that of Améry's torture and imprisonment are quickly corrected. He notes that this book puts him "into the formidable thematic neighborhood of 'Albertine disparue'" (Proust's story of lost love), and in a later letter writes that the manuscript is about a certain "Paulette" and "the mystery of [his] so-called 'feelings'" for her (Améry 2008b, p. 545). A novel about lost love and heartbreak then, with no trace of Auschwitz, it seems. And not just a casual scribbling, either: In the letter to Ernst Mayer, Améry calls it "the last and uttermost I have to give. If it is good, my life will have had a meaning, if it is nothing, then I will know that I am a nothing" (Améry 2008a, p. 544). A tall order for a project that never made it beyond a pile of disconnected fragments, and which Améry never mentioned again after 1950. What made him abandon it? And what made him take it up in the first place? At first sight, both questions seem to bear a connection to Améry's earlier work *Die Schiffbrüchigen*. When he first started working on his new project, he believed the former lost. The fact that many of the protagonists reappear in the later manuscripts suggests a desire to rewrite the lost novel, however differently. In 1949, he chanced upon a manuscript of *Die Schiffbrüchigen* in the offices of a Viennese editor and for a while made a new, unsuccessful attempt to have it published. Eventually, Améry abandoned both—the attempt to publish the novel of the 1930s, and the unfinished manuscripts from after the war. It would be twenty-five years until he turned to fiction again.

Whether or not Améry intended to leave out of his post-war novel the ordeal he had just endured, it did find its way in. While on the face of it, the majority of texts seem to ignore it (with mixed results—more on that below), at least one fragment confronts the experience head-on. Likely intended as a chapter of the novel, it marks Améry's first attempt to bring to paper the horrors he had experienced. The text, entitled *Journey Around Death: The Fortress Derloven*, tells of Eugen Althager's imprisonment and torture by the Gestapo in the Belgian fortress Derloven. While the fragment is clearly a fictional predecessor to Améry's famous 1966 essay "On Torture", the two have little in common beyond the subject matter. *Journey Around Death* begins with a pastoral description of the Belgian countryside:

> Between Mechelen and Antwerp, a gentle countryside unfolds into peaceful meadows and fields, crisscrossed by leafy brooks, pastures, poplar alleys and flemish farmhouses. The fields are brown, blue, and golden yellow (...) Carriage horses with aloof, majestic necks march silently along the freshly tilled earth, their beautiful heads tilting with each step. (Améry 2008c, p. 583)

And so on. Améry starts out in a style reminiscent of the *Heimatliteratur*[8] he had once admired as if to belie the chapter's threatening title. When we finally arrive at the scene of the crime, the tone changes:

> In the middle of this countryside... stands the fortress Derloven. Derloven was a battlefield of death. Of slow death and galloping death; death of hunger and death of cold; of sudden-fear-apoplexy, spinal-cord-death and

> broken-neck-death; of death by the wheel of torture, by rifle butt, or by kicking boots; and finally, of the comparatively humane death by the orderly firing squad. (Améry 2008c, pp. 583–586)

In its clinical matter-of-factness, the list could have been penned by the murderers themselves: *Angst-Apoplexie, Genickbruch-Sterben, Stiefeltritt—Tod*... There is something singularly strained about both the bucolic description at the outset and this unwieldy, aseptic list of ways to die. Yet Améry seems undeterred: When he finally turns to Althager's (i.e., his own) ordeal, he doubles down, almost drowning the experience in words. His detailed description of the torture tools and of the act itself leaves nothing to the imagination, ironically calling to mind what Améry himself would much later write about a painting by Dürer: "And absolutely diabolical is a dignified naturalism which represents the torments of hell and makes sure that no fleck is left empty, which, with an incomparably skillful hand, puts even the emperor's pinscher into the representation of the hellish roast and meticulously draws every single hair" (Améry 1971). Améry is not Dürer, but there is something of that "diabolical naturalism" in his meticulous rendering of barbarity. The malaise deepens when, as the story progresses, the primary plot of love and deception gradually takes center stage again. Suddenly the description of torture appears as little more than a literary foil, a suffering evoked so as to magnify the protagonist's true trial: the loss of the unfaithful lover. When the fragment breaks off, Eugen Althager is planning a trip to Venice to reconquer Odette, and Améry is turning his back again to the experience that had, in this particular fragment, so forcefully tried to assert itself.

There is little doubt that Améry's failure to turn into literature the experience that he would twenty years later so brilliantly relate in an essay, is at least partly due to the difficulty that lies at the heart of his criticism of Dürer. There is something "diabolical" in the effort of the artist/writer who turns agony into art, and no artist, not even the most talented one, can completely avoid that trap. The moment suffering is turned into *material* for an artwork, even if it is to honor the victims, the honor due is already partially betrayed. Adorno spells out the aporia in a passage on Schönberg's "A Survivor from Warsaw":

> By turning it, despite all its brutality and irreconcilability, into an image, it is as if the dignity of the victims was violated. Something is made out of them, artworks prepared for consumption by the world that killed them. The so-

> called artistic rendering of the naked bodily pain of those bludgeoned with rifle butts holds, however remotely, the potential to squeeze out pleasure. Morality, which obligates art not to forget even for a second, slithers into the abyss of its opposite. By virtue of the aesthetic principle of stylization (...), the unthinkable fate appears as if it had some meaning: it is haloed, something of its horror taken away. By this alone, injustice is done to the victims, while no art that avoids their plight could pass the test of justice. Even the cry of despair pays its dues to the despicable affirmation. (Adorno 2003d, pp. 423–424)

There is something of that aporia in *Journey Around Death*. Even if the potential to squeeze out pleasure seems “however remote”, it is implicitly contained in the “so-called artistic rendering of the naked bodily pain”, in Améry’s effort to find the right turn of phrase, to integrate his story into the greater plot—“the aesthetic principle of stylization”. The fact that his style seems at times awkward only underscores the challenge of *any* stylization of atrocity.[9] Yet while Améry no doubt felt that challenge acutely, his struggle seems to go far beyond the actual literary *representation* of suffering. As I pointed out, *Journey around Death* was an exception, its intended place in the novel unclear. For the most part, the post-war fragments ignore Eugen’s broken body to focus on his broken heart. That did little, however, to save the novel. The reader who takes the time to decipher the stack of mostly handwritten pages now archived as “Eugen-Althager-Komplex” in the German Literary Archives in Marbach, is struck by the sense of loss that emanates from them. Not only is there constantly question of loss: love lost, lives lost, dreams lost, but the author himself seems lost. Far from the masterful stylist Jean Améry of later years, the writer Hans Mayer[10] is at a loss for words. Pages and pages of beginnings, snippets, crossed out paragraphs and unfinished sentences, where the same words, the same story return again and again, even if the names sometimes differ. And just in case the repetitiveness and scattered nature of the manuscripts aren’t enough to convey a feeling of helplessness, Améry integrates his sense of failure into the text, by having his alter ego protagonist repeatedly deplore the writer he has not become. He speaks of his “bungled poetic calling [*verpatztes Dichtertum*]”,[11] mourns his “first novel”, and asserts wistfully that he “could have become a writer”.[12] In one grotesque yet poignant passage, the main character (and through him Améry) is cruelly mocked by the specter of Karl Kraus:

> Well, he had begun to work as a journalist, despite the fact that way back in his youth, there had been a consensus that he possessed the authentic, true soul of a poet. Yes, he had become a miserable newspaper slave, and at night, he was frequently visited by the German [sic] carnival figure Karl Kraus, who stood at the foot of his bed and read newspaper articles with a soul rending snicker, dropping comments and [*illegible*] with incredibly contemptuous gestures. Which woman would be stupid enough to climb up into his drafty attic, to a poor heartbroken fool, who was on top of it a traitor, a traitor to the *Geist*? That's right. Hadn't the Cain's mark of the newspaper scribbler long been imprinted on his forehead?[13]

There is a lot of suffering in these scattered pages, but it is not the one that would later come to define—for better and for worse—Améry's career. The newspaper slave, the widower, the betrayed lover—but the survivor? Only incidentally. If torture and imprisonment are mentioned outside of *Journey around Death*, it happens casually, sometimes cryptically, without any importance to the flow of the story: one of the protagonists is—in passing—identified as a survivor,[14] Améry's Auschwitz prisoner number is found on the spine of a book,[15] or there is a very brief mention of torture.[16] This sidelining of an obviously traumatic experience, which finds itself grafted like a foreign object onto texts that desperately try to ignore it, only exacerbates the feeling of helplessness the manuscripts convey.

15.3 "*Man schrieb schön und spielte Piano...*"

How is Améry's literary struggle related to the experience he could neither work in nor leave out? The post-war manuscripts seem to suggest that the actual representation of that experience is only one piece of the puzzle. How else did the shadow of the recent past prevent Améry from being the *Dichter* he longed to be? A comment in his 1967 essay on "Life with books" gives us a clue, one that reads like a belated condemnation of the efforts of the writer Hans Mayer:

> Literature erstwhile termed 'beautiful'[17] irritates me.... 'One wrote beautifully and played the piano', Karl Kraus once said.... There can be no such thing today as writing beautifully and playing the piano: the state of our times and our civilization does not allow it.[18]

Remarkably, the last sentence appears almost identical in *Lefeu*, except that there, the author quoted is not Karl Kraus but—Hans Mayer. Jean Améry cites Hans Mayer as an example for the kind of literature that is no longer possible—without revealing to the reader that he is, in fact, disavowing himself: "For now you are sleeping. And my heart is heavy [*Denn nun schläfst du. Und mein Herz ist schwer*]—which is true, but which cannot be said anymore, for the state of *Geist* and culture does no longer allow it. There are no lullabies left, Irene" (Améry 1982, p. 81). The two first sentences are taken from a poem that Améry published in 1934 in the journal *Die Brücke*, and took up again in his novel *Die Schiffbrüchigen*: "Are you sleeping Lili? My heart is heavy [*Schläfst Du schon Lili? Mein Herz ist schwer!*]"[19] It is hard to imagine a greater disavowal than this veiled self-criticism.

Why can there be no such thing in 1967 as writing beautifully? Why can the poem Améry wrote in 1934 not be said anymore? At a primary level, it seems to be once more the aesthetically pleasing that is at stake here. Even when it isn't squeezed from the pain of the victims, it can wrong them, as Adorno notes in a text written in 1944 in the shadow of the horror unfolding in Europe: "Even the tree that blossoms lies the moment one perceives its bloom without the shadow of terror; even the innocent 'How beautiful!' becomes an excuse for the infamy of a reality that is different" (Adorno 2003a, p. 26). Just like Adorno, Améry struggled with this "lie"—with the glaring dissonance between the beautiful prose and the piano playing, and the very different reality he had himself experienced. Améry's assertion that "the state of *Geist* and culture" no longer allow to write like that, however, goes beyond the visceral rejection of the too beautiful to point toward a more complicated truth: the fact that both the culture, and the horrors of Auschwitz that seem to negate it, are fruit of the same tree—and the inevitable implications that has for the culture in question. That Améry was aware of these implications early on becomes clear in another post-war fragment that, like *The Fortress Derloven*, stands apart: a fictitious letter addressed by Eugen Althager to a friend. Entitled "Letter into Uncertainty" and dated September 1945 (which is likely when it was written) the letter anticipates some of the reflections—even some of the wording—that Améry would use in *At the Mind's Limits* twenty-one years later. For our purpose particularly significant is what the letter says about culture and its civilizing power—or lack thereof:

> 'Culture is differentiation.' Do you remember this definition that I gave in our 1935 journal 'Die Brücke'? Well, by God! These fates between bombs and concentration camps, between standing in line and desolation, these millions of lives caught between mass graves, hunger, cold and homelessness are diabolically and despicably simple. I have been there, and I have not become deeper nor dumber, smarter nor more frivolous, I have not become better or worse. (...) The soul, dear friend, or the spirit [*Geist*] have nothing to do with this bloody movie. And neither does art.[20]

With the same self-irony that will distinguish the later essayist, Améry declares nothing less than the bankruptcy of culture. Through the mouth of his alter ego, he rejects with a disillusioned "Well, by God!" the highest ideal of Enlightenment: culture's ability to differentiate, and to make a difference. Six years before the publication of Adorno's *Diktum*, Améry denies art the competence to say anything about the German catastrophe—and thus, ultimately, to say anything of significance altogether. Even if he is not as explicit as Adorno will be in 1949, his text contains in nuce the idea with which the Frankfurt philosopher will scandalize—that it is impossible to write poetry after Auschwitz. For the claim that art and *Geist* "have nothing to do in this bloody movie" has at least three implications: (1) that art and *Geist* were not able to prevent these "diabolically and despicably simple" atrocities, (2) that art and *Geist* are incapable to grasp this horror, and (3) that art and *Geist* are incapable to express it, to represent it, to explain it, with all that this means for the future of art, literature, and philosophy. *They have nothing to do in this bloody movie.* There is only a small step from Améry's laconic phrase: "And neither does art" to Adorno's *Diktum*. In fact, it is Adorno who will spell out, twenty years after Hans Mayer, what the latter only alluded to:

> [Culture's] palace, as Brecht says in a magnificent passage, is built from dog shit. Years after this passage was written, Auschwitz has irrefutably demonstrated the failure of culture. That it could happen in the midst of all the traditions of philosophy, art and enlightening sciences says more than simply the latter's inability to move and transform people. It is in these traditions themselves, in their emphatic claim to autarky, that the untruth lies. (Adorno 2003b, p. 359)

The disillusionment voiced here almost certainly played a decisive role in Améry's abandoned novelistic attempts after the war. Beyond the trauma that kept creeping up on him, his early struggle points to the broken promises of the *Geist* and the culture he had once adored, to what they (and therefore the *Dichtung* he believed himself destined to) claimed to stand for and so utterly betrayed. While this failure will be a central topic of *At the Mind's Limits*, it is only in *Lefeu*, his return to literature forty years after *Die Schiffbrüchigen*, that he—quite literally—spelled out what this means for art *after* Auschwitz, and for himself as the writer trying to create it.

15.4 *Lefeu* or *The Demolition*

Lefeu is a book as hard to retell as it is to pin down. The main plotline is simple enough: Lefeu, an unsuccessful painter in his sixties, lives in a run-down Paris garret room where he paints dark, austere paintings of Parisian streetscapes. He faces expulsion because a real estate developer wants to replace his building with a luxury apartment tower. Meanwhile, Lefeu is courted by agents from a German art gallery who have set their eyes on him and are hoping to "launch" him "with big publicity pomp and under the heading 'metaphysical realism'" (Améry 2008d, p. 650). Lefeu resists both, refusing to do what the world expects from him, his saying no [*Neinsage*] an existential response to the word of glittery ruin [*Glanz-Verfall*] he abhors. His girlfriend Irene, an avant-garde poet, resists in her own way, her disintegrating poems mirroring her own disintegrating self. The recent past is a constant presence in the book. On a trip to the outskirts, at the sight of large factory chimneys, Lefeu is overwhelmed by the memory of his parents who were deported and gassed, and it suddenly dawns on him why he has his entire life said no to the world. At the end, he sets his garret room on fire, with his paintings and himself in it.

Lefeu or The Demolition is far from a conventional novel. The book is written as one long and almost uninterrupted stream of consciousness by Lefeu himself, which makes the "story" less of a story than a reflection on the story. While the details of the plot are often "shrouded in an ambivalent darkness", as Améry himself puts it, the reflection drives the book forward, a sign of "the author's commitment to human reason in the face of the unreason of being" (Améry 2008d, p. 651). To top it off, Améry ends the book with a chapter (which he explicitly wanted to be a chapter and not an afterword) entitled "Why and How", a "kind of *Entstehung des Doktor Faustus* (*toute proportion gardée*,[21*] of course)",[22] a "reflection of the reflection" (Améry 2008d, p. 659), where Améry analyzes his own writing process and reflects on the result. The novel-*essay* is indeed just that, and as it strings together Lefeu's free-wheeling associative monologues, with frequent literary references, French asides and barely a paragraph break, the reader breathlessly follows along—or doesn't. Indeed, the novel's distinct form and style were precisely what many critics objected to. "Bantering", "incoherent", "a literary degeneration",[23] "obtrusively autobiographical",[24] "literature is only 'signaled'",[25] "no confidence in the narrating word",[26] "this non-thing and non-concept of a novel-essay"[27]—these are just some of the critiques leveled against *Lefeu*. Even more positive reviewers pointed out that the book is "not 'readable' in the conventional sense"[28], that it will need a "focused" and "courageous reader", and they questioned whether the reading public "will persevere".[29] That the book is not an easy read seems to be the one thing all critics agree on. Those who praise it (and they are more numerous than Améry's own assessment of the reception suggests) speak of an "enormous problematic nexus",[30] a "very dense tapestry of language and thought", a "highly intellectual" book that "cannot be remotely paraphrased".[31] This novel, so the consensus, is not really a novel—at least not a novel as we know it. Some swiftly conclude that Améry has "no talent as a fiction writer",[32] that he has succumbed unprepared to "the temptation of fiction [Reich-Ranicki uses the German *Belletristik*, from the French *belles lettres*, beautiful literature…]".[33]

Is that really it? The novel itself and Améry's own reflections on it suggest a different story. If Améry didn't write the *Belletristik* Reich-Ranicki and others wanted to see, it seems to have less to do with a lack of talent than with what he called, in the book itself, "the state of *Geist* and culture" in his day. To examine this hypothesis, let us start with his own reflections on how *Lefeu* came about.

After linking *Lefeu* to his "obsession to write fiction", Améry turns to the historical events unfolding while he was working on his manuscript—and immediately relates them to the latter:

> In the days in which I wrote my first chapters, the completely unacceptable happened in Vietnam: the cities Hanoi and Haiphong were "erased" by Nixon—just as Hitler had promised to do with the cities of England, with the difference that in 1972, the rodomontades had become reality, moreover accompanied by slick freedom chatter. A profound disgust came over me that hasn't lifted since. There is no doubt that his disgust went into the work. Let me come back here to the word "glittery ruin [*Glanz-Verfall*]" Wasn't it the land of glittery ruin par excellence that in

> Vietnam horribly revealed itself as enemy of the world and humanity? Wasn't it the reality of our times that triumphed there with B-52 bombers? (Améry 1982, p. 181)

Améry goes on to denounce the "very real global conspiracy of capitalism", voices his conviction that the "literary and artistic America of protest" is not "the contradiction … but rather the luxury waste product [of the murderous one]" (Améry 1982, p. 181), and adds that, given the reports coming in from "the countries calling themselves socialist", he had "no concrete hope to oppose to [this] outrage" (Améry 1982, p. 182). The only thing left is Lefeu's "*Neinsage* [saying no]"—a complete refusal to be part of it, to the point of self-extinction.

Is it all about capitalism, then? Is Lefeu's *Neinsage*, and through it Améry's refusal—or inability—to write the "beautiful" novel that is expected of him, a reaction to the ravages of imperialist late capitalism? It is, and it isn't. It isn't in a one-dimensional way, but it is in the sense that for Améry, these ravages are closely linked to the slaughter he himself only narrowly escaped. In a world where a bloody war, far away and mostly invisible, is contrasted and justified by economic comfort and consumption at home (and its supposed endangerment), Améry sees the entanglement of money, power and murder, and senses the intimate connection between the war-mongering and the race for profit and power (be it small-scale—Lefeu's real estate developer, or big scale: Nixon's America) of 1972, and the horrors that happened thirty years earlier—the coldness, indifference and greed that are the conditions of possibility of both. There is no straight line from capitalist crimes to Nazi atrocities, but they are connected through the reification, dehumanization, and greed that fed (and feed) them. In remarkable affinity with Adorno's critical theory of society, Améry points to this nexus in a paragraph of "Why and How" that spells out the relationship between Vietnam, Auschwitz, consumerist society and his (and Lefeu's) struggle, and reads as a devastating indictment of a post-Auschwitz world that continues business as usual—not so much because it has forgotten Auschwitz, but because the latter was never more than a small hiccup in the forward march of the glittery ruin:

> But there are a few things that I do grasp, and they have to do with Lefeu and my stronger than planned identification with him. As my disgust with the political events of 1972/73 grew, I felt suddenly certain, with obsessive intensity, that Hitler and his Reich of ignominy had opened the trap door

> through which humanity had fallen into the void of its own negation. Back when I longed, battered and shivering, in five to six different German KZ for a day that never came, the infamously famous 'qualitative jump' must have occurred. There was no more *Jasage* [saying yes] since: the realm of death had opened up in the world. One could not survive it. Only lemurs had arisen from this night. Or, as it is written in *Lefeu*: One did not have the right to survive the survival. The absurdity of my existence stood there in front of me. Why did I continue to play the game long lost? Why did I correspond with publishers and radio stations, took ridiculous daily worries stupidly serious? Why did I play writer, me, who should have taken my place in a mass grave long since grown over? And how could a world of shameful affluence dare to admire its reflection in the phosphorescent laughter of the glittery ruin? (Améry 1982, pp. 186–187)

For Améry, there is no doubt: Auschwitz was the end of the world, the world as we knew it (or thought we did). As humanity fell down the trap door of its own negation, "history ended with the tombs in the air" (Améry 1982, p. 187), Améry writes in a nod to Celan. Adorno had come to the same conclusion thirty years earlier: "Karl Kraus was right to call his play 'The last days of mankind'. What happens today would have to be called 'After the end of the world'" (Adorno 2003a, p. 60), he wrote in 1944 in *Minima Moralia*. The world, however, sees it differently. Giddy with "shameful affluence", it blithely continues on its path as if nothing had happened. Rather than stand petrified, the world of glittery ruin, built on the mass graves barely grown over, rears its head with the phosphorescent laughter of someone who has not only survived their own end but gotten stronger from it. The French-Jewish philosopher Emmanuel Lévinas powerfully evokes the shock of the survivor who, after witnessing the pillars of Western civilization crumble, realizes that outside, the world has not ended: "We expected a new sky, a new world ... We were infinitely naive." He speaks of the "perplexed looks" exchanged among survivors when they realized that "there was no apocalypse", of their "stupor at the impassibility of a world that continued business as usual" (Lévinas 1984, pp. 319–320). Améry echoes a similar sentiment in his autobiographical *Unmeisterliche Wanderjahre* (addressing himself): "You suffered ... because of a real, car-driving, house-building, factory-creating Germany whose force and obvious placidity you begrudged. More than anything, you were irritated by its intellectual hustle and bustle, in output and potential almost equal to its economic counterpart. Incapable of grief, these people did not mourn. They were here, forcefully affirming their existence" (Améry 2002b, pp. 301–302). Mankind had fallen through the trap door of its own negation, but it obviously didn't care. What Améry and other survivors experienced like a complete caesura, with a before and after separated by an abyss, seemed not to have shaken much the people in whose midst it happened. One of the few who was as shocked as Améry and Levinas was Adorno: "The thought that, after this war, life could go on 'normally' or that our culture could be 'rebuilt'—as if any rebuilding of culture weren't already its negation—is idiotic. Millions of Jews were murdered, and this is supposed to be a mere intermezzo and not the catastrophe itself. What exactly is this culture waiting for?" (Adorno 2003a, p. 61). Améry, as we have seen, suffered greatly from this disconnect. The culture that had shaped and nurtured him had brought forth an evil so great that it put into question everything that culture stood for, and with it the claim, as Althager/Améry had written, that culture can make a difference. And as if the fact that it happened wasn't bad enough, the post-Auschwitz world, instead of confronting the apocalypse (and thus keeping alive the possibility of some sort of mending), continued business as usual, not even seeing that the glittery ruin was a ruin. Améry's *J'accuse*, "And how could a world of shameful affluence dare to admire its reflection in the phosphorescent laughter of the glittery ruin?", is echoed by Adorno's stark verdict in *Negative Dialectic*: "All culture after Auschwitz, including its urgent critique, is garbage. By restoring itself after what happened in its world without resistance, it has fully become the ideology that it potentially always was" (Améry 2003b, p. 359). This state of affairs, quite possibly more even than the memory of the traumatic past, is what made Lefeu/Améry unable to "survive his own survival".[34] By continuing as if nothing had happened, the world effectively erased the experience of the survivors, making them silenced outcasts in a world that did not want its forward thrust hampered by any kind of reckoning with the past. By failing to acknowledge the magnitude of the disaster, it perpetuated the conditions that had brought it about in the first place. The culture that saw it happen "in its world without resistance" eschewed the self-reflection that alone could have saved it. That makes most its productions henceforth garbage, if not outright barbaric—because if you write poetry after Auschwitz as if nothing happened, you become accomplice of the evil that relies on precisely that forgetfulness.

Lefeu, in all its unwieldy intensity, is the product of Améry's struggle with that reality. In "Why and How", he repeatedly speaks of Vietnam and of its effect on his writing. The reason Vietnam shook him to the core is because in it he saw at work, in a different form, the same evil that had brought forth Auschwitz—in a world which once more showed mostly indifference, thus allowing that evil to "continuously engender [more] evil": "Inevitably, as my identification with the main character grew, I came to a point where I saw all the issues of our times centered around this evil that continuously engendered more evil. One may object that this is falsification of history, even historical blindness, and ask what on Earth the glittery ruin has to do with the murderous spectacle that killed Lefeu's parents" (Améry 1982, pp. 187–188). One may ask, but for Améry, the intimate entanglement is not in doubt. The Nazis lost on the battlefields, but the evil that they brought to a paroxysm is not defeated. While Améry did not attempt to theorize the social and historical roots of this evil nor its different incarnations, he understood intuitively its embeddedness in a cultural, socioeconomic, and political framework that at first sight seems to have little to do it. What Lefeu denounces: the greed, the callousness, the marketization, and commercialization of everything (notably art), and the violence that undergirds it all—in other words, the *Glanz-Verfall*—is simultaneously the condition of possibility of the evil in question, and part of its manifestation. As mentioned, this realization was more intuitive for Améry than the result of reflection. He speaks of "subjective evidence" and concedes that "to ascribe the current misery to the evil that he experienced and to the non-sense of his survival, betrays the reason that avoids metaphysical Hegelian leaps and sticks nicely to the path of common sense" (Améry 1982, pp. 500–501)—in other words, the very reason that Améry had for the most part of his life passionately defended. For his claim that the glittery ruin is linked to the "murderous spectacle that killed Lefeu's parents", he has "as good as no argument, just this one: that everyone in history experiences their own story, and that the subjective evidence (a feeling, no more, a feeling that freed itself from objectifying historiography and overcame it) claims its right to exist, against all rational objections" (Améry 1982, p. 500). Maybe Améry would have been pleased to know that the illustrious philosopher he despised had a lot of arguments to support his subjective feeling and connect the glittery ruin—modern capitalist, or as Adorno called it: *bourgeois* society—with the murder that happened in its midst. Here is not the place to explore them in depth, suffice it to say that Adorno's analysis of the deadly core of capitalist-bourgeois society points to numerous (interrelated) factors, many of which are prominent in *Lefeu*: the dominance of scientific-rational thought over a more broad way of engaging the world, the compartmentalization of society (which, amongst other things, turns art into an inconsequential leisure retreat), the rejection of difference (which is quickly "subsumed" at best, eliminated at worst), the increasingly transactional nature of social interactions and the experiential paucity and coldness that go with it, and so on. Calling coldness the "fundamental principle of bourgeois subjectivity, without which Auschwitz would not have been possible" (Adorno 2003b, p. 356), Adorno asserts that if the people were not "profoundly indifferent toward whatever happens to everyone else except for the few to whom they are closely bound, possibly by tangible interests, Auschwitz would not have been possible, people would not have accepted it". He goes on to pinpoint "the inability to identification [with the other]" as "without doubt the most important psychological precondition [for Auschwitz]", one that is connected to the economic substructure of society, to what Adorno calls "business interest: that one pursues one's own advantage before anything else" (Adorno 2003b, p. 687). It goes without saying that this economic substructure defines the world of the *Glanz-Verfall* Lefeu abhors and plays a prominent role in its violence. It is also central in the swift return to the aptly termed "*business* as usual" after the horrors of Auschwitz. The latter were never allowed to earnestly put into question the "car-driving, house-building, factory-creating" society, lest they undermine its very foundation.

Realizing that the *Glanz-Verfall* not only accommodates itself with the murdering and inhumanity past and present, but feeds on it, Lefeu/Améry concludes that his "survival was countersensical", that it "must be taken back" (Améry 1982, p. 501)—for that survival was implicitly tethered to the hope that the world would rise from its ashes *transformed*, that it wouldn't simply go back to the way it was before because it *could not*—because it is impossible to write a poem after Auschwitz. Améry shared the shock Adorno's *Diktum* tried to give voice to, and the conclusion that stemmed from it: that everything the culture which had produced and enabled such horror was built on, everything it took for granted, had to be rethought, reassessed, questioned. Améry was aware (at first dimly, later acutely) that this included the literature he held dear: the old masters that shaped him as much as his own attempts to create literature. We see it not only in his early struggle to pick up the threads of his interrupted life and become a *Dichter*, but also prominently in *Lefeu*, and in *At the mind's limits*, where the impact of Auschwitz on the culture that preceded it is omnipresent. Thus for example in the chilling passage where Améry recalls how, during a long and cold *Appell* in Auschwitz, the sight of a flag flapping in the wind made him murmur "as if by mechanic association": "The walls stand speechless and cold/In the wind, flags clatter"—the end of one of Hölderlin's most famous poems, "*Hälfte des Lebens*" [Life at midpoint]. Result? "Nothing". The association doesn't evoke the "spiritual and emotional model that I had for years associated with this poem by Hölderlin". Auschwitz superimposed itself on Hölderlin: "So and so and the kapo yells left and in the wind, the flags clatter". The verse does not call forth the images hoped for—it calls forth absolutely nothing. The reality, whose horror exceeds the imaginable, has deprived the words of their capacity to affect imagination: "The poem no longer transcends reality" (Améry 2002a, p. 32). It is as if the Nazi hell had made reality intranscendable.

15.5 The Disavowed Heritage

If reality had indeed become intranscendable, one of the first victims of that new state of affairs would be literature—any literature created after the event (which leads us straight to Adorno's *Diktum*, and to Améry's various fictional attempts), but also, in hindsight, any literature that preceded it.

In *Lefeu or The Demolition*, literature's lost innocence is omnipresent. It is brought to evidence through the countless quotations that are, more or less overtly, woven into the text. There is something obsessive, almost desperate, about their ubiquity, as if Lefeu/Améry wanted to hold on to them at all costs as if he was conjuring them up in the hope of some redemption. But the hope is vain: Just like Hölderlin's poem, the literary evocations no longer have the desired effect. On the contrary, they disturb. They become "word dams that block the view on reality" (Améry 1982, p. 124), singularly out of place—at best. At worst, they take on a cynical or ironical connotation that was certainly far from their authors' intentions. Let me give just a few examples. Hofmannsthal: "(…) hit by the certainty that he couldn't survive his survival, after all of his name and kin, had, with *the weariness of peoples quite forgotten* [*samt ganz vergessner Völker Müdigkeiten*], gone up in flames in the furnaces of the germanized East" (Améry 1982, p. 148). Hölderlin, again: "*The world's pleasures I enjoyed while they did last*, the joys of life, *long gone! long gone! are past* [*Das Angenehme dieser Welt hab' ich genossen*, des Lebens Freuden *sind, wie lang, wie lang, verflossen*"] (Améry 1982, p. 57). And then there is Mörike, of course, whose poem "The Fire-Rider" serves as the book's leitmotiv: "*Thronging crowds and carriages turned back home from all the horror* [*Volk und Wagen im Gewühle kehrten hein von all dem Graus*], and started diligently to rebuild, thinking neither of the fire-rider nor of those who croaked" (Améry 1982, p. 128). Quoting The Fire-Rider's "*Hush! There it flaked into ash* [*Husch, da fiel's in Asche ab*]" (Améry 1982, pp. 128–129), Lefeu goes as far as to accuse the poet of sacrilege: "There it is: survival was countersensical, and as much sacrilege [*Frevel*] as the fire-rider's discussion of the embers" (Améry 1982, p. 131). And finally there's von Platen: "*He who has seen beauty with his own eyes* [*Wer die Schönheit angeschaut mit Augen*]. Or something like that. But that doesn't touch my soul anymore. These are propositions to whose meaning I strictly adhere. *To suck poison from every whiff of air and to smell death in every flower* [*Jedem Hauch der Luft ein Gift entsaugen und den Tod aus jeder Blume riechen*]: that means what it says" (Améry 1982, p. 54). The reference to the gas chambers is hard to miss.

Even the writer who Améry arguably admired more than any other, Thomas Mann, cannot escape Lefeu's reassessment. He comes up when Lefeu tries to give himself a pep talk: "Hang in there [*Durchhalten*], Gustav von Aschenbach said, it was even his favorite word" (Améry 1982, p. 9). Even if Lefeu did find some consolation in Mann's irony, one can only hope that Améry himself did not quote the hero of his favorite author when he "longed, battered and shivering, in five to six different German KZ for a day that never came" (Améry 1982, p. 186)—inevitably, the weary bourgeois' motto would have become cruel cynicism. Just like the same Gustav von Aschenbach's 'heroism of weakness' would have turned into sarcasm in the face of the "SS doctor who, in 1944, palpated my bones to see if I was already ripe for slaughter" (Améry 1982, p. 192).

On the face of it, there is nothing wrong with Thomas Mann's "ironical objectivism", as he himself called it. It is when placed in the context of the death camps that it inescapably turns into sarcasm, cruelly exposing the abyss between the Germany where Mann wrote *Death in Venice* and created his persevering bourgeois, and Nazi Germany where persevering was not only a question of life and death but generally not enough to survive. As Améry writes in *At the mind's limits*: "There was no bridge leading from death in Auschwitz to the 'Death in Venice'" (Améry 2002a, p. 47). Adorno comes to the same conclusion in a 1947 comment on Rilke's poem "Oh Lord, give to each his own fitting death". "Rilke's prayer about an own, fitting death is but a deceit over the fact that nowadays people only croak [krepieren]", he writes, after reflecting on what "the Nazis inflicted on millions of people, the selection of the living as dead", and on death "administratively decreed over innumerable lives" (Adorno 2003a, p. 266). He repeated the accusation in a 1967 open letter to Rolf Hochhuth: "Rilke's verse of the own, fitting death, which you refer to, has become bloody cynicism [*Hohn*] in the face of those murdered in the camps" (Adorno 2003e, p. 593). In the meantime, Améry had seized upon the same verse to illustrate the aestheticization of death that Auschwitz had made unbearable: "Unbearable was any literary evocation of death, be it Hesse's 'Dear Brother Death' or the death of Rilke, who famously sang: 'Oh Lord, give each their own fitting death'" (Améry 2002a, p. 47).

What both Améry and Adorno denounce here is not so much the inadequacy of the words as the poet's detached gaze on a reality that bears no transcending. By putting himself above reality, he betrays it. In a world where death is "administratively decreed, where 'it is no longer the individual that dies, but the exemplar'" (Adorno 2003b, p. 355), Rilke's prayer becomes a fraud. The blatant disconnect between Rilke's meditations, and the reality Adorno and Améry see, unmasks the potential immorality in the gesture of any artist, who contemplates "in a world in which the contemplative attitude has become cynicism [*Hohn*]" (Adorno 2003f, p. 46). Art, "through its distance from action, in the face of the deadly threat, through harmlessness, has by its form alone, even before any content, become ideology" (Adorno 2003c, p. 371), Adorno writes, and Améry, reflecting on his favorite literary heroes, comes to a similar conclusion: "The human you long for and who you cannot find in contemporary literature or philosophy or sociology, was—you should at least consider it—maybe never anything else but ideology: be it Faust, or Adrian Leverkühn, or wise Nathan, or Roth's Hiob" (Améry 2002b, p. 334).

What makes art potentially ideology "by its form alone" is, paradoxically, what makes it art in the first place: the fact that it rises above the down-to-earth, transcends reality. If reality can no longer be transcended, does that mean that art is no longer possible? That is of course precisely the question that Améry and Adorno grapple with. Both are acutely aware that the situation is aporetic. Adorno, in fact, spells it out in the very same sentence that contains his *Diktum*. Taken in its entirety, the sentence reads: "Cultural criticism finds itself faced with the final stage of the dialectic of culture and barbarism: to write a poem after Auschwitz is barbaric, and that corrodes even the knowledge of why it has become impossible to write poetry today" (Adorno 2003h, p. 30). In other words, the claim that writing poetry after Auschwitz is barbaric may be just as barbaric. He puts it even more explicitly in *Negative Dialectic*: "He who pleads for maintaining the radically guilty and shabby culture becomes an accomplice, while he who rejects culture directly promotes the barbarity that culture turned out to be. Not even silence escapes the vicious circle" (Adorno 2003b, pp. 359–360). This is precisely the aporia that Lefeu the painter, and *Lefeu* the novel, are caught up in. Améry knew that "schönschreiben" was no longer possible, that, as Adorno wrote, "culture in the traditional sense is dead" (Adorno 2003i, 455). Two years before the publication of *Lefeu*, he wrote in a letter to his friend and fellow writer Rudolf Hartung: "[I have] the feeling that the aesthetic sphere is falling apart, that art and literature have come to an end".[35] The literary quotations that haunt the pages of *Lefeu* are epitaphs to the culture that is no more. Yet at the same time, Améry longs to be a *Dichter*, and senses intuitively that the promise literature, and art in general, hold (as much as they may have betrayed it) is the only thing that has the potential to prevent the *Glanz-Verfall* from having the last word. In other words, art's ability to transcend reality, the very trait that makes it problematic, is at the same time what gives it its power and its subversive potential.

This is the context in which Améry wrote *Lefeu*, and the novel-essay not only reflects his struggle but also "the state of *Geist* and culture" it inscribes itself in. The mixed reviews now appear in a different light, particularly if we consider that the broken culture sits "on a heap of debris where even the awareness of its own brokenness is broken" (Adorno 2003g, p. 285), as Adorno put it. "Literature is only 'signaled'",[36] one reviewer complained, while another called the book "a literary degeneration".[37] Could it be anything else, given what we have just discussed? The "temptation of *Belletristik* [literally: beautiful literature]" that Améry allegedly succumbed to unprepared also reads differently now, not to speak of the review that deplores his lack of "confidence in the narrating word".[38] The latter is outright baffling and makes one wonder whether the reviewer even read the book. For the gradual loss (or rather, the gradual realization of the loss) of that confidence is the thread that goes through the entire book, until in the end, the trust in words is as demolished as Lefeu's home, and with it Lefeu's ability to go on pretending that he has survived his survival. For Lefeu/Améry, this linguistic demolition (incidentally, it becomes clear that the *Abbruch* in the title refers to much more than just real estate) carried enormous weight. Language had always played a prominent role in Améry's life. It was a reflection on language, through the philosophy of Fritz Mauthner, that ended the love affair between the young Hans Mayer, "a foolish and blind petty bourgeois" (Améry 2002b, p. 189), and the nationalistic *Heimatliteratur*. It led him to the Viennese Circle and to positivism, which he remained attached to until the very end, even if he became more critical as time went by.[39] "The meaning of a sentence is the method of its verification"[40]—this statement by Wittgenstein, widely relayed by the positivists, became Améry's favorite weapon against all metaphysics and jargons, notably Adorno's "jargon of dialectic" (see Améry 2004). It is omnipresent in his essays, articles, and letters—and in *Lefeu*. There, however, its fate seems to have turned, as becomes clear from its very first occurrence. Criticizing his avant-garde poet girlfriend Irene, Lefeu points out that "one has to stick strictly to the meaning of a sentence"—until here, all is well—"*trusting that there is one*. One can say of this meaning that it is the method of its verification" (Améry 1982, p. 8). And it is all downhill from there. From this first questioning of the meaning of the sentence, Lefeu/Améry gradually loses all hope "that there is one" until in the end, the *Sinn* [meaning] of the positivists is defeated by the *Widersinn* [countersense] of survival. In between, Améry, "carried and led along by language" (Améry 1982, p. 179), has words and meaning disintegrate. "Deutschl. (...) Man kann darüber spr." (Améry 1982, p. 29), we read in the second chapter, baffled to see such language debris come from the pen of Améry, unconditional champion of the integrity of words and virulent critic of experimental poetry. That it is the word Germany, and the statement "One can speak about it" that are the first to fall apart, is, of course, no coincidence. The reflection follows, and soon Lefeu wonders aloud (in a concession to Irene) whether "certain forms of poetry that renounce (...) first the meaning of words, then that of sentences, are the cause or the *consequence* of alienation" (Améry 1982, p. 70). The confidence in words gradually diminishes, as Lefeu muses that even "in crucial moments of one's existence" the "words that offer themselves have become worn out by documentary and literary use ('a tomb in the sky')" so that one has no choice but to "push away the importunate word constructs—in disgust" (Améry 1982, p. 122). Finally, reflecting on the deportation of his parents, Lefeu concludes that all one is left with is a sarcastic smirk at the "impotence of word and paintbrush in the face of reality" (Améry 1982, pp. 122–123), and that "words, whatever their relationship to reality may be, must be suppressed: for the sake of reality's deadly honor". The same goes for "literary evocations, which only delegate the impotence of one's own word and feeling in order to bear witness. No place for Celan" (Améry

1982, p. 123). No poetry after Auschwitz. And yet, as much as the word "destroys" reality, the latter, "if it is to be grasped, apprehended, depends on the word"—"to remain silent means to silence" (Améry 1982, p. 125). Améry is conscious of that aporia and painfully aware that by insisting on the inadequacy of the word, the impotence of literature (and culture more broadly), he is pulling the rug under his own feet: "As I kept rereading the parts I had written, I had more and more the feeling that I had caused my own defeat" (Améry 1982, p. 191), he writes in "Why and How". A defeat that goes far beyond that of Améry the *Dichter*—for, as we know, there is only a small step from the *Unsinn* of words to the *Widersinn* of survival. Lefeu, after confessing that he "wished, with unbearable intensity, to see the Glanz-Verfall, or any of its symbols, go up in flames", after realizing that "everything [he] did, everything [he] omitted to do, was determined, since 1945, by the fact that [he] couldn't survive his survival" (Améry 1982, p. 161), concedes defeat and sets his little garret room on fire, and with it himself, the fireman ("Lefeu recte Feuermann" [Améry 1982, p. 123], as he reminds us). In his self-reflection, Améry will take the *Widersinn* of survival a step further, going as far as to declare that "one *has no right* to survive one's survival" (Améry 1982, p. 186). Without knowing, he is echoing once again Adorno, who wrote in 1955: "The only way we have a chance to withstand the experience of the last decades is if we never forget for a single moment the paradox that after what happened, we continue to live" (Adorno 2003j, p. 142). And in *Negative Dialectic*, in yet another unconscious nod to Améry/Lefeu (and in what was often falsely read as a retraction of his *Diktum*), Adorno will draw a line from the impossibility of poetry after Auschwitz to the impossibility of survival: "Perennial suffering has as much right to express itself as the tortured has the right to scream. That's why it may have been wrong to say that after Auschwitz, one could no longer write poetry. Not wrong, however, is the equally cultural question whether one can still live after Auschwitz, whether he who escaped by chance and should have been murdered even has the right to do so" (Adorno 2003b, p. 354). For Améry, the question was not rhetorical. For him, just like for Adorno, questioning words, culture, the literature he so loved, was tantamount to questioning life, and when he wrote that in writing *Lefeu*, he had defeated himself, he meant it. On February 16, 1974, he finished the manuscript of Lefeu. On February 20, a mere four days later and long before the first negative reviews came in, Améry tried to kill himself with sleeping pills. A friend found him in time and he was "saved". Two years later, he wrote in *On Suicide*: "The rescue, which the doctor was so proud of, is one of the worst things ever done to me—and that says something" (Améry 2005a, p. 265).

15.6 Epilogue

In the end, and despite his own intentions, *Lefeu, or The Demolition* was not the last word of Améry the *Dichter*. In 1977, he wrote *Charles Bovary. A country doctor*, another novel-essay where he tried to give a voice to Emma Bovary's deceived husband and where once again, reflection and fiction interweave. More revealing, however, is Améry's very last project, a novella of which all that remains is a plot summary of a dozen pages. Little to go on, in other words, but enough to be struck by the very different nature of this novella compared to what preceded it. *Rendezvous in Oudenaarde*, thus the title, seems to be far removed from *Lefeu or The Demolition*, at least at first sight. No more criticism of the *Glanz-Verfall*, no more *mise en scène* of saying no—this time, it is the novella itself that says no. *Rendezvous in Oudenaarde* is a flight into the past, a return to the other side of the abyss. As Améry explains in his exposé, it is the story of an "alienation":

> The main thought is the power of imagination (…) The imaginative has a dreamlike as well as a literary character: The reality of literary figures will be solidified. Hans Castorp is more real than any uncle; Niels Lyhne is a better companion than any acquaintance; there are characters from Hermann Bang, Proust, Flaubert, Joyce, Musil, Thomas Mann, etc. (…) They all symbolize the dream as life. (Améry 2003b, p. 11)

It is a fully accepted alienation—a novella as they are no longer written, according to Améry's own conclusions in *Lefeu*. As if the writer who had made "permanent revision" one of his mantras had set out to contradict himself one last time, Améry resuscitates the literature whose end he had declared. The plot has once more autobiographical aspects: it is the story of a certain Vanderleyden (whose Flemish name evokes the German "Leiden", suffering), who goes on a search for his dead wife Litta after she appears to him in a dream and tells him to meet her in the small town of Oudenaarde. During his journey, he meets many a literary hero, all "more real than any uncle" (Améry 2003b, p. 11). The dreamlike nature of the narrative is fully intentional: "Life as dream and the dream as life become congruent" (Améry 2003b, p. 22).

Rendezvous in Oudenaarde has something of the condemned man's last cigarette. Améry allows himself everything, giving himself completely to a world that no longer exists, and writing as he always wanted to, had the state of *Geist* and culture not prevented him: *er schreibt schön*. As Irene Heidelberger-Leonard notes: "In this furious flight forward, the idealist [*Weltverbesserer*] Jean Améry turns his back to the imperfections of the present and focuses fully on the literary beyond" (Heidelberger-Leonard 2004, p. 320). Does that mean that Améry revises his verdict on the impossibility of *Schönschreiben*? Not exactly. The end of the dream as life suggests that Améry knows that the literary beyond will forever be out of reach. After a long quest, Vanderleyden finally finds Oudenaarde. He sees Litta, she smiles at him, he runs toward her, but collapses in a hail of police bullets before reaching her—before reaching Litta, who, as the narrator told us earlier, "was, due to a whim of her amateur writer father, in fact named Littera" (Améry 2003b, p. 12). Does this ending mean a reunion, as Heidelberger-Leonard reads it? "Reunion of Vanderleyden with Littera—in death: *unio mystica* with literature. Améry has arrived home, here he is safe" (Heidelberger-Leonard 2004, p. 322). It seems unlikely to me that the atheist Améry would find comfort in the idea of a *unio mystica* in the afterlife. Even if there was such a union, confining literature to the realm of death could hardly have been a victory for somebody who considered death "absolute negation" (Améry 2005b, p. 148). I am inclined to put the focus on the fact that Vanderleyden collapses before reaching Litta-Littera. Vanderleyden-Améry fails—literature eludes him, one last time. The sentence that Améry planned to put at the end of his novella, Litta-Littera's last words to Vanderleyden/Améry, seems to corroborate this interpretation: "'You are too late, you were always too late…' (Finis)" (Améry 2003b, p. 22).

Too late to write *Rendezvous in Oudenaarde*. Améry can't help but destroy his dream as life and confirms in doing so what his work incessantly proclaimed: in our life that is not a dream, literature, as it used to be, has come to an end. Hans Castorp, Herbert Törless, and Eugen Althager cannot be resuscitated. Henceforth, in a world after Auschwitz, the only poetry possible is one that assimilates its own impossibility—one which, like *Lefeu*, never forgets for a single moment the paradox of its own existence.

Notes

1. For an example of Améry's criticism of Adorno, see Améry, J. (2004). Jargon der Dialektik. In *Werke, Band 6*. Stuttgart: Klett-Cotta.
2. The German word *Dichter* is used indiscriminately for poets and novelists, and it is in this sense that I use it here.

   Likewise, for Adorno, "poem [*Gedicht*]" stands not only for literature broadly speaking, but ultimately for any artistic creation (see below, and my discussion of the *Diktum* in Silberbusch, O. (2018)).
3. Jean Améry to Ernst Mayer. 17.1.1975. Fonds Jean Améry, Deutsches Literaturarchiv Marbach, HS.2002.0083.
4. Jean Améry to Inge Werner. 3.3.1975, Fonds Jean Améry, Deutsches Literaturarchiv Marbach, 86.784a/58.
5. Jean Améry to Ernst Mayer, 26.1.74. Fonds Jean Améry, DLA Marbach.
6. Jean Améry to Ernst Mayer, 16.11.71. Fonds Jean Améry, DLA Marbach.
7. This part of the plot is—like most others—based on Améry's life. His wife died of a heart attack in 1944, which he found out only after months of uncertainty. See Heidelberger-Leonard, I. (2004).
8. *Heimatliteratur* is a genre of pastoral, often nationalistic literature of Germany and Austria that came into vogue at the end of the nineteenth century and was later enlisted by the National-Socialist blood-and-soil movement.
9. Twenty years after *Journey around Death*, Améry will denounce the stylization of horror in a review of Michel Tournier's critically acclaimed novel *The Ogre*, calling out the book's "aestheticism of barbarity" and accusing the author of "conveying exotic charm to the morally unbearable" (Améry 2003a, pp. 174–175). While Améry's early attempts to bring his own suffering to paper have admittedly little in common with Tournier's tableau of horrors, the 'estheticization of barbarity' seems to have played a role in his struggle.
10. Jean Améry was born Hans Mayer. After the war, he translated the German Hans into Jean and turned Mayer into the French-sounding anagram Améry.
11. Mayer H. [Améry, J.] (n.d.). *Grenzwanderungen*. Fonds Jean Améry, DLA Marbach, 81.1349.
12. Mayer H. [Améry, J.] (n.d.). *Der Schierlingstrunk*, Fonds Jean Améry, DLA Marbach, 81.1349.
13. Mayer H. [Améry, J.] (n.d.). *Fritz Griebner und die Mühsal des Sterbens*. Fonds Jean Améry, DLA Marbach.
14. See Mayer H. [Améry, J.] (n.d.) *Beate, Die Eingemauerten, Grenzwanderungen, Fritz Griebner und die Mühsal des Sterbens, Eine*

europäische Tragödie, Prosa o. T., or as “Prisoner of war Nr. 172364” in *Die Selbstmörder*. Fonds Jean Améry, DLA Marbach, 81.1349.
15. Mayer H. [Améry, J.] (n.d.). Pierre 172364, A la recherche du temps perdu, In: *Filmskript o. T.*, Fonds Jean Améry, DLA Marbach, 81.1349.
16. Mayer H. [Améry, J.] (n.d.). *Heinrich Greyt, Dornenkrone der Liebe*. Fonds Jean Améry, DLA Marbach, 81.1349.
17. In German, *schöne Literatur* used to designate what in English is simply called literature. The term emerged in the nineteenth century, as a translation of the French “belles lettres” and as a way to distinguish literature from scientific literature and nonfiction. Today, the term is dated.
18. Améry, J. (1973), “Leben mit Büchern”. Fonds Jean Améry, DLA Marbach, 81.1275.
19. Frühwirth, P. [Améry, J.], “Beim Einbruch der Nacht” in *Die Brücke*, Mai 1934. DLA Marbach. 81.1354.
20. Mayer, H. (n.d.) *Ein Brief ins Ungewisse*. Fonds Jean Améry, DLA Marbach, 81.1349.
21. * in French in the original.
22. Letter to Rudolf Hartung, 12.12.1973. Fonds Jean Améry, Deutsches Literaturarchiv Marbach, 81.1593.
23. Reich-Ranicki, M. (1974). Schrecklich ist die Verführung zum Roman. In *Frankfurter Allgemeine Zeitung*, 1.6.1974.
24. No Author (1974). “Trümmerhaufen der Ideen”, in *Neue Zürcher Zeitung*, 10.7.1974.
25. Henschen, H. (1974). Auf der Suche nach dem Roman. In *Die Zeit*, 21.6.1974.
26. Wolken, K. (1974). Leben und Sterben des Malers Lefeu. In *Die Welt*, 12.9.1974.
27. Kraus, W. (1974). Der Tod des Glasperlenspielers. In *Rhein-Neckar-Zeitung*, 23.6.1974.
28. Altwegg, J. (1975). “Jean Améry schrieb einen Roman-Essay in zwei Sprachen”, in Tages-Anzeiger, Nr. 186, 08/14/1975.
29. Bettinger, S. (1974). Nein-Sagen oder Kompromisse? In *Tribüne* 13 (1974), 5799.
30. Herzog, S. (1974). Lefeu oder Der Abbruch. In *Rias Berlin*, 18.9.74.
31. Wallmann, J. (1974). Zwischen den Stühlen. Jean Améry’s “Bilanz der eigenen Existenz”. In *Rheinischer Merkur*, 19.4.1974.
32. Günther, J. (1974). Jean Améry: Lefeu oder der Abbruch. In *Neue deutsche Hefte* 21, 598.
33. Reich-Ranicki, M. (1974). Schrecklich ist die Verführung zum Roman. In *Frankfurter Allgemeine Zeitung*, 1.6.1974.
34. This puts him in the company of not only his creator Améry, but also of Primo Levi, Paul Celan, Jerzy Kosinski, Piotr Rawicz, Tadeusz Borowski,

and Bruno Bettelheim, to name but a few (well-known) survivors who committed suicide.

35. Jean Améry to Rudolf Hartung, 30.1.1971. Fonds Jean Améry, DLA Marbach, 81.1591.
36. Henschen, H. (1974). Auf der Suche nach dem Roman. In *Die Zeit*, 21.6.1974.
37. Reich-Ranicki, M. (1974). Schrecklich ist die Verführung zum Roman. In *Frankfurter Allgemeine Zeitung*, 1.6.1974.
38. Wolken, K. (1974). Leben und Sterben des Malers Lefeu. In *Die Welt*, 12.9.1974.
39. Gerhard Scheit speaks rightly of Améry's "gratitude" to positivism (Scheit 2004, p. 607), which "remained all his life the reference point of his thought" (ibid., p. 613).
40. The statement was first made by Ludwig Wittgenstein, then taken up by the Viennese Circle, which explains that it is often falsely attributed to Carnap, Mach, or Schlick (see Wittgenstein 2001, p. 79).

References

Adorno, T. W. (2003a). *Minima Moralia. GS Bd 4.* Frankfurt/M.: Suhrkamp.

Adorno, T. W. (2003b). *Negative Dialektik. GS Bd 6.* Frankfurt/M.: Suhrkamp.

Adorno, T. W. (2003c). *Ästhetische Theorie. GS Bd 7.* Frankfurt/M.: Suhrkamp.

Adorno, T. W. (2003d). Engagement. In *Noten zur Literatur. GS Bd. 11* (pp. 409–430). Frankfurt/M.: Suhrkamp.

Adorno, T. W. (2003e). Offener Brief an Rolf Hochhuth. In *Noten zu Literatur. GS Bd. 11* (pp. 591–598). Frankfurt/M.: Suhrkamp.

Adorno, T. W. (2003f). Standort des Erzählers im zeitgenössischen Roman. In *Noten zur Literatur. GS Bd. 11* (pp. 41–47). Frankfurt/M.: Suhrkamp.

Adorno, T. W. (2003g). Versuch, das Endspiel zu verstehen. In *Noten zur Literatur. GS Bd. 11* (pp. 281–321). Frankfurt/Main: Suhrkamp.

Adorno, T. W. (2003h). Kulturkritik und Gesellschaft. In *Kulturkritik und Gesellschaft. GS Bd. 10* (pp. 11–30). Frankfurt/Main: Suhrkamp.

Adorno, T. W. (2003i). Die auferstandene Kultur. In *Vermischte Schriften. GS Bd. 20* (pp. 453–464). Frankfurt am Main: Suhrkamp.

Adorno, T. W. (2003j). Wird Spengler recht behalten? In *Vermischte Schriften, GS Bd. 20* (pp. 140–148). Frankfurt am Main: Suhrkamp.

Améry, J. (1971). Absolut teuflisch ist ein gediegener Naturalismus. *In Frankfurter Rundschau, 3*(7), 71.

Améry, J. (1982). *Lefeu oder Der Abbruch.* Stuttgart: Klett-Cotta.

Améry, J. (1992). *Der Grenzgänger. Gespräch mit Ingo Hermann.* Göttingen: Lamuv.

Améry, J. (2002a). Jenseits von Schuld und Sühne. In *Werke, Bd. 2* (pp. 7–177). Stuttgart: Klett-Cotta.

Améry, J. (2002b). Unmeisterliche Wanderjahre. In *Werke, Bd. 2* (pp. 179–349). Stuttgart: Klett-Cotta.

Améry, J. (2003a). Ästhetizismus der Barbarei. In *Werke, Bd. 5* (pp. 174–187). Stuttgart: Klett-Cotta.

Améry, J. (2003b). Rendezvous in Oudenaarde: Projekt einer Novelle. In *Werke, Bd. 5* (pp. 11–23). Stuttgart: Klett-Cotta.

Améry, J. (2004). Jargon der Dialektik. In *Werke, Bd. 6* (pp. 264–296). Stuttgart: Klett-Cotta.

Améry, J. (2005a). Hand an sich legen. In *Werke, Bd. 3* (pp. 173–343). Stuttgart: Klett-Cotta.

Améry, J. (2005b). Über das Altern. In *Werke, Bd. 3* (pp. 7–171). Stuttgart: Klett-Cotta.

Améry, J. (2005c). Die Zeit der Rehabilitierung. In *Werke, Bd. 7* (pp. 90–102). Stuttgart: Klett-Cotta.

Améry, J. (2008a). Brieffragment, vermutlich and Ernst Mayer [undatiert]. In *Werke, Bd. 1* (pp. 544–545). Stuttgart: Klett-Cotta.

Améry, J. (2008b). Brief an Maria Leitner [10. Mai 1949]. In *Werke, Bd. 1* (p. 545). Stuttgart: Klett-Cotta.

Améry, J. (2008c). Die Festung Derloven. In *Werke, Bd. 1* (pp. 583–608). Stuttgart: Klett-Cotta.

Améry, J. (2008d). Lefeu oder Der Abbruch. Konzept zu einem Roman-Essay (1972). In *Werke, Bd. 1* (pp. 649–660). Stuttgart: Klett-Cotta.

Heidelberger-Leonard, I. (2004). *Jean Améry*. Stuttgart: Klett-Cotta.

Heidelberger-Leonard, I. (2008). Editorische Notiz. In J. Améry (Ed.), *Werke, Bd. 1* (pp. 514–520). Stuttgart: Klett-Cotta.

Lévinas, E. (1984). Tout est-il vanité ? (1946). In *Cahiers de la nuit surveillée. Emanuel Lévinas* (pp. 319–321). Paris: Verdier.

Scheit, G. (2004). Nachwort. In J. Améry (Ed.), *Werke, Bd. 6* (pp. 607–642). Stuttgart: Klett-Cotta.

Silberbusch, O. (2018). *Adorno's Philosophy of the Nonidentical. Thinking as Resistance*. New York: Palgrave Macmillan.

Wittgenstein, L. (2001). *Wittgenstein und der Wiener Kreis: Gespräche aufgezeichnet von Friedrich Waismann*. Frankfurt am Main: Suhrkamp.

CHAPTER 16

Realism Contested: Jean Améry's *Charles Bovary, Country Doctor*

Adrian Switzer

Realism is reality contested: Realist works of art are representations of this contest; they are records of what Barthes terms "the reality effect." Articulating the terms of this contestation has been the task of much nineteenth-and twentieth-century art history and theory—well before Barthes' seminal essay, and long after it. Writing in the pages of the journal *Le Réalisme* in the mid-nineteenth century, Duranty places the then new aesthetic in opposition to the good and beautiful: "The beautiful, the true and the good is a fine slogan [for art] and yet it is specious. If I had a slogan it would be the true, the true alone" (Nochlin 1971, p. 36). Similarly, G.H. Lewes writing on *Realism in Art* in 1858 claims, "Realism is [...] the basis of all art, and its antithesis is not Idealism but Falsism" (Nochlin 1971, p. 35). By contrast, and against Realism, Baudelaire privileged poetry as what is most real, and "true in another world"; the things of the world with which Realist art is concerned are mere hieroglyphs that indicate this other truth (Nochlin 1971, p. 14).

A. Switzer (✉)
Department of Philosophy, Colby College, Waterville, ME, USA

Department of Philosophy, University of Missouri-Kansas City, Kansas City, MO, USA
e-mail: aswitzer@colby.edu

Y. Ataria et al. (eds.), *Jean Améry*,
https://doi.org/10.1007/978-3-030-28095-6_16

Realism is fascinating, perhaps even more so than reality. We tend to overlook our everyday objects and surroundings. In Heideggerian terms, things recede into the "equipmental" background of our daily lives, and this because of their ready usefulness (Heidegger 1993, pp. 154–155). By comparison, the viewer looks again at a painting by Courbet—*A Burial at Ornans* (1849–50), for example—in thrall of its verisimilitude. This aesthetic experience is premised on much the same assumption as traditional art historical and theoretical accounts of Realism. As Fried (1992) defines this shared assumption, "[the] tende[ncy] [is] to view realist paintings [...] as if they were nothing more than accurate transcriptions of reality outside themselves" (Fried 1992, p. 3). While equating "a realist painting's representation" with the "actual scene itself," Fried suggests that the appeal of Realism for the art spectator, historian, and critic might lie elsewhere.

Realism, generally, and Courbet's Realism, in particular, is less a matter of its faithful depiction of reality than its handling of the artist/spectator relation, or, what Fried calls, "the relationship between painting and beholder" (Fried 1992, p. 6). The painting/beholder relationship has a historical precedent in eighteenth-century debates about depictions of dramatic scenes and theatricality, generally. In this context, Fried argues, "Courbet's art belongs to the anti-theatrical tradition" of the early nineteenth century; but it does so while employing techniques and strategies of "overcoming the theatrical" that "radical[ly] break with the values and effects of the dramatic as such" (Fried 1992, p. 46). The thrall in which Courbet's paintings hold us, then, might not be because of how true to reality they are—Fried notes the oblique orientation of the grave to the picture plain in *A Burial at Ornans* and the awkward placement of one of the candle-bearing children to the funeral procession to show how unrealistic the work is (Fried 1992, p. 4)—but how we as spectators (or historians or critics) relate to them as scenes or figures to behold.

The human figure as subject of Realist art, and ultimately we will be interested, with Améry, in the meaning of the figure, might be counted real as it approximates anatomical exactitude. Eakins' paintings are often treated as exemplary in this respect. As Leja (2004) reports, the curriculum Eakins developed for his students at the Pennsylvania Academy of the Fine Arts in the late nineteenth century included a "grueling routine of dissection and anatomical study" (Leja 2004, p. 60). The results of such meticulous study are on display, for example, in *The Champion Single Sculls* (1871). Eakins portrays a rower in careful, anatomical detail; as Leja describes Eakins' detail: "[The rower's] arm and shoulder are modeled with an emphasis that picks them out from the pictorial field more strongly than any contemporary daylight photograph" (Leja 2004, p. 62). Truer to physical reality than photography—the musculature and integument of the rower's shoulder emerge out from within the flat plane of his pale skin and the dark water background—Eakins' Realism is figured in the physicality of his subject. The spectator, or, again, the critic or historian, wonders at the painting; in this case, viewers wonder at the exact corporeality of its central figure.

Yet, what is fascinating about *The Champion Single Sculls* and other figurative paintings by Eakins, might not be located so specifically on the body of its subject as in the incongruity between it and its surrounding details. For one, as Leja points out, Eakins leaves a trail of intact circles in the wake of the boat's advance across the water. What with the passage of time and of the scull would dissipate are in the painting shown as the perfectly preserved points at which the rower successively dipped his oars into the water and subsequently withdrew them. Equally, red-and-white latticework bridges are pictured in the painted distance though no such bridges cross the Schuylkill River; further, overhead clouds fail to reflect on the surface of the water (Leja 2004, p. 64). If medical-scientific accuracy is fundamental to Eakins' Realism, it may be so in contest with other modes of knowing and seeing, or so Leja suggests: "Eakins's commitment to truthful vision through systematic knowledge gave rise to irreconcilable conflicts, which animated his paintings" (Leja 2004, p. 61).

The art historian, the art critic, and the cultural theorist write endlessly about Realist works. From its inception, a mass of critical literature has grown up around Realism: Duranty, Lewes, and Baudelaire, cited earlier, were just a few among its many earliest critics; Barthes, Fried, and Leja are only three of the many critics working on Realism in contemporary theory. As Foucault writes in reference to Velásquez's *Las Meninas* at the beginning of *The Order of Things*:

> [T]he relation of language to painting is an infinite relation. It is not that words are imperfect, or that, when confronted by the visible, they prove insuperably inadequate. Neither can be reduced to the other's terms: it is in vain that we say what we see; what we see never resides in what we say. And it is in vain that we attempt to show [...] what we are saying. (Foucault 2002, p. 10)[1]

But, it is not the language/painting, or word/image, relation that is infinite. Foucault casts the central issue of Realism in derivative terms. Rather, and basically, it is the reality/Realism relation that is infinite. The looking-again that is looking at Courbet or Velasquez, the re-writing of the same, again, by the art historian or critic or theorist: such is the nature of aesthetic experience, whether scholarly or everyday, in Realist modernity.

The reality/Realism relation is also the contested space of Flaubert's *Madame Bovary* and Jean Améry's *Charles Bovary, Country Doctor: Portrait of a Simple Man* (hereafter, *Charles Bovary, Country Doctor*). Though Flaubert rejected the title—"I hate what is conventionally called Realism, though people regard me as one of its high priests" (Nochlin 1971, p. 49)—his novel of disillusioned love and life in the Northern French provinces has been taken to be exemplary of the aesthetic. Améry's book, in turn, is many genres in one. It is a defense of Charles and of the bourgeoisie, generally; the book is also a *cri de cœur*, and a love and lust letter to Emma Bovary—the prose seethes, at times, with necrophilic desire. Further, *Charles Bovary, Country Doctor* is a comparative study of competing realities between a literary character and his creator, and an imagined court trial of Flaubert, with the author ending up in the docket, guilty of the charges brought against him. Améry's novel of sorts is also a theory of Realism contested. It is the last of these myriad aspects of Améry's book that will interest us in the present chapter.

Inspired by the literary theory of Heinrich Vormweg, Améry undertook the literary project late in his life of becoming, or, of becoming again—he had begun as a young man as a writer of prose—a "story-teller [*Erzähler*]" (Zisselberger 2011, p. 152). Dissatisfied with his reputation as an essayist and memoirist, specifically of the atrocities of the Second World War and Holocaust, Améry wanted to assume what he took to be his rightful place among the modern *literati*. Following Vormweg, Améry rejected literary trends in the contemporary German *Kulturbetrieb* of treating language as autonomous and literature as an object of formal, structuralist analysis (Zisselberger 2011, p. 156). The referentiality and authority of language were suspended in the *Neue Literatur*; literature and its theorization had become merely formal aesthetic exercises (Zisselberger 2011, pp. 156–157). Against these trends, Améry undertook in his late fictions—*Lefeu, or the Demolition* [*Lefeu oder Der Abbruch*] (1974) and *Charles Bovary, Country Doctor*, published four years later—to restore a lost "faith in language [*Sprachvertrauen*]" (Zisselberger 2011, p. 156), or, in terms of Realism, and from a letter written in 1972 about

Vormweg's theory, Améry aimed to "contest contestation with production [*die Kontestation zu kontestieren durch Produktion*]" (Zisselberger 2011, p. 157).

In his last novel, published the year of his suicide, Améry contests Realism in a series of questions. Under the chapter heading, "The Reality of Charles Bovary [*Die Wirklichkeit Charles Bovarys*]", Améry asks, "What is 'real'? What is 'real-ism'? This has never been fully plumbed but only acquiesced to, in line with the commonsense equilibrium of everyday speech" (Améry 2018, p. 102).[2] The task of the present chapter is to develop Améry's theory of Realism contested in critical exchange with its Flaubertian original. In the end, Améry rejects *Madame Bovary* as a failed Realist work, undermined by an "improbabl[e]" depiction of the life and death of a country doctor and its unrealistic premise of the blind trust of a "simple man [*einfachen Mannes*]"—a reclamation of the term "simple" from Flaubert who titled his early story of a faithful servant, a devout Catholic and fawning pet-owner, "A Simple Heart [*Un Cœur simple*]."

As Améry rhetorically articulates his critical engagement with the Realist aesthetic and art historical tradition and does so under the chapter heading, "The Reality of Gustave Flaubert [*Die Wirklichkeit Gustave Flauberts*]," "what does this even mean: the reality of a figure of art? [*was soll das überhaupt bedeuten: Realität einer Kunstfigur?*]" (Améry 2018, p. 52). This question marks the very divide between Realism and the real: "meaning [*bedeuten*]," on one side of the colon, stands over and against the figure [*Figur*] and the real [*Real*] on the other side of the non-equation. Continuing, Améry acknowledges that "if we take the word 'reality' with reference not to its epistemological content, but in the slipshod […] sense granted it by everyday usage [*wenn man das Wort 'Wirklichkeit' nicht auf seinen erkenntnistheoretischen Gehalt untersucht, es vielmehr hinnimmt, wie eben der Sprachgebrauch es liederlich*]," then Charles Bovary, whose name is recorded in no "church registry" nor in any "historical documents," may be examined as to his possibilities. Restated in this way in the language of the everyday, which for all its lack of epistemological justification is "not arbitrary [*willkürlich nicht*]," Bovary's possibilities seem to be reduced to one of two options: "Things had to be this way and only this way, says one; no, that cannot have been, says [an]other, disagreeing [*So und nur so mußte es kommen, sagt der eine; neine, so konnte das doch nicht gewesen sein, redert der andere dagegen*]" (Améry 2018, p. 52).

Realism returned to the everyday seems to admit of almost no critical discourse. At most, Améry counts two diametrically opposed perspectives on the character: one is either for Charles as real or against him as unreal. But, in recalling Flaubert's work to the commonsensical, Améry is not thereby reducing it to the "for" or "against" of personal readerly opinion. The everyday—and, as we will see, the "everyman [*jedermann*]" (Améry 2018, p. 115)—is that from which Realism must borrow its language, particularly when the narrative touches upon real historical events, or when the body of a character is put to the page. To the extent that Améry counts *Madame Bovary* a successful work of Realist literature, it is so in just these moments of historical factuality and real figuration told in the everyday: "To the degree that [Flaubert] was a realist storyteller [...] he achieved realism [...] as a writer who never fully withdrew from everyday language, instead *refining* it [*Sofern* [Flaubert] *ein realistischer Erzähler war* [...] *gelangte er zum Realismus* [...] *als ein Schriftsetller, der sich der Alltagssprache nicht völlig entzog, sie nur läuterte*]" (Améry 2018, pp. 117–118). Cliché refined in *le beau style*, such is the Realism of *Madame Bovary*; or, by Flaubert's own rule of thumb: "To write well is to think well, to feel well, and to render well [*Bien écrire, c'est à la fois bien penser, bien sentir, bien* [*rendre*]]" (Améry 2018, p. 116).

Consider in this regard Emma's piano lessons. Weekly visits to Rouen under the pretense of Emma learning piano are really a cover for an affair with Léon—a cover that falters when Charles meets the piano teacher Mlle Lempereur who has no knowledge of "Mme. Emma Bovary, a doctor's wife from Yonville-l'Abbaye [...] There must be some mistake, she has not had the pleasure of making the lady's acquaintance" (Améry 2018, p. 53). Améry interjects as he does again and again in *Charles Bovary, Country Doctor*, giving voice to the readerly experience of finding aspects of the novel to defy good sense. Unrealistic, the whole scenario: "No. That does not work, no one believes that, the storyteller's invention is a bad one—this one, and so many more! [*Nein. Das geht nicht, das glaubt keiner, das ist schlect erfunden vom Geschichtenerzähler—das und so vieles andere!*]" (Améry 2018, p. 54; translation modified).

Impossible, Améry argues, that Charles would not have noticed his wife's first flirtations with Léon; impossible, he further charges, that Charles would unwittingly encourage his wife to spend so much time alone with the "notorious ladykiller Rodolphe Boulanger" (Améry 2018, p. 54). What is more, and most improbable, is bourgeois Charles unaware of his wife's exorbitant spending. "[T]he reader can hardly accept all that

[[*E*]*s ist dem Leser kaum zumutbar*]" (Améry 2018, p. 54). What is the basis of these complaints? Améry's own tastes and sensibilities? No. The charges against Flaubert's Realism are not put in the idiosyncratically singular. Rather, Améry objects to Flaubert in commonsensical terms and from the general perspective of "the reader [*dem Leser*]," and in the impersonal plural: that is, "no one believes" Flaubert's contrivances. Emphasizing the resonance between "common" in the sense of the everyday and "common" as a generic designation—or, as Améry puts it, "[c]ommon is what belongs to all of us, in common. Common sense is the sense of the community [[*g*]*emein ist, was allen gemeinsam gehört. Gemeiner Sinn ist Gemeinsinn*]" (Améry 2018, p. 85; translation modified)—the voice in which Améry raises objection to Flaubert echoes the plural, common voice with which *Madame Bovary* begins.

Charles Bovary is first on the scene in Flaubert's novel, titled though it is for his future wife who comes into the story only much later. Flaubert begins in the first-person plural: "We were in study hall when the headmaster entered, followed by a new bourgeois student and by the handyman carrying a large desk [*Nous étions à l'étude, quand le Proviseur entra, suivi d'un nouveau habillé en bourgeois et d'un garçon de classe qui portrait un grand pupitre*]" (Flaubert 1992, p. 3; translation modified). The "we" with whom the book begins is a group of young students; we the readers join the narrative with Charles' entrance as the new student into the classroom; among the "we" in whose voice Flaubert begins is Flaubert himself—or, so Améry asserts *in voce* Charles:

> The others walked home from school, many arm-in-arm, and exchanged clever banter [...] None of them paid me any mind. Gustave Flaubert, gangly, blond, gimlet-eyed like the Norman heroes in our schoolbooks [...] Gustave Flaubert, I was nothing to you. (Améry 2018, pp. 31–32)[3]

How quite to countenance Améry's claim, we will consider in a moment. But, to continue as Flaubert continues. Again and again in its first pages the narrative is told in the first-person plural: for example, "We began to recite our lessons [*On commença le récitation des leçons*]," "We were in the habit, upon entering class, of tossing our caps on the ground to free our hands [...] that was how it was done [*Nous avions l'habitude, en entrant en classe, de jeter nos casquettes par terre, afin d'avoir ensuite nos mains plus libres* [...] *c'était là le genre*]" (Flaubert 1992, p. 4; translation modified).

If Charles is figured from the beginning as other than the "we" in whose voice we are introduced into the narrative, there is a sense in which he too is in common company with the other students. Failing to do what everyone does with their hats, Charles is left standing before the class, hat in hand, to give his name: "Stand up, said the professor, and tell me your name [...] Charbovari! [*Levez-vous, dit le professeur, et dires-moi votre nom* [...] *Charbovari!*]" (Flaubert 1992, p. 5). Charles' mispronunciation of his own name sets the class off, collectively, in chorus: "We were screaming, barking, stamping and repeating: Charbovari! Charbovari! [[*O*]*n hurlait, on aboyait, on trépignait, on répétait: Charbovari! Charbovari!*] (Flaubert 5; translation modified). The "we" that narrates Flaubert's book from the start merges in chorus with Charles' commonness; Charles' general status is announced in his name being rendered in the singular-plural: that is, "Charles Bovary" as "Charbovari." As Marder (2001) comments on the beginning of the novel in her study of Baudelaire and Flaubert, "[Charles] [...] has no access to his proper name. He fails to speak under the sign of his proper name and hence never manages to make that name remembered by others" (Marder 2001, pp. 96–970). Rather than read the opening scene of *Madame Bovary* in terms of the modern "temporal disorder" of remembering and forgetting, as Marder does, Améry uses it to point out what is generally real at the heart of Realism.

Realism speaks from and of common reality, or so Améry asserts in weighing in on the art critical debate about the aesthetic. As noted above, Flaubert, for Améry, "achieved Realism [*gelangte* [...] *zum Realismus*]" by writing in "everyday language [*der Alltagssprache*]" (Améry 2018, pp. 117–118). The language of the everyday is the shared voice of the first-person plural: "*On*," *en Française*; "*Wir*," *auf Deutsch*, or, generally, in Latin as the *lingua franca* of bourgeois modernity. To punish him for making a scene, the schoolmaster tasks Charles in the first chapter of Flaubert's novel to, "copy out for me twenty times the verb tenses of *ridiculus sum* [*vous me copierez vingt fois le verbe ridiculus sum*]" (Flaubert 6; translation modified). Note the blending of persons and voices that occurs in carrying out this conjugation: [*R*]*idiculus sum, ridiculi es* [...] *ridiculum sumus* [I am ridiculous, you are ridiculous [...] we are ridiculous]. From this, Améry concludes, "*Charbovari, charbovari, charbovari, numquam ridiculus erat* [Charles Bovary was never ridiculous]" (Améry 2018, p. 35), and this because of the work he did as a provincial doctor. Charles' specialized medical knowledge is written and spoken in the common language of the vulgate; further, as a country doctor Charles contributed to the common lot of the petit bourgeoisie after *La Grande Révolution*: "He who does his work is not ridiculous [*Wer seine Arbeit tut, ist nicht lächerlich*]" (Améry 2018, p. 34). That Améry numbers Gustave Flaubert one among the "we" of the schoolboys from whose perspective *Madame Bovary* begins is a matter of his being the son of a public servant and general practitioner: "Docteur Achille-Cléophas Flaubert [...] from the big city of Rouen" (Améry 2018, p. 33).

There is another reality to *Madame Bovary* from which Améry raises his common objections, and does so in the name of Realism: "[Flaubert's] masterpiece conceals from us what was actual and real in the imagined life of poor Charles Bovary. How, then, shall we find some trace of what is hidden?" (Améry 2018, p. 54; translation modified).[4] What is "actual [*wirkend*]" and "real [*wirklich*]" in the otherwise merely imagined life of Charles Bovary is his work [*Werk*] as country doctor and bourgeois citizen [*Bürger*]. If Gustave Flaubert is a Realist, it is insofar as he speaks in the common, everyday language of the people and of the history to which he belonged as the son of a bourgeois doctor not unlike Doctor Bovary—though, belonged with a difference or at a distance given the Flaubert's status as haute bourgeoisie.

Political history, then, is the reality of *Madame Bovary* as a work of Realist literature. Améry intimates this "hidden" reality of the book in his choice of terms to refer to Flaubert as an artist. Instead of referring to Flaubert as a "*Schriftsteller* [author]," or "*Erzähler* [story-teller]," Améry, as noted above, uses the German "*Geschichtenerzähler*," which translated somewhat literally means, "historical story-teller." Figuring himself an artist in the purest form—explaining in various letters from the mid-1850s that "[the] aesthetic significance [of an artwork rests] entirely on the style, which must attain an abstract beauty of its own absolutely independent of the subject" (Fried 1992, pp. 267–268)—Flaubert nevertheless wrote historical fictions of a sort. Indeed, in a letter from the same period, Flaubert acknowledged the historical task of literature: "The leading characteristic of our century is its historical sense. This is why we have to confine ourselves to relating the facts" (Nochlin 1971, p. 23). Accordingly, *Sentimental Education* is one of the great novelistic depictions of the revolutionary events of 1848, and this despite Flaubert's distaste for the *quarante-huitard* ideals of democratic equality and liberty (Nochlin 1971, pp. 48–49).

The hidden reality of *Madame Bovary* is political and historical; specifically, it is the political history of the bourgeoisie after the 1830 July

Revolution and up to the Second Republic: "In his artist's arrogance, his estrangement from reality, Gustave Flaubert has not seen, has not *wanted* to see [...] bourgeois progress [[*I*]*n seiner Künstler-Hoffart nicht gesehen, nicht sehen wollen* [...] *des bürgerlichen Fortschritts*]" (Améry 2018, p. 62). Exemplified in the character of Homais, the Yonville apothecary who in the novel's last sentence is awarded "*la croix d'honneur* [the cross of the Legion of Honor]" (Flaubert 1992, p. 411), the early history of the bourgeoisie portends the progressivism of the Radical Party of the Third Republic and of Zola and Clemençeau's political support of Captain Dreyfus during his antisemitically motivated court martial (Améry 2018, p. 62). Yet, Flaubert reduces Homais' bourgeoism and his enlightened scientific ideas and prescriptions to "grotesque prattle [*grotesken Geschwätz*]" (Améry 2018, p. 62).

Recall, in this regard, that it is Homais who suggests to Charles the operation on Hippolyte. Having "lately read an article extolling a new method of curing clubfoot," and being a "partisan of progress [*partisan du progress*]," Homais conceives of "the patriotic idea that Yonville, to keep abreast of the times, should have its own operation on strephopodia [*cette idée patriotique que Yonville, pour se mettre au niveau, devait avoir des operations de stréphopodie*]" (Flaubert 1992, p. 203; translation modified). Cursorily studied in the musculature of the foot and ankle, Charles cuts Hippolyte's Achilles tendon: "[T]here was a sharp snap. The tendon was cut; the operation was over [[*O*]*n entendit un craquement sec. Le tendon était coupé, l'opération était finie*]" (Flaubert 1992, p. 207). Overnight, Homais writes up the seemingly successful operation for the *Fanal de Rouen*, the local newspaper; he sounds the call for medical, scientific progress:

> Despite the prejudices that still cover part of the face of Europe, the light is beginning to penetrate into our country districts. Just this Tuesday our small city of Yonville was the scene of a surgical experiment that was also an act of pure philanthropy. (Flaubert 1992, p. 208; translation modified)[5]

Homais' eloquence does not "alter the course of events" (Flaubert, 1992, p. 209). Set in a make-shift cast built by the town cabinetmaker and locksmith, Hippolyte's foot quickly becomes infected, then gangrenous. The boy's pain is torturous: his screams disturb the travelers staying over in the inn where Hippolyte lives and works; sobbing and stammering, he pleads with Charles during a visit, "When will I be cured? Ah! Help me! I am miserable! [*Quand est-ce que je serai guéri?—Ah! sauvez-moi!... Que je suis malheureux! qui je suis*]" (Flaubert, 1992, p. 211; translation modified). Finally, Canivet, a surgeon in nearby Neufchâtel, is called in to amputate Hippolyte's leg at mid-thigh. Canivet upbraids the self-important apothecary with his naïve idealism:

> But everybody wants to be smart nowadays, and they stuff you full of remedies without caring about the consequences! We do not pretend to be so smart, such miracle-workers, such silly-hearts; we are general practitioners, healers, and we would never imagine operating on something that is working well. Straighten a clubfoot! Who ever heard of straightening a clubfoot? (Flaubert, 1992, p. 213; translation modified)[6]

Flaubert locates the post-revolutionary promise of bourgeois progress onto the body of Hippolyte, thereby exposing its rottenness. At worst, scientific enlightenment is a murderous exercise in stupidity; at best, it can be cut out before it maims and kills more innocents. Améry interjects, "What is happening here? [*Was ging hier vor?*]"; he immediately answers his own query: "Undoubtedly this: the reality of Gustave Flaubert, of this specific 'I,' this 'bundle of perceptions,' stands opposed to historical reality [*Gewißlich dies: die Wirklichkeit Gustave Flauberts, dieses Ichs, dieses singulären 'Bündels von Empfindungen,' stand der historischen Wirklichkeit entgegen*]" (Améry, 2018, pp. 62–63). Continuing, Améry suggests that Flaubert as an 'I' and in settling accounts with his own father—a general practitioner and political freethinker—discarded bourgeois moralism and progressive history as what, according to Lessing, gives "meaning to the meaningless [*Sinngebung des Sinnlosen*]" (Améry, 2018, p. 63). The self as Humean, phenomenological "bundle of perceptions," is in Flaubert given priority to historical meaning; Flaubert *L'Auteur*, "pioneer of a new novel," thus becomes a "forefather of the nineteenth- and twentieth-century anti-Enlightenment [*Verantwortlichen der Gegenaufklärung des XIX. und des XX. Jahrhunderts*]" (Améry, 2018, p. 63).

If Realism/real is the master term, in the deconstructive sense, of the aesthetic and its theorization, another binary operates therein: past/present. On the one hand, the socio-economic determinants of bourgeois history lead in a somewhat continuous chain from the period of Bourbon Restoration of Achille-Cléophas Flaubert to the July Revolution and July Monarchy to 1848 and the Second Republic of his literary son—who began *Madame Bovary* in Paris just months before the December *coup d'état* (Flaubert, 1992, p. 7)—to the Third Republic, which Améry takes to have been the last bulwark against the rise of twentieth-century totalitarianism. That Flaubert interrupts this sequence, and does so for the sake of style and in the name of the singular "I," or the "existential freedom" of the individual (Améry, 2018, p. 62), allows, in part, for the future ruin wrought by the twentieth century—where meaninglessness prevails over the meaning-making potential of real historical discourse. As we will see, part of the meaninglessness to which Flaubertian realism condemns modernity is also a silencing or a rendering insignificant of the body—a link between bourgeois history and the body suggested by the central plot point of Charles' failed surgery on Hippolyte's foot.

"*Je vous accuse, Monsieur Flaubert!*" Charles proclaims again and again in the last chapter of Améry's book: "*Liberté*: You denied it to me. *Egalité*: You could not bear seeing me, the petit bourgeois, as an equal of the *haute bourgeois* Gustave Flaubert. *Fraternité*: You do not care to be my brother in suffering, you preferred to play the role of the indulgent judge" (Améry 2018, p. 141).[7] Flaubert denies Charles "the opportunities inscribed in the principles of 1789 [*die Chancen, die in den Prinzipien von 1789 eingezeichnet*]" (Améry 2018, p. 142), and this because Flaubert denies the real of the Revolution:

> Was the Bastille never stormed? Did Monsieur Delacroix not bring freedom to the masses at the barricades? [...] The bourgeois revolution to you was nothing but deluded sound and fury, just as later you saw the *Commune de Paris* as an uncouth annoyance. (Améry 2018, p. 143)[8]

Among those who stand accused at the end of *Charles Bovary, Country Doctor*—and in its last pages, the book becomes a legal and moral proceeding—Homais for keeping the arsenic with which Emma kills herself and Charles for his necrophilic desire for his dead wife, only Flaubert is condemned for his crimes against history.

Here is the other order of time that defines the Realism/reality contest. Let us call this other order the time of the real. Améry, in the name of the reality of Charles Bovary, turns "fate is to blame [*c'est le faute de la fatalité*]," the last words the character utters in *Madame Bovary* before dying (Flaubert 1992, p. 410), and the only memorable thing Charles ever said in his life, according to his author (Améry 2018, p. 151, n. 2), back on Flaubert in final judgment. Fate, by which Flaubert "negates the bourgeois subject [...] and any social engagement with subjectivity [*das bürgerliche Subjekt* [...] *und damit jegliche gesellschaftliche Verbindlichkeit der Subjectivität negiert*]" (Améry 2018, p. 68), is in itself real in history. Indeed, fate is the real of history. Against those who would render it a literary device—who would stylize it and narrativize it—fate is unremittingly swift in its judgment. Such is the other order of time, one whose determinate reality grounds the absolute normative force of justice; or, as Nietzsche puts it in "On the Uses and Disadvantages of History for Life," anticipating Amérian history, "[h]istorical justice [...] is a dreadful virtue" because it is unconditional (Nietzsche 1997, p. 91).

Inherently, the Realist historical novel is a vexed form. Taking its tack from reality, or, purporting to represent reality as it really is, Realism tends to foreshorten history to the present. Such foreshortening is an erasure of the past. What was, or, how things were, is treated as significant only insofar as they show up as traces of the past that mark present reality. If there is a historicism to Realism, then, it is presentist in its focus and practice. Flaubert's particular relationship with historical fiction is still more complex. Early in his career, Flaubert wrote two expressly historical works: *The Temptation of Saint Anthony*, which tells the early history of the Church and the collapse of the Roman Empire as a conflict with "Oriental heresies and religions" figured in Anthony's hallucinations (Green 2004, p. 89) and *Salammbô* set in third-century Carthage (Green 2004, p. 92). In being untrue to the history of late antiquity, Flaubert was not thereby denying its significance. Foucault, for one, finds in Flaubert's *Temptation* the fundamental historical work of "return[ing] history to the origin of time and the beginning of things" (Foucault 1998, p. 117). Flaubert composes his early works as one might experience history: unevenly, partially, and distortedly—as facts blend into memory and forgetting.

Flaubert's mature works, *Madame Bovary, Sentimental Education* and *Bouvard and Pécuchet*, are more of the moment than his early historical fantasies. Nevertheless, they are for that reason no less historical, in a sense. Drafts of *Madame Bovary* included explicit reference to 22 February 1848, the day on which the Revolution began, and 4 December 1851, the date of the *coup d'état* that issued in the Second Republic. Reflecting on Flaubert's inclusion and subsequent omission of these historically significant dates in drafts of the novel, Green (2004) concludes that their absence "only emphasizes their significance": "*Madame Bovary* challenges us not to forget the past but to read from the ironic perspective of historical hindsight" (Green 2004, p. 92).

Ironic historical hindsight is something different than cynical presentism or ahistorical modernism. The real history, as it were, of the nineteenth-century bourgeoisie signifies out from within *Madame Bovary*: Flaubert renders it ironically; Flaubert's irony is a stylized signification of historical reality. Against irony, Améry would have the historically real—what in *At the Mind's Limit* he terms the "moral truth" of the past (Améry 1980, p. 70)—sound out loudly and clearly. In terms borrowed from nineteenth-century literary theoretical debates about Realist historical fiction, we can rephrase the respective difference between Flaubert and Améry as a writerly, poetic commitment to "*la vérité*" and a moral-historical insistence on "*le vrai*" (Green 2004, p. 87). Flaubert was unconvinced that the novel could represent the latter, leaving accounts of *le vrai* to the historians. Améry, by contrast, found traditional literary concerns with *la vérité* historically, which is to say, morally and politically, suspect. Accordingly, one task of the genre-defying *Charles Bovary, Country Doctor* as novel-essay, or essay-novel—Améry used the terms interchangeably to refer to his late fictions—is to reveal what is historico-morally true [*vrai*] out from within the merely literary truth [*vérité*] of Flaubert's novel.

If bourgeois historicity is the other reality of *Madame Bovary*, or, better, if the historico-moral truth of the real is somehow written into the novel—even if only as the trace of the specific historical dates Flaubert erased as he prepared the final version of the text—the second question, again, is, "[h]ow [...] shall we find some trace of what is hidden?" (Améry 2018, p. 54). Améry does not simply dismiss Flaubert out-of-hand. Though odder than all other works in the secondary literature—with the exception, perhaps, of Sartre's multi-volume, semi-biographical *The Family Idiot* to which Améry refers in his own study (Améry 2018, p. 69)—*Charles Bovary, Country Doctor* is a long, sustained critical engagement with the novel of its near namesake and its author. Joining company with Flaubert's contemporaries who esteemed it the great Realist novel of the nineteenth century, Améry admits, "I too, despite everything that may be marshaled in objection, believe this singular creation to be a Realist book and masterpiece [*Als ein realistisches Buch und Meisterwerk verstehe auch ich, entgegen allem, was soeben eingworfen wurde, diese einzigartige literarische Schöpfung*]" (Améry 2018, p. 108).

There is something to *Madame Bovary* that bears critical interrogation; there is some sign of the other, historical reality in its pages, and this despite Flaubert's personal, account-settling overwriting of that reality. Heidelberger-Leonard's (2010) reading of Améry's philosophy of history, such as it is, as an anticipation of the *Historikerstreit* in Germany in the late 1980s applies equally well to his contestation of Realism: "[T]here can be [...] two ways of doing history, and that where the subjective premises of this discrepancy cannot be expressed, there can be no exchange of ideas" (Heidelberger-Leonard 2010, pp. 164–165). Equally, were historical reality silenced completely in *Madame Bovary*—did "22 February 1848" and "4 December 1851" not leave a trace in the finished text—then no "exchange of ideas," in Heidelberger-Leonard's sense, could occur in the contested space between Flaubert's novel and Améry's novel-essay. In conclusion, we will argue that it is the real literary figure, and, specifically, the literary figure as corporeally real, that is the point of common if contested exchange between Flaubert and Améry.

In his reading of the various voices and different perspectives in which Nietzsche writes, Derrida discerns a style—a particular way of signifying—of the body (Derrida 1978, p. 71). The same is discernable in the styles-upon-styles that describe the literary, essayist, confessional, historicist, and moral-juridical discourses between Flaubert and Améry. Recall, in this regard, the form of Améry's initial challenge to Realism—"[W]hat does this even mean: the reality of a figure of art? [[*W*]*as soll das überhaupt bedeuten: Realität einer Kunstfigur*?]." The real is on the side of the figure; the body is and must needs be the real of Realism. Similarly, recall that for Flaubert, to write well [*bien écrire*] is to feel well [*bien sentir*]; or, what is the same, it is to write the body in such a way as to represent its reality with style. And bodies abound in *Madame Bovary*, from Monsieur Rouault's broken leg—the occasion of Charles first meeting Emma as he treats her father's injury (Flaubert 1992, p. 16)—to Homais' strephopodic foot, to Emma's dying body, destroyed from within by the arsenic: "Soon, she was vomiting blood. Her lips pressed together more tightly. Her limbs were tense; her body was covered with brown blotches [*Elle ne tarda pas à vomir du sang. Ses lèvres se serrèrent advantage. Elle avait les membres crispés, le corps couvert de taches brunes*]" (Flaubert 1992, p. 376; translation modified).

Améry, rather, would have the body speak for itself, to emerge from stylized speech and say what is real in its raw undress. Wandering the empty house, Charles, according to Améry, still smells Emma's body—a scent that bleeds across the boundary between the living and dead:

> The white skin of my beloved, with its slight shading of cinnamon, smelled so intoxicating that I swooned as she lay next to me in our humble marriage bed [...] I steal off to the alcove, where her scent still lingers [...] [it is the smell of] the chlorine powder [...] strew[n] in lavish quantities in the name of hygiene and public health. (Améry 2018, p. 17)[9]

Living flesh, the color of cinnamon and sweet to smell, becomes the rot of a corpse awash in acrid disinfectant. But, how does the body signify reality? Elided from this last excerpt is the sentence, "I call for the dead: not too loud, but enough that I hear my own voice [*Ich rufe nach der Toten: nicht allzulaut, aber stark genug, daß ich die eigne Stimme höre*]" (Améry 2018, p. 17). How does the mute stuff of flesh, which is barely audible to itself, come to speak out from and of what is real?

In conclusion, we will follow Foucault's suggestion of multiplying discourses at the Realist/real juncture to allow the latter, the body, to signify out from within the former. Foucault's insight into the multiplication of discourses around Realism is well at work in Améry's novel-essay. Consider Améry's description of Charles finding and reading the letters Léon wrote to Emma after their affair in Rouen:

> I turned the key, pressed the spring: a whole packet of letters lay there. I read. Appalled, and with burning desire [...] They were not signed, '*votre ami*' [...] *Pour toujours, ton Léon. Je t'aime comme jamais un homme a aimé une femme. Notre chambre à l'Hôtel de Boulogne. Notre lit. Le parfum de ton corps* [Forever, your Léon. I love you as a man has never loved a woman. Our room at the Hôtel de Boulogne. The scent of your body]. (Améry 2018, p. 76)[10]

Frenzied at reading these letters—and they would be countless: Flaubert describes Léon as writing to Emma ceaselessly after their first weekend together at the Hotel de Boulogne (Flaubert 1992, p. 305)—Charles kicks the top off a crate standing beside Emma's rosewood desk: "Rodolphe's name leapt at my eyes from among a pile of other letters [[*D*]*a sprang mir das Bild Monsieur Rodolphes in die Augen, mitten in einem Haufen anderer Briefe*]" (Améry 2018, pp. 76–77). From one of his dead wife's liaisons to another, Charles is overwhelmed with their words:

> The letters only brought to me in words what my wordless world had been. When I read them, I bellowed like a pig being dragged to slaughter, but I bellowed as a matter of form; duty is duty, after all. Léon: *Je sense toujours*

> *ton corps contre le mien et compte les heures pour que mon rêve s'accomplisse.* Rodolphe: *Lorsque je vous enveloppais dans mon grand manteau, je me jurais qu'aucune autre femme jamais* [Léon: I still feel your body against mine and count the hours until my dream comes true. Rodolphe: When I wrapped you in my overcoat, I swore that no other woman ever...]. (Améry 2018, p. 78)[11]

Charles emerges from his wordlessness in and through the words of others; much of this passage, as the one above, is Charles repeating Léon and Rodolphe's words. Elsewhere in the book, Améry has Charles speak aloud these same sentences, but now as his own words: "Now that I am enlightened, through mourning and the letters in the secret drawer, I would say to you, as your ear yearned to hear, *ma petite chatte, tendre petite chatte, je t'aime comme jamais un homme a aimé une femme, mon adorée, je compte les heures* [my little kitten, tender little kitten, I love you as no man ever loved a woman, my adored one, I am counting the hours...]" (Améry 2018, p. 92).[12]

Unattributed in Améry's book, these are Rodolphe's words to Emma, now passed from the lips of her husband to her expectant ears. Except, they are not. Rodolphe writes these words to Emma in breaking off plans to flee Yonville together; but they are not his words, not exactly.

> [W]hen [Rodolphe] had his pen in hand, he could find nothing to write [...] Emma seemed to have receded into the distant past [...] In order to recapture some feeling of her he went to the wardrobe at the head of his bed and took out an old Rheims biscuit box where he stored letters from women. (Flaubert 1992, pp. 234–235; translation modified)[13]

Drawing excerpts from among this pile of letters—"tender or jovial, facetious, melancholy; there were some that asked for love and others that asked for money [*tendres ou joviales, facétieuses, mélancoliques; il y en avait qui demandaient de l'amour et d'autres qui demandaient de l'argent*]" (Flaubert 1992, p. 236; translation modified)—Rodolphe pieces together his farewell to Emma: a dismissive that will be delivered at the bottom of a basket of apricots on the morning Rodolphe escapes the elopement. These are the words Charles speaks to Emma, repeating Rodolphe who was himself repeating countless women who had written him over the years. The exchange of discourse between Flaubert's novel and Améry's novel-essay is multiple and plural: words multiply in the Realist space of reality contested.

Flaubert's novel, too, is a patchwork of borrowings and repeatings. Though not quite a *Dictionnaire des idées reçues*, which Fairlie (1962) defines as, "a compendium of the obligatory trite ideas of mid-nineteenth-century [persons] and of the mechanical clichés in which [they] express [themselves]" (Fairlie 1962, p. 30), *Madame Bovary* anticipates Flaubert's later compilation of such a form. Often, characters in the novel speak in empty platitudes. Fairlie identifies the agricultural fair [*comices agricoles*]—the scene where Rodolphe and Emma, hidden away from the crowds, trade in banal love discourse while prize pigs and cows are announced in the name of science, patriotism, and progress (Flaubert 1992, pp. 174–175)—as "the most sustained exampl[e]" of Flaubert's mimicry of characters trading in so-called received ideas (Fairlie 1962, p. 30). Equally exemplary of the clichéd character of much of what is said in *Madame Bovary* is the scientific-religious debate between Homais the apothecary and Bournisien the priest at Emma's bedside as she lies dying: obliviously, the two men of letters and learning trade in truisms about God and science while the patient writhes and shutters in pain (Flaubert 1992, pp. 387–389).

Though put in terms of the literary detail, Barthes' account of the "reality effect" applies well to Flaubert's polyvocal style. About Flaubert's description of Rouen late in the novel, seen from Emma's vantage as she takes the Hirondelle from Yonville for piano lessons, that is, for her weekly try[st] with Léon, Barthes writes, "the description of Rouen is quite irrelevant to the narrative structure of *Madame Bovary* (we can attach it to no functional sequence nor to any characterial, atmospheric, or sapiential signified)" (Barthes 1986, p. 145). Yet, the irrelevance of the description of Rouen, and its lacking all significance, does not introduce the geographical reality of the place—Barthes calls it "a real referent if ever there was one" (Barthes 1986, p. 144)—into Flaubert's novel at the expense of all narratological and characterial sense. Rather, a "'realistic' imperative" governs Flaubert's description; "aesthetic constraints," which delimit a description that otherwise could go on and on, are "steeped—at least as an alibi—in referential constraints" (Barthes 1986, p. 145). Reality represented in description disrupts narrative, but, in turn, lends structure to a "view," in this case, of the French town of Rouen, which otherwise "would be inexhaustible in discourse: there would always be a corner, a detail, an inflection of space or color to report" (Barthes 1986, p. 145). Rouen as it really is is both a disruptive intrusion into Flaubert's Realist novel and, when recast as description, a positive restraint on the "inexhaustib[ility] [of] discourse" (Barthes 1986, p. 145).

All of this, though, is reality at one remove: it is the real as discursively depicted. Detail draws writing away from literature, making of it something akin to painting. Continuing, Barthes acknowledges "concrete reality," the "real," or "what is" as the "irreducible residu[e]" of all literary analysis (Barthes 1986, p. 146).

> The pure and simple 'representation' of the 'real,' the naked relation of 'what is' [...] appears as a resistance to meaning; this resistance confirms the great mythic opposition of the true-to-life [...] and the intelligible [...] reference to the 'concrete' [...] is always brandished like a weapon against meaning. (Barthes 1986, p. 146)

Barthes' tone tells of his being unconvinced. Unconvinced not by the idea that the real is the indissoluble residue of literature and literary theory; rather, Barthes is unconvinced by the implicit conclusion that the real is thereby opposed to the intelligible, or that it is "against meaning." Invoking concrete reality to bludgeon interpretive efforts into silence, leaving the reader, critic, and theorist with nothing left to say other than that Flaubert had depicted Rouen as it really is or was—this is the (non) reading of Realism that Barthes rejects.

Note the logic by which what, essentially, is an antirealist conclusion is drawn and drawn in the name of Realism. Reality is treated as something in itself, with its own defining characteristics and marks, namely, that it is insignificant. Barthes puts the same point in the converse: "[A]s if, by some statutory exclusion, what is alive cannot not signify—and vice versa" (Barthes 1986, p. 146). Yet, the stipulation that "what is alive cannot not signify," or, conversely, that reality is insignificant, comes from the position of signification. Thus, reality is made meaningful in and by the very act of stipulating that it is not. Positively, Barthes explains real meaning, or, the meaning of the real, as a matter of the "concrete detail" being "constituted by the direct collusion of a referent and a signifier" (Barthes 1986, p. 147).

"Rouen" (as signifier) points directly to Rouen (as referent); the ostensive significance of the former is enveloped by and exhausted in the latter. This is not the end of Realism but its beginning. Now settled as a denotative signifier pointing, wordlessly, at the city that is its referent, "Rouen" is free in the pages of *Madame Bovary* to connote. What it connotes, specifically, is the real:

> [E]liminated from the realist speech-act as a signified of denotation, the 'real' returns to it as a signified of connotation; for just when these details are reputed to denote the real directly, all they can do [...] is signify it; Flaubert's barometer [...] say[s] nothing but this: [I am] the real; it is the category of 'the real' [...] which is then signified. (Barthes 1986, p. 148)

By "Flaubert's barometer" Barthes has in mind a detail from the beginning of Flaubert's short story "A Simple Heart." Drawing the reader into the home of Madame Aubain in Pont-l'Évêque, the house in which Félicité works as a servant, whose religious faith and singular devotion to a pet parrot are the referent of the "simple" in the title of the story, Flaubert sets out a wealth of decorative detail: "Against the white-painted paneling [of the living room] were ranged eight mahogany chairs. On an old piano, beneath a barometer, rested a pyramid of piled-up boxes and cartons. A tapestry wing-chair stood on each side of a yellow marble mantelpiece in Louis XV style" (Flaubert 1991, p. 3). The detailed description of the interior of the house—and it goes on for another two paragraphs—is a moment, as Porter (2004) puts it, of "slowed or zero narrative speed" (Porter 2004, p. 127).

Signifier of a barometer on a wall in a parlor in a provincial French town, "barometer" in Flaubert's story is free to signify reality. This is the "reality effect" as Barthes develops the concept in the eponymous essay; this effect is, for Barthes, the basis of aesthetic Realism. In a double-gesture that Realism carries out and then conceals, and does so in the name of portraying reality as it really is, a sign is first made the denotative signifier of its referent, and then takes on another significance, namely, of the real itself. Far from the latter being insignificant and meaningless, it is one half of a differently constituted meaningfulness: that is, the literary detail and its expression of reality. On a Foucauldian note, Barthes ends his argument: "[T]he realis[t] enterprise [...] [establishes the significance of the real] in the name of a referential plenitude" (Barthes 1986, p. 148).

The body, in Améry's contested Realism, is the real of Barthes' "reality effect." The real figure crosses the threshold into significance—the body signifies—precisely at the point where it is made to signify something other than itself: for example, bourgeois romanticism, as in Rodolphe and Léon's love letters to Emma, or, scientific progress, as in the medical details of Hippolyte's surgery. Here is where Améry contests Flaubert's Realism, and does so in the name, or in the significance of the body. While Flaubert writes his figures, realistically depicted, in close proximity to the reality they are to represent, for example, Homais' patriotic bourgeoism or Emma's idealistic romanticism, Améry would have the reality of the literary figure be a matter of their corporeality—seemingly insignificant though the body, at first, seems. Améry signals this corporeal contestation of Flaubert's realism in describing Charles as having lived in a "wordless world," and of his first utterance being an animal-like bellow. The real of the body is at first mute and dumb; what is merely bodily is wordless and inarticulate; when first brought to the threshold of signification, as it is by Charles when reading the letters of his dead wife's lovers, reality first sounds out as an animal howl. But, it is a wordlessness that subsequently flourishes through the countless texts-upon-texts from which Charles learns the lover's discourse. If the body sounds, at first, in brute noise, shortly thereafter it speaks in the florid prose of love and lust.

Charles Bovary, Country Doctor is thus a sentimental education, but of the body becoming articulate, rather than, as Flaubert would have it in his novel of the same title, of the provincial idealist losing his illusions in cosmopolitan Paris. As Améry signals this borrowing from and reworking of Flaubert, he titles the middle chapter of the book "The Bourgeois as Lover [*Der Bürger als Liebhaber*]" (Améry 2018, p. 76). Here, Charles' sentimental education comes complete: "[N]ow I am a bourgeois, *bourgeois-citoyen*, *bourgeois-amant*, fully conscious of his human rights and exercising them with a passion that is no longer the sacred privilege of the distinguished classes" (Améry 2018, p. 88).[14] The common realities of bourgeois history and the feeling, wanting body converge in Améry's contestation of Flaubertian Realism: "*Passion et virtu*—and the former is actually the latter [*und jene ist dieser eigentlich*]" (Améry 2018, p. 88; translation modified).

The real body of Charles, wordlessly animal, learns to speak by reading the letters his wife's lovers sent her. Yet, the borrowed language in which Charles first addresses Emma in love and ardor is not from among the secret stack of letters hidden in the crate by Emma's desk. The letter Rodolphe composes of borrowed phrases from other women is lost until the last pages of Flaubert's novel. Upon receiving word of their broken elopement, Emma retreats with the letter to the attic of the house: "Leaning against the window frame she read the letter with sneers of anger [...] She cast her eyes about her, longing for the earth to open up. Why not end it all? What was holding her back? [...] And she moved forward, looking down at the pavement: 'Jump! Jump!'" (Flaubert 1992, p. 240; translation modified).[15] Emma is called back by Charles, unaware of the state she is in; Félicité, the maid, leads her down to the dining room for supper. At the table, Emma is thrown into a panic: "Suddenly, the memory of the letter came back to her. Had she lost it? Where would she find it? [*Tout à coup, le souvenir de la lettre lui revint. L'avait-elle donc perdue? Où la retrouver?*]" (Flaubert 1992, p. 241; translation modified). Within the hour, Emma collapses in a hysterical fit from which she does not recover for months—emerging, once, yelling, "[a]nd the letter? And the letter? [*Et la lettre? Et la lettre?*]" (Flaubert 1992, p. 245; translation modified).

Flaubert's novel goes on. Emma poisons herself with arsenic stolen from Homais' storeroom; Charles' reputation as a doctor is lost, and with it all of his clientele; the outstanding debt the Bovary's owe to Lheureux the dry goods merchant come due in a flurry of promissory notes, none of which Charles can pay; all of the wares and furniture in the house are sold at auction to pay down the principle. One day, Charles, widowed, mournful, penniless, wanders into the attic of the empty house and stumbles across Rodolphe's last letter:

> [Charles] felt under his slipper a thin ball of paper [...] It was Rodolphe's letter. It had fallen to the floor in among some boxes where it had remained, and now the draught from the dormer had blown it toward the door. Charles stood there motionless and gaping. (Flaubert 1992, p. 402; translation modified)[16]

Charles' lessons, then, in love discourse, and from the letters received by his adulterous wife, are from Rodolphe's borrowings—but as first encountered by the body, specifically, by the foot. Upon first encounter, Charles says nothing: "Charles stood there [...] gaping [*Charles demeura* [...] *béant*]." If Charles becomes a bourgeois lover by reading the stack of secret letters, as Améry would have it, his own first utterance is borrowed from a letter that he first feels wordlessly with his body.

* * *

Améry's late foray into literature was meant as an escape from the caricature into which his early autobiographical and memoirist essays had made him. The renown that came to him with publication of *At the Mind's*

Limit—a collection of essays that present in often excruciating detail his tortured experience as a political prisoner in the Belgian fortress of Breendonk and at Auschwitz—also reduced him to a "moral instance [...] [and] a writer who sought to rescue the experiences of Shoah victims from the fate of cultural amnesia" (Zisselberger 2011, p. 152). But, Améry always wanted to be something else. From the start, Améry's hope was to be a "literary writer [*Schriftsteller*]" and *Romancier* whose fictions were read critically and popularly (Zisselberger 2011, p. 152). Améry's first, late novel, *Lefeu, or The Demolition*, achieved neither of these ends. Widely unread, the novel was panned in the literary press by the influential critic Marcel Reich-Ranicki. Améry was no *Schriftsteller*, Reich-Ranicki wrote in review, but merely a "scribbler [*Schreiber*]" (Zisselberger 2011, p. 153). The failure of *Lefeu* precipitated Améry's first suicide attempt; it was during his recovery that Améry conceived of writing *Charles Bovary, Country Doctor*.

We would do injustice to Améry's late literary aspirations to reduce them to his earlier, more famous and better regarded writings. Still, the interest we have found in the real significance of the body in Améry's last novel-essay has precedent in his writings on torture. Somewhere, Proust writes, "[*r*]*ien n'arrive ni comme on l'espère, ni comme on le craint*," Améry reminds us: "Nothing really happens as we hope it will, nor as we fear it will" (Améry 1980, p. 25). Our failure consists in being unable to imagine reality—and this because the latter is different in kind from the former. We are lulled by the everyday into thinking otherwise. In Améry's example of buying a newspaper, the image of the act and its everyday reality basically coincide. Moreover, there is no difference between one's singular act of buying a newspaper and everyone else's same act: "The act does not differ from the image through which I anticipated it, and I hardly differentiate myself personally from the millions who performed it before me" (Améry 1980, p. 26). Everyday reality is an abstraction, one that enables common action and the "codifi[cation]" of those acts to others in speech and practice, that is, we can speak to one another and can be understood because of the irreal space-and-time we collectively shape and share.

Occasionally, if only rarely, all general forms of speech and action are lost. There are times when the real emerges out from within what, commonly, the individual and their community were in the habit of calling everyday reality: "[I]n rare moments of life [...] we truly stand face-to-face with the event and, with it, reality" (Améry 1980, p. 26). Torture is one such moment. In the event of torture, Proust's comment on the unimaginability of the real rings truest: it is not as one imagined or feared. But, an unimaginable reality, which comes screaming at the body in a flurry of torturous fists, is not thereby insignificant—this is the point at which Améry's writings on torture anticipate his historical, political, and moral contestation, in the name of the body, of Flaubertian Realism. While bodily sensation, and particularly pain, "defies communication through language," nevertheless Améry writes on and on about torture, as he writes on and on about the bodily reality of Charles Bovary: "Whoever is overcome by pain through torture experiences [their] body as never before. In self-negation, [their] flesh becomes a total reality [...] [I]n torture [...] the transformation of the person into flesh becomes complete" (Améry 1980, p. 33). Animal-like, the tortured person screams—of and from their body. Yet, in sounding out in the contested space of Realism, this bodily howl proliferates into the writing and re-writing of our shared modern political history.

Notes

1. *[L]e rapport du langage à la peinture est un rapport infini. Non pas que la parole soit imperfaite, et en face du visible dans un déficit qu'elle s'efforcerait en vain de rattraper. Ils sont irréductibles l'un à l'autre: on a beau dire ce qu'on voit, ce qu'on voit ne loge jamais dans ce qu'on dit, et on a beau fair voir* [...] *ce qu'on est en train de dire* (Foucault 1966, p. 25).
2. *Was heißt 'wahr'? Was ist 'wahr-scheinlich'? Es wurde nicht durchgedacht, nur hingenommen, dem common-sense-Äquilibrium der Alltagsrede vertrauend* (Améry 1978, p. 111).
3. *Die anderen gingen heim von der Schule, manche Arm in Arm, und redeten gewitzt und städtisch* [...] *Keiner nahm mich wahr. Gustave Flaubert, hochaufgeschossen, blond, wie die normannischen Helden in unseren Schulbüchern, sternäugig* [...] *Gustave Flaubert, ich war Luft für dich* (Améry 1978, p. 36).
4. *Was wirkend und wirklich war in dem au seiner Phantasie geschöpften Leben des armen Charles Bovary, es verhalt uns der Meisterroman. Wie den also die Spuren dieser Verhohlenheit auffinden?* (Améry 1978, p. 60).
5. *'Malgré les préjugés qui recouvrent encore une partie de la face de l'Europe comme un réseau, la lumière cependant commence à pénétrer dans nos campagnes. C'est ainsi que, mardi, notre petite cite d'Yonville s'est vu le théâtre d'une experience chirurgicale qui est en même temps un acte de haute philanthropie* (Flaubert 1966, p. 206).

6. *Mais on veut faire le malin, et l'on vous fourre des remèdes sans s'inquiéter des consequences. Nous ne sommes pas des savants, des miriflores, des jolis cœur; nous sommes des practiciens, des guérisseurs, et nous n'imaginerions pas d'opérer queleu'un qui se porte à merveille! Redresser des pieds bots? Est-ce qu'on peut redresser les pieds bots?* (Flaubert 1966, p. 210).
7. *Liberté: Sie verweigerten sie mir. Egalité: Sie duldetern nicht, daß ich, der Kleinstbürger, ein Gleicher sei mit dem Großbürger Gustave Flaubert. Fraternité: Sie wollten nicht mein Bruder sein im Elend, gefielen sich vielmehr in der Rolle des toleranten Richters* (Améry 1978, p. 158).
8. *Wurde nicht die Bastille gestürmt? Und hat nicht Monsieur Delacroix die Freiheit das Volk auf die Barrikaden führen lassen?* [...] *Die bürgerliche Revolution war nichts als irrer Lärm und Furor, so wie nachmals Ihnen die Commune de Paris ein pöbelhaftes Ärgernis* (Améry 1978, p. 154).
9. *Die weiße Haut der Geliebten, die nur eben eine leichte Tönung ins Bräunliche hatte hatte, roch so betäubend, daß mir schwindelte, wenn sie im ehrsam ehelichen Bette an meiner Seite lag* [...] [*I*]*ch schleiche mich nach dem Alkoven, in dem noch immer ihr Duft hängt [...] den Chlorkalk* [...] *verschwenderischer Güte* [...] *der Hygiene wegen und für die Volksgesundheit* (Améry 1978, pp. 21–22).
10. *Ich drehte den Schlüssel, drückte auf die Feder: ein ganzes Paket von Briefen lag da. Ich las. Mit Entsetzen und brennender Begierde* [...] *Die Signatur war nicht 'Votre ami'* [...] *Pour toujours, ton Léon. Je t'aime comme jamais un homme a aimé une femme. Notre chambre à l'Hôtel de Boulogne. Notre lit. Le parfum de ton corps* (Améry 1978, p. 84).
11. *Die Briefe brachten mir nur in Wörten zu, was meine wortlose Welt gewesen war. Als ich sie las, da brüllte ich wie ein Ferkel, das man am Ohr zur Schlactbank zerrt, aber ich brüllte der Ordnung wegen, Pflicht ist Pflicht. Léon: Je sense toujours ton corps contre le mien et compte les heures pour que mon rêve s'accomplisse. Rodolphe: Lorsque je vous enveloppais dans mon grand manteau, je me jurais qu'aucune autre femme jamais* (Améry 1978, p. 86).
12. *Nun, da ich aufgeklärt bin, durch Totenklage und Briefe aus Geheimfach, würde ich dir sagen, wonach dein Ohr in Brünstigkeit verlangte, ma petite chatte, tendre petite chatte, je t'aime comme jamais un homme a aimé une femme, mon adorée, je compte les heures* (Améry 1978, p. 100).
13. *Mais, quand* [Rodolphe] *eut la plume entre les doigts, il ne sut rien trouver* [...] *Emma lui semblait être reculée dans un passé lointain* [...] *Afin de ressaisir quelque chose d'elle, il alla chercher dans l'armoire, au chevet de son lit, une vieille boîte à biscuits de Reins où il enfermait d'habitude ses lettres de femmes* (Flaubert 1966, p. 228).

14. *Zu dieser Stunde erst bin ich Bürger, bourgeois-citoyen, bourgeois-amant, der sein Menschenrecht erkennt und wahrnimmt in der Passion, die nicht länger der vornehmen Stände heileges Privileg ist* (Améry 1978, p. 97).
15. *Elle s'était appuyée contre l'embrasure de la mansard et elle relisait la letter avec des ricanements de colère* [...] *Elle jetait les yeux autour d'elle avec l'envie que la terre croulât. Pourquoi n'en pas finir? Qui la retenait donc? [...] Et elle s'avança, elle regarda les pavés en se disant: – Allons! allons!* (Flaubert 1966, p. 232).
16. [Charles] *sentit sous sa pantoufle une boulette de papier fin* [...] *C'était la lettre de Rodolphe tombée à terre entre des caisses, qui était restée là, et que le vent de la lucarne venait de pousser vers la porte. Et Charles demeura tout immobile et béant* (Flaubert 1966, p. 360).

References

Améry, J. (1978). *Charles Bovary, Landarzt: Porträt eines einfachen Mannes.* Stuttgart, Germany: Klett-Cotta.

Améry, J. (1980). *At the Mind's Limit: Contemplations by a Survivor on Auschwitz and its Realities* (S. Rosenfeld & S. P. Rosenfeld, Trans.). Bloomington, IN: Indiana University Press.

Améry, J. (2018). *Charles Bovary, Country Doctor: Portrait of a Simple Man* (A. N. West, Trans.). New York: New York Review of Books.

Barthes, R. (1986). The Reality Effect. *The Rustle of Language* (R. Howard, Trans.) (pp. 141–148). Oxford: Basil Blackwell.

Derrida, J. 1978. *Spurs: Nietzsche's Styles* (B. Harlow, Trans.). Chicago: University of Chicago Press.

Fairlie, A. (1962). *Flaubert: Madame Bovary.* Great Neck, NY: Barron's.

Flaubert, G. (1966). *Madame Bovary.* Paris: Garnier-Flammarion.

Flaubert, G. (1991). A Simple Heart. *Three Tales* (A. J. Krailsheimer, Trans.) (pp. 3–40). New York: Oxford University Press.

Flaubert, G. (1992). *Madame Bovary* (F. Steegmuller, Trans.). New York: Vintage.

Foucault, M. (1966). *Les Mot et les choses: Une archéologie des sciences humaines.* Paris: Gallimard.

Foucault, M. (1998). Afterword to The Temptation of St. Anthony. In J. D. Faubion (Ed.), *Essential Works of Foucault 1954–1984, Volume Two: Aesthetics, Method and Epistemology* (pp. 103–122). New York: New Press.

Foucault, M. (2002). *The Order of Things: An Archaeology of the Human Sciences* (A. Sheridan, Trans.). New York: Routledge.

Fried, M. (1992). *Courbet's Realism.* Chicago, IL: University of Chicago Press.

Green, A. (2004). History and Its Representation in Flaubert's Work. In T. Unwin (Ed.), *The Cambridge Companion to Flaubert* (pp. 85–104). New York: Cambridge University Press.

Heidegger, M. (1993). The Origin of the Work of Art. In D. F. Krell (Ed.), *Basic Writings* (pp. 139–212). New York, NY: Harper Collins.
Heidelberger-Leonard, I. (2010). *The Philosopher of Auschwitz: Jean Améry and Living with the Holocaust*. London: I.B. Tauris.
Leja, M. (2004). *Looking Askance: Skepticism and American Art from Eakins to Duchamp*. Berkeley, CA: University of California Press.
Marder, E. (2001). *Dead Time: Temporal Disorders in the Wake of Modernity (Baudelaire and Flaubert)*. Stanford: Stanford University Press.
Nietzsche, F. (1997). On the Uses and Disadvantages of History for Life. In D. Breazeale (Ed.), *Untimely Meditations* (pp. 57–124). New York: Cambridge University Press.
Nochlin, L. (1971). *Realism: Style and Civilization*. Middlesex, UK: Penguin Books.
Porter, L. M. (2004). The Art of Characterization in Flaubert's Fiction. In T. Irwin (Ed.), *The Cambridge Companion to Flaubert* (pp. 122–144). New York: Cambridge University Press.
Zisselberger, M. (2011). *Aufbrechen/Abbrechen*: Toward an Aesthetics of Resistance in Jean Améry's Novel-Essay *Lefeu oder der Abbruch*. In M. Zolkos (Ed.), *On Jean Améry: Philosophy of Catastrophe* (pp. 151–192). Lanham, MD: Lexington Books.

Index[1]

[1] Note: Page numbers followed by 'n' refer to notes.

Y. Ataria et al. (eds.), *Jean Améry*,
https://doi.org/10.1007/978-3-030-28095-6

The manufacturer's authorised representative in the EU is Springer Nature Customer Service Centre GmbH, Europaplatz 3, 69115 Heidelberg, Germany. If you have any concerns regarding our products, please contact ProductSafety@springernature.com

Printed and bound by CPI Group (UK) Ltd, Croydon, CR0 4YY
05/10/2026
02228125-0013